Ewa Dąbrowska and Dagmar Divjak (Eds.)
Cognitive Linguistics – Key Topics

This volume is part of a three-volume set on Cognitive Linguistics

1   **Cognitive Linguistics** – Foundations of Language
    Ewa Dąbrowska and Dagmar Divjak (Eds.)

2   **Cognitive Linguistics** – A Survey of Linguistic Subfields
    Ewa Dąbrowska and Dagmar Divjak (Eds.)

3   **Cognitive Linguistics** – Key Topics
    Ewa Dąbrowska and Dagmar Divjak (Eds.)

Cognitive Linguistics
Key Topics

Edited by
Ewa Dąbrowska and Dagmar Divjak

ISBN 978-3-11-062299-7
e-ISBN (PDF) 978-3-11-062643-8
e-ISBN (EPUB) 978-3-11-062312-3

Library of Congress Control Number: 2018968028

Bibliographic information published by the Deutsche Nationalbibliothek
The Deutsche Nationalbibliothek lists this publication in the Deutsche Nationalbibliografie;
detailed bibliographic data are available in the Internet at http://dnb.dnb.de.

© 2019 Walter de Gruyter GmbH, Berlin/Boston
Cover image: Viorika E+/gettyimages.de
Typsetting: Meta Systems Publishing & Printservices GmbH, Wustermark
Printing and Binding: CPI books GmbH, Leck

www.degruyter.com

Contents

Maria Koptjevskaja-Tamm
Chapter 1: Semantic typology —— 1

Stefan Th. Gries
Chapter 2: Polysemy —— 23

Kenny R. Coventry
Chapter 3: Space —— 44

Vyvyan Evans
Chapter 4: Time —— 66

Luna Filipović and Iraide Ibarretxe-Antuñano
Chapter 5: Motion —— 87

Teenie Matlock and Till Bergmann
Chapter 6: Fictive motion —— 109

John R. Taylor
Chapter 7: Prototype effects in grammar —— 127

Devin M. Casenhiser and Giulia M. L. Bencini
Chapter 8: Argument structure constructions —— 148

Rachel Giora
Chapter 9: Default nonliteral interpretations. The case of negation as a low-salience marker —— 166

Laura A. Janda
Chapter 10: Tense, aspect and mood —— 191

Johan van der Auwera, Daniël Van Olmen, and Denies Du Mon
Chapter 11: Grammaticalization —— 212

Ewa Dąbrowska
Chapter 12: Individual differences in grammatical knowledge —— 231

Sherman Wilcox
Chapter 13: Signed languages —— 251

Brian MacWhinney
Chapter 14: Emergentism —— 275

Index —— 295

Maria Koptjevskaja-Tamm
Chapter 1: Semantic typology

Definitions of cognitive linguistics normally emphasize the interaction of language and cognition, cf. "[c]ognitive linguistics is the study of how language relates to the human mind" (Kibrik 2011: 15). As is customary, such programmatic statements operate with generic nouns, in this case "language" and "mind", and abstract away from the concrete manifestations of human languages and human minds. This is certainly justified for a research agenda, but it is important not to overlook the reality behind it. Leaving the issue of the diversity of minds to cognitive scientists, as a typologist I will focus here on language diversity: there are between 6,000 and 8,000 languages currently spoken in the world, and "[t]he crucial fact for understanding the place of language in human cognition is its diversity" (Evans and Levinson 2009: 431).

Linguistic diversity does not imply that any generalizations over language properties and the language-mind relations are meaningless or premature before these have been studied for all the world's languages, the majority of which still lack any decent description. It does imply, though, that such generalizations gain a lot from careful systematic cross-linguistic studies that may unveil cross-linguistic regularities behind diversity. This chapter focuses on the discipline for which cross-linguistic comparison is foundational, namely linguistic typology, and in particular on its semantically oriented direction, *semantic typology*. Section 1 introduces semantic typology, section 2 gives examples of central research within semantic typology. Section 3 discusses the major methodological challenges that semantic typologists face, section 4 summarizes the lessons to be drawn, and section 5 points out a few directions for further research. The chapter's overarching goal is to show the value of bringing linguistic diversity and semantic typology into research on "how language relates to mind".

1 Introducing semantic typology

Typology is "the study of linguistic patterns that are found cross-linguistically, in particular, patterns that can be discovered solely by cross-linguistic comparison" (Croft 2003: 1). Typological research takes linguistic diversity as its point

---

Maria Koptjevskaja-Tamm, Stockholm, Sweden

https://doi.org/10.1515/9783110626438-001

of departure, assumes that the variation across languages is restricted, and aims at discovering the systematicity behind it.

The typological research angle that is probably most interesting for cognitive linguists is *semantic typology*, which comprises "the systematic cross-linguistic study of how languages express meaning by way of signs" (Evans 2011: 504). Semantic typology is orthogonal to the more traditional compartments of typology, such as phonetic/phonological, grammatical or lexical, since meanings are normally expressed by an intricate interplay among signs of various kinds – words, morphological markers, syntactic constructions, prosody, gestures, etc.

This chapter will focus on some of the linguistic domains where painstaking semantic comparison according to the standards of linguistic typology has demonstrated significant linguistic diversity coupled with regularities of great value for cognitive research. Purely grammatical phenomena (e.g., tense), as well as those that have mainly figured in grammatical discussions (e.g., word classes) are left out here. The majority of cases discussed will involve meanings expressed by lexical items, often in combination with particular constructions (*lexical semantic typology*, or just *lexical typology*). But even with these restrictions, it is not possible to do justice to all the semantic-typological research within the limited space of this chapter (for overviews and references cf. Brown 2001; Goddard 2001; Koptjevskaja-Tamm 2008; Koch 2001; Evans 2011).

The main emphasis will be on the *linguistic categorization* of different cognitive domains and/or on *different meanings* that can be expressed by one and the same word (often coupled with different constructions) or by words related to each other (either synchronically or historically), with somewhat different relative weight attached to these issues in different cases. Both categorization within cognitive domains (onomaseology) and questions of polysemy and semantic shifts, and in particular universal metaphoric and metonymic processes (semasiology) are, of course, central issues in cognitive semantics. The discussion will touch upon the following questions:

– How do speakers of different languages categorize a particular cognitive domain by means of words and other linguistic expressions?
– To what extent is linguistic categorization universal or language- and culture-specific?
– What semantic shifts are frequent across languages?
– What is the interplay among the various factors that shape linguistic categorization and patterns of semantic shifts?

2 Semantic typology: selected major examples

2.1 Colour

COLOUR has figured prominently in linguistic and anthropological research, in cognitive research in general and in cognitive linguistics in particular, among others, in discussion of prototypes (cf. Taylor volume 2) and embodiment. It is a popular textbook example of striking cross-linguistic diversity in *linguistic categorization*, which has been claimed to be severely restricted, at least with respect to basic terms (allegedly present in all languages) and their foci. In the universalist view, stemming from Eleanor (Heider) Rosch's experiments on colour cognition among the Dugum Dani (Heider 1972) and the colour-naming survey by Berlin and Kay (1969), all languages choose their subsets of basic terms from a universal stock according to a universal hierarchy. Universality in linguistic colour categorisation is supposed to originate in the neurophysiology of vision (Kay and McDaniel 1978), and/or in the visual environment of humans (Shepard 1992).

This view has been strongly challenged by "relativists", such as Levinson (2001), Lucy (1997), or Wierzbicka (2005). They have, among other things, questioned the validity of the decontextualized denotation-based methodology (various tasks based on Munsell chips) underlying the lion's share of colour studies in the Berlin-Kay paradigm. It is, for instance, doubtful whether COLOUR constitutes a coherent semantic domain in many languages once their putative "basic" colour terms have undergone proper linguistic analysis (cf. Levinson 2000), not to mention the fact that the word 'colour' is absent from many (most?) of the world's languages. People use colour words (or words that come up as colour words in the Berlin-Kay paradigm) for communicating meanings that can hardly be reduced to the physiology of seeing but are most probably based on comparison with salient visual prototypes in the environments – universal (sky, fire or blood) or more local (such as local minerals) (Wierzbicka 2005). And surely, the word for 'red' in a language that only has 'black', 'white' and 'red' simply cannot *mean* the same as 'red' in a language with a richer repertoire of colour words.

Significantly, the distribution of the different colour systems across the languages of the world shows remarkable geographic differences (cf. Kay and Maffi 2005; Kay et al. 2009). For instance, many of the languages that do not distinguish 'blue' and 'green' (the "grue" languages, the majority of the 120 languages in Kay and Maffi 2005) are concentrated to the tropics. The inhabitants of these areas are exposed to sunlight with high proportions of ultraviolet-B, which, in turn, often leads to deficiency in colour vision (Lindsey and Brown

2002; Bornstein 2007). This casts additional doubts on the universality of the focal colour categories available to all (sighted) human beings.

COLOUR remains the most widely cross-linguistically studied domain in terms of the languages covered by systematic methodology and the intensity of theoretical discussions (cf. Malt and Wolff [eds.] 2010 for recent overviews; MacLaury et al. 2007 and references therein; and http://www.icsi.berkeley.edu/wcs/ for the World Color Survey Site).

2.2 From COGNITION to PERCEPTION

The well-known and putatively universal *metaphor* KNOWING IS SEEING (a special case of the THINKING IS PERCEIVING metaphor in the MIND-AS-BODY system) has been central in the discussions of embodiment (Sweetser 1990; Lakoff and Johnson 1999; Bergen volume 1). In her influential study, Sweetser (1990) notices that in Indo-European languages, verbs of seeing often demonstrate metaphorical extensions to meanings of thinking and/or knowing. This contrasts them with verbs for other perception modalities. In particular, verbs of hearing often show semantic extensions to understanding and/or to obeying (social interaction). In Sweetser's (1990: 37) words, "[t]he objective, intellectual side of our mental life seems to be regularly linked with the sense of vision", because vision is our "primary source of data about the objective world", because it has "the ability to pick out one stimulus at will from many", and because it may be shared by different people in the same place. Hearing, on the other hand, is primarily connected to linguistic communication and is therefore a person's powerful means of intellectual and emotional power over other people. Sweetser hypothesizes that "[t]he link between physical hearing and obeying or heeding – between physical and internal receptivity or reception – may well, in fact, be universal, rather than merely Indo-European" (1990: 42) and that "[i]t would be a novelty for a verb meaning 'hear' to develop a usage meaning 'know' rather than 'understand', whereas such a usage is common for verbs meaning 'see'" (1990: 43).

However, as shown by Evans and Wilkins (2000) and contrary to Sweetser's hypotheses, the most recurrent semantic extension in Australian Aboriginal languages is between the auditory sense and cognition, whereas the visual sense mostly gives rise to social interaction readings such as desire and sexual attraction, aggression, etc. Also in Vanhove's (2008) sample of twenty-five languages from eight linguistic phyla, verbs of hearing normally have at least one extension to cognition, while the shift from vision to cognition is less common.

The discussion of these different patterns revolves in fact around the interaction between universal and cultural sides of embodiment. For Evans and

Wilkins, the extensions from 'hear' to 'know' and 'think' in the Australian Aboriginal languages are rooted in social and cultural practices, among them the avoidance of literal face-to-face conversation and particular cultural scripts connecting learning to hearing stories and 'song lines'. In fact, the anthropology of senses suggests that the primacy of vision in modern societies is partly a social construct, possibly privileged by literacy, whereas oral traditions might privilege other senses, chiefly audition (Classen 1993). However, the straightforward connection between literacy vs. oral traditions and extensions from vision vs. hearing to cognition has not been confirmed (Vanhove 2008).

Vision does, however, appear to be primary within the linguistic domain of perception itself. Quite a few languages do not have dedicated verbs for the different sense modalities, but "conflate" several senses in one and the same verb. The Papuan language Kalam offers probably the most widely-quoted example, where "[i]n different contexts *nŋ-*, occurring as the lone content verb in a clause, may be glossed as 'know, be conscious, be aware, be awake, think, see, hear, smell, taste, feel, recognize, notice, understand, remember, learn, study'" (Pawley 1994: 392). There are, however, ways of making the intended "reading" more specific, e.g., by adding 'eye' vs. 'ear' for 'seeing' vs. 'hearing'. Would that mean that the Kalam speakers simply have one under-differentiated linguistic category for PERCEPTION and COGNITION? Or should *nŋ-* be analyzed as primarily meaning 'know' with extensions to perception, as primarily meaning 'perceive' with extensions to cognition, or as multiply polysemous and distinguishing between the senses of 'see', 'hear', and 'know' (cf. Goddard 2001 for an outline of the possible solutions)? In his influential work on perception verbs in fifty languages, Viberg (e.g., 2001) analyzes such cases as polysemy and shows that lexicalization of perception by verbs across languages and the patterns of sense conflation follow the sense-modality hierarchy

```
                touch
sight > hearing > taste
                smell
```

That is, if a language has a dedicated verb for touching, tasting or smelling, it will distinguish between hearing and seeing verbs. Also 'see' or 'hear' may be used for the lower sense modalities (cf. *slyšat' zapax* 'lit. hear a smell' in Russian), but no languages will use tasting or smelling verbs for talking about vision. Later research has, by far and large, confirmed these cross-linguistic findings.

To conclude, the metaphor THINKING IS PERCEIVING seems to hold across languages, although its more concrete manifestation, KNOWING IS SEEING, is less universal than has been suggested in Sweetser (1990) and Lakoff and Johnson (1999), at least when it comes to verbs. Research on the semantics and grammar of perception and cognition is on the whole very active (cf. Aikhenvald and Storch 2013 for a recent addition).

2.3 MOTION events

For cognitively minded linguists and cognitive scientists, cross-linguistic research on MOTION is, most probably, firmly associated with the tradition stemming from Talmy's seminal chapter (1985) (cf. Filipović this volume), where much of the recent research focuses on Talmy's later distinction between verb-framed and satellite-framed languages.

However, the latest systematic investigations of languages that were not represented in Talmy's research and a closer attention to some of those that were have led to significant modifications of the Talmy typology. These involve both the addition of new types and the insight that languages make use of multiple constructional types depending on which particular motion event is involved (Croft et al. 2010: 233). Verkerk (2014) provides a statistical corroboration to the latter insight on the basis of a parallel corpus for sixteen Indo-European languages, which employ the different motion constructions to different extents. This is very much in line with the dominant position in modern typological research that classifications normally apply to particular phenomena rather than to whole languages. Languages as wholes are seldom purely isolating, agglutinating or flectional, exclusively nominative-accusative or ergative, etc., but normally have different mixtures of these properties.

The linguistic motion domain is, however, very complex and heterogeneous and lends itself to cross-linguistic research from different angles (e.g., the distinction between the 'DEICTIC' MOTION verb ['come'] and the 'non-deictic' verb ['go'] in Ricca 1993; Wilkins and Hill 1995; Wälchli and Cysouw 2012; or verbs of motion in a liquid Ground, AQUA-MOTION, http://aquamotion.narod.ru/index-eng.html; Maisak and Rakhilina 2007; Koptjevskaja-Tamm et al. 2010).

2.4 BODY from different angles

BODY is one of the most crucial domains for cognitive linguistics and for cognitive research in general, given the strong commitment to embodiment (cf. Bergen volume 1). A particularly interesting topic is the use of BODY-PART terms in conventionalised descriptions of EMOTIONS, MENTAL STATES and PERSONAL TRAITS, where languages differ significantly in which body-parts can be seats for which emotions and mental states (e.g., Enfield and Wierzbicka 2002; Sharifian et al. 2008; Maalej and Yu 2011).

Body-part terms also often develop into markers for SPATIAL RELATIONS (e.g., 'head' > 'on' or 'back' > 'behind'), numbers ('hand' > 'five'), etc., following cross-linguistically common grammaticalization patterns with interesting geographic variations (see Koptjevskaja-Tamm 2008: 27–31 for details).

However, the body itself, in its concrete physical manifestation, and consisting of seemingly self-evident parts, is also a fascinating object for cross-linguistic studies. The basic issue here is which parts of the body are labelled across languages, i.e., conceptualized as categories of their own, and what factors underlie this. There are some well-known "deviations" from what seems to be normal for speakers of English or French: Russian uses *ruka* for both hand and arm, *noga* for both 'foot 'and 'leg', and *palec* for both 'finger' (including the thumb) and 'toe'. But still, aren't there any clear partitions of the body? Aren't there universal linguistic body-part concepts?

Now, the Russian *ruka*, covering both 'hand' and 'arm', turns out not to be exotic against the background of the world's languages: 228 languages in Brown's (2005a) sample of 617 (i.e., 37%) languages show the same pattern. Even more strikingly, quite a few languages of the world (72 languages of the 593 languages, i.e., 12% in Brown 2005b) have the same word for 'hand' and 'finger'.

Research on the whole body covers only a handful of languages, but is an important example of cross-linguistic generalizations on linguistic categorization. For instance, Brown (1976) and Andersen (1978) suggest the following two *generalizations*:
- There will be distinct terms for BODY, HEAD, ARM, EYES, NOSE and MOUTH
- If there is a distinct term for FOOT (as opposed to LEG), then there will be a distinct term for HAND (as opposed to ARM).

'Body' has also been suggested to be a universally lexicalized concept within the Natural Semantic Metalanguage (cf. Goddard 2001; Wierzbicka 2007). However, many of the earlier generalizations have been challenged by the studies of ten lesser-known languages in Majid et al. (2006). For instance, Lavukaleve, a Papuan language isolate spoken on the Russell islands within the central Solomon Islands (Terrill 2006: 316), has one and the same word, *tau*, for both ARM and LEG, but none for ARM or LEG specifically, contradicting the claim that ARM is always lexicalized by a distinct term. Lavukaleve has also a distinct simple word, *fe*, for reference to FOOT, but nothing comparable for HAND – contradicting therefore the second claim above. Some of the languages in Majid et al. (2006) and elsewhere (e.g., Wilkins 1996) seem to lack the distinct label for

BODY itself, as e.g., opposed to 'person', 'skin' or 'body', contradicting the first of the above-mentioned generalizations (and strongly contested in Wierzbicka 2007).

Majid (2010) gives an excellent summary of how a cross-linguistic categorization of the body challenges many of the current views on body parts in perception. Vision has been privileged over other senses in discussions about "natural" segments of the body, most of which use various versions of visual processing models such as the 3D theory by Marr (1982) whereby the different parts of human body are represented by a three-dimensional hierarchical model. However, "[t]here is now an emerging literature on how body parts are represented and organized in different perceptual modalities, as well as how these sensorial representations are pooled together to create an integrated and holistic representation of the body and its parts" (Majid 2010: 59–60). For instance, intentional actions may either disrupt or unify perception of body parts. Thus, two tactile stimuli applied to either the hand or to the arm are perceived closer than when one of them applies to the hand and the other to the arm. However, the perceptual distance between the hand and the arm decreases when the person has to move his/her hands (de Vignemont et al. 2009). Majid concludes that there are different body partonomies for different representational systems, but joints – and the concomitant perceptual discontinuities – appear to constitute landmarks for segmentation and provide limits on where languages may draw boundaries in their body-part nomenclature.

Some of the factors behind the cross-linguistic differences in how languages categorize the body may also be sought in the physical, socio-historical and cultural environment. Brown (2005a, 2005b) suggests that the significant statistical asymmetries in the distributions of the languages with the same word for FINGER and HAND, and of those with the same word for HAND and ARM are correlated either with geography/climate or with culture. Thus, languages without the HAND-ARM distinction tend to occur more frequently near the equator, which may be accounted for by the fact that people living in other parts of the world often need extensive clothing, which greatly increases the distinctiveness of arm parts. Languages without FINGER-HAND distinction tend to be spoken by traditional hunter-gatherers or by groups having a mixed economy of cultivation and foraging. These often lack the habit of carrying finger rings, which makes fingers salient as distinct hand parts (Brown 2005a, 2005b).

2.5 Temperature

Cross-linguistic research on temperature is a relatively new addition to semantic typology. The TEMPERATURE domain constitutes the focus of a recent collaborative project covering more than fifty genetically, areally and typologically diverse languages (Koptjevskaja-Tamm 2015). Significantly, where English has a fairly rich inventory of temperature words (*hot, warm, lukewarm, chilly, cool, cold*, etc.), many languages manage with a simple opposition between two, 'hot/warm' vs. 'cool/cold'. In addition, the temperature systems often consist of several subparts that behave differently. For instance, languages often single out personal-feeling temperatures ('I feel cold') by special words or by particular constructions, as compared to tactile temperatures ('The stones are cold') and to ambient temperature ('It is cold here'). On the other hand, the linguistic encoding of ambient temperature may share properties with those of either tactile or personal-feeling temperature. The motivation for this lies in the conceptual and perceptual affinities of ambient temperature with both of the other frames of temperature evaluation. Thus, ambient and personal-feeling temperature are rooted in the same type of experience, thermal comfort, whereas tactile temperature relates to evaluation of the temperature of other entities, based on perception received by the skin. However, both tactile and ambient temperatures are about temperatures that can be verified from "outside", whereas personal-feeling temperature is about a subjective "inner" experience of a living being. In addition some entities, for instance water, may require particularly elaborated subsystems of temperature expressions, with additional expressions for extreme temperature values, such as 'ice-cold' and 'boiling hot', or for in-between temperatures like 'tepid'. This is, in turn, linked to the omnipresence and importance of water in human life, where its functioning for different purposes requires a particular temperature. This questions the universality of TEMPERATURE as a coherent semantic domain in many languages, an assumption usually held in cognitive research and in cognitive linguistics (see Clausner and Croft 1999; cf. the discussion of colour in section 2.1).

The interest of cognitive linguists and cognitive researchers in temperature has so far been mainly related to metaphors underlying emotions, e.g., AFFECTION IS WARMTH (Lakoff and Johnson 1999: 50) and ANGER IS HEAT (Kövecses 1995). An important question raised in Geeraerts and Grondelaers (1995) is to what degree such extensions reflect universal metaphorical patterns or are based on common cultural traditions. The results in Koptjevskaja-Tamm (2015) show that while some languages demonstrate elaborated systems of such uses, quite a few languages lack them altogether. Languages also vary as to which temperature term has predominantly positive associations in its extended uses (e.g., 'cold' rather than 'warm'), partly due to the different climatic conditions.

Section 2 has hopefully demonstrated the value of bringing in linguistic diversity into research on "how language relates to mind". Due to the space limitations, much of the other important research has been left out here, e.g., the foundational work on space (Levinson and Wilkins 2006, Levinson and Meira 2003, Ameka and Levinson 2007) – some of which is reported on in Coventry (this volume) – or the abundant literature on KINSHIP and EMOTIONS across languages. Some of the new areas addressed in recent cross-linguistic studies include CUT and BREAK (Majid and Bowerman 2007), LOCATION (Ameka and Levinson 2007), PUT and TAKE (Narasimhan and Kopecka 2012) and PAIN (Reznikova et al. 2012). The rest of the chapter will present the methodological, theoretical and typological insights accumulated in all this research.

3 Methodological challenges in semantic typology

Semantic typology has to find its own way for balancing the methodological and theoretical ambitions of both theoretical semantics and general typology.

Serious work in semantics presupposes taking a stance on two major and partly interrelated problems: what can be meant by meaning and how to solve the issue of *polysemy/semantic generality/vagueness*. For most semanticists, semantic analysis stands for understanding *descriptive meaning, sense,* or *intension*, rather than *denotation/extension*. This is especially true for cognitive semantics, for which linguistic meanings always imply a certain construal of a particular situation (cf. Langacker volume 1) and are laden with particular associations, intimately related to the speakers' "world" knowledge. In line with the general usage-based view within cognitive linguistics, the meanings of linguistic expressions are consequences of their uses, and word meanings are always associated with certain constructions. Conversely, conventional meanings associated with linguistic expressions only partially sanction the senses evoked in particular contexts. As a consequence, there are different opinions on what counts as polysemy both within Cognitive Linguistics and also among different semantic theories, practices (such as dictionary entries) and language users (see Riemer 2005 and Gries this volume).

Typological and cross-linguistic research has its own methodological issues. First of all, it is dependent on comparable data from (many) different languages. Cross-linguistic identification of studied phenomena presupposes a procedure which ensures that we compare like with like. Crucially, it should involve theory-neutral or framework-neutral definitions and concern observable phenomena. Another big issue concerns language sampling: a large sample representing the world's languages is a preferred option if we want to say something general about cross-linguistic variation and its limits. Languages often share similarities because of common ancestry, but also because of direct and indirect contacts among them. Therefore something you find by comparing English, French, German, Czech, Hungarian and even Basque does *not* have to be a universal, but might be a result of combined genetic and prolonged contact factors: a "Standard Average European" property. In general, modern typological research is very cautious in declaring "universals", i.e., properties that are believed to be present in all or most languages. Most universals suggested by cross-linguistic comparison have either been falsified or have been shown to have many counter-examples (cf. The Universals Archive in Konstanz, http://typo.uni-konstanz.de/archive/intro/index.php). The World Atlas of Language Structures (Haspelmath et al. 2005; Dryer and Haspelmath 2011) is the currently most ambitious and most quoted collective achievement in linguistic typology, primarily devoted to grammatical and phonetic phenomena.

Most of the cross-linguistic research on semantics, and in particular, on lexicon is based on elicited data. The "Nijmegen method" of semantic typology uses standardized stimuli, such as sets of pictures, videoclips and films for collecting data on a number of cognitive domains directly in the field (cf. http://fieldmanuals.mpi.nl/). Each set covers a shared denotational grid allowing systematic comparisons of semantic distinctions potentially relevant for the domain and may be used under different elicitation conditions, including games. Data for many studies is collected by means of questionnaires, ranging from simple translational questionnaires (e.g., Viberg's 2001 research on perception verbs) to much more sophisticated questionnaires which elicit verbal descriptions of various situations (e.g., deictic verbs in Ricca 1993 and Wilkins and Hill 1995; pain descriptions in Reznikova et al. 2012; temperature descriptions in Koptjevskaja-Tamm 2015). Comparison of parallel texts (translations of one and the same text) is now gradually gaining ground as a relatively new and promising method for data collection in cross-linguistic work, where the number of translations vary from just a few to more than 100 (cf. Wälchli and Cysouw 2012). Cross-linguistic semantic studies based on secondary sources, like dictionaries, are quite limited (some of the exceptions include Andersen 1978; Brown 1976, 2005a, 2005b; Sweetser 1990 and François 2008).

Each data collection method has its merits and drawbacks. Elicitation techniques are designed as a systematic grid for targeting the key aspects of the relevant linguistic phenomena, but non-elicited data may disclose interesting and unexpected sides of the phenomena that the researcher was not aware of. Also many meanings hardly lend themselves to being investigated via stimuli: for instance, mental states such as *think*, or abstract domains such as POSSESSION and EXISTENCE (cf. also Evans and Sasse 2007).

Elicited data are most often decontextualized, although the degree of decontextualization varies significantly between different techniques and studies.

Retelling a film for someone who has not seen it or exchanging verbal instructions during a game more closely reflect language in normal use than describing a series of disconnected videoclips or naming colour chips. Parallel texts have a clear advantage here as a source of context-embedded natural data that are semantically comparable across languages, even though translational equivalents across languages, in particular within a longer text, are never completely equivalent. The one text available in many languages are the various versions of the New Testament, which has severe limitations, but is a good source for studying motion events (cf. Wälchli and Cysouw 2012).

A successful study in semantic typology benefits from a combination of different types of data. Most of the recent enterprises with this orientation have been carried out as joint projects involving experts on particular languages. Because of this, studies in semantic typology usually operate with much more limited language samples (between ten and fifty languages) than is the norm in grammatical and phonetic typology.

A further issue is how the data are analyzed and how the results of the analysis are represented. Much of the current research in semantic typology sees the meanings of linguistic expressions as sets of uses, or as "etic definitions". To quote Levinson and Wilkins (2006: 8), "an 'etic' metalanguage (coined on the model of 'phonetic' by Pike) is some objective description of the domain which makes maximal discriminations, so that we can specify precisely how a language groups these discriminations within its own 'emic' (cf. 'phonemic') concepts". The step from "etic" to "emic" concepts is, however, far from trivial (cf. Evans 2011) and involves decisions as to which of the uses count as the same meaning viz. as instances of polysemy. Different decisions lead to different consequences, e.g., in conclusions about linguistic categories. For instance, Wierzbicka (2007) argues that it is far from clear to what extent the exclusively denotationally oriented research on body in Majid et al. (2006) gets to grips with the "real" meanings of the expressions under study and, consequently, with the categories perceived as different by those who use them. In other words, even though *ruka* in Russian covers both ARM and LEG, there might be reasons for distinguishing between the two meanings rather than lumping them into one. Only in the latter case is it legitimate to claim that the language does not conceptualize arm and leg as two distinct parts of the body.

The problem of a consistent meta-language for describing meaning across languages is enormous. This, in turn, relates to the general gap between theoretical semantics and actual lexicographic practices. Although cognitive semanticists oppose their "encyclopaedic" view on lexical meanings with the usual "dictionary view" (e.g., V. Evans and Green 2006: 207–222), there is little practical lexicographic work done in this tradition, with the notable exception of the

FrameNet project (www.isci.berkeley.edu/framenet/). A growing praxis in semantic typology is to represent its findings by means of semantic maps, which are more or less explicitly agnostic about the distinction between polysemy and semantic generality. Standard "implicational" semantic maps, originally used for grammatical devices (Haspelmath 2003: 231), and further successfully extended to lexicon (François 2008) compete with "probabilistic" semantic maps, built automatically by means of statistical analysis techniques, e.g., multidimensional scaling (Cysouw and Wälchli 2012; Majid et al. 2007). Such maps are normally produced for the purpose of a particular study, which, unfortunately, creates obstacles for evaluating cross-linguistic connections even between studies of high semantic and lexicographic quality.

An important candidate for a consistent metalanguage for the purposes of cross-linguistic comparison is the Natural Semantic Metalanguage (NSM), originally advocated by Anna Wierzbicka. The proponents of the NSM strive to compare descriptive meanings rather than denotational ranges and aim at providing meaning definitions by means of reductive paraphrases based on a principled set of "universal semantic primitives" (e.g., Goddard and Wierzbicka 1994; Goddard 2001; Wierzbicka 2007). NSM linguists have recently proposed a systematic approach to lexical typology using the notions of semantic molecules and templates (e.g., Goddard 2012). The theory has both positive and negative sides, its strong basic assumption is debatable (cf., e.g., Riemer 2005 and Evans 2011), but on the whole it deserves more attention in the typological enterprise and in cognitive linguistics than it has enjoyed so far.

4 Lessons from semantic typology

Cross-linguistic research on categorization (onomaseological semantic typology) starts from the basic assumption that experiences systematically encoded by one and the same linguistic label are perceived as representing one and the same category or categories closely related to each other. The question is then to what extent linguistic categorization is universal or language- and culture-specific. Some researchers consider categorization universal, at least when it comes to basic, universal and daily situations, so that lexical meanings "originate in non-linguistic cognition, and are shaped by perceptual and cognitive predispositions, environmental and biological constraints, and activities common to people everywhere" (Majid et al. 2007: 134). The radically relativistic view holds that the cross-linguistic variation in categorization is hardly limited at all and that meanings of linguistic expressions across languages are largely incommensurable.

The achievements of semantic typology provide evidence for an in-between position, i.e., that the cross-linguistic variation in how languages categorize one and the same domain operates within a constrained space, which in each case is defined in terms of cross-linguistically important dimensions. Some of these dimensions may, further, be explained by the human anatomy, and/or by general perceptual and cognitive predispositions. The examples of such explanations include neurophysiology of vision for colour (section 2.1) and its primacy within perception for categorization of perception by means of verbs (section 2.2), interaction of different perceptual modalities for the categorization of the body (section 2.3), or the structure of temperature perception (section 2.5). Perceptually salient topological features such as containment vs. support, properties of the figure (including animacy and agency) vs. ground are decisive for structuring various space- and motion-related domains (Levinson and Wilkins 2006; Ameka and Levinson 2007; Narasimhan and Kopecka 2012). The preferable attention to endpoints of motions rather than to sources may explain why the expression system for taking events in a language never displays a higher degree of elaboration than the one for putting events (cf. Narasimhan and Kopecka 2012 for the details and references).

Environmental factors, typical human activities (including communication), socio-cultural patterns, etc., are also often evoked as responsible for the shaping of linguistic categorization and for its instantiation in a particular language (cf. section 2.4 on TEMPERATURE and section 2.2 on the 'hand'/'arm', and 'hand'/'finger' distinctions).

Now, even though linguistic categorization of a particular domain normally operates within a constrained space, languages manifest an amazing cross-linguistic variation. First of all, there is an enormous diversity in the sheer number of lexical categories for carving up a certain domain. For instance, for describing 61 distinct cutting and breaking videoclips, the speakers of Yélî Dnye (Papuan) used only three verbs (Levinson 2007), whereas the Tzeltal (Mayan) speakers used more than fifty (Brown 2007).

In addition, even systems with comparable degrees of elaboration may differ in the details of the partitioning, e.g., in the placement of category boundaries. Categories, as they emerge in the course of cross-linguistic research, do not look like classical Aristotelian categories with necessary and sufficient meaning components, but have fuzzy boundaries and are rather organized in terms of prototypes, in the tradition of the mainstream cognitively oriented semantic research. One and the same situation may often be construed in different ways and may, consequently, be expressed by two different categories.

Much of what has been said above on onomaseological semantic typology applies, mutandis mutandi, to its semasiological counterpart, i.e., research on cross-linguistically recurrent metaphorical and metonymical patterns and other semantic associations. There are, however, unique methodological complications inherent in systematic cross-linguistic research on metaphor and metonymy. Conceptual Metaphor Theory emphasizes conceptual association that does not boil down to individual metaphorical uses or to linguistic convention. But to quote Gibbs (volume 1), "cognitive linguists, and others, should articulate criteria for identifying metaphoric patterns in language and inferring specific conceptual metaphors from discourse. These procedures should be specified with sufficient detail so that other researchers can possibly replicate the analysis and emerge with similar conclusions". Translated into the methodology of systematic cross-linguistic research, this means that we can only test the extent to which some concrete manifestations of suggested metaphors hold (e.g., whether verbs for seeing are systematically extended to perception, or whether words for 'warm' are systematically extended to emotions), rather than whether the conceptual metaphors KNOWING IS SEEING or AFFECTION IS WARMTH as a whole are universal.

There are cross-linguistically recurrent patterns in semasiological typology, and the roots for them and for the cross-linguistic variation in their manifestations may again be found in human biology, perception, cognition, physical environment, typical human activities, history or socio-cultural patterns (cf. sections 2.4 and 2.5 on the use of body and temperature for talking about emotions and section 2.2 for the connection between perception and cognition). Pain is often described by means of cross-linguistically recurrent and conventionalized metaphors (Reznikova et al. 2012), and there are cross-linguistically recurrent metaphorical and metonymical patterns underlying body part nomenclature (Wilkins 1996; Koch 2008; Urban 2012).

A final reflection concerns the traditional separation between grammatical typology, focusing on the grammatical behaviour of words and on morphosyntactic patterns, and lexical typology, that has largely been restricted to domain-categorization by lexical means. This somewhat artificial distinction is coupled with fundamental problems. As Lucy (1997) points out, the mainstream tradition of research into colour terms across languages does not presuppose any deeper linguistic analysis of these terms. "Articles surveying terms in a dozen or more languages never mention anything about those languages, or even about the structural value of the terms. *You do not need to know anything about languages or linguistics at all to read this literature or even to conduct research within the tradition*" (1997: 330).

Fortunately, the recent developments within semantic typology witness an ambition to reconcile the lexical and grammatical interests and to engage in a dialogue with linguistic grammatical theory. Much of the research on space and motion explicitly transcends the lexicon-grammar distinction (Levinson and Wilkins 2006; Ameka and Levinson 2007.) Another example is the project on categorization of the CUT and BREAK domain (Majid and Bowerman 2007), where one of the leading issues has been the interface between syntax and lexical semantics, i.e., to what extent and how the argument structure properties of a verb are predictable from its meaning. An even more ambitious research agenda aiming at comparing wholesale verbal lexical profiles of different languages and their repercussions for the grammatical characteristics has been proposed by Kibrik (2012).

Cognitively minded linguists will certainly appreciate the rise of Construction Grammar (Casenhiser and Bencini this volume) as an appropriate framework for semantic-typological research, e.g., on PAIN predicates (Reznikova et al. 2012), on TEMPERATURE (Koptjevskaja-Tamm 2015), and on LOCATION–EXISTENCE–POSSESSION (Koch 2012). The Construction-Grammar inspired schemas are capable of covering linguistic phenomena on different levels (lexicon and grammar), are both sufficiently systematic for capturing cross-linguistic (dis)similarities and sufficiently flexible for leaving room for language- and phenomenon-specific details.

5 Further research questions

Systematic research in semantic typology has so far been carried out on rather limited language samples. These are often sufficient for falsifying some assumptions on the universality of a particular phenomenon and for unveiling major patterns in its cross-linguistic variation, but are hardly adequate for drawing reliable conclusions on the interplay among the various factors behind it and for clearly distinguishing between universal determinants and those due to historical relations among the languages. Systematic research in semantic typology needs, therefore, to be extended to more linguistic phenomena and to more languages. In particular, sign languages have been largely missing in most studies of semantic typology.

But there are further fascinating research issues that will benefit from taking into consideration linguistic diversity and findings in semantic typology, for instance

- How do linguistic and non-linguistic categories relate to each other? (See Malt et al. 1999 on a difference between linguistic and non-linguistic categorization of household storage containers among the speakers of American English, Argentinean Spanish and Mandarin Chinese.)

- How do linguistic and non-linguistic domains relate to each other? For instance, although COLOUR or TEMPERATURE languages are usually assumed to be coherent cognitive domains, languages do not necessarily treat them as such, cf. sections 2.1 and 2.5.
- Do semantic differences in the linguistic categorization systems and in the metaphorical/metonymical patterns affect cognition, perception and/or non-verbal behaviour in speakers of different languages? Compare here the revived interest for the issue of linguistic relativity (Li and Gleitman 2002; Levinson et al. 2002; Slobin 2003; Malt and Wolff [eds.] 2010).
- Will there be differences in linguistic categorization, cognition and perception in bilingual speakers as compared to monolingual ones and will these differences depend on the differences among the languages involved? (See Athanasopoulos et al. 2010 or A. Brown and Gullberg 2008 on the gradual conversion in the speakers' linguistic descriptions, cognitive processing, gestures and unconscious perception between the L1 and L2 systems.)
- Will there be substantial differences in how children acquire linguistic categories in different languages? (See Bowerman and Choi 2003 and Parish-Morris et al. 2010 on the gradual replacement of children's pre-language sensitivity to many different properties of specific spatial situations by selective sensitivity to the categories relevant in the language that the child is acquiring.)
- To what extent will semantic differences in the linguistic categorization systems and in the metaphorical/metonymical patterns find correlates in how these are represented in the brain (cf. Kemmerer 2010)?
- What is the division of labour across different sign modalities in expressing meaning? Can the semantic choices made in one subsystem affect the choices made in the other(s) (cf. "semiotic ecology" in Evans 2011)? We know very little about how information is distributed across different sign modalities, but some forms seem to be better for expressing certain things than others. For instance, in spite of all the rich lexical and grammatical resources for talking about space and emotions, precise spatial localization often requires deictic gestures, while emotion and emotional intensity is better captured by prosody, often together with gestures.

By pursuing these captivating questions, cross-linguistic diversity and semantic typology can make a substantial contribution to the study of how language relates to the human mind.

6 References

Aikhenvald, Alexandra Y. and Anne Storch (eds.) (2013): *Perception and Cognition in Language and Culture*. Leiden: Brill.

Ameka, Felix K. and Stephen C. Levinson (eds.) (2007): The typology and semantics of locative predication: Posturals, positionals and other beasts. *Linguistics* 45(5/6): 847–871.

Andersen, Elaine (1978): Lexical universals of body-part terminology. In: J. H. Greenberg (ed.), *Universals of Human Language*, 335–368. Stanford: Stanford University Press.

Athanasopoulos, Panos, Benjamin Dering, Alison Wiggett, Jan-Rouke Kuipers, and Guillaume Thierry (2010): Perceptual shift in bilingualism: Brain potentials reveal plasticity in pre-attentive colour perception. *Cognition* 116(3): 437–443.

Bergen, Benjamin (volume 1): Embodiment. Berlin/Boston: De Gruyter Mouton.

Berlin, Brent and Paul Kay (1969): *Basic Color Terms: Their Universality and Evolution*. Berkeley: University of California Press.

Bornstein, Marc H. (2007): Hue categorization and color naming: Cognition to language to culture. In: R. MacLaury, G. V. Paramei and D. Dedrick (eds.), *Anthropology of Color: Interdisciplinary Multilevel Modeling*, 3–27. Amsterdam: John Benjamins.

Bowerman, Melissa and Soonja Choi (2003): Space under construction: language-specific spatial categorization in first language acquisition. In: D. Gentner and S. Goldin-Meadow (eds.), *Language in Mind: Advances in the Study of Language and Thought*, 387–427. Cambridge: MIT Press.

Brown, Amanda and Marianne Gullberg (2008): Bidirectional crosslinguistic influence in L1-L2 encoding of manner in speech and gesture. *Studies in Second Language Acquisition* 30: 225–251.

Brown, Cecil H. (1976): General principles of human anatomical partonomy and speculations on the growth of partonomic nomenclature. *American Ethnologist* 3: 400–424.

Brown, Cecil H. (2001): Lexical typology from an anthropological point of view. In: M. Haspelmath, E. König, W. Oesterreicher and W. Raible (eds.), *Language Typology and Language Universals*, Volume 2, 1178–1190. Berlin: Walter de Gruyter.

Brown, Cecil H. (2005a): Hand and arm. In: M. Haspelmath, M. Dryer, D. Gil and B. Comrie (eds.) *The World Atlas of Language Structures (WALS)*, 522–525. Oxford: Oxford University Press.

Brown, Cecil H. (2005b): Finger and hand. In: M. Haspelmath, M. Dryer, D. Gil and B. Comrie (eds.) *The World Atlas of Language Structures (WALS)*, 526–529. Oxford: Oxford University Press.

Brown, Penelope (2007): 'She had just cut/broken off her head': Cutting and breaking verbs in Tzeltal. *Cognitive Linguistics* 18(2): 319–330.

Casenhiser, Devin and Giulia Bencini (this volume): Argument structure constructions. Berlin/Boston: De Gruyter Mouton.

Classen, Constance (1993): *Worlds of Sense: Exploring the Senses in History and Across Cultures*. London: Routledge.

Clausner, Timothy C. and William Croft (1999): Domains and image-schemas. *Cognitive Linguistics* 10: 1–31.

Coventry, Kenny (this volume): Space. Berlin/Boston: De Gruyter Mouton.

Croft, William (2003): *Typology and Universals* (Cambridge Textbooks in Linguistics). Cambridge: Cambridge University Press.

Croft, William, Jóhanna Barðdal, Willem Hollmann, Violeta Sotirova, and Chiaki Taoka (2010): Revising Talmy's typological classification of complex events. In: H. C. Boas (ed.), *Contrastive Construction Grammar*, 201–235. Amsterdam/Philadelphia: John Benjamins.

de Vignemont, Frédéreque, Asifa Majid, Corinne Jolla, and Patrick Haggard (2009): Segmenting the body into parts: evidence from biases in tactile perception. *Quarterly Journal of Experimental Psychology* 62: 500–512.

Dryer, Matthew S. and Martin Haspelmath (eds.) (2011): *The World Atlas of Language Structures Online*. Max Planck Digital Library. http://wals.info/

Enfield, N. J. and Anna Wierzbicka (eds.) (2002): The body in description of emotion. *Pragmatics and cognition*, special issue 10(1–2).

Evans, Nicholas (2011): Semantic typology. In: J. J. Song (ed.), *The Oxford Handbook of Typology*, 504–533. Oxford: Oxford University Press.

Evans, Nicholas and Stephen Levinson. (2009): The myth of language universals: Language diversity and its importance for cognitive science. *Behavioral and Brain Sciences* 32: 429–492.

Evans, Nicholas and Hans-Jürgen Sasse (2007): Searching for meaning in the Library of Babel: Field semantics and problems of digital archiving. *Archives and Social Studies: A Journal of Interdisciplinary Research* 1. (http://socialstudies.cartagena.es/index.php?option=com_contentandtask=viewandid=53andItemid=42)

Evans, Nicholas and David P. Wilkins (2000): In the mind's ear: The semantic extensions of perception verbs in Australian languages. *Language* 76: 546–592.

Evans, Vyvyan and Melanie Green (2006): *Cognitive Linguistics. An Introduction*. Mahwah/London: Lawrence Erlbaum.

Filipović, Luna and Iraide Ibarretxe-Antuñano (this volume): Motion. Berlin/Boston: De Gruyter Mouton.

François, Alexandre (2008): Semantic maps and the typology of colexification: Intertwining polysemous networks across languages. In M. Vanhove (ed.), *From Polysemy to Semantic Change*, 163–215. Amsterdam/Philadelphia: John Benjamins.

Geeraerts, Dirk and Stef Grondelaers (1995): Looking back at anger: Cultural traditions and metaphorical patterns. In: J. R. Taylor & R. E. MacLaury (eds.), *Language and the Cognitive Construal of the World*. 153–179. Berlin: de Gruyter.

Gibbs, Raymond W. Jr. (volume 1): Metaphor. Berlin/Boston: De Gruyter Mouton.

Goddard, Cliff (2001): Lexico-semantic universals: A critical overview. *Linguistic Typology* 5: 1–65.

Goddard, Cliff (2012): Semantic primes, semantic molecules, semantic templates: Key concepts in the NSM approach to lexical typology. In: M. Koptjevskaja-Tamm and M. Vanhove (eds.), New directions in lexical typology. A special issue of *Linguistics* 50(3): 421–466.

Goddard, Cliff and Anna Wierzbicka (eds.) (1994): *Semantic and Lexical Universals – Theory and Empirical Findings*. Amsterdam/Philadelphia: John Benjamins.

Gries, Stefan Th. (this volume): Polysemy. Berlin/Boston: De Gruyter Mouton.

Haspelmath, Martin (2003): The geometry of grammatical meaning: Semantic maps and cross-linguistic comparison. In: M. Tomasello (ed.), *The New Psychology of Language* 2. 211–242. Mahwah: Lawrence Erlbaum.

Haspelmath, Martin, Matthew Dryer, David Gil, and Bernard Comrie (2005): *The World Atlas of Language Structures (WALS)*. Oxford: Oxford University Press.

Haspelmath, Martin, Ekkehard König, Wulf Oesterreicher, and Wolfgang Raible (eds.) (2001): *Language Typology and Language Universals*, Volumes 1–2. Berlin: Walter de Gruyter.

Heider, Eleanor R. (1972): Universals in color naming and memory. *Journal of Experimental Psychology* 93: 10–20.

Kay, Paul, Brent Berlin, Luisa Maffi, William R. Merrifield, and Richard Cook (2009): *The World Color Survey*. Stanford: Center for the Study of Language and Information.

Kay, Paul and Lisa Maffi (2005): Colour terms. In: M. Haspelmath, M. Dryer, D. Gil and B. Comrie (eds.), *The World Atlas of Language Structures (WALS)*, 534–545. Oxford: Oxford University Press.

Kay, Paul and Chad McDaniel (1978): The linguistic significance of the meanings of basic color terms. *Language* 54: 610–46.

Kemmerer, David (2010): How words capture visual experience: the perspective from cognitive neuroscience. In: B. C. Malt and P. Wolff (eds.), *Words and the Mind. How Words Capture Human Experience*, 287–327. Oxford: Oxford University Press.

Kibrik, Andrej (2011): *Reference in Discourse*. Oxford: Oxford University Press.

Kibrik, Andrej (2012): Toward a typology of verb lexical systems: A case study in Northern Athabaskan. In: M. Koptjevskaja-Tamm and M. Vanhove (eds.), New directions in lexical typology. A special issue of *Linguistics* 50(3): 495–532.

Koch, Peter (2001): Lexical typology from a cognitive and linguistic point of view. In: M. Haspelmath, E. König, W. Oesterreicher and W. Raible (eds.), *Language Typology and Language Universals*, Volume 2, 1142–1178. Berlin: Walter de Gruyter.

Koch, Peter (2008): Cognitive onomasiology and lexical change: around the eye. In: M. Vanhove (ed.), *From Polysemy to Semantic Change*, 107–137. Amsterdam/ Philadelphia: John Benjamins.

Koch, Peter (2012): Location, existence, and possession: A constructional-typological exploration. In: M. Koptjevskaja-Tamm and M. Vanhove (eds.), New directions in lexical typology. A special issue of *Linguistics* 50(3): 533–604.

Koptjevskaja-Tamm, Maria (2008): Approaching lexical typology. In: M. Vanhove (ed.), *From Polysemy to Semantic Change*, 3–52. Amsterdam/Philadelphia: John Benjamins.

Koptjevskaja-Tamm, Maria (ed.) (2015): *The Linguistics of Temperature*. Amsterdam/ Philadelphia: John Benjamins.

Koptjevskaja-Tamm, Maria, Dagmar Divjak, and Ekaterina Rakhilina (2010): Aquamotion verbs in Slavic and Germanic: A case study in lexical typology. In: V. Driagina-Hasko and R. Perelmutter (eds.), *New Approaches to Slavic Verbs of Motion*, 315–341. Amsterdam/ Philadelphia: John Benjamins.

Koptjevskaja-Tamm, Maria and Martine Vanhove (eds.) (2012): New directions in lexical typology. A special issue of *Linguistics* 50(3).

Kövecses, Zoltan (1995): Anger: Its language, conceptualization, and physiology in the light of cross-cultural evidence. In: J. R. Taylor and R. E. MacLaury (eds.), *Language and the Cognitive Construal of the World*, 181–196. Berlin: Mouton de Gruyter.

Lakoff, George and Mark Johnson (1999): *Philosophy in the Flesh. The Embodied Mind and its Challenge to Western Thought*. New York: Basic books.

Langacker, Ronald W. (volume 1): Construal. Berlin/Boston: De Gruyter Mouton.

Levinson, Stephen (2001): Yélî Dnye and the theory of basic color terms. *Journal of Linguistic Anthropology* 10(1): 3–55.

Levinson, Stephen (2007): Cut and break verbs in Yélî Dnye, the Papuan language of Rossel Island. *Cognitive Linguistics* 18(2): 207–218.

Levinson, Stephen and Sergio Meira (2003): 'Natural concepts' in the spatial topological domain – adpositional meanings in cross-linguistic perspective: an exercise in semantic typology. *Language* 79(3): 485–516.

Levinson, Stephen, Sotaro Kita, Daniel B. M. Hauna, and Björn H. Rasch. (2002): Returning the tables: Language affects spatial reasoning. *Cognition* 84: 155–188.
Levinson, Stephen and David Wilkins (2006): *Grammars of Space*. Cambridge: Cambridge University Press.
Li, Peggy and Lila Gleitman (2002): Turning the tables: language and spatial reasoning. *Cognition* 83: 265–294.
Lindsey, Delwin T. and Angela M. Brown (2002): Color naming and the phototoxic effects of sunlight on the eye. *Psychological Science* 13(6): 506–512.
Lucy, John (1997): The linguistics of 'color'. In: C. L. Hardin and L. Maffi (eds.), *Color Categories in Thought and Language*, 320–346. Cambridge: Cambridge University Press.
Maalej, Zouheir A. and Ning Yu (eds.) (2011): *Embodiment via Body Parts. Studies from Various Languages and Cultures*. Amsterdam/Philadelphia: John Benjamins Publishing Company.
MacLaury, Robert E., Galina V. Paramei, and Don Dedrick (eds.) (2007): *Anthropology of Color: Interdisciplinary Multilevel Modeling*. Amsterdam: John Benjamins.
Maisak, Timur and Ekaterina Rakhilina (eds.) (2007): *Glagoly dviženija v vode: leksičeskaja tipologija*. [Verbs of motion and location in water: Lexical typology]. Moskva: Indrik.
Majid, Asifa (2010): Words for parts of the body. In: B. C. Malt and P. Wolff (eds.), *Words and the Mind. How Words Capture Human Experience*, 58–71. Oxford: Oxford University Press.
Majid, Asifa and Melissa Bowerman (2007): Cutting and breaking events: A crosslinguistic perspective. *Cognitive Linguistics* 18(2): 133–152.
Majid, Asifa, Nicholas J. Enfield, and Miriam van Staden (eds.) (2006): Parts of the body: Cross-linguistic categorisation. [Special issue] *Language Sciences*, 28(2–3).
Malt, Barbara C., Sloman, Steven A., Gennari, Silvia, Shi, Meiyi, and Wang, Yuan (1999): Knowing versus naming: Similarity and the linguistic categorization of artifacts. *Journal of Memory and Language* 40: 230–262.
Malt, Barbara C. and Philipp Wolff (eds.) (2010): *Words and the Mind. How Words Capture Human Experience*. Oxford: Oxford University Press.
Marr, David (1982): *Vision: A Computational Investigation into the Human Representation and Processing of Visual Information*. New York: W. H. Freeman.
Narasimhan, Bhuvana and Anetta Kopecka (eds.) (2012): *Events of 'Putting' and 'Taking': A Crosslinguistic Perspective*. Amsterdam/Philadelphia: John Benjamins.
Parish-Morris, Julia, Shannon M. Pruden, Weiyi Ma, Kathy Hirsh-Pasek, and Roberta Michnick Golinkoff (2010): A world of relations: relational words. In: B. C. Malt and P. Wolff (eds.), *Words and the Mind. How Words Capture Human Experience*, 219–242. Oxford: Oxford University Press.
Pawley, Andrew (1994): Kalam exponents of lexical and semantic primitives. In: C. Goddard and A. Wierzbicka (eds.), *Semantic and Lexical Universals – Theory and Empirical Findings*, 387–422. Amsterdam/Philadelphia: John Benjamins.
Reznikova, Tatiana, Ekaterina Rakhilina, and Anastasia Bonch-Osmolovskaya (2012): Towards a typology of pain predicates. In: M. Koptjevskaja-Tamm and M. Vanhove (eds.), New directions in lexical typology. A special issue of *Linguistics*, 50(3): 421–466.
Ricca, Davide (1993): *I verbi deittici di movimento in Europa: Una ricerca interlinguistica*. Firenze: La Nuova Italia Editrice.
Riemer, Nick (2005): *The Semantics of Polysemy*. Berlin/New York: Mouton de Gruyter.
Sharifian, Farzad, René Dirven, Ning Yu, and Susanne Niemeier (eds.) (2008): *Culture, Body and Language. Conceptualizations of Internal Body Organs Across Cultures and Languages*. Berlin: Mouton de Gruyter.

Shepard, Roger N. (1992): The perceptual organisation of colors: An adaptation to regularities of the terrestrial world? In: J. H. Barkow, L. Cosimedes, and J. Tooby (eds.), *The Adapted Mind: Evolutionary Psychology and the Generation of Culture*, 495–532. New York: Oxford University Press.

Slobin, Dan I. (2003): Language and thought online: Cognitive consequences of linguistic relativity. In: D. Gentner and S. Goldin-Meadow (eds.), *Language in Mind: Advances in the Study of Language and Thought*, 157–191. Cambridge: MIT Press.

Sweetser, Eve (1990): *From Etymology to Pragmatics: Metaphorical and Cultural Aspects of Semantic Structure*. Cambridge: Cambridge University Press.

Talmy, Leonard (1985): Lexicalization patterns. In: T. Shopen (ed.), *Language Typology and Synchronic Description*, Volume 3, 47–159. Cambridge: Cambridge University Press.

Taylor, John R. (this volume): Prototype effects in grammar. Berlin/Boston: De Gruyter Mouton.

Terrill, Angela (2006): Body-part terms in Lavukaleve, a Papua language of the Solomon Islands. In: A. Majid, N. J. Enfield and M. van Staden (eds.), Parts of the Body: Cross-Linguistic Categorisation [Special issue] *Language Sciences* 28(2–3): 304–322.

Urban, Matthias (2012): *Analyzibility and Semantic Associations in Referring Expressions. A Study in Comparative Lexicology*. PhD Dissertation. Leiden University.

Vanhove, Martine (2008): Semantic associations between sensory modalities, prehension and mental perceptions: A crosslinguistic perspective. In: M. Vanhove (ed.), *From Polysemy to Semantic Change*, 342–370. Amsterdam/Philadelphia: John Benjamins.

Verkerk, Annemarie (2014): Where Alice fell into: Motion events from a parallel corpus. In B. Szmrecsanyi, and B. Wälchli (eds.), *Linguistic Variation in Text and Speech, Within and Across Languages*, 324–354. Berlin: de Gruyter.

Viberg, Åke (2001): Verbs of perception. In: M. Haspelmath, E. König, W. Oesterreicher and W. Raible (eds.), *Language Typology and Language Universals*, Volume 2, 1294–1309. Berlin: Walter de Gruyter.

Wächli, Bernhard and Michael Cysouw (2012): Lexical typology through similarity semantics: Toward a semantic map of motion verbs. In: M. Koptjevskaja-Tamm and M. Vanhove (eds.), New directions in lexical typology. A special issue of *Linguistics*, 50(3): 671–710.

Wierzbicka, Anna (2005): There are no "color universals". But there are universals of visual semantics. *Anthropological Linguistics* 47(2): 217–244.

Wierzbicka, Anna (2007): Bodies and their parts: an NSM approach to semantic typology. *Language Sciences* 29: 14–65.

Wilkins, David P. (1996): Natural tendencies of semantic change and the search for cognates. In: M. Durie and M. Ross (eds.), *The Comparative Method Reviewed. Regularity and Irregularity in Language Change*, 264–304. New York/Oxford: Oxford University Press.

Wilkins, David P. and Deborah Hill (1995): When GO means COME: Questioning the basicness of basic motion verbs. *Cognitive Linguistics* 6(2/3): 209–259.

Stefan Th. Gries
Chapter 2: Polysemy

1 The notion of polysemy

The probably most widely accepted definition of polysemy is as the form of ambiguity where 2+ related senses are associated with the same word; consider the meanings of *glass* in *I emptied the glass* ('container') and *I drank a glass* ('contents of the container'). Ever since this notion was proposed by Bréal (1897), it has been puzzling researchers from many disciplines: linguists, lexicographers, psycholinguists, psychologists, computer scientists, etc. In the componential Classical Theory of Meaning (Katz and Fodor 1963; Katz 1967), (i) meanings[1] of words were defined on the basis of necessary and sufficient conditions (or features/markers) without reference to contexts, (ii) therefore, a particular entity was either a full member of the category defined by a word or not, and (iii) the similarity of meanings of different words, or senses of the same word, could be quantified by counting the number of features/markers shared by meanings/senses. Thus, a word was ambiguous if it had more than one definition using such features (where no distinction between different kinds of ambiguity – homonymy and polysemy – was made).

Cognitive linguistics (CL), or cognitive semantics, drew on research in philosophy, anthropology, and cognitive psychology and adopted a perspective in which polysemy became an omnipresent property associated with lexical items but also morphemes, grammatical constructions, and whole grammatical classes. Section 2 sketches the development of polysemy in CL. Section 3 explores how polysemy was addressed in neighboring fields (psycholinguistics and corpus linguistics), and section 4 points out desiderata for future CL research on polysemy.

2 Polysemy in cognitive linguistics

In this section, I will discuss the "history" of polysemy in CL; as in most of CL, I will mostly focus on lexical semantics.

---
[1] I use *meanings* for unrelated interpretations and *senses* for related interpretations.

Stefan Th. Gries, Santa Barbara, United States of America

https://doi.org/10.1515/9783110626438-002

The treatment of polysemy in CL involves (i) viewing meaning/sense as categorization, (ii) recognizing the importance of context for meaning/senses and that linguistic and encyclopedic knowledge are hard to keep separate, and (iii) incorporating prototype theory into linguistics. As for (i), meaning/sense is viewed as categorization such that, e.g., learning/recognizing that a sparrow is a bird amounts to establishing birds as a category of which sparrows are a member. That is, lexical items are the linguistically coded subset of all conceptual, mentally represented categories.

As for (ii), meanings of lexical items are difficult to pin down without considering both their *context* and *encyclopedic real-world knowledge*, an assumption from Fillmore's (1975, 1982) Frame Semantics. An early example involves what Cruse (1995: 44) calls cooperative readings: The presence of zeugma in (1a) appears to indicate that *dissertation* is polysemous with at least two senses ('intellectual content' vs. 'physical object'), but the slight change to (1b) results in an absence of zeugma, which does not support a similar polysemy (following Geeraerts 1993 and, ultimately, Norrick 1981):

(1) a. Judy's dissertation is thought-provoking and yellowed with age
    b. Judy's dissertation is still thought-provoking although yellowed with age

(2) the splinter in my hand

In fact, Taylor (2012: 220 ff.) points out it is often unclear where in an utterance polysemy resides – in a lexical item or its context. Is (2) polysemous because of the polysemy of *in* or of *hand* or do both senses co-select each other? Similarly, Taylor (2012: 226) illustrates how the meaning of *cut the lawn* changes from the prototypical one to the meaning of 'cut someone a piece of instant lawn (as *cut someone a piece of cake*)' that it may have in an instant lawn business. Finally, Labov (1973) has shown that speakers presented with something that looks like something between a bowl and a cup prefer to call it *bowl* when it contains potatoes, and *cup* when it contains coffee.

As for (iii), CL has drawn on research in cognitive psychology (much of it by Heider/Rosch, e.g., Rosch 1975, 1978) that showed subjects/speakers do not categorize objects using necessary/sufficient features but by comparing their similarity to the *prototype* (see Taylor this volume) of the candidate category/categories. Specifically, prototypical members of a category are listed more often/earlier in experiments where subjects are asked to list members of a category, their category membership is verified more quickly, and they give more rise to generalizations about the category. The notion of a prototype has been defined/operationalized in different ways (see Lakoff 1987): the prototypical sense of a word may be the most frequent and/or salient and/or most concrete one, the earliest attested one (historically or acquisitionally), the one from which most others can be derived best, but these criteria need not converge. I will consider a prototype (say, of *bird*) to be an abstract conceptual entity that combines attributes with a high cue validity for that category ('flies', 'has feathers', 'lays eggs', 'has a beak', etc.).

This perspective gave rise to the notions of (i) *radial categories* – categories with a central element combining many high-cue validity attributes and motivating the existence of less central members; the most-cited example is probably *mother* – and (ii) *family resemblance categories* – categories in which not all members share the same set of attributes but in which members are disjunctively related by sharing at least some attributes with each other; the usual example is Wittgenstein's ([1953] 2001) *game*. That means that prototype effects and category structure can be found on the level of the individual senses, on multiple levels of more schematic elements subsuming similar senses, and on the level of the whole category of interrelated senses of an element; thus, "the semantic value of a word need no longer be a single, unitary structure, but rather, [...] a set of interrelated senses" (Cuyckens and Zawada 2001: xiii). For example, Norvig and Lakoff (1986) discuss the structure of senses of the polysemous verb *take*. The prototype is exemplified by *John took the book from Mary* and different links are postulated to connect senses; for example,

- *profile shift*, relating the prototype to *John took the book to Mary*, which profiles the movement of the Agent$_i$ to the Recipient$_j$;
- metaphoric links (see Gibbs volume 1): *John took the book to Mary* is connected to *John took the book at Mary* via the metaphor APPLYING FORCE IS TRANSFERRING AN OBJECT;
- metonymic links (see Barcelona volume 1) and frame-addition links: *John took the book to Chicago* is connected to *John took Mary to the theater* via the metonymy GOING TO (public establishment) D STANDS FOR DOING C (activity conventionally done at D).

Additional important types of links connecting senses are generalizations, specializations, and image-schema transformations. The latter is exemplified by *John walked over the bridge* (involving a SOURCE schema) being related via an image-schema transformation to *John lives over the hill* (involving an ENDPOINT schema). This also means that, ultimately, some relations between senses of a word are motivated by speakers' conceptualizations of real-world events and concrete bodily/sensori-motor experience (cf. Lakoff and Brugman 1986, Gibbs and Matlock 2001).

2.1 Phase 1: extreme splitting

Considering studies of word senses on a continuum from extreme lumpers (strict monosemy analyses, e.g., Ruhl 1989) to extreme splitters (highly granular polysemy analyses), the initial phase of CL research on polysemy would be in the latter extreme. Beginning with Brugman's (1981) analysis of the preposition *over* (cf. also Lakoff 1987: 416 ff. and Brugman and Lakoff 1988) and Lindner (1981) on *up* and *out*, cognitive-semantic studies involved the above theoretical notions and many minimally different senses in the so-called *full-specification approach*. For instance, in Brugman's/Lakoff's account of *over*, (3) and (4) constitute different senses since they differ with regard to whether the trajectors (*Sam, the bird*) are in contact with the landmark (*the wall*) or not:

(3) The bird flew over the wall.

(4) Sam climbed over the wall.

(5) John walked over the bridge.

(6) John walked over the hill.

Similarly, (5) and (6) are considered different senses, because only (6) involves a landmark (*the hill*) that is vertically extended (Lakoff 1987: 422). Brugman's/Lakoff's analysis involves more than twenty senses arranged in a radial category around *over*'s prototypical sense, which they claim is exemplified by *The plane flew over*. Two crucial notions of such analyses are those of *cognitive/ representational reality* and *motivation* (of links and senses). Regarding the former, many studies did not topicalize the ontological status of the lexical networks of polysemous items, but some literature assumed some cognitive reality: "a network-style mode of storage is cognitively real" (Brugman and Lakoff 1988: 477). Langacker offered less bold characterizations:

> It is not suggested that a strong claim of psychological reality can be made for any particular linguistic analysis as currently constituted. The description of a language is nevertheless a substantive hypothesis about its actual cognitive representation. (1987: 56, see also p. 382)

Regarding the latter, motivation is situated between unpredictable arbitrariness and perfect predictability. For instance, if one extended the analysis of *over* to non-prepositional cases – e.g., as a particle or prefix – one would encounter uses like *sleep overpowered him*. If one wanted to express the concept 'to overpower' but did not know the verb *overpower*, one might not *predict* there *must* be an English verb *overpower*. Nevertheless, once one considers the prototypical spatial meaning of *over* and the independently-postulated metaphor CONTROL IS UP, then a verb such as *overpower* "makes sense" (Lakoff 1987: 448).

For ten to fifteen years, this approach was extremely influential. In fact, since CL (i) viewed lexical items as categories, (ii) abandoned a strict separation between lexis and syntax, and (iii) therefore, viewed constructions as categories, too, polysemy analyses soon surfaced outside of lexical semantics: cf. Nikiforidou (1991) on genitives, Panther and Thornburg (2002) on *-er* nominalizations, Smith (2001) on Icelandic datives, Hendrikse (2001) on the Southern Bantu noun class system, Selvik (2001) on Setswana noun classes, etc. However, the most far-reaching extension was to the semantics of syntactic constructions. Goldberg's work (e.g., 1992, 1995) on argument structure constructions was particularly influential. First, it affected the decision where to localize polysemy: instead of assuming that different intransitive verbs such as *sneeze* or *cough* are polysemous in having a caused-motion sense (e.g., *Pat sneezed/coughed the napkin off the table*), she argued the syntactic pattern V-NP-PP itself has a meaning (here, 'caused-motion') and that, say, verbs in a constructional verb slot elaborate the construction's meaning; for instance, the prototypical transfer-of-possession sense of *give* elaborates the prototypical 'X causes Y to receive Z' meaning of the ditransitive construction V-NP-NP.

The second important extension was that constructions, just like words, were assumed to have multiple senses related by polysemy links. For instance, apart from the prototypical sense of the ditransitive, the ditransitive was argued to also have the senses listed in (7) (Goldberg 1995: section 3.3.3.2), and other analyses have posited constructional polysemy in other domains (cf. Michaelis and Lambrecht 1996 or Jackendoff 1997).

(7) a. Joe permitted Chris an apple.   'X enables Y to receive Z'
    b. Joe baked Bob a cake.   'X intends to cause Y to receive Z'
    c. Joe refused Bob a cake.   'X causes Y not to receive Z"

2.2 Phase 2: discussion and revision

While polysemy analyses became increasingly popular, scholars also began to discuss their shortcomings. One discussion was triggered by Sandra and Rice (1995); see also Rice (1996):
- how is the prototype defined? For *over*, Brugman/Lakoff postulated 'above-across' is the prototype, Tyler and Evans (2001) postulated 'above' to be central, Deane (2005) "characterized the preposition in terms of a trajector entity which intervenes between [an] observer and the landmark" (Taylor 2012: 236), etc.;

- how are different senses distinguished and is the fine level of resolution often adopted really warranted? Do (5) and (6) need to be distinguished as different senses or can they be conflated into one? (Are there even different word senses?)
- what motivates the different representational formats (cf. Lewandowska-Tomaszczyk 2007: section 4.2 for a comparison) and what is the ontological status of the proposed networks? Cognitive linguists often argued their analyses were compatible with, or stood for, some sort of cognitive reality, but how much do such linguistic analyses warrant psychological/psycholinguistic claims? (Cf. also Riemer (2005: Ch. 1)

Another discussion involved how much (cognitive) linguists can really say about mental representation (especially on the basis of something as volatile as introspection; cf. Nisbett and Wilson 1977). First, Croft (1998) argued that the typical introspective linguistic evidence – e.g., grammatical/semantic idiosyncrasies – can exclude more general models of mental representation (i.e., more schematic/monosemic models), but that, conversely, grammatical/semantic generality does not automatically support more general models – for that, additional experimental/observational evidence is required (e.g., sentence-sorting, sentence-similarity judgments, or [lack of] similar distributional behavior in corpora).

Sandra (1998) limited the purview of linguistic studies even more, arguing that "linguists have a very minor role to play when issues of mental representations are at stake […] At most they can restrict the range of potential options" (1998: 361) Sandra also cautions CL to avoid the *polysemy fallacy* to automatically postulate very fine-grained sense distinctions (when more schematic subanalyses might be sufficient) and to consider such analyses a rendering of the language user's mental representation of the linguistic data. This view, which appears to exhibit a slightly old-fashioned and non-interdisciplinary division of linguists vs. non-linguists/psycholinguists as well as a lack of recognition of, say, Tuggy's (1993) introduction of multiple levels of schematization, was addressed by Tuggy (1999). Tuggy points out shortcomings in Sandra's characterization of Croft's positions and the polysemy fallacy, but also argues that introspective data are "extremely important evidence" because "[w]hen such intuitions line up impressively, they acquire a degree of objectivity" (1999: 352). This argument actually reinforces Sandra's point since proper experimentation is a way to get intuitions by multiple speakers to "line up". Also, Tuggy proposes additional polysemy diagnostics such as direct intuitions about sense relations, perceptions of puns, evidence from speech errors, and "holes in the pattern", as when particular usages that should go with a particular form do not. (See Riemer 2005: Ch. 3 for discussion.)

Another point of critique involves the relation of the *polysemies of words and/in constructions*. One account discussed above with regard to (7) argued that constructions such as the ditransitive are polysemous just as the lexical items are. However, Croft (2003: 55) argued that the senses of, say, the ditransitive construction appear to be more due to the classes of verbs inserted into them: "It is not an accident that the verbs found with ditransitive sense E ['X enables Y to receive Z' from (7a)] are verbs of permission [...]. That is, it seems that the different 'senses' of the ditransitive construction are very closely tied to the verb classes that each 'sense' occurs with" (2003: 56). Croft proceeds to make a case for verb-class specific constructions and even verb-specific constructions (cf. also Boas 2008), which testifies to the many difficulties of locating at which level(s) polysemy is situated.

2.3 Phase 3: newer developments

As a result of the research mentioned above, research on polysemy went, simplistically speaking, two different ways. First, new theoretical approaches were developed, most notably Tyler and Evans's Principled Polysemy framework (but cf. also Kreitzer 1997); this approach will be discussed briefly in this section. Second, polysemy research turned to more diverse data, using psycholinguistic experimentation and corpus data, which is the topic of section 3.

The *Principled Polysemy approach* (cf. Tyler and Evans 2001; Evans 2005) targeted the first of the two problem areas. First, they proposed criteria to determine when two usages constitute different senses by doing more justice to the role of context and distinguishing polysemy from vagueness; second, they proposed criteria to identify the prototype, or sanctioning sense, of a polysemous category. As for the former, for some usage to count as a distinct sense of *x*, it must contain additional meaning not apparent in other senses associated with *x* (the meaning criterion) and it will feature unique or highly distinctive syntagmatic/collocational patterns (the concept elaboration criterion) and similarly distinctive structural dependencies (the grammatical criterion); the latter two criteria, thus, make an implicit reference to the study of corpus data. As for the latter, Evans (2005) lists four linguistic criteria (and mentions additional empirical evidence of the type discussed by Sandra and Rice [1995] or Croft [1998]): diachronic primacy, predominance in the lexical network, predictability regarding other senses, and – for *time* – a sense involving experience at the phenomenological level or – for *over* – relations to other prepositions.

This approach is promising as it is among the first to propose more rigorous "decision principles"; however, the concept elaboration and the grammatical criterion and many of the prototype criteria (which, curiously, do not feature acquisitional primacy) are gradable and may not converge. Nonetheless, these criteria help make decisions more replicable especially as more empirical evidence guiding linguists' decision is gathered.

3 Polysemy in neighboring fields

This section discusses how neighboring fields such as corpus linguistics and psycholinguistics have dealt with polysemy. This is essential because, as became apparent above, CL regularly points to findings/methods in neighboring fields (without, however, really integrating much of such work); cf. Cuyckens et al. (1997) for discussion. In general, one can make a coarse distinction between (i) corpus-linguistic work, which by its very nature is concerned more with *associative/co-occurrence relations* (cf. section 3.1) and psycholinguistic experimentation, which targets more *semantic/categorical relations* (cf. section 3.2).

3.1 Corpus linguistic approaches

Corpus-linguistic work on polysemy within CL comes in three kinds: first, there are studies where the corpus-linguistic component consists merely of using a corpus as a source of examples – ideally, examples are not just cherry-picked to support a particular point but also considered if they constitute counterexamples; given the limited role that corpus methods other than mere retrieval play in such work, this will not be discussed here. Second, there are analyses which involve the retrieval of, ideally, many examples of the element to be analyzed, which are then annotated for various characteristics, which are then analyzed statistically. Third, there are studies straddling the boundary between corpus linguistics and computational (psycho)linguistics, which differ from the previous kind of analyses in that many do not (i) involve (semi-)manual annotation and (ii) aim at uncovering something about human language *per se* but rather test/evaluate computational models of linguistic data (with no pretense of cognitive realism).

The main assumption underlying the latter two approaches is what Miller and Charles discuss as the *co-occurrence approach*, the assumption that distributional similarity is correlated with functional (semantic, pragmatic, etc.) similarity, as expressed in Harris's (1970: 785 f.) famous dictum that "difference of meaning correlates with difference of distribution". Miller and Charles (1991) contrast this with the *substitutability approach*, which essentially amounts to an experiment in which subjects fill gap in sentences with one of several words whose similarity is tested. From this they argue for the notion of a *contextual representation* of a word, which is

> a mental representation of the contexts in which the word occurs, a representation that includes all of the syntactic, semantic, pragmatic, and stylistic information required to use the word appropriately. (1991: 26)

Correspondingly, different levels of statistical complexity can be distinguished in this second approach. The earliest relevant corpus work is largely monofactorial in nature and does not yet include the more advanced statistics characteristic of much of contemporary corpus linguistics; relevant examples include Schmid (1993) and Kishner and Gibbs's (1996) work on how senses of *just* are correlated with different parts of speech in *just*'s environment.

More advanced analyses in "multidimensional corpus-based cognitive semantics" were then developed in particular in Gries's and Divjak's *Behavioral Profile* approach. This approach is similar in spirit to corpus-linguistic work such as Atkins (1987) and Hanks (1996, 2000) and has been applied to both polysemy and synonymy. It typically (i.e., not always) consists of four steps: (i) retrieving a sample of the expression(s) in question; (ii) annotating the concordance lines for a large number of features; (iii) converting these data into a table of percentage vectors that state how much of the data in percent exhibits a particular feature; (iv) statistically analyzing the data with exploratory tools (such as cluster analysis). Gries (2006) was the first to apply this approach in the study of polysemy, studying the verb *run* (cf. Glynn 2014 for a replication) and showing how the correlations of percentage vectors helps decide where to locate senses in a network, whether to lump or split senses, what the prototypical sense may be. Berez and Gries (2009) use cluster analysis as a corpus-based equivalent to psycholinguistic sense-sorting experiments to explore what senses of *get* exhibit high inter-sense similarity. Divjak and Gries (2009) extend this approach to the senses of near-synonymous phrasal verbs in English and Russian, and other work has targeted near synonymy (Divjak and Gries 2006; Divjak 2006; Gries and Otani 2010).[2] In addition, the BP approach has stimulated interesting extensions using different kinds of exploratory statistics and corpus data: Glynn (2010) applies what amounts to the BP approach to *bother* but instead of using cluster analysis he uses multiple correspondence analysis (MCA); Levshina (2015) uses an MCA to discover structure in the semantic field of seat-

---

[2] BP analyses were first presented independently by Gries and Divjak in 2003 at the ICLC; a similar but otherwise unrelated approach is Speelman et al. (2003).

ing furniture; Janda and Solovyev (2009) apply very similar methods to constructional similarities.

Finally, there are more computational approaches based on unannotated texts. Biber (1993) studies how the polysemy of the word *right* is reflected in the distribution of its collocates. More technical approaches involve NLP applications based on co-occurrence vectors in multi-dimensional space; cf. Schütze (2000) for a discussion of word, sense, and context vectors. However, much of this work is more concerned with ambiguity, not polysemy. Other similar work more concerned with psychological realism/applications is Burgess and Lund's (1997) HAL or Landauer and Dumais's (1997) LSA, which are both based on large co-occurrence matrices of words and have been used successfully in many domains, which may point to promising applications within cognitive semantics once the "symbol grounding problem" is addressed, possible via the notion of embodiment (cf. Traxler 2012: 89 f.).

Corpus data have been useful in cognitive semantics, but they usually do not allow researchers to make definitive statements about cause-effect relations or online processing. The studies discussed in the next section target these aspects.

3.2 Psycholinguistic approaches

Psycholinguistics was probably the field that CL related to first: Even when CL was still far from adopting experimental/observational approaches, there were attempts to integrate the psycholinguistic models/findings regarding into CL. Deane (1988), for instance, is an attempt to unite the theory of image schemas, Relevance Theory, and Anderson's architecture of cognition. Geeraerts (1985) discusses how various characteristics of the human mind all motivate why the human mind should exhibit the type of conceptual organization around prototypes. But what about psycholinguistics proper?

Polysemy was not represented much in psycholinguistic research before the 1960s and some early work (Asch and Nerlove 1960 or Macnamara et al. 1972) was concerned with questions that may seem unrelated to CL work on polysemy. However, that is not entirely true. For instance, the former studied how children acquire and distinguish words denoting both a physical and a psychological quality, such as *hard*, *deep*, *bright*, etc., certainly a topic of current relevance. The latter study tests the hypotheses that speakers store meanings associated with a phonological form in a particular order, that this order is very similar across speakers, and that during comprehension speakers try meanings in that order. While this may seem far-fetched, given the lexical networks that have been developed, a usage-based approach that accords frequencies of words, senses etc. a primary role, implies at least some sort of rank-ordering of senses based on their frequencies. Indeed, the experimental results refuted that simplest rank-ordering hypothesis but also showed that (i) the first 1–2 senses named by subjects often coincided and (ii) context plays an important role in rapid online meaning disambiguation.

Such examples notwithstanding, most early work on the subject was concerned with ambiguity or homonymy and explored

- the *time course of activation* of word senses: are only relevant or relevant *and* irrelevant senses of words activated and how does the presence of multiple meanings or senses affect word recognition (cf. Hino and Lupker 1996 and Azuma and Van Orden 1997)?
- the importance of *context* for sense selection: does it have an effect at all, what exactly is it, and when does it kick in?
- the importance the *frequency/dominance of senses* plays for sense selection: less frequent meanings take longer to access (Hogaboam and Perfetti 1975);
- interactions of the above.

That is, most earlier studies on lexical access/disambiguation neither included any systematic distinction between homonymy and polysemy in their designs/ explanations; in fact, some psychological/psycholinguistic studies use *polysemy* to refer to cases such as *ball* ('spherical object' vs. 'dance event'), which linguists would class as homonymy, others use *ambiguity* as meaning 'polysemy'. (In fact, some recent introductions to psycholinguistics – e.g., Byrd and Mintz (2010) or Menn (2011) – do not feature *polysemy* or *ambiguity* as index entries). Therefore, some early work speaks directly to many questions of CL, but much is 'only' indirectly related to CL since, e.g., it hardly explores the nature of the relations between senses or adopt the same fine degree of sense granularity; cf. Gibbs and Matlock (2001) or Klein and Murphy (2001). While the exact nature of lexical access is still debated, there is evidence that

- all meanings of a word are accessed even if they are contextually inappropriate (semantic or syntactic context cannot constrain initial access);
- context both before and after the word can help make subordinate but contextually appropriate meanings more available for selection; also, context helps suppress contextually inappropriate meanings of homonyms within approximately 200 ms and can make reactions to dominant senses as fast as to unambiguous controls;
- dominant and subordinate senses react differently to context (cf. Lupker 2007 for a detailed overview).

An early study that *does* speak to cognitive semanticists is Caramazza and Grober (1976). They first report results of three different tasks on the word *line* – acceptability judgments of concordance contexts, similarity judgments of such contexts, and a sentence production task – which produce highly interrelated results. Interestingly, they applied multidimensional scaling and cluster analysis to the similarity judgments and obtained a clear and interpretable 5-cluster/sense solution. On the whole, their model of how polysemy is represented in the mental lexicon, the Process Theory of Meaning, is similar to the monosemy approach and assumes a single or a small set of very general meanings. However, it also accords crucial roles to context and encyclopedic knowledge (cf. also Anderson and Ortony 1975 for similar conclusions): senses other than the central one are derived by extension/analogy, or "instruction rules", and an encyclopedic dictionary, which stores all factual information a speaker has about a word, constrains the application of the instruction rules.

Another relevant study is Durkin and Manning (1989). For nearly 200 words (11 % of them homonyms), they collected typical senses from subjects and relatedness ratings of all senses to central ones. They find that senses of polysemous words are rated as more similar to each other than senses of homonymous words, but also that, while contexts boosts senses' salience ratings, dominant senses enjoy a larger degree of salience even in contexts biasing subordinate senses. Also, the ease with which subordinate senses can be accessed differs considerably across words.

A classic study on the processing of homonymous meanings vs. polysemous sense is Frazier and Rayner (1990). Their eye-movement data indicate that, in the absence of a disambiguating context, fixation times for words with multiple meanings are longer while fixation times for words with multiple senses are not. They explain that as a consequence of having to immediately disambiguate such homonyms so as not to maintain inconsistent representations and selecting one meaning involves suppression of others, which requires extra processing time. Similarly, Pickering and Frisson (2001: 556) propose that, upon hearing a homonymous word in a non-disambiguating context, speakers make an early selection of a meaning whereas, upon hearing a polysemous word in such a context, the user "activates one underspecified meaning and uses context to home in on the appropriate sense".[3] Additional evidence in particular for the higher relatedness of senses of polysemous words (compared to the meanings of homonyms) comes from Williams (1992). He shows that senses of polysemous adjectives resulting in zeugma in the *do so* test prime contextually irrelevant related senses: "it does not appear to be possible to suppress the irrelevant

---

[3] This approach is compatible with Frisson and Pickering's (1999) study, which shows that both literal and metonymic senses can be accessed immediately, "perhaps through a single under-specified representation" (1999: 1366).

meanings of a polysemous adjective in the same way as [those] of a homonym" (1992: 202). In addition, the time course of activation is similar to that of dominant properties of monosemous nouns. Finally, the direction of priming is significant, too: priming from non-central senses to central ones was significant at all delays, but not the other way round, which Williams interprets as possibly related to category structure/similarity effects (e.g., prototype effects).

Similar differences were found in Brisard et al. (2001), who demonstrated significant priming effects for polysemous and vague adjectives, but not for homonymous adjectives. Also, consider Rodd et al. (2002, 2004). In the former study, they find that the unrelated senses of homonymous words (and their wider attractor basin) slow recognition down whereas the related senses and richer semantic representations (and deeper attractor basins) of polysemous words speed recognition up. In the latter, they propose a distributed-semantic-representation model of lexical knowledge that accommodates these effects by assuming that the related senses of polysemous words share overlapping regions in semantic space. Similarly, Beretta, et al. (2005) show that the meanings of homonymous words are accessed more slowly than senses of polysemous words; cf. also Azuma and Van Orden (1997).

On the other hand, in experiments similar to Light and Carter-Sobell's (1970) and Bainbridge et al.'s (1993), Klein and Murphy (2001, 2002) show that both memory performance and sensicality judgments suggest that senses of *paper* are related but not similar, stored separately or at least functionally distinct. In fact, senses of one word may be excited and inhibited at the same time. Also, Klein and Murphy (2001: exp. 3) find no performance difference between homonyms and polysemous words but, in Klein and Murphy (2002: exp. 1–3), conclude that the similarity of polysemous senses is graded, and that polysemous senses share more connections than homonymous meanings (not unlike what a family resemblance approach would predict).

In sum, there is some agreement on some issues, but most hypotheses implicit in CL polysemous analyses are far from as unambiguously supported as many in the CL mainstream would hope for – a great deal of work lies ahead.

4 Desiderata

Given the huge amount of research on polysemy and ambiguity, this overview was selective and much interesting work could not be discussed. While psycholinguistic work has yielded some robust findings, many of the central questions of CL regarding senses' distinctness, relatedness, representation, and their right level of granularity, remain largely unanswered. Across all three areas – CL,

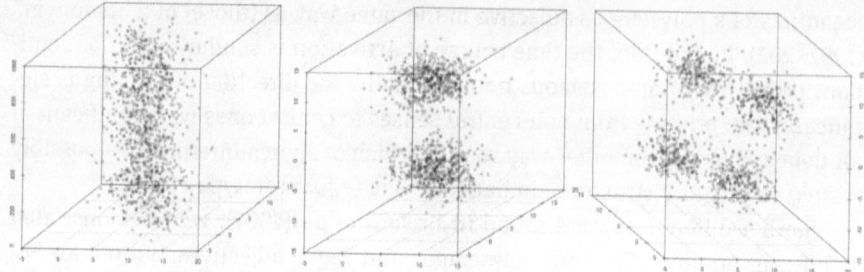

Fig. 2.1: A point cloud in three-dimensional 'semantic space', from three different angles.

corpus linguistics, and psycholinguistics – a consensus is emerging to assume a multidimensional semantic space in which usages or senses are located such that their spatial proximity reflects distributional and/or semantic similarity; cf., e.g., Gries (2010) and Taylor (2012) for cognitive/corpus linguistics and, Rodd et al. (2004: 89) for psycholinguistics. Thus, while integral to early CL, the notion of distinct senses appears more of a descriptive device rather than a claim about psycholinguistic reality. This conception does justice to the fact that the same word/sense – i.e., region of semantic space – can be accessed or traversed at different levels of resolution and from different angles/trajectories. A simple example is shown in Figure 1, which represents the same usages (as dots) in semantic space from three different angles. The left panel suggests there is one group of relatively coherent usages, maybe corresponding to one sense. However, the other two panels show the same usages from different angles (e.g., from different semantic/discourse contexts), and these panels give rise to two or four senses. That is, context facilitates sense recognition by imposing a particular view on, or trajectory through, stored exemplars, and the possibility of creativity is afforded by the speaker's freedom to (i) approach the same region from different perspectives or (ii) see similarities between different point clouds in semantic space and exploit this linguistically by means of, say, analogy, or (iii) condense regions of space.

In what follows, I discuss a few areas for future research. First, corpus-based work needs to be developed further both in terms of scope (words, senses, and features included) and methodology. Current developments are promising and future work may evolve by including powerful new tools such as network models, fuzzy clustering, etc.

More importantly, CL must approach polysemy more interdisciplinarily. Many experimental studies in psycholinguistics on ambiguity should be replicated on the basis of CL analyses to shed more light on whether the fine-grained senses distinctions, the nature of links, etc. are supported. Similarly, we need better evidence on the role of prototypes in online processing and on how word senses interact with constructions and their senses.

With regard to language acquisition, there seem to be only few studies targeting polysemy from a CL perspective. The few studies that there are – e.g., Dowker (2003), Nerlich et al. (2003) on *get*, Rice (2003) on prepositional networks, Kidd and Cameron-Faulkner (2005) on *with* – have unfortunately not left enough of a mark on CL in spite of their relevance. Rice (2003: 275) makes the interesting suggestion that

> a lexical category for a young child does not start out as either monosemous or polysemous, but as potentially very homonymous. Additional senses do not emerge through extension. Rather, they *may* be integrated through some sort of schematization process at a much later date.

This is an area that needs more experimental/observational research, but also maybe computational modeling; cf., e.g., Parisien and Stevenson (2009) for a study of *get*.

Finally, neurolinguistics offers a completely new range of applications; cf. Coulson (2004) for an overview of EEG/ERP or Stringaris et al.'s (2006) fMRI study of semantic relatedness. Burgess and Simpson (1988) tested whether the brain's two hemispheres respond identically to target words more associated with the dominant or the subordinate meaning of an ambiguous word and found that "the two hemispheres have opposite responses to subordinate meanings. The left hemisphere deactivates subordinate meanings, but the right hemisphere increases them over time" (Traxler 2012: 528 f.). Mason and Just (2007) showed that the brain activity arising from processing lexically ambiguous words differs as a function of meaning dominance and working memory capacity (i.e., individual differences). Finally, CL has approached the polysemy of content and function words in the same way, but the two types of words seem to be lateralized differently (Bradley and Garrett 1983); in fact, Damasio and colleagues suggest that nouns vs. verbs and even different categories of concrete objects are represented in different neural regions, which has implications for polysemous words (cf. Lupker 2007: 169). Only by combining multiple approaches/tools will CL be able to develop polysemy analyses that are compatible with the cognitive commitment to make one's account of human language accord with what is generally known about the mind and brain from disciplines other than linguistics.

5 References

Anderson, Richard C. and Andrew Ortony (1975): On putting apples into bottles. *Cognitive Psychology* 7(2): 167–180.

Asch, Solomon and Harriet Nerlove (1960): The development of double function terms in children. In: B. Kaplan and S. Wapner (eds.), *Perspectives in Psychological Theory*, 47–60. New York: International Universities Press.

Atkins, Beryl T. Sue (1987): Semantic ID tags: Corpus evidence for dictionary senses. In *Proceedings of the Third Annual Conference of the UW Centre for the New Oxford English Dictionary*, 17–36.

Azuma, Tamiko and Guy C. Van Orden (1997): Why *safe* is better than *fast*: The relatedness of a word's meanings affects lexical decision times. *Journal of Memory and Language* 36(4): 484–504.

Bainbridge, J. Vivian, Stephan Lewandowsky, and Kim Kirsner (1993): Context effects in repetition priming are sense effects. *Memory and Cognition* 21(5): 619–626.

Beretta, Alan, Robert Fiorentino, and David Poeppel (2005): The effect of homonymy and polysemy on lexical access. *Cognitive Brain Research* 24(1): 57–65.

Berez, Andrea L. and Stefan Th. Gries (2009): In defense of corpus-based methods: A behavioral profile analysis of polysemous *get* in English. In: S. Moran, D. S. Tanner, and M. Scanlon (eds.), *Proceedings of the 24th Northwest Linguistics Conference. University of Washington Working Papers in Linguistics* Vol. 27, 157–166. Seattle, WA: Department of Linguistics.

Biber, Douglas (1993): Co-occurrence patterns among collocations: A tool for corpus-based lexical knowledge acquisition. *Computational Linguistics* 19(3): 531–538.

Boas, Hans C. (2008): Resolving form-meaning discrepancies in Construction Grammar. In: J. Leino (ed.), *Constructional Reorganization*, 11–36. Amsterdam/Philadelphia: John Benjamins.

Bradley, Dianne C. and Merrill F. Garrett (1983): Hemisphere differences in the recognition of open and closed class words. *Neuropsychologia* 21(2): 155–159.

Bréal, Michel (1897): The history of words. In: G. Wolf (ed./transl.), *The Beginnings of Semantics: Essays, Lectures and Reviews*, 152–175. London: Duckworth.

Brisard, Frank, Gert Van Rillaer, and Dominiek Sandra (2001): Processing polysemous, homonymous, and vague adjectives. In: H. Cuyckens and B. Zawada (eds.), *Polysemy in Cognitive Linguistics*, 261–284. Amsterdam/Philadelphia: John Benjamins.

Brugman, Claudia (1981): The story of *over*. M. A. thesis. University of California, Berkeley.

Brugman, Claudia and George Lakoff (1988): Cognitive topology and lexical networks. In: S. L. Small, G. W. Cottrell, and M. K. Tanenhaus (eds.), *Lexical Ambiguity Resolution*, 477–508. San Mateo, CA: Morgan Kaufman.

Burgess, Curt and Kevin Lund (1997): Modelling parsing constraints with high-dimensional context space. *Language and Cognitive Processes* 12(2/3): 177–210.

Byrd, Dani and Toben H. Mintz (2010): *Discovering Speech, Words, and Mind*. Chichester: John Wiley.

Caramazza Alfonso and Ellen Grober (1976): Polysemy and the structure of the subjective lexicon. In: C. Rameh (ed.), *Semantics: Theory and Application*, 181–206. Washington, DC: Georgetown University Press.

Coulson, Seana (2004): Electrophysiology and pragmatic language comprehension. In: I. Noveck and D. Sperber (eds.), *Experimental Pragmatics*, 187–206. Basingstoke: Palgrave MacMillan.

Croft, William (1998): Linguistic evidence and mental representation. *Cognitive Linguistics* 9(2): 151–173.
Croft, William (2003): Lexical rules vs. constructions: A false dichotomy. In: H. Cuyckens, T. Berg, R. Dirven, and K.-U. Panther (eds.), *Motivation in Language: Studies in Honour of Günter Radden*, 49–68. Amsterdam/Philadelphia: John Benjamins.
Cruse, D. Alan (1995): Polysemy and related phenomena from a cognitive linguistic viewpoint. In: P. Saint-Dizier and E. Viegas (eds.), *Computational Lexical Semantics*, 33–49. Cambridge: Cambridge University Press.
Cuyckens, Hubert, Dominiek Sandra, and Sally Rice (1997): Towards an empirical lexical semantics. In: B. Smieja and M. Tasch (eds.), *Human Contact through Language and Linguistics*, 35–54. Frankfurt a. M.: Peter Lang.
Cuyckens, Hubert and Britta Zawada (2001): Introduction. In: H. Cuyckens and B. Zawada (eds.), *Polysemy in Cognitive Linguistics*, ix–xxvii. Amsterdam/Philadelphia: John Benjamins.
Deane, Paul D. (1988): Polysemy and cognition. *Lingua* 75(4): 325–361.
Deane, Paul D. (2005): Multimodal spatial representation. In: B. Hampe (ed.), *From Perception to Meaning: Image Schemas in Cognitive Linguistics*, 235–282. Berlin/New York: Mouton de Gruyter.
Divjak, Dagmar S. (2006): Ways of intending: Delineating and structuring near synonyms. In: S. Th. Gries and A. Stefanowitsch (eds.), *Corpora in Cognitive Linguistics: Corpus-Based Approaches to Syntax and Lexis*, 19–56. Berlin/New York: Mouton de Gruyter.
Divjak, Dagmar S. and Stefan Th. Gries (2006): Ways of trying in Russian: Clustering behavioral profiles. *Corpus Linguistics and Linguistic Theory* 2(1): 23–60.
Divjak, Dagmar S. and Stefan Th. Gries (2009): Corpus-based cognitive semantics: A contrastive study of phrasal verbs in English and Russian. In: K. Dziwirek and B. Lewandowska-Tomaszczyk (eds.), *Studies in Cognitive Corpus Linguistics*, 273–296. Frankfurt a.M.: Peter Lang.
Dowker, Ann (2003): Young children's and adults' use of figurative language: How important are cultural and linguistic influences? In: B. Nerlich, Z. Todd, V. Herrman, and D. D. Clarke (eds.), *Polysemy: Flexible Patterns of Meaning in Mind and Language*, 317–332. Berlin/New York: Mouton de Gruyter.
Durkin, Kevin and Jocelyn Manning (1989): Polysemy and the subjective lexicon: Semantic relatedness and the salience of intraword senses. *Journal of Psycholinguistic Research* 18(6): 577–612.
Evans, Vyvyan (2005): The meaning of *time*: Polysemy, the lexicon and conceptual structure. *Journal of Linguistics* 41(1): 33–75.
Fillmore, Charles J. (1975): An alternative to checklist theories of meaning. *Proceedings of the First Annual Meeting of the Berkeley Linguistics Society*, 123–131.
Fillmore, Charles J. (1982): Frame semantics. In: The Linguistic Society of Korea (ed.), *Linguistics in the Morning Calm*, 111–137. Seoul: Hanshin Publishing Co.
Frazier, Lyn and Keith Rayner (1990): Taking on semantic commitments: Processing multiple meanings vs. multiple senses. *Journal of Memory and Language* 29(2): 181–200.
Frisson, Steven and Martin J. Pickering (1999): The processing of metonymy: Evidence from eye movements. *Journal of Experimental Psychology: Learning, Memory, and Cognition* 25(6): 1366–1383.
Geeraerts, Dirk (1985): Cognitive restrictions on the structure of semantic change. In: J. Fisiak (ed.), *Historical Semantics. Historical Word-Formation*, 126–153. Berlin/New York: Mouton de Gruyter.

Geeraerts, Dirk (1993): Vagueness's puzzles, polysemy's vagaries. *Cognitive Linguistics* 4(3): 223–272.

Gibbs, Raymond W. Jr. and Teenie Matlock (2001): Psycholinguistic perspectives on polysemy. In: H. Cuyckens and B. Zawada (eds.), *Polysemy in Cognitive Linguistics*, 213–239. Amsterdam/Philadelphia: John Benjamins.

Glynn, Dylan (2010): Testing the hypothesis: Objectivity and verification in usage-based Cognitive Semantics. In: D. Glynn and K. Fischer (eds.), *Quantitative Methods in Cognitive Semantics: Corpus-Driven Approaches*, 239–629. Berlin/New York: De Gruyter Mouton.

Glynn, Dylan (2014): The many uses of *run*: Corpus methods and socio-cognitive semantics. In: D. Glynn and J. Robinson (eds.), *Corpus Methods for Semantics: Quantitative Studies in Polysemy and Synonymy*, 117–144. Amsterdam/Philadelphia: John Benjamins.

Goldberg, Adele E. (1992): The inherent semantics of argument structure: The case of the English ditransitive construction. *Cognitive Linguistics* 3(1): 37–74.

Goldberg, Adele E. (1995): *Constructions: A Construction Grammar Approach to Argument Structure*. Chicago: University of Chicago Press.

Gries, Stefan Th. (2006): Corpus-based methods and cognitive semantics: The many meanings of *to run*. In: S. Th. Gries and A. Stefanowitsch (eds.), *Corpora in Cognitive Linguistics: Corpus-Based Approaches to Syntax and Lexis*, 57–99. Berlin/New York: Mouton de Gruyter.

Gries, Stefan Th. (2010): Behavioral Profiles: A fine-grained and quantitative approach in corpus-based lexical semantics. *The Mental Lexicon* 5(3): 323–346.

Gries, Stefan Th. and Naoki Otani (2010): Behavioral profiles: A corpus-based perspective on synonymy and antonymy. *ICAME Journal* 34: 121–150.

Hanks, Patrick (1996): Contextual dependency and lexical sets. *International Journal of Corpus Linguistics* 1(1): 75–98.

Hanks, Patrick (2000): Do word meanings exist? *Computers and the Humanities* 34(1/2): 205–215.

Harris, Zelig S. (1970): *Papers in Structural and Transformational Linguistics*. Dordrecht: Reidel.

Hendrikse, A. P. (2001): Systemic polysemy in the Southern Bantu noun class system. In: H. Cuyckens and B. Zawada (eds.), *Polysemy in Cognitive Linguistics*, 185–212. Amsterdam/Philadelphia: John Benjamins.

Hino, Yasushi and Stephen J. Lupker (1996): Effects of polysemy in lexical decision and naming: An alternative to lexical access accounts. *Journal of Experimental Psychology: Human Perception and Performance* 22(6): 1331–1356.

Hogaboam, Thomas W. and Charles A. Perfetti (1975): Lexical ambiguity and sentence comprehension: The common sense effect. *Journal of Verbal Learning and Verbal Behavior* 14(3): 265–275.

Jackendoff, Ray (1997): Twistin' the night away. *Language* 73(3): 534–559.

Janda, Laura A. and Valery D. Solovyev (2009): What constructional profiles reveal about synonymy: A case study of Russian words for *sadness* and *happiness*. *Cognitive Linguistics* 20(2): 367–393.

Katz, Jerrold J. (1967): Recent issues in semantic theory. *Foundations of Language* 3. 124–194.

Katz, Jerrold J. and Jerry A. Fodor (1963): The structure of a semantic theory. *Language* 39(2): 170–210.

Kidd, Evan and Thea Cameron-Faulkner (2005): Overcoming polysemy in first language acquisition: The case of *with*. *Proceedings of the 29th Annual Boston Conference on Language Development*, 341–352.
Kishner, Jeffrey M. and Raymond W. Gibbs Jr. (1996): How *just* gets its meanings: Polysemy and context in psychological semantics. *Language and Speech* 39(1): 19–36.
Klein, Deborah E. and Gregory L. Murphy (2001): The representation of polysemous words. *Journal of Memory and Language* 45(2): 259–282.
Klein, Deborah E. and Gregory L. Murphy (2002): Paper has been my ruin: Conceptual relations of polysemous senses. *Journal of Memory and Language* 47(4): 548–570.
Kreitzer, Anatol (1997): Multiple levels of schematization: A study in the conceptualization of space. *Cognitive Linguistics* 8(4): 291–326.
Labov, William (1973): The boundaries of words and their meanings. In: C.-J. Bailey and R. W. Shuy (eds.), *New Ways of Analyzing Variation in English*, 340–371. Washington, DC: Georgetown University Press.
Lakoff, George (1987): *Women, Fire, and Dangerous Things: What Categories Reveal about the Mind*. Chicago: The University of Chicago Press.
Lakoff, George and Claudia Brugman (1986): Argument forms in lexical semantics. In: V. Nikiforidou, M. van Clay, M. Niepokuj, and D. Feder, (eds.), *Proceedings of the Twelfth Annual Meeting of the Berkeley Linguistics Society*, 442–454. Berkeley: Berkeley Linguistics Society.
Landauer, Thomas K. and Susan T. Dumais (1997): A solution to Plato's problem: The latent semantic analysis theory of acquisition, induction, and representation of knowledge. *Psychological Review* 104(2): 211–240.
Levshina, Natalia (2015): *How to Do Linguistics with R: Data exploration and statistical analysis*. Amsterdam: John Benjamins.
Lewandowska-Tomaszczyk, Barbara (2007): Polysemy, prototypes, and radial categories. In: D. Geeraerts and H. Cuyckens (eds.), *The Oxford Handbook of Cognitive Linguistics*, 139–169. Oxford: Oxford University Press.
Light, Leah L. and Linda Carter-Sobell (1970): Effects of changed semantic context on recognition behavior. *Journal of Verbal Learning and Verbal Behavior* 9(1): 1–11.
Lindner, Susan (1981): A lexico-semantic analysis of English verb-particle constructions with *up* and *out*. Ph.D. dissertation. University of California, San Diego.
Lupker, Stephen J. (2007): Representation and processing of lexically ambiguous words. In: M. G. Gaskell (ed.), *The Oxford Handbook of Psycholinguistics*, 159–174. Oxford: Oxford University Press.
Macnamara, John, Ann O'Cleirigh, and Thomas Kellaghan (1972): The structure of the English lexicon: The simplest hypothesis. *Language and Speech* 15(2): 141–148.
Menn, Lise (2011): *Psycholinguistics: Introduction and Applications*. San Diego: Plural.
Michaelis, Laura A. and Knud Lambrecht (1996): Towards a construction-based theory of language function: The case of nominal extraposition. *Language* 72(2): 215–247.
Miller, George A. and Walter G. Charles (1991): Contextual correlates of semantic similarity. *Language and Cognitive Processes* 6(1): 1–28.
Nerlich, Brigitte, Zazie Todd, and David D. Clarke (2003): Emerging patterns and evolving polysemies: The acquisition of *get* between four and ten years. In: B. Nerlich, Z. Todd, V. Herrman, and D. D. Clarke (eds.), *Polysemy: Flexible Patterns of Meaning in Mind and Language*, 333–357. Berlin/New York: Mouton de Gruyter.
Nikiforidou, Kiki (1991): The meanings of the genitive: A case study in semantic structure and semantic change. *Cognitive Linguistics* 2(2): 149–205.

Nisbett, Richard E. and Timothy DeCamp Wilson (1977): Telling more than we know: Verbal reports on mental processes. *Psychological Review* 84(3): 231–259.

Norrick, Neal R. (1981): *Semiotic Principles in Semantic Theory*. Amsterdam/Philadelphia: John Benjamins.

Norvig, Peter and George Lakoff (1986): Taking: a study in lexical network theory. In: J. Aske, N. Beery, L. A. Michaelis, and H. Filip (eds.), *Proceedings of the Thirteenth Annual Meeting of the Berkeley Linguistics Society*, 195–206. Berkeley: Berkeley Linguistics Society.

Panther, Klaus-Uwe and Linda L. Thornburg (2002): The roles of metaphor and metonymy in English *-er* nominals. In: R. Dirven and R. Pörings (eds.), *Metaphor and Metonymy in Comparison and Contrast*, 279–319. Berlin/New York: Mouton de Gruyter.

Parisien, Christopher and Suzanne Stevenson (2009): Modelling the acquisition of verb polysemy in children. *Proceedings of the CogSci2009 Workshop on Distributional Semantics beyond Concrete Concepts*, 17–22.

Pickering, Martin J. and Steven Frisson (2001): Processing ambiguous verbs: Evidence from eye movements. *Journal of Experimental Psychology: Learning, Memory, and Cognition* 27(2): 556–573.

Rice, Sally (1996): Prepositional prototypes. In: M. Pütz and R. Dirven (eds.), *The Construal of Space in Language and Thought*, 135–165. Berlin/New York: Mouton de Gruyter.

Rice, Sally A. (2003): Growth of a lexical network: Nine English prepositions in acquisition. In: H. Cuyckens, R. Dirven, and J. Taylor (eds.), *Cognitive Approaches to Lexical Semantics*, 243–260. Berlin/New York: Mouton de Gruyter.

Riemer, Nick (2005): *The Semantics of Polysemy: Reading Meaning in English and Warlpiri*. Berlin/New York: Mouton de Gruyter.

Rodd, Jennifer M., Gareth Gaskell, and William D. Marlsen-Wilson (2002): Making sense of semantic ambiguity. *Journal of Memory and Language* 46(2): 245–266.

Rodd, Jennifer M., Gareth Gaskell, and William D. Marlsen-Wilson (2004): Modelling the effects of semantic ambiguity in word recognition. *Cognitive Science* 28(1): 89–104.

Rosch, Eleanor (1975): Cognitive reference points. *Cognitive Psychology* 7(4): 532–547.

Rosch, Eleanor (1978): Principles of categorization. In: E. Rosch and B. B. Lloyd (eds.), *Cognition and Categorization*, 27–48. Hillsdale: Lawrence Erlbaum.

Ruhl, Charles (1989): *On Monosemy: A Study in Linguistic Semantics*. Stony Brook: State University of New York Press.

Sandra, Dominiek (1998): What linguists can and can't tell you about the human mind: A reply to Croft. *Cognitive Linguistics* 9(4): 361–378.

Sandra, Dominiek and Sally A. Rice (1995): Network analyses of prepositional meaning: Mirroring whose mind – the linguist's or the language user's? *Cognitive Linguistics* 6(1): 89–130.

Schmid, Hans-Jörg (1993): *Cottage and Co., idea, start vs. begin*. Tübingen: Max Niemeyer.

Schütze, Hinrich (2000): Disambiguation and connectionism. In: Y. Ravin and C. Leacock (eds.), *Polysemy: Theoretical and Computational Approaches*, 205–219. Oxford: Oxford University Press.

Selvik, Kari-Anne (2001): When a dance resembles a tree. A polysemy analysis of three Setswana noun classes. In: H. Cuyckens and B. Zawada (eds.), *Polysemy in Cognitive Linguistics*, 161–184. Amsterdam/Philadelphia: John Benjamins.

Smith, Michael B. (2001): Why Quirky Case really isn't quirky. Or how to treat dative sickness in Icelandic. In: H. Cuyckens and B. Zawada (eds.), *Polysemy in Cognitive Linguistics*, 115–160. Amsterdam/Philadelphia: John Benjamins.

Speelman, Dirk, Stefan Grondelaers, and Dirk Geeraerts (2003): Profile-based linguistic uniformity as a generic method for comparing language varieties. Computers and the Humanities 37(3): 317–337.
Stringaris, Argyris, Nicholas Medford, Rachel Giora, Vincent C. Giampietro, Michael J. Brammer, and Anthony S. David (2006): How metaphors influence semantic relatedness judgments: The role of the right frontal cortex. *NeuroImage* 33(2): 784–793.
Taylor, John R. (2012): *The Mental Corpus*. Oxford: Oxford University Press.
Taylor, John R. (this volume): Prototype effects in grammar. Berlin/Boston: De Gruyter Mouton.
Tuggy, David. (1993): Ambiguity, polysemy, and vagueness. *Cognitive Linguistics* 4(3): 273–290.
Tuggy, David (1999): Linguistic evidence for polysemy in the mind: A response to William Croft and Dominiek Sandra. *Cognitive Linguistics* 10(4): 343–368.
Traxler, Matthew J. (2012): *Introduction to Psycholinguistics: Understanding Language Science*. Malden/Oxford: Wiley-Blackwell.
Tyler, Andrea and Vyvyan Evans (2001): Reconsidering prepositional polysemy networks: the case of *over*. *Language* 77(4): 724–765.
Williams, John N. (1992): Processing polysemous words in context: Evidence for interrelated meanings. *Journal of Psycholinguistic Research* 21(3): 193–218.
Wittgenstein, Ludwig (1953, 2001) *Philosophical Investigations*. Malden: Blackwell.

Kenny R. Coventry
Chapter 3: Space

1 Introduction

Space has long been viewed as one of the fundamental building blocks in cognitive linguistics. For almost four decades it has been argued that both language and thought are grounded in more "basic" perceptual and experiential constructs, and the geometry of space has figured, arguably, as the most basic (Langacker 1986; Lakoff 1987; Talmy 1983). Candidate spatial relations that have been proposed as important underlying constructs for language and thought include containment, support, verticality, and contiguity, and (non-spatial) domains such as emotion, time, and metaphors in language are often assumed to be parasitic on these spatial concepts (Lakoff and Johnson 1980; Casasanto and Boroditsky 2008; see also chapters by Gibbs & Bergen in volume 1, and Evans this volume). But what exactly are these spatial constructs, and how do they map onto language?

A useful starting point to get at these basic spatial building blocks for language is to focus on language that overtly relates to space – spatial language.

Several decades of research on spatial terms of various types reveals a series of findings that are illuminating regarding the nature of these basic primitives. Here I consider what we have learned about spatial language during this time, and what this tells us about the fundamental building blocks of language and thought. Two central themes will emerge; the importance of experimental approaches in cognitive linguistics (testing and complementing theoretical insights), and the importance of vision and **action** as underlying constraints on spatial language comprehension and production.

2 Spatial language defined

One can define spatial language as language that enables a hearer to narrow a search (usually visual) for the location of an object (Landau and Jackendoff 1993; Talmy 1983). Under this rubric come a range of types of term, including spatial adpositions (e.g., the spatial prepositions in English; such as *in*, *over*, *in front of*, etc.) and motion terms describing how an object is moving through

Kenny R. Coventry, East Anglia, United Kingdom

space. Terms including spatial demonstratives (e.g., *this* and *that*) are also regarded as spatial, although the extent to which they define where an object is located is controversial (see for example Enfield 2003).

Word limits prevent me from surveying all areas of spatial language in this chapter (motion is covered by Filipović and Ibarretxe-Antunano this volume). Here my focus is on spatial adpositions and spatial demonstratives. The choice of the former is a reflection of the high frequency of these terms across languages as well as the versatility of these terms. The choice of the latter is motivated again by frequency concerns, but also by the universality of demonstratives, their philological importance, and the fact that they are among the first words children across cultures produce. Both categories also illustrate how experimental approaches are important for an understanding of the mapping between language and space.

3 Spatial adpositions

The spatial prepositions in English have received a lot of attention from linguists over many years, and indeed have formed a cornerstone of activity in cognitive linguistics. The so-called "locative/relational" prepositions in English have been categorized into simple "topological" terms, proximity terms, and "projective/dimensional" terms (Coventry and Garrod 2004). In many ways these distinctions are somewhat arbitrary – they all share features to some extent – but for our present purposes they will suffice. Here we do not review all the work done on spatial adpositions, but by necessity will be rather selective, focusing on the topological terms *in* and *on*, and the projective terms *over, under, above* and *below*. However, some general remarks are in order.

It has long been noted that spatial terms are highly polysemous, both in terms of the same words cropping up in spatial and non-spatial contexts (e.g., contrast *under the table* with *under the weather*), and also the same terms used spatially in different ways (contrast *the hand is over the table* with *the tablecloth is over the table*). One of the fundamental features of cognitive linguistic approaches to language is the notion that words are associated with a multitude of senses which are related, but do not all share exactly the same features. This idea can be traced backed to Wittgenstein (1953), and has been developed both theoretically and empirically as a kernel theme in cognitive linguistics (see for example the early data from Rosch and Mervis 1975; see Lakoff 1987 for review). Spatial adpositions can be regarded as "radial" categories, with central, "prototypical" image schemata, and more peripheral senses related to, and generated from, these schemata (Brugman 1988; Herskovits 1986). For example Brugman

(1988) provides analyses of *over*, with three central image schemata representing the geometric relations underpinning dozens of senses, with more specific senses, both spatial and metaphorical, emerging from these central "prototypical" geometric conceptualizations. As we shall see, the range of parameters associated with spatial terms has moved away from the purely geometric, with empirical evidence for a wider range of relevant experiential constraints associated with the comprehension and production of these terms.

3.1 Topological terms – focus on *in* and *on*

Understanding of containment and support begins to emerge early in development, as do a range of spatial (binary) concepts (see Quinn 2005). Containers appear to exert a special fascination for children, revealed in their play (Bower 1982; Clark 1973), and several studies have shown knowledge of containment in infants of only a few months of age. For instance, when an object is shown lowered into a container, and the container is moved, 2.5 month olds are surprised when the object does not move with the container (e.g., Hespos and Baillargeon 2001; see also Casasola et al. 2003). Understanding of support is somewhat more protracted in development and emerges later than containment (Casasola and Cohen 2002). In terms of language acquisition, it has long been recognized that *in*, *on*, and *under* are among the earliest of all the prepositions across languages, appearing in the second and third years (Bowerman 1996; Johnson and Slobin 1979; Piaget and Inhelder 1956), building on the spatial concepts already well (but not fully) developed.

In and *on* can be used in a variety of ways. The spatial relation associated with *coffee in a cup* is different from the relations associated with *flowers in a vase*, and *a crack in a vase*. Moreover, one would say that a marble is *in a cup* when the cup is upright, but not when the cup is overturned with the marble *under* it, even though the marble is geometrically contained in both cases. Such examples have led to the view in cognitive linguistics that spatial terms are highly polysemous. But why are there so many different relations associated with these terms, and how best can one deal with the apparent polysemy? This is the first issue we wrestle with in this section.

Coventry and Garrod (2004) reviewed a body of empirical findings on the mapping between language and space, beginning with the basic question of how spatial language and the spatial world covary. In addition to examining how words co-occur/collocate with other words, such as the corpus linguistic work discussed elsewhere in these three volumes, it is equally important for spatial language to understand the real-world correlates of spatial language. To do so, an experimental approach to this question was pursued beginning in the 1980s, systematically manipulating visual scenes to examine how language comprehension and production is affected by changes in spatial relations and the objects those relations pertain to. Synthesizing the results from this experimental work, together with theoretical insights from both the perceptual sciences and linguistics, the "functional geometric framework" for spatial language was proposed by Coventry and Garrod involving three interconnected parameters that conjointly underpin the comprehension and production of spatial prepositions.

First, there are geometric relations or routines that capture the spatial relation between objects. In the case of *in*, the geometry of containment itself can account for many of the various uses/senses of *in*. Coventry and Garrod (2004) appealed to the region connection calculus (RCC) of Cohn and colleagues (Cohn et al. 1997) as a means of capturing the geometric constructs underlying *in* and *on* (moving a step beyond the somewhat abstract geometric constructs in image schemata). RCC is a qualitative geometry that defines containment and enclosure using just two primitives – connection and convexity – and these primitives have the attraction of being able to apply to a wide range of spatial relations that at first sight might appear to be different relations or senses or image schemata. For example, using the same essential formalism, RCC accounts for a range of ways in which one object can be in another object or objects. The strongest form of enclosure is when a region an object occupies is topologically inside (that is, completely surrounded by) the region the other object occupies, as in *a crack in a vase*, or *jam in a (sealed) jar*. However, this same basic notion allows for a range of weaker forms of enclosure as licensed in the calculus, dependent on the different ways in which an object has an inside. This includes subparts and overlaps in "convex hull" regions (e.g., *The flowers in a vase; tea in a cup*) and scattered insides (*The island in the archipelago*). The main point is that RCC (and later variants of qualitative geometry) give a formal and perceptually grounded account of the flexibility of spatial relations that allows a range of specific realizations of the same primitive spatial relations without the need for a multitude of separate senses of spatial relations (see also Tyler and Evans 2003, for a different approach to polysemy; see also Gries this volume). The way the geometry applies is dependent on the types of insides objects possess, thus accounting for enclosure in both 2D and more real-world 3D settings. Moreover, such an approach is also consistent with how spatial relations might be computed by the visual system (see for example Ullman 1996).

But geometric routines on their own are not enough to account for the myriad of uses of *in* and *on*. The second key component associated with *in* and *on* has to do with a second component of spatial relations – how objects interact with each other and how we interact with them. Coventry and Garrod (2004) coined the term "dynamic-kinematic routines" as a label for the types of routines – different from geometric routines – that are computed when looking at spatial scenes. For *in* and *on*, the specific dynamic-kinematic routine of "location control" was proposed originally in Garrod and Sanford (1989), and a similar notion was also suggested by Vandeloise (1991), and although not explicitly linked to containment and support, this is also related to the force dynamics proposed by Talmy (1988). Location control is the function of constraining the location of an object(s) over time, such that if one object moves, the contents will move with it. In a gravitational plane, containers afford constraining the location of contents, and this notion of location control is related to the geometry of enclosure, but is also empirically testable as being separate from it.

In a series of experiments we varied the geometry of spatial scenes and the degree of location control those scenes exhibited. For example, scenes with filmed (real) objects showed an apple perched on top of other fruit in a glass bowl at various heights, sometimes overhanging past the convex hull of the container. The scenes were static, or displayed various forms of movement. In the "strong location control" condition, the bowl plus fruit was shown moving from side-to-side at the same rate such that the bowl was controlling the location of the contents over time. In contrast, in a weak location control condition, the located object (e.g., the apple) was shown moving by itself, wiggling from side-to-side (but remaining in contact with the object immediately below it) while the rest of the objects (bowl and other fruit) remained stationary (see Figure 3.1 for examples). The consequences of these manipulations for spatial language have been examined using a range of measures, including free production studies where participants are asked "Where is the apple?" and rating studies where participants rate the appropriateness of sentences of the form *The apple is PREPOSITION the bowl* to accurately describe the pictures/videos. And the manipulations of geometry (i.e., height of pile) and location control have been tested both with adults (Coventry 1998; Garrod et al. 1999) and children (Richards et al. 2004). The results of these studies show that both geometry **and** location control are important predictors of both the choice of *in* and *on* to describe object arrangements, and also the acceptability ratings given to sentences to describe spatial scenes. For example, Richards et al. (2004) found that children as young as four years of age preferred to describe the scenes using *in* as first or only mention in their spatial descriptions when the scenes showed strong location control, and in contrast used *in* as first or only mention least when the scenes showed weak location control. Garrod et al. (1999) have also shown that there is a direct relationship between independent judgments of location control and language to describe the same (static) spatial scenes. They had one group of participants rate the likelihood that the located object and

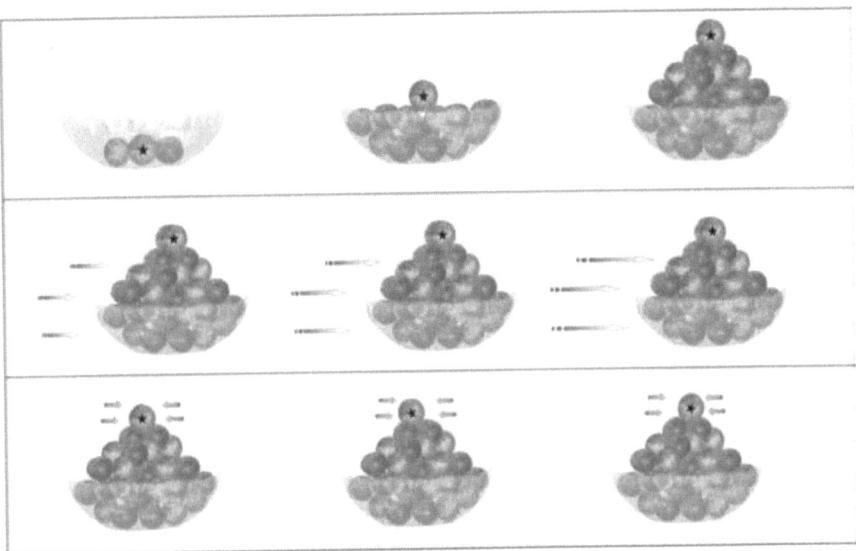

Fig. 3.1: Examples of scenes from Richards et al. (2004) showing geometry and location control manipulations. The top row shows manipulation of geometry. The middle row shows a schematic of strong location control; the bottom row, weak location control.

reference objects would remain in the same relative positions were the reference object to be moved from side-to-side, and another group of participants rated the appropriateness of spatial expressions (e.g., *the ball is in the bowl*) to describe the same scenes. Significant correlations were found between the location control judgments and the language ratings for the same scenes, indicating that location control seems to systematically underpin the comprehension of *in* and *on*.

Location control may well be an important construct for non-spatial uses of prepositions also, as in the case of spatial metaphors such as *on the bottle* or in *a trance* (see Garrod and Sanford 1989 for discussion). However, while a combination of geometric routines and dynamic-kinematic routines is undoubtedly powerful, and can account for a wide range of uses of *in* and *on* (see also Tyler and Evans 2003, for discussion), on their own geometric and dynamic-kinematic routines do not account for the mapping between *in* and *on* and the spatial world. Particular objects have particular functions, and one learns about these through interaction with particular objects in particular situations and through the mapping words have with other words in a language.

In a series of studies (Coventry et al. 1994; Coventry and Prat-Sala 2001; Feist and Gentner 1998, 2003) the objects involved in a spatial relationship have been manipulated, showing consequences for spatial description across a range of

Fig. 3.2: The coffee capsule is *in the dish* or *on the plate* (*on the dish*/*in the plate* are less preferable descriptions).

methods. For example, Coventry et al. (1994) showed objects positioned at various heights in a bowl or in a jug (of similar dimensions). They found that *in* was judged to be a more appropriate description of a solid object (e.g., an apple) in *a bowl* compared to the same object in *a jug*. Moreover, adding liquid to the jug further diminished the appropriateness of *in* to describe the position of the apple with respect to the jug, but did not impact upon judgments for the apple in the bowl. These types of data suggest that objects come to have specific functions by virtue of the co-occurrence of objects together in particular configurations (more evidence of this is provided for vertical prepositions; see below).

Associating objects with particular functions does not only occur through perception – the collocation of prepositions and nouns in language is also important. For example in English two different nouns can be used for a receptacle with the same level of concavity – a *dish* versus a *plate*. In Figure 3.2, the coffee capsule can be described as *in the dish* or *on the plate*; *on the dish* or *in the plate* are less acceptable descriptions. In a series of studies manipulating labeling of the same objects (Coventry et al. 1994; Coventry and Prat-Sala 2001), we found that changing the name for the same viewed object affects the preposition chosen to refer to that spatial relation. The implications of this are that the situation-specific meaning of spatial language is a combination of different types of co-occurrence relations – the likelihood with which words co-occur with other words, the likelihood with which objects occur in particular spatial configurations and exhibit particular geometric and dynamic-kinematic relations, and how these constraints mesh together (see also Speed et al. volume 1).

In summary, geometric routines, the dynamic-kinematic routine of location control, and rich situation knowledge about object associations, object-specific functions and collocations between nouns and prepositions are all necessary to give an account of the semantics of *in* and *on* (and equivalent terms in other languages: see Feist 2008 for discussion). Three points merit recapitulation.

First, we have gone beyond drawing pictures of spatial relations in the form of image schemata to more grounded representations, both geometric and extra-geometric, that are more plausibly computed by the vision and action systems. Second, such an account is able to deal with a wide range of senses of these prepositions using only a few parameters, thus avoiding the need for the explicit representation of extensive polysemy in some earlier cognitive linguistic accounts. Third, the empirical approach to spatial language gives good information regarding the mapping between language and space, using methods that go beyond relying on one's own intuitions about spatial relations (Sandra and Rice 1995).

3.2 Projective terms – focus on *over, under, above* and *below*

The projective prepositions in English include *left, right, in front of, behind, over, under, above,* and *below*. These terms require a reference frame from which a spatial direction is generated. For instance *above* is usually employed with respect to the gravitational axis (*above* an object is usually higher in the gravitational plane). However, one can also use *above* from the viewers' perspective (when performing a hand stand, viewing an object *above* can be lower in the gravitational plane). And when looking at someone else doing a handstand, one can also say that an object is *above her head* using her body as the axes rather than gravity. Levinson (1996, 2003) distinguishes between three classes of reference frame; the absolute reference frame (e.g., the gravitational plane, cardinal directions, and so on and so forth), the relative frame (determined by the changing position of the viewer), and the intrinsic frame (determined by the axes of the reference object).

There is a literature examining preferences for particular reference frames, as well as constraints on their use. Often reference frames are collapsed – for instance, *above* is usually used when the absolute (gravitational) and relative frames are aligned. Empirical work by Carlson and colleagues has played an important part in unpacking constraints on reference frames using experimental paradigms as well as event-related brain potentials that tease apart the use of individual frames (e.g., Carlson et al. 2002). Carlson-Radvansky and Irwin (1993) found that English projective terms display a distinct pattern of preferences on their use, with distinct preferences for the absolute frame for *above*, followed by the intrinsic frame, with less evidence for the use of a relative frame when the absolute and intrinsic frames do not coincide with relative use.

Once a reference frame has been selected for a projective term, the geometric routines for the vertical prepositions have been well articulated, with computational frameworks for these proposed and developed by Regier and Carlson

Fig. 3.3: Examples of scenes used by Coventry et al. (2001).

(2001), and Regier (1996) building on earlier empirical results (e.g., Hayward and Tarr 1995; Logan and Sadler 1996). For example, the Attention Vector Sum model developed by Regier and Carlson (2001), partly inspired by population vector encoding in several neural subsystems (e.g., Georgopolous et al. 1986), elegantly computes acceptability ratings for *above* that map onto human judgments for varying positions of located objects in relation to various shapes of reference object.

In addition to geometric routines, evidence for dynamic kinematic routines for these terms has also been forthcoming. The comprehension and production of vertical prepositions is affected by the extent to which objects are shown to fulfill, or are expected to fulfill, their functions (e.g., Carlson-Radvansky et al. 1999; Coventry et al. 2001). For example, Coventry et al. (2001) presented participants with pictures of people holding objects with a protecting function, such as a person holding an umbrella (see Figure 3.3). The geometry of the scene was manipulated with the umbrella positioned either directly over the person, or at varying angles from the vertical. The scenes also manipulated the extent to which the protecting object was shown to protect the person from falling objects. In the functional condition, rain was shown falling on the umbrella, protecting the person. In the non-functional condition, rain was shown missing the protecting object, and making contact with the person. Participants rated the appropriateness of sentences containing the prepositions *over, under, above* and *below* to describe the relative positions of the objects (e.g., *The umbrella is over the man / The man is under the umbrella*). Several findings of interest emerged. First, both the relative positions of the located and reference objects

Fig. 3.4: Examples of scenes used by Coventry et al. (2010).

and function affected ratings. For geometry, ratings were highest when the protecting object was directly over the person's head, and for function, ratings were highest when the protecting object was protecting and lowest when it was not. Second, there was an effect of function even when the protecting object was in the prototypical geometric position (i.e., directly above the person's head). Third, there were interactions between geometry and function and specific prepositions. While ratings for *above* and *below* were more affected by the relative positions of objects than those for *over* and *under*, the reverse was true for function. This latter finding suggests that English has two sets of vertical prepositions which are not synonyms, but rather pick out a differential focus on geometry (*above, below*) versus function (*over, under*).

Building on these earlier results, the dynamic-kinematic routine for vertical prepositions has been investigated using eye tracking and brain imaging methods. For example, in the scenes shown in Figure 3.4, the box and the bowl are in the same relative positions, but the objects falling from the box are not shown either directly reaching or missing the bowl. Coventry et al. (2010) posited that, if dynamic-kinematic routines are real, participants would have to project the path of falling objects in order to establish whether the box and bowl are interacting as one would typically expect when these objects occur together before they are able to give acceptability judgments. Eye tracking revealed that participants spent more time looking to the side of the bowl when the falling objects looked like they would miss the container (the right picture in Figure 3.4) than when the objects would be expected to end up in the container (middle picture) during a sentence-picture rating task.

This provides evidence that participants were indeed looking down the path of the falling objects prior to making their judgments about the suitability of spatial prepositions to describe the pictures. Moreover, in some recent brain imaging work (Coventry et al. 2013) we found that spatial language judgments when looking at similar pictures are associated with "mentally animating" the visual scene when viewing it. Using functional Magnetic Resonance Imaging, we localized the brain regions associated with motion processing (middle temporal and middle superior temporal regions). Participants performed a sentence picture verification task in the scanner; they first read sentences containing prepositions (e.g., *the box is over the bowl*) or comparative adjectives (*the box* is bigger than the bowl) followed by a picture (examples in Figure 3.4). Among the findings, we found that there was reliably more motion processing activation for the static images when they were preceded by sentences containing prepositions compared to sentences containing comparative adjectives. This shows that spatial language actually drives how a visual scene is processed when one is looking at it. Moreover, in whole brain analyses, we also found more premotor and motor activations during picture presentation when the pictures were again preceded by sentences containing prepositions as compared with comparative adjectives. This confirms that spatial language goes beyond geometric relations, pointing to the importance of the action system as well as the visual system as components associated with it.

Just as *in* and *on* require more than geometric and dynamic-kinematic routines to understanding the mapping with the spatial world, so too do the vertical prepositions. For example, in the protecting object experiments of Coventry et al. (2001), the influence of objects without a usual protecting function was also considered, but in situations where those objects could nevertheless afford protection. For instance, the umbrella in Figure 3.3 was substituted with a suitcase, which presumably does not have a lexicalized protecting function. Nevertheless, ratings of *the suitcase is over the man*, etc., were affected by the position of the falling rain. In another study, adding holes to an umbrella where the function is no longer afforded (i.e., when the rain a distance away from the object is expected to pass through the umbrella even though it is falling towards it) has been found to eliminate the influence of the position of the rain on spatial language ratings (Coventry et al., 2010). These examples (among others) show that consideration of situational and object knowledge is required for vertical spatial terms, just as it is for the prepositions *in* and *on*.

4 Spatial demonstratives

Spatial demonstratives, such as *this* and *that*, are particularly important to examine with respect to the mapping between language and space. These terms, like topological prepositions, are among the first words all children acquire (Clark 1973, 2003) but they are more closely associated with deictic gestures than other spatial terms, and other linguistic items in general (H. Clark 1996; Diessel 2006). They also occur in all languages, are high frequency terms within a language, and philologically emerge as the earliest traceable words in languages (Deutscher 2005; Diessel 2006). For these reasons spatial demonstratives should be one of the first ports of call when examining the mapping between language and space, but rather surprisingly they have received much less attention than spatial prepositions.

A useful starting point when considering demonstratives is the impressive cataloguing of demonstrative systems across languages by Diessel (1999, 2005). In a large-scale analysis of demonstrative systems across over 200 languages, Diessel found that the most basic distinction languages make is a binary distinction (54% of languages sampled; English among them). From this Diessel argues that a proximal-distal contrast underlies demonstrative systems across languages (Diessel 2005, 2006). As Enfield (2003) has argued, typologies are however not based on studies of real demonstrative use – and only recently have experimental studies begun to examine the mapping between demonstratives and perceptual space.

Using a methodology designed to elicit spatial demonstratives without speakers realizing that their language was being tested, Coventry et al. (2008) tested the mapping between spatial demonstrative use and perceptual space across two languages. English and Spanish-speaking participants were instructed to produce either *this* or *that* (or the Spanish equivalents: *este, ese, aquel*) to identify the position of coloured geometrical shapes/disks placed on a table at varying distances from them (whilst believing the experiment was about memory for object location; see Figure 3.5). First, an object was placed on a coloured dot various distances from the participant. Next, the participant had to point at the object saying either *this/that* colour shape (e.g., *this red triangle*). (Participants were told that they were in the 'language' condition in the memory experiment, and therefore it was important to stick to only three words in their descriptions [while pointing at the object] so that everyone in the language condition had the same amount of language.) When the object was placed within arm's reach, participants used *this* (*este* in Spanish) more often than *that*, with *that* used more than *this* when the object was positioned outside of arm's reach. Participants also used *this/este* more frequently when they had placed the object rather than when the experimenter had placed the object. Finally, an extension of the use of *this/este* to describe positions beyond arm's reach was found when participants pointed using a stick.

These data (and data from other studies; see for example Bonfiglioli et al. 2009; Maes and De Rooij 2007) map onto findings in neuroscience and neuropsychology that has identified two separate brain systems representing peripersonal (near) and extrapersonal (far) space (e.g., Berti and Rizzolatti 2002; Làdavas 2002). Indeed the extension of *this* using a stick and the manipulation of who places the object prior to description in Coventry et al. (2008) were motivated directly by findings on peripersonal space showing that peripersonal space can be extended through tool use and contact (e.g., Berti and Frassinetti 2000; Longo and Lourenco 2006).

Fig. 3.5: The setup for the memory game experiments (Coventry et al., 2008), and some of the shaped used.

So it appears that *where* an object is located is important for demonstrative choice, mapping into a basic distinction the perceptual system makes. But are demonstratives also affected by other extrageometric variables just as prepositions are?

Linguistic typological work across languages has shown that demonstrative systems vary quite considerably across languages, and some of the distinctions relate to the nature of the objects placed rather than their location. Some languages have three-term demonstrative systems, usually regarded as distance oriented (Spanish: Kemmerer 1999; Levinson 2003), or person oriented (e.g., Japanese: Diessel 2005), but other languages make distinctions such as whether an object is visible or not (e.g., Tiriyó: Meira 2003; Quileute: Diessel 1999), whether or not an object is owned by the speaker (e.g., Supyire: Diessel 1999), and whether the object is elevated on the vertical plan (e.g., Dyirbal, Lahu: Diessel 1999). Such cross-linguistic differences have led some to argue that de-

Fig. 3.6: The visibility manipulations in Coventry et al. (2014).

monstratives simply do not map onto perceptual space (see for example Enfield 2003; Kemmerer 1999, 2006 for discussion). However, an alternative possibility is that spatial demonstratives, just like adpositions, are associated with multiple constraints on their use. In a series of recent studies with English speakers using the memory game (Coventry et al. 2014) we varied whether the object placed was owned by the participant or not, whether the object was visible, and whether the object was familiar to the participant or not. For the visibility experiment, an object was placed and was then left uncovered, covered with a glass (so the object was still visible), or covered with a metal cover (so the object was occluded; see Figure 3.6). *This* was used least to describe the object when covered with the metal cover, with no difference between the glass cover and uncovered conditions. Although English does not make an explicit distinction in its binary demonstrative system between visible and hidden objects, English speakers nevertheless use that parameter to select demonstratives in their language.

For the ownership manipulation, participants at the start of the experiment were given participation payment in the form of coins, which were then used as stimuli in the experiment. Either the participant's coins were placed prior to description, or coins owned by the experimenter were placed. Participants used *this* significantly more than *that* to describe the location of their own coins compared to the coins owned by the experimenter.

If English demonstrative use is affected by object properties that are explicit in the demonstrative systems of some other languages, we wondered if further object properties might also be important, motivated by work we have conducted earlier on other types of spatial language. In the final experiment in this series, we examined familiarity of objects. The objects placed were either familiar colour-shape combinations (e.g., red square) or less familiar combinations (e.g., vermillion ranunculoid). Participants in this experiment used *this* more frequently to describe the location of the familiar objects compared to the unfamiliar objects.

So the results of the memory game experiments in Coventry et al. (2014) show that demonstrative choice is affected by knowledge of the objects being described. And in all the experiments the object manipulations did not interact with distance (note that there was also an effect of peripersonal versus extrapersonal space on demonstrative choice in all experiments). But do these results also map onto the perception of space? To test this we ran further non-linguistic experiments. Objects were placed as in the memory game scenario, but this time participants had the task of remembering where an object had been placed immediately after its placement. We then compared estimated distance (participants instructed the experimenter to move a stick to where the object had been placed) to the actual object placement distance from the participant. The results directly mirrored the results of the language memory game experiments. Objects owned by the participant were remembered as being closer than objects owned by someone else; covered (invisible) objects were remembered as being further away than covered visible objects or uncovered objects; familiar objects were remembered as being nearer than unfamiliar objects. And just like the language data, the object effects did not interact with distance.

Overall demonstrative use in English appears to be affected by object properties that are explicitly distinguished in the demonstrative systems of some other languages. Moreover, it would appear that the factors that affect demonstrative choice mirror the factors that affect (non-linguistic) memory for object location. Thus demonstrative distinctions across languages as well as demonstrative choice within a language appear to be related to distinctions affecting the perception of space as reflected in memory for object location.

An important caveat is to note that the experimental approach we have briefly overviewed in this chapter should not be viewed as a substitute for other methods. For example, with respect to demonstratives, other parameters affecting their use have been documented in addition to the parameters we have investigated empirically, including joint attention (see Diessel 2006) and the shared knowledge states of interlocutors (e.g., Piwek et al. 2008), with insights from cross-linguistic and typological analyses. It is to the issue of cross-linguistic variation that I briefly turn.

5 Cross-linguistic differences and "linguistic relativity"

The fact that languages carve up space in different ways is challenging for the view that a set of basic universal primitive spatial concepts underlie all spatial language (Levinson and Meira 2003; Bowerman 1996; see also Koptjevskaja-Tamm this volume). For example, containment and support relations do not always cluster in the same way across languages when speakers of different languages are charged with sorting or describing spatial scenes. While English distinguishes between containment (*in*) and support (*on*) relations, Dutch is among a cluster of languages that more finely differentiates support relations, with a distinction between vertical attachment (*aan*: a picture on a wall, a handle on a door), and horizontal support (*op*: a cup on a table). In contrast, Spanish collapses containment and support relations with a single term, *en*, appropriate for containment and support (Bowerman 1996). Such differences lead to two questions that merit mention. First, does the language one learns affect how one structures space? Second, do speakers of different languages actually "think" spatially in different ways? I take each of these issues in turn.

It is tempting to think that the distinctions a language makes are revealing about the type of non-linguistic concepts and processes that speakers of that language employ. Indeed, with respect to *in* and *on*, differences in the way Korean and English languages carve up these relations has been the subject of a series of fascinating studies. While English distinguishes between containment and support events as the end points of motion actions, Korean distinguishes between tight-fit and loose-fit path events. In Korean the verb *kkita* is used for tight-fit path events (putting a video cassette in a video cassette box/putting a lid on a jar) while *nehta* is used for loose-fit containment paths and *nohta* for loose-fit support relations (Bowerman 1996). Choi et al. (1999), using a preferential looking method, showed that 1.5–2 year old Korean and English learning children already look at language-appropriate aspects of spatial relations when looking at visual scenes paired with words in their language. However, McDonough et al. (2003) and Hespos and Spelke (2004) found that younger infants learning Korean or English look at both geometric distinctions between containment and support and tight-fit loose-fit distinctions, suggesting that learning a language might focus on some perceptual distinctions more than others, rather than language structuring space uniquely for that language. Indeed, as I reviewed above, even English adults are sensitive to degrees of location control when using *in* and *on*, and therefore it might be mistaken to argue that language completely filters out distinctions. However, one has to be cautious; as Casasola (2008) notes, it is likely that the extent to which language structures spatial categories in development varies as a function of spatial category.

It has also been claimed that the language ones speaks affects performance on a range of non-linguistic tasks (i.e., a test of "linguistic relativity"; see Wolff and Holmes 2010 for discussion). A much-discussed example is that of Pederson and colleagues (1998), who found differences across a range of tasks between speakers of languages differing in their use of references frames. For example, Tzeltal speakers, who use the absolute frame of reference even in small-scale/table-top space, have a tendency, when they rotate 180 degrees, to rearrange objects absolutely, while Dutch and English speakers rotate the object arrangement in alignment with body rotation (i.e., they produce relative arrangements). The interpretation of these results as evidence for a strong form of the Whorfian hypotheses has been controversial (see Majid et al. 2004; Li and Gleitman 2002 for different views). What *is* clear is that speakers of languages can use their language a tool to aid performance on non-linguistic tasks (see Trueswell and Papafragou 2010). However, while speakers of a language may use the distinctions they have in their language when performing non-linguistic tasks, those distinctions may not capture how those terms are actually used within a language by speakers (cf. Coventry et al. 2014).

6 Conclusions

Spatial language is a natural place to start to examine the spatial constructs that are important for language. This brief (and highly selective) review of empirical research on spatial language has illustrated how experimental approaches to spatial language have helped to unpack the multiple constraints underpinning the mapping between language and space. Cross-linguistic data collected using multiple methods will continue to play an important role in understanding not only the extent of possible universal perceptual parameters underpinning spatial language across languages, but also the full range of constraints speakers may employ to use the spatial language they have within their own language.

7 References

Bergen, Benjamin (volume 1): Embodiment. Berlin/Boston: De Gruyter Mouton.
Berti, Anna and Francesca Frassinetti (2000): When far becomes near: Remapping of space by tool use. *Journal of Cognitive Neuroscience* 12: 415–420.
Berti, Anna and Giacomo Rizzolatti (2002): Coding near and far space. In: H.-O. Karnath, A. D. Milner, and G. Vallar (eds.), *The Cognitive and Neural Bases of Spatial Neglect*, 119–129. New York: Oxford University Press.
Bonfiglioli, Claudia, Chiara Finocchiaro, Beno Gesierich, Francesco Rositani, and Massimo Vescovi (2009): A kinematic approach to the conceptual representations of *this* and *that*. *Cognition* 111: 270–274.
Bower, Thomas G. R. (1982): *Development in Infancy* (2nd Edition). San Francisco: W. H. Freeman.
Bowerman, Melissa (1996): Learning how to structure space for language: a cross-linguistic perspective. In: P. Bloom, M. A. Peterson, L. Nadel, and M. F. Garrett (eds.), *Language and Space*, 385–436. Cambridge: MIT Press.
Brugman, Claudia (1988): *The Story of "over": Polysemy, Semantics and the Structure of the Lexicon*. New York: Garland.
Carlson, Laura A., Robert West, Holly A. Taylor, and Ryan S. Herndon (2002): Neural correlates of spatial term use. *Journal of Experimental Psychology: Human Perception and Performance* 28(6): 1391–1407.
Carlson-Radvansky, Laura A., Eric S. Covey, and Kathleen M. Lattanzi (1999): "What" effects on "where": Functional influences on spatial relations. *Psychological Science* 10: 516–521.
Carlson-Radvansky, Laura A., and David E. Irwin (1993): Frames of reference in vision and language: where is above? *Cognition* 46: 223–244.
Casasanto, Daniel and Lera Boroditsky (2008): Time in the mind: Using space to think about time. *Cognition* 106: 579–593.
Casasola, Marianella (2008): The development of infants' spatial categories. *Current Directions in Psychological Science* 17: 21–25.
Casasola, Marianella and Leslie B. Cohen (2002): Infant categorization of containment, support, and tight-fit spatial relationships. *Developmental Science* 5: 247–264.
Casasola, Marianella, Leslie B. Cohen, and Elizabeth Chiarello (2003): Six-month-old infants' categorization of containment spatial relations. *Child Development* 74: 679–693.
Choi, Soonja, Laraine McDonough, Melissa Bowerman, and Jean M. Mandler (1999): Early sensitivity to language-specific spatial categories in English and Korean. *Cognitive Development* 14: 241–268.
Clark, Eve V. (1973): Nonlinguistic strategies and the acquisition of word meanings. *Cognition* 2: 161–182.
Clark, Eve V. (2003): *First Language Acquisition*. Cambridge: Cambridge University Press.
Clark, Herbert H. (1996): *Using Language*. Cambridge: Cambridge University Press.
Cohn, Anthony G., Brandon Bennett, John Gooday, and Nicholas M. Gotts (1997): Qualitative spatial representation and reasoning with the region connection calculus. *Geoinformatica* 1: 1–42.
Coventry, Kenny R. (1998): Spatial prepositions, functional relations and lexical specification. In: P. Oliver and K. Gapp (eds.), *The Representation and Processing of Spatial Expressions*, 247–262. Hillsdale: Lawrence Erlbaum Associates.

Coventry, Kenny R., Richard Carmichael, and Simon C. Garrod (1994): Spatial prepositions, object-specific function and task requirements. *Journal of Semantics* 11: 289–309.

Coventry, Kenny R., Thomas Christophel, Thorsten Fehr, Berenice Valdés-Conroy, and Manfred Herrmann (2013): Multiple routes to mental animation: Language and functional relations drive motion processing for static images. *Psychological Science* 24(8): 1379–1388.

Coventry, Kenny R. and Simon C. Garrod (2004): *Saying, Seeing and Acting. The Psychological Semantics of Spatial Prepositions*. Hove and New York: Psychology Press, Taylor and Francis.

Coventry, Kenny R., Debra Griffiths, and Colin J. Hamilton (2014): Spatial demonstratives and perceptual space: Describing and remembering object location. *Cognitive Psychology* 69: 46–70.

Coventry, Kenny R., Dermot Lynott, Angelo Cangelosi, Lynn Monrouxe, Dan Joyce, and Daniel C. Richardson (2010): Spatial language, visual attention, and perceptual simulation. *Brain and Language* 112(3): 202–213.

Coventry, Kenny R. and Merce Prat-Sala (2001): Object-specific function, geometry and the comprehension of 'in' and 'on'. *European Journal of Cognitive Psychology* 13(4): 509–528.

Coventry, Kenny R., Merce Prat-Sala, and Lynn Richards (2001): The interplay between geometry and function in the comprehension of 'over', 'under', 'above' and 'below'. *Journal of Memory and Language* 44: 376–398.

Coventry, Kenny R., Berenice Valdés, Alejandro Castillo, and Pedro Guijarro-Fuentes (2008): Language within your reach: Near-far perceptual space and spatial demonstratives. *Cognition* 108: 889–898.

Deutscher, Guy (2005): *The Unfolding of Language: An Evolutionary Tour of Mankind's Greatest Invention*. New York: Metropolitan Books.

Diessel, Holger (1999): *Demonstratives. Form, Function, and Grammaticalization*. John Benjamins: Amsterdam.

Diessel, Holger (2005): Distance contrasts in demonstratives. In: M. Haspelmath, M. Dryer, D. Gil, and B. Comrie (eds.), *World Atlas of Language Structures*, 170–173. Oxford: Oxford University Press.

Diessel, Holger (2006): Demonstratives, joint attention, and the emergence of grammar. *Cognitive Linguistics* 17: 463–489.

Enfield, Nick J. (2003): Demonstratives in space and interaction: data from Lao speakers and implications for semantic analysis. *Language* 79: 82–117.

Evans, Vyvyan (this volume): Time. Berlin/Boston: De Gruyter Mouton.

Feist, Michele I. (2008): Space between languages. *Cognitive Science* 32: 1177–1199.

Feist, Michele I. and Dedre Gentner (1998): On plates, bowls and dishes: Factors in the use of English IN and ON. In: M. A. Gernsbacher and S. J. Derry (eds.), *Proceedings of the Twentieth Annual Meeting of the Cognitive Science Society*, 345–349. Hillsdale: Lawrence Erlbaum Associates.

Feist, Michele I. and Dedre Gentner (2003): Factors involved in the use of in and on. In: R. Alterman and D. Kirsh (eds.), *Proceedings of the Twenty-fifth Annual Meeting of the Cognitive Science Society*, 390–395. Hillsdale: Lawrence Erlbaum Associates.

Filipović, Luna and Iraide Ibarretxe-Antuñano (this volume): Motion. Berlin/Boston: De Gruyter Mouton.

Garrod, Simon, Gillian Ferrier, and Siobhan Campbell (1999): *In* and *on*: Investigating the functional geometry of spatial prepositions. *Cognition* 72(2): 167–189.

Garrod, Simon C. and Anthony J. Sanford (1989): Discourse models as interfaces between language and the spatial world. *Journal of Semantics*, 6, 147–160.

Georgopolous, Apostolos P., Andrew B. Schwartz, and Ronald E. Kettner (1986): Neuronal populating coding of movement direction. *Science* 233(4771): 1416–1419.

Gibbs, Raymond W. (volume 1): Metaphor. Berlin/Boston: De Gruyter Mouton.

Gries, Stefan Th. (this volume): Polysemy. Berlin/Boston: De Gruyter Mouton.

Hayward, William G. and Michael J. Tarr (1995): Spatial language and spatial representation. *Cognition* 55: 39–84.

Herskovits, Annette (1986): *Language and Spatial Cognition: An Interdisciplinary Study of the Prepositions in English*. Cambridge: Cambridge University Press.

Hespos, Susan J. and Renée Baillargeon (2001): Reasoning about containment events in very young infants. *Cognition* 78: 207–245.

Hespos, Susan J. and Elizabeth S. Spelke (2004): Conceptual precursors to language. *Nature* 430(6998): 453–456.

Johnson, Judith and Dan I. Slobin (1979): The development of locative expressions in English, Italian, Serbo-Croatian and Turkish. *Journal of Child Language* 6: 529–546.

Kemmerer, David (1999): "Near" and "far" in language and perception. *Cognition* 44: 1607–1621.

Kemmerer, David (2006): The semantics of space: Integrating linguistic typology and cognitive neuroscience. *Neuropsychologia* 44: 1607–1621.

Koptjevskaja-Tamm, Maria (this volume): Semantic typology. Berlin/Boston: De Gruyter Mouton.

Làdavas, Elisabetta (2002): Functional and dynamic properties of visual peripersonal space. *Trends in Cognitive Science* 6: 17–22.

Lakoff, George (1987): *Women, Fire, and Dangerous Things*. Chicago: Chicago University Press.

Lakoff, George and Mark Johnson (1980): *Metaphors We Live By*. Chicago: Chicago University Press.

Landau, Barbara and Ray Jackendoff (1993): 'What' and 'where' in spatial language and cognition. *Behavioural and Brain Sciences* 16(2): 217–265.

Langacker, Ronald W. (1986): *Foundations of Cognitive Grammar*, Vol. 1. Stanford: Stanford University Press.

Levinson, Stephen C. (1996): Frames of reference and Molyneux's question. In: P. Bloom, M. A. Peterson, L. Nadel, and M. F. Garrett (eds.), *Language and Space*, 109–169. Cambridge: MIT Press.

Levinson, Stephen C. (2003): *Space in Language and Cognition. Explorations in Cognitive Diversity*. Cambridge University press: Cambridge.

Levinson, Stephen C. and Sergio Meira (2003): 'Natural concepts' in the spatial topological domain – adpositional meanings in crosslinguistic perspective: An exercise in semantic typology. *Language* 79(3): 485–516.

Li, Peggy and Lila Gleitman (2002): Turning the tables: Language and spatial reasoning. *Cognition* 83: 265–294.

Logan, Gordon D. and Daniel D. Sadler (1996): A computational analysis of the apprehension of spatial relations. In: P. Bloom, M. A. Peterson, L. Nadel, and M. F. Garrett (eds.), *Language and Space*, 494–530. Cambridge MIT Press.

Longo, Matthew R. and Stella F. Lourenco (2006): On the nature of near space: Effects of tool use and the transition to far space. *Neuropsychologia* 44: 977–981.

Maes, Alfons and C. De Rooij (2007): How do demonstratives code distance? In: A. Branco, T. McEnery, R. Mitkov, and F. Silva (eds.), *Proceedings of the 6th Discourse Anaphora and Anaphor Resolution Colloquium DAARC 2007*, 83–89. Lagos, Pt: Centro Linguistica da Universidade do Porto.

Majid, Asifa, Melissa Bowerman, Sotara Kita, Daniel B. M. Haun, and Stephen C. Levinson (2004): Can language restructure cognition? The case for space. *Trends in Cognitive Science* 8: 108–114.

McDonough, Laraine, Soonja Choi, and Jean M. Mandler (2003): Understanding spatial relations: Flexible infants, lexical adults. *Cognitive Psychology* 46: 226–259.

Meira, Sergio (2003): 'Addressee effects' in demonstrative systems: The cases of Tiriyó and Brazilian Portuguese. In: F. Lenz (ed.), *Deictic Conceptualization of Space, Time and Person*. Amsterdam: John Benjamins.

Pederson, Eric, Eve Danziger, David Wilkins, Stephen Levinson, Sotaro Kita, and Gunter Senft (1998): Semantic typology and spatial conceptualization. *Language* 74(3): 557–589.

Piaget, Jean and Bärbel Inhelder, B. (1956): *The Child's Conception of Space*. London: Routledge and Kegan Paul.

Piwek, Paul, Robbert-Jan Beun, and Anita Cremers (2008): 'Proximal' and 'distal' in language and cognition: Evidence from demonstratives in Dutch. *Journal of Pragmatics*, 40: 694–718.

Quinn, Paul C. (2005): Developmental constraints on the representation of spatial relation information: Evidence from preverbal infants. In: L. A. Carlson and E. van der Zee (eds.), *Functional Features in Language and Space: Insights from Perception, Categorization, and Development*. New York: Oxford University Press.

Regier, Terry (1996): *The Human Semantic Potential. Spatial Language and Constrained Connectionism*. Cambridge: MIT Press.

Regier, Terry and Laura A. Carlson (2001): Grounding spatial language in perception: An empirical and computational investigation. *Journal of Experimental Psychology: General* 130(2): 273–298.

Richards, Lynn V., Kenny R. Coventry, and John Clibbens (2004): Where's the orange? Geometric and extra-geometric factors in English children's talk of spatial locations. *Journal of Child Language* 31: 153–175.

Rosch, Eleanor and Carolyn B. Mervis (1975): Family resemblances: Studies in the internal structure of categories. *Cognitive Psychology* 7(4): 573–605.

Sandra, Dominiek and Sally Rice (1995): Network analyses of prepositional meaning. Mirroring whose mind – the linguist's or the language user's? *Cognitive Linguistics* 6: 8–130.

Speed, Laura, David P. Vinson, and Gabriella Vigliocco (volume 1): Representing meaning. Berlin/Boston: De Gruyter Mouton.

Talmy, Leonard (1983): How language structures space. In: H. Pick, and L. Acredolo (eds.), *Spatial Orientation: Theory, Research and Application*, 225–282. New York: Plenum Press.

Talmy, Leonard (1988): Force dynamics in language and cognition. *Cognitive Science* 12: 49–100.

Trueswell, John and Anna Papafragou (2010): Perceiving and remembering events cross-linguistically: Evidence from dual-task paradigms. *Journal of Memory and Language* 63: 64–82.

Tyler, Andrea and Vyvyan Evans (2003): *The Semantics of English Prepositions: Spatial Scenes, Embodied Meaning and Cognition*. Cambridge: Cambridge University Press.

Ullman, Shimon (1996): *High-level Vision. Object Recognition and Visual Cognition.* Cambridge: MIT Press.
Vandeloise, Claude (1991): *Spatial Prepositions. A Case Study from French.* Chicago: University of Chicago Press.
Wittgenstein, Ludwig (1953): *Philosophical Investigations.* Oxford: Blackwell.
Wolff, Phillip and Kevin J. Holmes (2010): Linguistic relativity. *WIREs Cognitive Science* 2: 253–265.

Vyvyan Evans
Chapter 4: Time

1 Introduction

Research on time, in cognitive linguistics, is concerned with how time manifests itself in language and thought. Cognitive linguists study time as a cognitive phenomenon, which can be investigated, in part, from its linguistic reflexes. Being interdisciplinary in nature, cognitive linguistics has approached the study of time from various perspectives. In addition to linguistics, research on temporal cognition has been informed by findings from experimental psychology, philosophy, neuroscience, and (cognitive) anthropology. This chapter addresses the key questions that cognitive linguistics has raised and attempted to answer, with respect to time.

2 What is the nature and status of time?

Does time arise from an internal subjectively-real experience type? Or is it abstracted from external sensory-motor experiences arising in veridical reality – our experience of the world "out there"? Questions of this sort have been addressed, either directly or indirectly, by cognitive linguists working with sometimes different theoretical, analytic and descriptive goals.

Conceptual Metaphor Theory (see Gibbs volume 1), for instance, has provided much of the impetus for exploring these specific questions. Lakoff and Johnson (1980, 1999) have argued that time is abstracted from veridical experiences, such as motion events: time is an abstract conceptual domain, while space is concrete. They put it as follows: "Very little of our understanding of time is purely temporal. Most of our understanding of time is a metaphorical version of our understanding of motion in space" (1999: 139). On this account time does not exist as a "thing-in-itself ... [w]hat we call the domain of time appears to be a conceptual domain that we use for asking certain questions about events through their comparison to other events." (Lakoff and Johnson 1999: 138). In short, time arises from the abstraction of relations between events that we perceive and experience in the world "out there". Once these relations have been

---

Vyvyan Evans, Bangor, United Kingdom

abstracted, they are structured in terms of spatial correlates, allowing us to conceptualise time. And once time has been conceptualised we can then experience it. In short, "our concept of time is cognitively constructed ... events and motion are more basic than time." (Lakoff and Johnson 1999: 167).

Other conceptual metaphor theorists have taken a more nuanced view. Grady (1997) holds that time and space evince a qualitative distinction that, and contrary to Lakoff and Johnson, is not best captured in terms of relative abstractness versus concreteness. Grady proposes that time derives from phenomenologically real, albeit subjective experience types, while spatial concepts are grounded in sensory-motor experiences. Moore (e.g., 2006), in his work on space-to-time conceptual metaphors concurs. He argues that time is as basic as space. Hence, time antecedes the conceptual metaphors that serve to structure it. The utility of metaphor, Moore contends, is to make time more accessible for conceptualisation, rather than creating it.

Evans (2004; see also 2013b), focusing on lexical concepts for time – rather than conceptual metaphors – argues that time is in some ways more fundamental than space, at least at the neurological level: it facilitates and underpins our ability to perceive and interact in the world, to anticipate, and to predict. Based on neurological evidence, Evans argues that the distributed nature of temporal processing is critical to our ability to perceive events. Event-perception is therefore facilitated by temporal processing, an issue we return to later.

In large part, the view taken on the nature and status of time depends on whether we are addressing temporal representations (concepts), or neurological representations (experiences). Indeed, the issue resolves itself into the following bifurcation: time is a subjectively real experience – as Grady, Moore and Evans hold – yet it is also a mental achievement, not something in and of itself, but rather abstracted from our perception of events in the world – the position argued for by Lakoff and Johnson.

One way out of this conundrum is to conclude that time is in fact both: temporal concepts are grounded in experiences that are independent of space (and sensory-motor experience more generally), but, time is also reified as an ontological entity, abstracted from the experiences which ground it, giving rise to an abstract category which can be deployed for intersubjective reflection. And in terms of the latter, this abstract category that can be structured, in part via conceptual metaphors, derives from sensory-motor experience.

There is now a very large body of evidence which supports the former view: not only is time directly experienced, its manifestation is often independent of our experience of motion events in space. Moreover, the human experience of time is, in principle, distinct from sensory-motor experience. For instance, Flaherty (1999) has found that our perception of duration is a function of how familiar subjects happen to be with particular tasks: training can influence our experience of task duration. Ornstein ([1969] 1997) has demonstrated that the complexity of a given perceptual array influences perception of duration. And Zakay and Block (1997) found that temporal perception is influenced by how interesting a particular activity is judged to be, or whether we are paying attention to a particular activity.

Other research reveals that our ability to judge duration is a consequence of physiological mechanisms, which vary in inter-subjectively predictable ways. For instance, if vital functioning is accelerated by the consumption of stimulants such as amphetamines, or due to increased body temperature, this results in an overestimation of time amongst subjects (Hoagland 1933; Fraisse 1963, 1984). In contrast, reduced body temperature leads to an underestimation of time (Baddeley 1966). In general, an increase or decrease in vital function consistently leads to perceiving duration as elapsing more quickly or slowly respectively (see Wearden and Penton-Voak 1995 for review).

Flaherty (1999) has found that the nature of experience types can influence our experience of time. For instance, the phenomenon of *protracted duration* – the phenomenologically real and vivid experience that time is proceeding more slowly than usual appears to be a consequence of events including boredom and near death experiences. In contrast, routine tasks with which we are familiar can give rise to the opposite effect: *temporal compression* – the phenomenologically real experience that time is proceeding more quickly than usual.

While findings such as these suggest that time is directly perceived, and phenomenologically real, there are types of temporal representation that appear not to be directly grounded in phenomenologically real experiences of this kind. One example of this is the *matrix* conceptualisation of time (Evans 2004, 2013b), also referred to as *time-as-such* (Sinha et al. 2011). This relates to our understanding of time as a manifold which, metaphorically, is draped across, and constitutes the whole of history; from this perspective, time is *the* event within which all other events take place. This view of time is exemplified by the linguistic example in (1):

(1) Time flows on (forever)

From this perspective, it makes sense to talk of time as having a beginning, as if it were an entity that lies outside us, in some sense providing reality with structure. It is this Matrix conceptualisation that is implicit in the conception of time in the classical mechanics of Newton, and to some extent, in post-Einsteinian physics. And by virtue of time as a Matrix being conceived as an ontological category independent of events, we can discuss and study it, and describe its "history", as evidenced by Steven Hawking's book title: *A Brief History of Time*.

In sum, temporal representations include those grounded in directly perceived temporal experiences. But representations for time can also be abstracted away from these experiences and reified as an ontological category independent of such experiences. This gives rise to mental achievements that are then available for intersubjective reflection without regard to directly experienced time. Representations of this type presume the existence of an objectively-real substrate that can be physically measured or observed, in some sense. And this conceptualisation presumably facilitates our ability to construct and interpret time-measurement systems such as calendars and clocks (Evans 2013b).

3 What is the relationship between time and space?

The relationship between temporal and spatial representation is, in a profound sense, paradoxical. On the one hand, space and time are, for many cognitive linguists, equally basic conceptual domains (Langacker 1987). They are basic in the sense that, although involving distinct types of representations, relating to matter and action, all other domains would seem to assume both space and time. In terms of the experiential level, we must have evolved mechanisms for processing the properties associated with space and time.

Some cognitive linguists have assumed that the fundamental nature of space and time results from a common structural homology (e.g., Talmy 2000). Linguistic evidence for this comes from what Talmy refers to as *conceptual conversion operations*. Talmy (2000) points out, on the basis of linguistic evidence, that acts and activities (from the domain of time) can be converted into objects and mass (from the domain of space). When a temporal concept is *reified*, this is conveyed by expressions exemplified by *a wash* and *some help* in (2) and (3) respectively:

(2) An act   reified as an object   (discrete)
    John washed her.   John gave her a wash.

(3) Activity   reified as a mass   (continuous)
    John helped her.   John gave her some help.

In example (2), the expression *washed* encodes an act, while *a wash* conceives of the same act as if it were an object. It is precisely because lexical concepts relating to time and space can be quantified, Talmy argues, that they can exhibit the conceptual alternativity evident in (2).

In example (3), the expression *helped* encodes an activity, while *some help* encodes a mass lexical concept. When an act is reified as an object, it can be described in terms consistent with the properties of objects. For example, physical objects can be transferred: *to call (on the phone)* becomes: *he gave me a call*. Physical objects can also be quantified: *to slap* becomes: *She gave him two slaps*. As Talmy observes, however, there are constraints upon this process of reification. For example, a reified act or activity cannot be expressed in the same way that prototypical physical objects can. Example (4) illustrates that the reified act, *a call* is incompatible with verbal lexical concepts that are prototypically physical.

(4) *John pushed/threw/thrust/slid Lily a call

The converse operation, which converts matter to action, is referred to as *actionalisation* (Talmy 2000). When units of matter are actionalised, they are expressed by lexical concepts encoded by verb phrase vehicles. This operation is illustrated by the following examples adapted from Talmy (2000: 45).

(5) *An object*   *actionalised as an act*   (discrete)
    Jane removed the pit from the olive. Jane pitted the olive.

(6) *A mass*   *actionalised as an activity* (continuous)
    Jane has a nosebleed.   Jane is bleeding from the nose.

In contrast, there are good reasons to think that, at the representational level, time and space are asymmetrically structured: time is supported by, and arguably parasitic on spatial representation: the position of Lakoff and Johnson (1980, 1999). Lakoff and Johnson argue that mappings recruit from the domain of space to provide structure for the domain of time, but not vice versa. Following seminal work by Clark (1973), Lakoff and Johnson have posited a "passage" conceptual metaphor, in which time recruits structure from (motion through) space. There are two versions of this conceptual metaphor, both based on linguistic evidence.

The first of these is the Moving Time Metaphor. In this conceptualisation there is a stationary Observer whose location corresponds to the present. The Observer faces the future, with the space behind corresponding to the past (Figure 4.1).

In Figure 4.1, events are represented by small circles. Motion is represented by the arrows. Events move from the future towards the Observer, and then behind into the past. The reason for thinking that speakers of English store this in their minds again comes from language:

PAST   PRESENT   FUTURE

Fig. 4.1: The Moving Time Metaphor.

Tab. 4.1: Mappings for the Moving Time Metaphor.

Source domain: MOTION OF OBJECTS	Mappings	Target domain: TIME
OBJECTS	→	TIMES
THE MOTION OF OBJECTS PAST THE OBSERVER	→	THE "PASSAGE" OF TIME
PROXIMITY OF OBJECT TO THE OBSERVER	→	TEMPORAL "PROXIMITY" OF THE EVENT
THE LOCATION OF THE OBSERVER	→	THE PRESENT
THE SPACE IN FRONT OF THE OBSERVER	→	THE FUTURE
THE SPACE BEHIND THE OBSERVER	→	THE PAST

(7) a. Christmas is *approaching*.
   b. The time for action *has arrived*.
   c. The end-of-summer sales *have passed*.

As these examples show, we employ the language of motion to refer to the passage of time. The regions of space in front of, co-located with, and behind the Observer correspond to future, present and past. In addition, we understand motion to relate to time's *passage*, as is clear by the use of *approaching*, in the first sentence. The series of mappings that allow us to understand these different aspects of the motion of objects in terms of TIME are captured in Table 4.2.

The second passage conceptual metaphor, which we can think of as being a reversal of the Moving Time Metaphor, is referred to as the Moving Ego, or Moving Observer metaphor. Here, time is conceived as a static "timescape" with events conceptualised as specific and static locations towards which the Observer moves and then passes (Figure 4.2).

As previously, events are represented by small circles in Figure 4.2, which are specific locations in the temporal landscape. Motion is represented by the arrows. In this case, it is the Observer, rather than the events, which is in motion. Here, we understand the passage of time *in terms of* the Observer's motion: the Observer moves across the temporal landscape towards and then past spe-

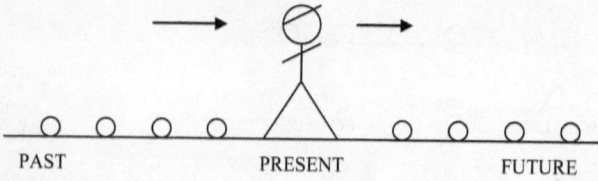

PAST   PRESENT   FUTURE

Fig. 4.2: The Moving Observer Metaphor.

Tab. 4.2: Mappings for The Moving Observer metaphor.

Source domain: MOTION OF OBSERVER	Mappings	Target domain: TIME
LOCATIONS ON OBSERVER'S PATH	→	TIMES
THE MOTION OF THE OBSERVER	→	THE "PASSAGE" OF TIME
THE LOCATION OF THE OBSERVER	→	THE PRESENT
THE SPACE IN FRONT OF THE OBSERVER	→	THE FUTURE
THE SPACE BEHIND THE OBSERVER	→	THE PAST
DISTANCE OF OBSERVER FROM LOCATION	→	TEMPORAL "DISTANCE" OF EVENT
RAPIDITY OF MOTION OF OBSERVER	→	IMMINENCE OF EVENT'S OCCURRENCE

cific events, expressed as fixed locations in space. Lakoff and Johnson again point to evidence from language for this conceptualisation:

(8) a. They're *approaching* crisis-point.
   b. The relationship *extended over* many years.
   c. He left *at* 10 o'clock.

Examples like these have been taken to reveal that, metaphorically, the Observer's motion is ascribed to time's passage. Time is being likened to a static landscape as we can see from expressions such as *extended over*. And the use of *at*, as in *He left at 10 o'clock* demonstrates that specific locations in the static landscape correspond to temporal events. See Table 4.2 for mappings that have been proposed for this metaphor.

In behavioural experiments, Boroditsky (2000; Boroditsky and Ramscar 2002) provided the first psycholinguistic support for Lakoff and Johnson's claim for asymmetric organisation between time and space. Boroditsky developed both spatial and temporal primes which she applied to temporal and spatial reasoning tasks. She reasoned that if spatial and temporal representations are structured symmetrically, which is to say, if temporal representation is just as useful for reasoning about space, as spatial representation is for time, then spatial cues should prime for temporal reasoning, while temporal cues should prime for spatial reasoning tasks. Boroditsky found evidence consistent with an asymmetric perspective: spatial cues appear to be useful for reasoning about time, but temporal primes appear not to be used when reasoning about space. More recently, Casasanto and Boroditsky (2008) have provided additional support for the asymmetric organisation of time in terms of space, making use of non-linguistic behavioural tasks.

One specific manifestation of the asymmetric organisation of space and time relates to *frames of reference* (FoRs). A FoR, in the domain of time, comprises three coordinates to locate or fix a temporal entity with respect to another (Zinken 2010). Early research focused on examining FoRs from the domain of space, investigating how they are recruited to structure temporal reference: the assumption being that FoRs from the domain of space are naturally mapped onto time. Two such taxonomies have been proposed (Bendner et al. 2010; Tenbrink 2011; see also Moore 2011). However, there is, as yet, little consensus on the nature of these taxonomies, or indeed whether spatial FoRs really do subserve temporal reference (see Bender et al. 2012 for critical evaluation). For instance, Evans (2013a, 2013b) has proposed that FoRs in the domain of time are qualitatively distinct from those in the domain of space. He has developed a time-based taxonomy of temporal FoRs deriving from the notion of *transience* (discussed below). Temporal FoRs is now one of the fastest developing areas of research in the study of temporal cognition.

At the neurological level, two proposals have been put forward to account for the relationship between time and space. Bonato et al. (2012) have proposed what they term the *Mental Time Line* (MTL) hypothesis. This hypothesis is consistent with the asymmetric organisation posited by Lakoff and Johnson's Conceptual Metaphor Theory. They posit that, at the neurological level, temporal experience is structured *in terms* of spatial characteristics.

A second possibility, one that would account for the data provided by Talmy, posits a single magnitude system. Such a system would provide a common metric allowing the different parameters associated with the domains of time and space to be quantified, and integrated. Such an approach has been proposed by Walsh (2003; Bueti and Walsh 2009) in *A Theory of Magnitude* (ATOM). Walsh proposes that there is a single generalised, neurologically-instantiated magnitude system, present at birth. This allows space and time to be quantified, in principle, in symmetrical ways.

Whichever of the two approaches, ATOM, or MTL, turns out to be correct – and there are arguments in favour of both – the only candidate brain region that might facilitate the interaction between spatial and temporal experience appears to be the inferior parietal cortex – this region of the brain is host to a series of closely-related sub-areas specialised for processing time, space and number (Bonato et al. 2012; Bueti and Walsh 2009; Walsh 2003).

4 What is the distinction between time and space?

If time does recruit structure from the domain of space, are the two domains distinct? In important work, Galton (2011) has proposed a number of parameters that allow representations for time and space to be compared and contrasted. This research demonstrates that time and space are qualitatively distinct conceptual domains. The relevant parameters enabling comparison of the two domains are: *magnitude*,[1] *dimensionality*,[2] and *directedness* (Galton 2011). I consider and nuance each of these parameters in turn.

The parameter of magnitude relates to the quantifiability of a given *substrate* – the stuff that makes up the domain. The substrate the makes up space is *matter*, of which two broad types can be distinguished: discrete entities (e.g., objects) and mass entities (e.g., fluids). This distinction, in types of matter, is reflected in the grammatical organisation of many languages, whereby a distinction between count versus mass nouns is encoded.

In addition, the substrate that makes up a domain exhibits a particular property allowing the substrate to be quantified: the way in which the substrate can be "cut up" into "amounts". The amounts, in the domain of space, relate to the property *extension*. Extension manifests itself in three distinct types – which is a function of the three-dimensionality of space, discussed further below. Space's extension involves length (one dimension), area (two dimensions), and volume (three dimensions).

The substrate that makes up time is that of *action* (Talmy 2000). As with space, action can also be broadly subdivided, as reflected in language. This relates to whether action is *bounded* versus *unbounded*, analogous to the distinction between discrete versus mass for the substrate matter. This is illustrated by the grammatical distinction between perfective versus imperfective aspect in many languages.

In the domain of time, the property exhibited by action, and hence, the means of "cutting up" action into amounts is *duration*, rather than extension. While duration can, self-evidently, be quantified by using *measurement systems*

---

[1] Galton (2011) uses the term "extension".
[2] Galton (2011) uses the term "linearity".

Tab. 4.3: Comparing the parameter magnitude for space and time.

Domain	Space	Time
Substrate	Matter	Action
Property	Extension	Duration
Distinction	Discrete vs. mass	Bounded vs. Unbounded

involving material artefacts such as clocks, duration (of relatively shorts periods) can be estimated without the need for measurement systems such as these. The distinctions between space and time in terms of the parameter of magnitude are summarised in Table 4.3.

Dimensionality, in physical terms, relates to the *constituent structure* of matter. The constituent structure of matter involves three distinct planes with respect to which points can be located. These are the transversal (left/right), sagittal (front/back) and vertical (up/down) planes. Hence, our everyday representation of space can be said to be three-dimensional.

In contrast, in the domain of time the constituent structure of action involves *succession*: the sequential relationship that holds between distinct units and sub-units of action (cf. Moore 2006; Núñez et al. 2006). In other words, our representation for time involves a relationship between units of action in a sequence. This involves just one dimension.

Physical theories that incorporate time, such as in the Theory of General Relativity (Einstein 1916), treat time as the fourth dimension of space, forming a space-time continuum, or Minkowski space, after the celebrated 19th century mathematician who first proposed incorporating time into space. On this view, points can be "located" in time, where units of action are strung out, all at once, across time. Yet this view is at odds with the human phenomenological experience of time (see Evans 2004: Chapter 19). Insofar as time, from a phenomenological perspective, can be said to exhibit dimensionality, this relates to the sequential relationship between events, providing one-dimensional constituent structure.

The final parameter, directedness, relates to whether the substrate in a given domain is *symmetric* (i.e., isotropic) or *asymmetric* (i.e., anisotropic). Space is isotropic: it has no inherent asymmetry. Indeed, it is possible to proceed in any direction: forward or back, or from side to side. In contrast, time is anisotropic: it manifests asymmetric organisation. From a phenomenological perspective, time is experienced as anisotropic. This concerns the anticipation of a future event, the actual experience of the event, and finally, the recollection of the event as past.

In his work, Galton (2011) discusses an additional feature which he argues is exhibited by time, but not by space. This he refers to as *transience*: the fleeting quality associated with temporal experience. For Galton, transience is the hallmark of time, and hence part of its inalienable character.

5 Is time homogenous or multifaceted?

Linguistic evidence demonstrates that the conceptual domain of time is multifaceted (Evans 2004, 2013b; Grady 1997; Moore 2006). For instance, the English word *time* covers a range of quite different lexical concepts (Evans 2004). Consider the following examples:

(9) The time for action has arrived

(10) a. Time flies when you're having fun
 b. Time drags when you have nothing to do

(11) a. The young woman's time [= labour/childbirth] approached
 b. His time [= death] had come
 c. Arsenal saved face with an Ian Wright leveller five minutes from time [BNC]

(12) [T]ime, of itself, and from its own nature, flows equably without relation to anything external [Sir Isaac Newton]

In these examples, all involving the vehicle *time*, a different reading is obtained. In (9), a discrete temporal point or moment is designated, without reference to its duration. The examples in (10) provide a reading relating to what might be described as "magnitude of duration". (10a) relates to the phenomenologically real experience whereby time proceeds "more quickly" than usual – this constitutes the phenomenon of temporal compression (Flaherty 1999) discussed briefly above. The example in (10b) relates to the experience of time proceeding "more slowly" than usual – the phenomenon of protracted duration, also discussed briefly above. In (11), the readings relating to *time* concern an event. In (11a) the event relates to the onset of childbirth, in (14b) the event designated relates to death, while in (11c) it concerns the referee blowing the whistle signalling the end of a game of soccer. In the sentences in (12) *time* prompts for an entity which is infinite, and hence unbounded in nature.

While English has one word for a range of (arguably) quite distinct experience types, other languages don't inevitably have a single word that covers the same semantic territory. For instance, recent research on the Amazonian language Amondawa reveals that there is no equivalent of the English word *time* in that language (Sinha et al. 2011). To give another example of a typologically and areally distinct language, it is also the case that Inuit languages don't have a single lexeme for *time*. Moreover, even genetically related languages utilise distinct lexical items to describe the semantic territory covered by the single lexical form, *time*, in English.

In sum, the English examples demonstrate that the form *time* relates to quite different types of representations – having a single word-form provides the illusion of semantic unity (Evans 2009), and gives rise to the myth that time relates to a homogenous set of experiences. The fact that other languages don't have a single word for the same set of experiences further underscores the cultural variability of cutting up the domain of time.

6 Are representations for time universal?

Some cognitive linguists have argued, or at least implied, that the motion-through-space conceptual metaphors for time are universal. For instance, Fauconnier and Turner put things as follows: "Time as [motion through] space is a deep metaphor for *all human beings*. It is common across cultures, psychologically real, productive and profoundly entrenched in thought and language" (2008: 54) [my emphasis]. But there are languages that appear not to have this conceptual metaphor. One example is the indigenous South American language Aymara; Aymara doesn't make use of motion on the sagittal plane to conceptualise time's passage (Núñez and Sweetser 2006).³

More strikingly, Sinha et al. (2011), based on their fieldwork of Amondawa, argue that motion-through-space metaphors for time are not transcultural universals. Amondawa is spoken by a small tribe of a little over 100 individuals located in remote western Amazonia. Official contact was not made until 1986. Based on their fieldwork, Sinha and colleagues make two claims. First, and in contrast to Indo-European languages, Amondawa does not make use of ascriptions from spatial language, and language relating to motion, to talk about time. Second, Amondawa does not make reference to time as an ontological category independent of events themselves: what Sinha et al. refer to as *time-as-such*. They maintain that there is no evidence from the Amondawa language

---

3 However, Aymara does make use of motion on the transverse plane to conceptualise the succession of events.

or culture that the Amondawa have time available, per se, as an object of conscious (intersubjective) reflection.

If correct, what do these claims say about time? First off, they don't imply that all aspects of time are not universal. As we have seen, time is a complex and multifaceted domain. Moreover, it is, at least in part, grounded in specialised, albeit distributed, neurobiological processes and structures that are purely temporal (Kranjec and Chatterjee 2010). Our experience of time is variegated, directly perceived via interoception, and subjectively real. The basal ganglia and cerebellum are implicated in fundamental timekeeping operations upon which the coordination of motor control is dependent (Harrington et al. 1998). Other neuroscientists have argued that temporal processing is widely distributed across brain structures, being intrinsic to neural function (e.g., Mauk and Buonomana 2004), and is fundamental to cognitive function (Varela 1999). Distinct brain structures are implicated in the experience of duration, succession, our experience of the present, our recollection of the past and pre-experience of the future (see Evans 2013b for a review). Indeed, the emerging view from neuroscientific research is that the exquisitely sophisticated timing structures in the brain are key to a raft of fundamental cognitive functions such as motor control, and perception and may provide the cognitive "glue" that facilitates learning and memory, behaviour planning, awareness, imagination and creativity (Pouthas and Perbal 2004; Pöppel 2009; Rubia et al. 2009).

Based on proposals in Evans (2013b), a taxonomy suggests itself for directly grounded temporal representations.[4] The most basic temporal concept is termed a *temporal element*. These are representations grounded in phenomenologically simple experience types that contribute to – or in some cases arise from – our experience of transience. Examples include felt experience types such as now, past, future, earlier and later, and are associated with the corresponding lexical forms (e.g., *now*, *past*, *future*, *earlier*, *later*, etc.).

The next type of temporal concept is grounded in the experience of transience, discussed earlier. Evans (2013b) suggests that there are three types of transience: *duration, succession*, and *anisotropicity*. Duration concerns the felt experience of the passage constituting an elapse – something greater than the *perceptual moment* – the smallest neurologically-instantiated unit of perceptual processing which is consciously accessible, and which is likely to constitute the basis for the human experience of now (Pöppel 1994, 2009). The perceptual moment has an outer limit of around 3 seconds (see Evans 2004, 2013b). Succession concerns the felt experience of the passage involving earlier and later expe-

---

[4] Cf. Pöppel (1978) who argues for what he terms "elementary time experiences".

Tab. 4.4: Transience types.

TRANSIENCE TYPE	DESCRIPTION
Duration	the felt experience of the passage constituting an elapse
Succession	the felt experience of the passage involving earlier and later experience types
Anisotropicity	the felt experience that the passage exhibits inherent asymmetry – a felt distinction between future, present and past

Tab. 4.5: Temporal qualities.

TEMPORAL QUALITY	DESCRIPTION
Change	a comparison, or awareness of a difference between two states at different temporal intervals
Frequency	the identification of a number of iterations of experiences, or experience types at different temporal intervals
Synchronicity	an awareness of two experiences or experience types occurring at the same temporal moment

rience types, which are sequenced with respect to each other. And anisotropicity concerns the felt experience that the passage exhibits inherent asymmetry – a felt distinction between future, present and past. Concepts associated with these transience types are encoded in language by lexical forms such as *duration*, *succession*, *passage*, and indeed *transience*. Table 4.4 summarises these transience types.

Transience logically supports more complex experience types: *temporal qualities*. Temporal qualities involve a comparison across events, with respect to transience. Examples include frequency, change and synchronicity. Change, for instance, involves a comparison, or awareness of a difference between two states at different temporal intervals, and hence, is processed with respect to transience. Frequency involves the identification of a number of iterations of experiences, or experience types at different temporal intervals. And synchronicity involves an awareness of two experiences or experience types occurring at the same temporal moment (see Table 4.5). Temporal qualities are more complex than either temporal elements or transience types as temporal qualities are presupposed by them.

While temporal elements, transience types and temporal qualities are all likely to be universal, there are representations for time that are not directly grounded in temporal experience. These can be thought of as mental achievements, in part supported (or constructed) by conceptual metaphors. A notable example concerns time conceptualised as a valuable resource which can be bought and sold, just like physical merchandise (Lakoff and Johnson 1999). Many languages – especially those associated with pre-industrialised cultures – do not conceptualise time in terms of a commodity or a resource (Evans 2004). This suggests that some temporal representations are cultural constructs. In short, Sinha and colleagues appear to be correct that some temporal representations are culture-specific.

The second claim made by Sinha and colleagues, recall, is that Amondawa lacks the concept of time-as-such (aka the Matrix conception). This conceptualisation is a prerequisite for time-measurement systems, which the Amondawa also lack. The Matrix conception entails a reification of duration as an entity distinct from and external to our subjective, and phenomenologically real, experience of duration. This particular concept also appears to be a mental achievement; after all, conceiving of time as *the* event in which all else unfolds cannot be directly grounded in embodied experience. This would require an eternal lifespan! However, when the Amondawa acquire Portuguese, they seemingly have little difficulty in acquiring expertise in the language and the time-measurement artefacts of Brazilian Portuguese culture. This suggests that this mental achievement is accessible to the cognitively modern human mind, even if it is not native to the Amondawa culture.

7 Why must time be represented in terms of sensory-motor experience at all?

While it appears that time is grounded in interoceptive experience types that are purely temporal, many temporal concepts do, nevertheless, appear to be represented, at least in part, in terms of sensory-motor representations, especially relating to space and motion through space. A perennial question that has exercised research in cognitive linguistics concerns why this should be the case.

The answer often advanced is that of *experiential correlation* (Lakoff and Johnson 1980, 1999). Time inevitably and ubiquitously correlates with some salient aspects of spatial experience. The best worked out version is the notion of *grounding scenarios* which capture the details of the correlation (Moore 2006).

But a correlation account doesn't, in fact, provide a complete answer. After all, correlation can't account for the asymmetrical relationship between spatial and temporal representations as proposed by Lakoff and Johnson. While duration correlates with spatial length, the correlation doesn't, in and of itself, explain why time recruits structure from space, but space doesn't recruit structure from the domain of time. Experimental findings illustrate that duration and physical length are asymmetrically organised in just this way (Casasanto and Boroditsky 2008).

A more sophisticated correlation solution is provided by Grady (1997). Grady argues that for correlations to give rise to cross-domain mappings of a fundamental sort – *primary metaphors* in his parlance – the correlation must be accompanied by a qualitative distinction in the type of experiences being correlated. For Grady, temporal experiences, and the concepts that accrue, are responses to sensory-motor experiences: when we experience motion along a path we subjectively experience temporal passage, which is a response to our experience of motion. Hence, temporal concepts have what Grady terms *response content*, while sensory-motor concepts have *image content*. On this account, what makes something a source versus a target concept is contingent on whether it is a response or image concept, with target concepts involving response content (rather than whether it is concrete or abstract).

This analysis appears to be on the right track. It is plausible that temporal mechanisms and structures evolved in order to coordinate and thereby facilitate the perceptual process (Evans 2013b). Events are widely acknowledged to be the units of perception (Cutting 1981; Gibson 1979; Heider 1959; Johansson et al. 1980; Pittenger and Shaw 1975; Zacks et al. 2001). Indeed, Cutting (1981: 71) describes events as "our very units of existence". Events appear to be centred on object/action units that are goal directed (Zacks et al. 2001): they involve correlated aspects of both space and time. In seminal work modelling the provenance of conscious awareness, Crick and Koch (1990) argued that the so-called *binding problem* – how percepts are formed in the absence of a central association area for the integration of perceptual information in the brain – is achieved via the coordinated oscillation of neurons. Hence, perceptual binding may result from temporal activities which *bind* perceptual information; binding arises via temporally coordinated activity, rather than integrating information at a specific "association" site in the brain. In short, temporal processes appear to have a critical role in facilitating our perception of sensory-motor experience.

Our experience of the world comes to us via the perception of events, and events are temporally structured. Hence, it may be that it is this temporal structuring that facilitates the perception of our world of sensory experience. Hence, spatial awareness may be facilitated by the temporal mechanisms which control and facilitate perception. In short, not only is there an inevitable correlation between invariant aspects of sensory-motor experience, and time, but temporal experience appears to arise, in part (perhaps large part), so that the spatio-sensory world around us can be perceived in the first place.

But if correct, this implies that our experience of time is epiphenomenal: it arose in order to facilitate the perceptual process. Perception is about sensory-motor experience, but enabled by temporal processes. And as time is not the object of perception, but the manner whereby it is facilitated, our representational systems re-utilise the perceptually-correlated sensory-motor reflexes for purposes of re-presentation of time in the conceptual system. While our experience of time and space are distinct and distinguishable at the neurological level, at the representational level they appear to be largely asymmetrically organised.

8 Empirical research on time in cognitive science

Cross-cultural and experimental research on the nature and organisation of time is now a lively area of investigation in cognitive science, building in part on pioneering research in cognitive linguistics. Some of the key questions being addressed relate to the complex interplay between language, culture and mental representations for time, as well as the representation of time in modalities other than language, especially gesture. Other research addresses cultural and linguistic influences on temporal representation such as the nature of orthographic systems. This section provides a brief summary of some representative highlights of this body of research.

It has been discovered that the Yupno language in Papua New Guinea construes deictic time spatially in terms of allocentric topography: the past is construed as downhill, present as co-located with the speaker and future is construed as uphill (Núñez et al. 2012). Moreover, the Pormpuraawns – a grouping of aboriginal languages – arrange sequential time from east to west, whereby time flows from left to right when a person is facing south, from right to left when a person is facing north, towards the body when a person is facing east, and away from the body when a person is facing west (Boroditsky and Gaby 2010).

Other research has investigated the consequences of orthographic systems on temporal representation. It has been found that the left-to-right orientation of time in English stems from culturally specific spatial representations, i.e., the direction of orthography. As a result, the direction in which time flows along a person's lateral mental timeline has been shown to differ systematically across cultures (e.g., Boroditsky et al. 2010 for Mandarin; Casasanto and Bottini 2010 for Dutch; Bergen and Lau 2012 for Taiwanese; Fuhrman and Boroditsky 2010 for Hebrew; Tversky et al. 1991 for Arabic).

An increasingly important line of research concerns the concurrent use of gesture during spoken language use. English speakers have been found to have an implicit mental timeline that runs along the lateral axis, with earlier times on the left and later times on the right of body-centred space. When producing co-speech gestures spontaneously, English speakers tend to use the lateral axis, gesturing leftwards for earlier times and rightwards for later times. This left-right mapping of time is consistent with the flow of time on calendars and graphs in English-speaking cultures, but is completely absent from spoken metaphors (Casasanto and Jasmin 2012; see also Cooperrider and Núñez 2009).

In the final analysis, research on the nature of time, in both language and thought, is now a lively and rapidly accelerating arena of investigation. Experimental and cross-linguistic/cultural investigations in cognitive science have been informed by the major research questions, reviewed in this chapter, as developed within cognitive linguistics.

9 References

Baddeley, Alan (1966): Time estimation at reduced body temperature. *American Journal of Psychology* 79(3): 475–479.

Bender, Andrea, Sieghard Beller, and Giovanni Bennardo (2010): Temporal frames of reference: Conceptual analysis and empirical evidence from German, English, Mandarin Chinese, and Tongan. *Journal of Cognition and Culture* 10: 283–307.

Bender, Andrea, Annelie Rothe-Wulf, Lisa Hüther, and Sieghard Beller (2012): Moving forward in space and time: How strong is the conceptual link between spatial and temporal frames of reference (FoRs)? *Frontiers in Psychology* 3: 486.

Bergen, Benjamin and Ting Ting Chan Lau (2012): Writing direction affects how people map space onto time. *Frontiers in Cultural Psychology* 3: 109.

Bonato, Mario, Marco Zorzi, and Carlo Umiltà (2012): When time is space: Evidence for a mental time line. *Neuroscience and Biobehavioral Reviews* 36(10): 2257–2273.

Boroditsky, Lera (2000): Metaphoric structuring: Understanding time through spatial metaphors. *Cognition* 75(1): 1–28.

Boroditsky, Lera, Orly Fuhrman, and Kelly McCormick (2010): Do English and Mandarin speakers think differently about time? *Cognition* 118(1): 123–129.

Boroditsky, Lera and Alice Gaby (2010): Remembrances of times east: Absolute spatial representations of time in an Australian Aboriginal community. *Psychological Science* 21: 1635–1639.

Boroditsky, Lera and Michael Ramscar (2002): The roles of body and mind in abstract thought. *Psychological Science* 13(2): 185–188.

Bueti, Domenica and Vincent Walsh (2009): The parietal cortex and the representation of time, space, number and other magnitudes. *Philosophical Transactions of the Royal Society B* 364: 1831–1840.

Casasanto, Daniel and Lera Boroditsky (2008): Time in the mind: Using space to think about time. *Cognition* 106: 579–593.

Casasanto, Daniel and Roberto Bottini (2010): Can mirror-reading reverse the flow of time? In: C. Hölscher, T. F. Shipley, M. Olivetti Belardinelli, J. A. Bateman and N. S. Newcombe (eds.), *Spatial Cognition* VII, 335–345. Berlin Heidelberg: Springer.

Casasanto, Daniel and Kyle Jasmin (2012): The hands of time: Temporal gestures in English speakers. *Cognitive Linguistics* 23(4): 643–674.

Clark, Herbert H. (1973): Space, time, semantics, and the child. In: T. Moore (ed.) *Cognitive Development and the Acquisition of Language*, 27–63. New York: Academic Press.

Cooperrider, Kensy and Rafael Núñez (2009): Across time, across the body: Transversal temporal gestures. *Gesture* 9(2): 181–206.

Crick, Francis and Christof Koch (1990): Towards a neurobiological theory of consciousness. *Seminars in the Neurosciences* 2: 263–275.

Cutting, James E. (1981): Six tenets for event perception. *Cognition* 10: 71–78.

Einstein, Albert (1916): Die grundlage der allgemeinen relativitätstheorie. *Annalen der Physik* 7: 769–822.

Evans, Vyvyan (2004): *The Structure of Time: Language, Meaning and Temporal Cognition*. Amsterdam: John Benjamins.

Evans, Vyvyan (2009): *How Words Mean: Lexical Concepts, Cognitive Models and Meaning Construction*. Oxford: Oxford University Press.

Evans, Vyvyan (2013a): Temporal frames of reference. *Cognitive Linguistics* 24(3): 393–435.

Evans, Vyvyan (2013b): *Language and Time: A Cognitive Linguistics Approach*. Cambridge: Cambridge University Press.

Fauconnier, Gilles and Mark Turner (2008): Rethinking metaphor. In: R. Gibbs (ed.), *Cambridge Handbook of Metaphor and Thought*, 53–66. Cambridge: Cambridge University Press.

Flaherty, Michael G. (1999): *A Watched Pot: How We Experience Time*. New York: New York University Press.

Fraisse, Paul (1963): *The Psychology of Time*. New York: Harper and Row.

Fraisse, Paul (1984): Perception and estimation of time. *Annual Review of Psychology* 35: 1–36.

Fuhrman, Orly and Lera Boroditsky (2010): Cross-cultural differences in mental representations of time: Evidence from an implicit nonlinguistic task. *Cognitive Science* 34: 1430–1451.

Galton, Antony (2011): Time flies but space doesn't: Limits to the spatialization of time. *Journal of Pragmatics* 43: 695–703.

Gibbs, Raymond W. Jr. (volume 1): Metaphor. Berlin/Boston: De Gruyter Mouton.

Gibson, James J. (1979): *The Ecological Approach to Visual Perception*. Boston: Houghton Mifflin.

Grady, Joseph E. (1997): *Foundations of meaning: Primary metaphors and primary scenes*. Ph.D. Dissertation, University of California at Berkeley.

Harrington, Deborah, Kathleen Haaland, and Robert T. Knight (1998): Cortical networks underlying mechanisms of time perception. *Journal of Neuroscience* 18(3): 1085–1095.

Heider, Fritz (1959): On perception, event structure and psychological environment. *Psychological Issues* 1(3): 1–123.

Hoagland, Hudson (1933): The physiologic control of judgments of duration: Evidence for a chemical clock. *Journal of General Psychology* 9: 267–287.

Johansson, Gunnar, Claes von Hofsten, and Gunnar Jansson (1980): Event perception. *Annual Review of Psychology* 21: 27–66.

Kranjec, Alexander and Anjan Chatterjee (2010): Are temporal concepts embodied? A challenge for cognitive neuroscience. *Frontiers in Psychology* 1(240): 1–9.

Lakoff, George and Mark Johnson (1980): *Metaphors We Live By*. Chicago: University of Chicago Press.
Lakoff, George and Mark Johnson (1999): *Philosophy in the Flesh*. New York: Basic Books.
Langacker, Ronald W. (1987): *Foundations of Cognitive Grammar:* Vol. I. Stanford: Stanford University Press.
Mauk, Michael D. and Dean V. Buonomano (2004): The neural basis of temporal processing. *The Annual Review of Neuroscience* 27: 307–40.
Moore, Kevin E. (2006): Space-to-time mappings and temporal concepts. *Cognitive Linguistics* 17(2): 199–244.
Moore, Kevin E. (2011): Ego-perspective and field-based frames of reference: Temporal meanings of FRONT in Japanese, Wolof, and Aymara. *Journal of Pragmatics* 43: 759–776.
Núñez, Rafael, Kensy Cooperrider, D. Doan, and Jürg Wassmann (2012): Contours of time: Topographic construals of past, present, and future in the Yupno valley of Papua New Guinea. *Cognition* 124: 25–35.
Núñez, Rafael, Benjamin E. Motz, and Ursina Teuscher (2006): Time after time: The psychological reality of the Ego-and Time-Reference-Point distinction in metaphorical construals of time. *Metaphor and Symbol* 21: 133–146.
Núñez, Rafael and Eve Sweetser (2006): With the future behind them: Convergent evidence from Aymara language and gesture in the crosslinguistic comparison of spatial construals of time. *Cognitive Science* 30: 401–450.
Ornstein, Robert E. (1969] 1997): *On the Experience of Time*. Boulder: Westview Press.
Pittenger, John B. and Robert E. Shaw (1975): Aging faces as viscal-elastic events: Implications for a theory of nonrigid shape perception. *Journal of Experimental Psychology: Human Perception Performance* 1: 374–382.
Pöppel, Ernst (1978): Time perception. In: R. Held, H. W. Leibowitz, and H.-L. Teuber (eds.), *Handbook of Sensory Physiology*, 713–729. Heidelberg: Springer.
Pöppel, Ernst (1994): Temporal mechanisms in perception. In: O. Sporns and G. Tononi (eds.), *Selectionism and the Brain: International Review of Neurobiology* 37: 185–201.
Pöppel, Ernst (2009): Pre-semantically defined temporal windows for cognitive processing. *Philosophical Transactions of the Royal Society B* 364: 1887–1896.
Pouthas, Viviane and Séverine Perbal (2004): Time perception does not only depend on accurate clock mechanisms but also on unimpaired attention and memory processes. *Acta Neurobiologiae Experimentalis* 64: 367–385.
Rubia, Katya, Rozmin Halari, Anastasia Christakou, and Eric Taylor (2009): Impulsiveness as a timing disturbance: Neurocognitive abnormalities in attention-deficit hyperactivity disorder during temporal processes and normalization with methylphenidate. *Philosophical Transactions of the Royal Society B: Biological Sciences* 364: 1919–1931.
Sinha, Chris, Vera da Silva Sinha, Jörg Zinken, and Wany Sampaio (2011): When time is not space: The social and linguistic construction of time intervals in an Amazonian culture. *Language and Cognition*, 3(1): 137–169.
Talmy, Leonard (2000): *Toward a Cognitive Semantics* (2 volumes). Cambridge: MIT Press.
Tenbrink, Thora (2011): Reference frames of space and time in language. *Journal of Pragmatics* 43: 704–722.
Tversky, Barbara, Sol Kugelmass, and Atalia Winter (1991): Cross-cultural and developmental trends in graphic productions. *Cognitive Psychology* 23: 515–557.
Varela, Francisco J. (1999): Present-time consciousness. *Journal of Consciousness Studies* 6(2/3): 111–140.

Walsh, Vincent (2003): A theory of magnitude: Common cortical metrics of time, space and quantity. *Trends in Cognitive Sciences* 7(11): 483–488.

Wearden, John H. and Ian S. Penton-Voak (1995): Feeling the heat: Body temperature and the rate of subjective time, revisited. *Quarterly Journal of Experimental Psychology* 48B: 129–141.

Zacks, Jeffrey M., Barbara Tversky and Gowri Iyer (2001): Perceiving, remembering, and communicating structure in events. *Journal of Experimental Psychology: General* 130: 29–58.

Zakay, Dan and Richard A. Block (1997): Temporal cognition. *Current Directions in Psychological Science* 6: 12–16.

Zinken, Jörg (2010): Temporal frames of reference. In: V. Evans and P. Chilton (eds.), *Language, Cognition and Space: The State of the Art and New Directions*, 479–498. London: Equinox Publishing.

Luna Filipović and Iraide Ibarretxe-Antuñano
Chapter 5: Motion

1 Motion in linguistics

There are converging reasons why linguists in particular feel obliged to talk about motion. One reason is that motion expressions are considered basic and omnipresent; they are widely used not only to express spatial and non-spatial meanings (Heine and Kuteva 2002) but may be also employed as structural templates for any other linguistic structure (cf. "localist approaches", e.g., Jackendoff 1983). Another reason is that spatial organisation and expression are paramount to human cognition and generally considered to be fundamental for our thinking (Miller and Johnson-Laird 1976) and as such space and motion have been considered a crucial testing ground for linguistic behaviour (especially from the relativistic viewpoint, e.g., Levinson 2003).

As a result, it is perhaps not too much of an exaggeration to say that every framework in linguistics has devoted some time and effort to describing how speakers think and talk about motion.[1]

In Cognitive Linguistics, motion is also a topic of special interest. Many cognitive linguists have devoted themselves to the study of motion, but the work of one scholar, Leonard Talmy, set the agenda for many subsequent studies in this area. We therefore start our discussion with a focus on his theory of lexicalization patterns (section 2) since this paradigm yielded the most prolific further research and novel theoretical and methodological developments in the field.

Motion is defined as change of location from a spatial position A to a different position B, whereby the moving figure was located at position A at time T1 and then located at position B at another time T2 (see Talmy 1985). Talmy distinguishes *motion* from *movement*, the latter being the state of motion at a location (e.g., wriggling at a single spot) rather than change of location, which is the defining feature of motion. The concept of *change*, which lies in the essence of motion events, is also relevant for distinctions among other events,

---

[1] A comprehensive database of references on motion linguistics from a variety of theoretical and empirical perspectives can be found at http://www.lit.kobe-u.ac.jp/~yomatsum/motionbiblio1.pdf.

Luna Filipović, East Anglia, United Kingdom
Iraide Ibarretxe-Antuñano, Zaragoza, Spain

such as change of state or change of posture. Part of the universality of human experience lies in the capability to perceive change, in the case of motion events, change of spatio-temporal location, and all languages of the world equip their speakers with means to talk about the change in spatial and temporal configurations that are the result of motion (see Filipović 2007a).

Much of the early research in this area was focused on prepositional meanings (static and dynamic; e.g., see Brugman 1988; Herskovits 1986; Vandeloise 1986) and subsequently expanded to the study of other spatial morphemes and to more complex constructions. The initial *localistic* approaches to spatial semantics, centered around one specific element of the sentence, have given way to more holistic approaches (*distributed spatial semantics*, Sinha and Kuteva 1995), with an addition of discourse analysis (see Hart volume 2) to the sentence analysis.

2 Lexicalization patterns and semantic typology

Much of Talmy's (1985, 1991, 2000) work is devoted to the study of the variation that languages show in mapping morphosyntactic and lexical resources onto semantic domains. Talmy argues that any event can be analyzed into a set of *semantic elements* which are valid for any language and that each language has its own *surface elements* to codify those semantic components. Surface elements refer to linguistic forms such as verbs, adpositions, subordinate clauses and "satellites" – a coinage that refers to "the grammatical category of any constituent other than a noun-phrase or prepositional-phrase complement that is in a sister relation to the verb root" and that can be "either a bound affix or a free word" (2000: 102). Talmy examines different semantic domains in the context of semantic vs. surface elements, but motion is by far the most widely known and studied of all.

Surface and semantic[2] components are useful to "dissect" motion events – in fact, these labels are now widespread and standard in motion event analysis – but they become much more interesting when one looks at these elements across languages. Talmy was not interested in providing details about every single possible codifying structure available in a given language, but just on those that are "characteristic" (2000: 27); that is, pervasive, frequent, colloquial

---

[2] For motion events, these components are: internal – Figure, Ground, Path, Motion, and co-event or secondary: Manner, Cause.

and, we can also add, commonly employed by native speakers, young or adult.³ In the case of motion events, Talmy (1985) considers the Path of motion to be the fundamental component of a motion event because without Path there is no motion (though there may be movement). The explicit presence of other components, such as Manner, though always present in reality, it is not obligatory for the verbalisation of a motion event.⁴

The result of his theoretical insights and exemplification from numerous genetically varied and geographically distant languages is a two-way language typology:⁵

- *Satellite-framed languages* (S-languages): Path is characteristically placed in the satellite. For instance, English *run **out***.
- *Verb-framed languages* (V-languages): Path is characteristically codified in the verb-root. For instance, French ***partir** en courant* 'leave running'.

Talmy's typological classification based on these lexicalization patterns is perhaps one of the most widely applied and well-known models in Cognitive Linguistics. As such it has generated positive as well as negative criticisms. We look at some empirical evidence from both camps.

2.1 Applications of the typology in linguistic research

Talmy's two-way typology has been applied now to a vast number of languages (see footnote 1 for references), and despite problems and caveats, it is safe to say that in the current motion literature, the distinction between satellite- and verb-framed languages, as well as his terminology for motion semantic compo-

---

3 This is a basic tenet in Talmy's proposal, which is only natural for a usage-based framework such as Cognitive Linguistics. Unfortunately, some critiques of the model (Croft et al. 2010; Kopecka 2006; Pourcel and Kopecka 2005) overlook this crucial premise, and consequently, insist on finding exceptions and problematic cases to the general framework. They focus their attention on all the possible motion structures a language may have available for the codification of motion instead of speakers' first/habitual/most frequent/preferred choices that Talmy talks about.
4 Interestingly enough, Path and Manner do not come online at the same time; Path is acquired before Manner (see Mandler 2004; Pruden et al. 2004; also Pulverman et al. 2004 and Filipović 2007a, 2010 for the fundamental importance of Path in spatial and temporal conceptualisation).
5 Talmy (1985) also proposed a previous three-way typology based on which semantic component was lexicalized in the verb root across languages (Manner-, Path-, and Figure-languages), but the crucial distinction still lies in the dichotomy based on whether the Path is lexicalized in the verb or out of the verb (see Filipović 2007a: 19).

nents is just the springboard for most studies. There is one particular application of Talmy's insights that has gained equal importance in motion studies nowadays, namely Dan Slobin's (1991, 1996, 2004, 2006) *thinking-for-speaking* hypothesis.

Slobin proposes that the use of different lexicalization patterns has important, and easily observable, relativistic consequences in the online use of language. Speakers of satellite- and verb-framed languages have to describe motion events with the linguistic resources (that is, surface components) available in their languages, and as such, their descriptions of motion events are constrained by what is available in their languages. Slobin employs verbal elicitation methodology, using various visual stimuli, most prominently the illustrations depicting motion events from the *Frog Story* (see Berman and Slobin 1994; Strömqvist and Verhoeven 2004 for more details). He concludes that speakers, guided by their own lexicalization patterns, direct their attention to different aspects of the same motion event, the result of which is a different *rhetorical style* as well as difference in the quality and quantity of available information about a motion event.

The structure and resources of satellite-framed languages allow speakers to describe both Manner and Path very often and in detail since they have rich and expressive Manner of motion verb lexicon, the possibility to attach several Path segments to a single main verb, free main verb slots for Manner (since Path is in the satellite). Verb-framed speakers, on the other hand, follow the opposite pattern. They tend to mention Path in the main verb, add, at most, one extra Path segment, and hardly describe Manner unless it is crucial for the discourse flow. Verb-framed languages do not usually exhibit rich and expressive Manner of motion verb lexicons,[6] and since the Path verb occupies the main verb slot, the only possibility for Manner is to be expressed outside the verb, in a separate expression (adverbs, gerunds, adpositional phrases or subordinate clauses). This restrains information content with regard to Manner due to the added extra processing cost.

A wide range of crosslinguistic studies covering different complementary research areas have been carried out within this methodological framework in order to test how well different languages fit in the bipartite typology and differ in their rhetorical styles.

---

6 This is always in comparison to satellite-framed languages (see Cardini 2008; Cifuentes-Férez 2010). There are however other studies that point out that verb-framed languages rich in ideophones do possess equally rich Manner sources (Basque: Ibarretxe-Antuñano 2006, 2009a; Emai: Schaefer (2001); Japanese: Akita and Matsumoto ms.; Sugiyama 2005).

Some studies incorporate the role of gesture to verbal elicitation. McNeill and collaborators (Kita and Özyürek 2003; McNeill 1992, 2000, 2005; Özyürek et al. 2005; Stam 2006), for instance, found similar results to those of Slobin. Using data from the *Tweety Cartoon*, another widely-used elicitation tool[7] (see McNeill 1992, 2005 for further details), they find that motion gestures are ubiquitous in all narrations but that their function differs depending on the lexicalization pattern. For instance, whereas verb-framed speakers use Manner gestures to talk about information not mentioned in speech (the so-called *Manner fogs*), satellite-framed speakers gesture to reinforce what is already in the speech.

Some other studies take a step forward and test whether fictive motion (see Matlock and Bergmann this volume) and metaphorical motion (see Gibbs volume 1) also match these lexicalization patterns and discourse tendencies. Özçalışkan (2004, 2005), for instance, examines English and Turkish texts only to find that the typological differences are kept in metaphorical motion. Based on English and Spanish data from three different genres (architecture, wine and sports), Caballero and Ibarretxe-Antuñano (forthcoming) refine Özçalışkan's findings. They argue that there are differences due to the genre specific discourse requirements; verb-framed metaphorical motion events are more expressive (i.e., a wider variety of Manner verbs are found more frequently) and dynamic (i.e., more details about Path and less about Ground) than their physical counterparts.

A significant amount of studies are produced from the applied perspective, especially examining the acquisition process of motion events in L1 and L2 across lexicalization patterns (see Cadierno 2017; Ellis and Cadierno 2009; Han and Cadierno 2010 for a review), and to a lesser extent translation (see Ibarretxe-Antuñano and Filipović 2013 for a review). Section 3 reports on some of these studies.

2.2 Problems and solutions

As just shown, many studies have confirmed the pervasive differences between Talmy's two contrasting lexicalization patterns. Over the years, however, some of its basic assumptions have also been challenged. The incorporation of new languages, the introduction of different tools and methodologies (e.g., electronic corpora and experimental design including response time and eye movement

---

[7] Another elicitation tool for gesture and motion are *The Tomato Man* movies (see Özyürek, Kita and Allen 2001 for further details).

detection) and the growing number of very detailed empirically-based descriptions of motion events has revealed certain problems and caveats. Here, we review some of the most recurrent problems in the literature as well as some of the proposed solutions. In general, criticisms revolve around two main problematic issues: the theory fails (i) to account for all possible motion structures, including finely grained distinctions, and (ii) to provide explanations for variation between and within lexicalization patterns.

2.2.1 Challenging motion structures

Talmy (2000: 101–128) introduces the notion of satellite, a closed-class type of surface element, to encompass grammatical forms such as verb particles (e.g., English), verb prefixes (e.g., Russian), incorporated nouns (e.g., Caddo) and polysynthetic affixes (e.g., Atsugewi), among others. He argues that these elements, typical of satellite-framed languages, are mainly involved in the expression of Path, but that they could also express Path+Ground, Patient (Figure/Ground) in noun-incorporating languages, Cause (Instrument) and only very rarely Manner (e.g., as in Nez Perce). Some authors (Beavers et al. 2010; Croft et al. 2010; Filipović 2007a) have noted that the notion of satellite per se is confusing. They argue that the differentiation between particles and prepositions in English is not clear-cut and propose to extend the notion of satellite to cover these other cases. Another problem concerning satellites has to do with certain structures that turn up in verb-framed languages. For example, languages such as Chantyal (Noonan 2003) and Basque (Ibarretxe-Antuñano 2004) possess directionals or spatial case-inflected locative nouns whose function comes quite close to that of a satellite. Romance languages also keep some traces of their Latin (satellite-framed) ancestry.[8] French and Spanish, for instance, still keep some Path prefixes, and Italian uses Path particles that look like satellites too. It has been argued that these elements could be considered satellites (Porquier 2001; Iacobini and Masini 2007), but other authors (Hijazo-Gascón and Ibarretxe-Antuñano 2013) prefer to classify these elements as *pseudosatellites* since their productivity and combinability – two key factors in this usage-based approach – are far more scarce and restricted than that of satellites in satellite-framed languages.

---

[8] For more information on the evolution from satellite-framed Latin to verb-framed Romance, see Ferrari and Mosca (2010); Iacobini and Fagard (2011); Slotova (2008). See also Verkerk (2014) for Indo-European and Kutscher and Werning (2013) for information on space in Ancient languages.

An early caveat in Talmy's typology is the boundary-crossing constraint, a term coined in Slobin and Hoiting (1994) but initially pointed out by Aske (1989). It refers to those cases in verb-framed languages where the semantics of the verb-root constraints the type of aspectual directional phrase it goes with. If the main verb conflates Motion+Path (the characteristic verb-framed pattern), then the directional phrase can depict a situation where the Figure traverses a boundary. If the main verb, on the other hand, contains the semantic component of Manner, this kind of translational motion event expression is not permitted. In order to describe both Path and Manner, the latter should be lexicalized outside the verb (e.g., *Javier entró en la casa corriendo* 'Javier entered in the house running'). The boundary constraint[9] has become a distinctive feature of verb-framed languages.

Another criticism arises from the nature of semantic components. Categories such as Path and, especially, Manner are considered too broad to capture similarities and differences across languages. They are suitable for a general lexicalization pattern typology, but once a finer-grained analysis is in place, they are too wide and general. Several authors therefore have proposed further subdivisions of Path (Berthele 2006; Filipović 2010; Narasimham 2003; Slobin 2008; Talmy 2000; Vulchanova and van der Zee 2013; Wälchli 2001) and Manner (Filipović 2010; Ibarretxe-Antuñano 2006; Özçalıskan 2004; Slobin 2005).

2.2.2 Constraints and variation in lexicalization patterns

As mentioned above, the list of new languages that have been incorporated to the study of lexicalization patterns grows larger every day; accordingly, as does the risk of the model not being able to account for all the empirical data-driven observations. Many of these new studies reveal that the two-way typology may not be quite so clear-cut and may also fail to acknowledge variation between and within lexicalization patterns.

Two kinds of phenomena can be included under the general label of *intertypological variation*. First, it concerns what we could informally label as "mixed" languages. This includes: (i) languages which, despite their affiliation to one lexicalization pattern, show patterns typical from the opposite lexicalization group. For instance, Aragonese (Hijazo-Gascón and Ibarretxe-Antuñano 2010)

---

[9] There are other restrictions on the type and complexity of directional information that a motion event clause can code. Bohnemeyer (2003), for instance, introduces the *Unique Vector Constraint* that states that all directional information in a single simple clause must keep the same direction vector.

is a verb-framed language but (pseudo-)satellite constructions are widely used; and (ii) languages where speakers indistinctively use both satellite- and verb-framed constructions on a regular basis. For example, Modern Greek (Soroli 2012) is reported to be such a language. Talmy himself (2000) acknowledges this variation and calls it a *parallel conflation system*. Second, some languages cannot be classified either as satellite- or verb-framed because they use a third way of codifying motion events. Slobin (2004) calls this lexicalization pattern *equipollently-framed* since the semantic components Path and Manner are lexicalized in equivalent surface elements (e.g., Mandarin Chinese). In order to account for blurred lines of the division between and among different lexicalization patterns, some authors have opted to propose new typologies for motion events: Matsumoto's (2003) Head- and non-head framed languages, Bohnemeyer et al.'s (2007) Type I-II-III, Grinevald's (2011) "working typology", and Slobin's (2008) Path-in-non-verb vs. Path-in-verb, to name just a few, but none of those proposals have been widely implemented.

Intratypological variation refers to variation within the same lexicalization pattern. That is, languages within the same group show diversity with respect to the level of salience and granularity of motion semantic components (see Goschler and Stefanowitsch 2013). This occurs not only in genetically different languages (Basque and Spanish; see Ibarretxe-Antuñano 2004), but also in languages with the same genetic filiations (see Ragnarsdóttir and Strömqvist 2004 for the Germanic family; Hijazo-Gascón and Ibarretxe-Antuñano 2013 for the Romance; and Huang and Tanangkingsing 2005 for western Austronesian verb-framed languages). In fact, these intratypological differences have led some authors to propose *clines of salience* for motion semantic components. This suggests that the whole typology can be seen as a cline rather than a dichotomy (see Ibarretxe-Antuñano 2004, 2009b; Filipović 2007a; Slobin 2004).

Finally, there is also room for *diatopic variation*. This is an area that has not yet received the attention it deserves, but recently a number of authors (such as Berthele 2006 for Swiss German and Romansch; Ibarretxe-Antuñano and Hijazo-Gascón 2012 for Spanish and Aragonese; and Schwarze 1985 for Italian) have discovered that dialects from the same language do not necessarily behave in the same way. Berthele (2006), for instance, reports that Muotathal, a Swiss German dialect spoken in the Schwyz canton, hardly uses Manner verbs but frequently describes Path by means of syntactically and semantically complex structures. This behaviour evident in *Frog Story* narratives is different from other Swiss dialects and the standard language.

3 Motion in acquisition, translation and beyond

The study of both agentive and caused motion events was instrumental in determining what kind of information about motion events tends to be given in some languages more often and in more detail than in others. It was also important for the differences in the kinds of details that we can expect to be expressed and remembered better or worse based on language-specific narrative habits and preferred patterns for habitual inclusion or exclusion of information. This is of immense importance in numerous applied research and professional fields, such as language acquisition, translation and interpreting, as well as forensic linguistics, to name just a few.

3.1 Motion in acquisition

Developmental psychology has offered important insights into how we become capable of thinking and speaking about motion. Specifically, studies in child language development have provided new knowledge of how motion verbs and constructions are initially acquired by infants, as well as how these findings can help us understand the overall relationship between language and cognition and the role of language in cognitive development in general. The pioneering cross-linguistic work of Berman and Slobin (1994) showed that children as young as three-years-old already attended to the linguistic requirements of their own languages. Although children (ages: 3, 5, 7, 9) had to describe identical pictures (*Frog Story*), the resulting stories were different depending on the language they were learning (English, German, Hebrew, Spanish or Turkish). Pulverman et al. (2008) tested infants' ability to note changes in Path and Manner – the fundamental requirement for learning relational terms such as verbs regardless of the native language. They found that 14- to 17-month-old infants succeeded at this task regardless of gender or cultural and linguistic differences, which suggests that this may be a robust ability common to all normally developing children. Pulverman et al. (2004) demonstrated further that the introduction of a label differentially heightens attention to motion components. The conceptual foundation for the relationships expressed by verbs in languages appears to be universal, but verb learning is complicated by the fact that verbs package actions and events in different ways across languages (see Gentner and Boroditsky 2001). The effect of language-specific packaging of information on attention has been attested on numerous occasions. Infants' initial attention to motion components is further modulated by individual languages (see Bowerman and Choi 2003; Choi and Bowerman 1991; Hickmann and Hendriks 2010; Ji et al. 2011) after an apparent universal bias at the outset. Thus, the developmental process appears to initially involve the universal ability to note Path and Manner changes and form language-general nonlinguistic constructs, which are gradually refined and tuned to the requirements of the native language. In effect, infants are *trading spaces*, maintaining their sensitivity to some relational distinctions while dampening other distinctions, depending on how their native language expresses these constructs (see Göksun et al. 2010; Maguire et al. 2010).

Research on motion events within second language acquisition paradigm has also yielded novel and important findings with respect to cross-linguistic interactions in the mind of the speaker, while simultaneously being a fertile testing ground for many theoretical assumptions in SLA (see Cadierno 2017; Ellis and Cadierno 2009; Han and Cadierno 2010; Pavlenko 2011 for a review). The motion lexicalization domain proved to be prone to cross-linguistic influence (see Jarvis and Pavlenko 2007), and it is an area where not only the occurrence of L1–L2 transfer can be expected, but also the reverse transfer (Brown and Gullberg 2008). This represents an ideal opportunity for testing assumptions as to when, where and why transfer may occur. In general, L2 studies inspired by Talmy's typology agree that L2 speakers need to learn to *readjust* their L1 motion structures to the narrative style of the L2 (Cadierno 2004, 2008; Robinson and Ellis 2008). This readjustment is not an easy or straightforward procedure. Learners need to learn not only the lexicalization pattern of the L2 (that is, linguistic structures – speech and gesture – for codifying L2 language) but also which aspects of the motion event are to be mentioned in the L2 motion description and when (that is, the rhetorical style in L2). According to Cadierno (2017), studies on L2 motion events have so far discovered that the learner's L1 influence is present in the L2 production (i) regardless of the type of L1 lexicalization pattern, satellite- or verb-framed (Cadierno 2004; Larrañaga et al. 2011; Negueruela et al. 2004); (ii) not only in speech but also in gesture (Brown and Gullberg 2008; Stam 2006), what Kellerman and van Hoof (2003) call *manual accent*; (iii) even in advanced learners (Choi and Lantolf 2008), and (iv) even in languages that belong to the same typological group. This applies to genetically-different (Hasko 2009) and genetically-similar languages (Hijazo-Gascón 2018). In addition to L1 effects, there is also an overall tendency to resort to the (potentially) *universal, economy-of-form strategy* (Filipović and Vidaković 2010).

3.2 Motion in translation and interpreting

Translation studies is another area that has benefited from findings in motion event lexicalization. Early work in translation already paid attention to the typological differences across languages. Vinay and Darbelnet (1958), for instance, talk about the *chasse-croisé pattern* to refer to the interchange that occurs between English and French structures when translating motion (see also Snell-Hornby 1983). However, translating motion events is not just a question of exchanging grammatically correct structures from one language into another; it is also a question of preserving the rhetorical style of the target language while adapting the content.

Most of the studies devoted to the study of motion events have analyzed the translation product, that is, how motion events have been translated from the source into the target domain. One of the first studies in this area is Slobin's (1996) analysis of Spanish and English novels and their respective translations. The research results seem to confirm that translators do actually adapt the source texts to the rhetorical style and resources of the target language (e.g., translation into Spanish contain less Manner information than the English originals and translations into English contain added Manner information that is not present in the Spanish original). This line of research has been followed up by similar studies on different language combinations. Ibarretxe-Antuñano and Filipović (2013) provide a summary of all proposed translation strategies to date (twenty in total), which are not restricted to just omission or addition of Path/Manner information, but also include substitution of one semantic component for another as well as adaptation of partial information. Ibarretxe-Antuñano and Filipović (2013) also report on a translation experiment whereby bilingual speakers judged original witness reports in Spanish (which contained sparse or no information about Manner) less aggressive and they were less likely to imagine the events described as extremely violent, in contrast to the English Manner-rich translations of the same events, which elicited higher values on the violence judgement scale. Thus, the effects of the typological differences go beyond the expressions themselves, and they can affect speakers' judgments regarding events they hear or read about. Further, in the context of forensic linguistic research, Filipović (2007b, 2013) has demonstrated that the crosslinguistic differences that play a role in expression and memory of motion events (see the next section) also affect the quantity and quality of information given by witnesses in translation-mediated communication with the police or in court. Studies such as these can raise awareness of what kind of information is easy or hard to express in a particular language, and subsequently translate into another, so that more attention can be paid to these precise points of conflict in order to prevent it through focused education of language professionals. This would lead to practical applications, such as improved efficiency and accuracy of language-mediated interactions including investigative legal interviews, translation practice and training, language learning and language teaching.

4 Motion in language and memory: Experimental psycholinguistic insights

Studying cross-linguistic differences in motion lexicalization inspired re-examinations of some of the long-lasting empirical puzzles such as whether and, if yes, when and why, we may encounter language-specific effects on cognition, and how they can co-exist with certain universal features of language processing and cognitive functions (such as perception and memory). These Whorfian questions have recently been revisited in many cognitive domains and most recent studies converge on the idea that both universal and language-specific forces are involved in the perception and in the cognitive organisation of categories in the domain of colour (e.g., Regier and Kay 2009), space (Landau 2010), and motion (Filipović 2010).

The interest in thinking and speaking about motion events has been intense in the psycholinguistic community. Numerous cross-linguistic studies of event description and cognition have had a specific focus on motion events (e.g., Filipović 2010, 2011; Filipović and Geva 2012; Finkbeiner et al. 2002; Gennari et al. 2002; Malt et al. 2003; Papafragou et al. 2002; Slobin 2006; Trueswell and Papafragou 2010). Some of these studies report evidence for typological differences affecting certain aspects of information content and cognition (e.g., Finkbeiner et al. 2002; Filipović 2011; Filipović and Geva 2012), and some argue that such differences are found only on restricted occasions that encourage the use of *language as a strategy in organising information* (e.g., Malt et al. 2003). These different studies also use different experimental methodologies to elicit data, for example, static illustrations (Papafragou et al. 2002), video clips triads (Malt et al. 2003), and contrastive video clip pairs (Filipović 2011), which together with the variation in the experimental stimuli (e.g., simple motion events in Papafragou et al. 2002 and Malt et al. 2003, and complex motion events in Filipović 2011) may impact the experimental outcomes.

There is substantial evidence that language can be used as a system for organising experience under specific conditions, such as sorting out events (as well as objects, see for example Lucy and Gaskins 2003), especially after prior verbalization, which instantiates language as a stable and reliable classification system. Language can also be evoked in difficult tasks, namely when memory is explicitly required, whereby a reliable system for the organization of information is necessary and language-specific structuring of perceptual stimuli is resorted to (see Finkbeiner et al. 2002). However, simple events stimuli, like "one Manner + one Path" motion events do not necessarily activate "language as a strategy" automatically and universal strategies may be employed instead, for example when Spanish speakers remembered subtle manner distinctions as well as English speakers (Filipović 2010). Other strategies are also used to render Manner of motion instead of arbitrary phonological labels that manner verbs are, such as ideophones in Basque (see Ibarretxe-Antuñano 2006) or mimetic expressions that give clues to the nature of the referent in Japanese (Imai et al. 2008). An ability to attend to both Path and Manner thus appears to be universal and, in order to determine the conditions under which language may start to play the mediating role in the conceptual organisation of information and memory of events, we had to look for the reasons when and why speakers may resort to their languages as aids to memory.

One such occasion is an enhanced cognitive load. In general terms, any kind of circumstance of added memory load, or other kind of cognitive pressure, tends to *encourage stereotyping* (adherence to preferred, entrenched patterns of reasoning) in general cognition, and by analogy, in language (see Mendoza-Denton 2010). We revert to familiar conceptualizations under such pressures, and we tend to do the same when using language as an aid to problem-solving, opting for the most characteristic, familiar, and frequent lexicalization patterns. For English speakers, that process involves speaking about the Manner of motion; for Spanish speakers Manner is less of a priority.

This line of reasoning underlies a study of memory for motion events under enhanced cognitive load and language effect on memory of motion events that was first reported in Filipović (2011). This study has shown that monolingual speakers of English perform better in a recognition task than their Spanish peers, when describing details of the event that are relevant to the recognition task. Using *complex motion events* stimuli (three manners per event) which enhanced the cognitive load in the specific area where the two languages differ, Filipović found that it was the language used explicitly (or tacitly) that helped recognition memory in the case of the English speakers but not the Spanish speakers. This typological advantage does not seem to be of much assistance in some other tasks, namely when free encoding is disabled (see Filipović and Geva 2012) or when simple motion events stimuli are used (e.g., Malt et al. 2003). Therefore, we can say that language effects can be detected in on-line (but not off-line) processing and some languages can be more of aid than others in complex tasks resulting from enhanced cognitive pressures or information load (see also Lai et al. 2013). As a result of lexicalization preferences in their respective languages, English speakers remember complex motion events (Filipović 2011) and agents (Fausey and Boroditsky 2011) better, while Spanish speakers are better at recalling whether causation was intentional or non-intentional (see Filipović 2013).

In sum, since languages differ with respect to the means they make available to their speakers to talk about different aspects of motion events (such as

Path, Manner, agentivity, causation), it is important to study those cross-linguistic contrasts in the domain of motion, and other domains alike, as they are indicative of the difficulties that may arise in different contexts of communication, and with respect to both linguistic expression and retrieval from memory. The studies briefly discussed here and similar ones provide central insights into both language-specific and universal factors in language processing. The fact that applied research into motion verbs and constructions leads to discoveries that shape our understanding of both domain-specific and general underlying principles of language use and language-mediated cognition is a testimony to the overall importance of the study of how we learn to think and speak about motion.

5 Conclusions

This chapter illustrated the current state of art in the domain of motion lexicalization research from a number of different linguistic and interdisciplinary perspectives. We can see that research in this domain is vibrant and multileveled, and that it brings about novel insights not just into how we speak and think about motion, but also how language processing mechanisms operate in different contexts such as acquisition or translation. Applied research in this area is developing rapidly and it is a testimony to the value of the insightful theoretical contributions made in the past that continue to inspire further research while at the same time informing the theory itself in return.

We saw that there is an interaction between both universal and language-specific factors, which co-exist when speakers use their language to relate their experience within their environments. Universal tendencies are moulded by language-specific preferences developmentally in first language acquisition, while in second language acquisition we seem to need to re-think-for-speaking, which is also a developmental process that moves along with L2 proficiency.

Finally, we witnessed an increasing number of current and future applications of this research in various practical and professional areas where language plays the central role. Language education and translation training stand to benefit immensely from raised awareness of the crucial cross-linguistic contrasts in motion lexicalization. Accuracy and efficiency of translation itself would be improved if we focused on the precise points of conflict between any two languages that can cause difficulties when framing the content of the message in two different systems respectively. The consequences of such conflicts may even go beyond the language itself and impact how we organize information for later judgment and for memory.

Studying the conditions under which we see the impact of linguistic habits beyond the text itself will lead to further understanding of the intimate relationship between language and the mind in this, as well as other, cognitive domains. It is not easy to capture the prolific output on motion research across the board, but we hope that this selective account depicts the multifaceted and dynamic field. The study of motion events in language and cognition has become a unifying platform for numerous disciplines, where empirically and methodologically diverse studies jointly afford new knowledge about a topic that can only be tackled in a truly interdisciplinary fashion. We hope that this account will inspire further research, especially in the domain that Filipović terms *applied linguistic typology* (see Filipović and Putz 2014; also Filipović 2017), namely where the academic scholarship both reflects upon and responds to the needs of users (i.e., learners or teachers of a language) by highlighting the phenomena that matter to their life and professional or personal involvement. Specifically, applied language typology studies the effects of typological contrasts that matter beyond the mere descriptions of languages and their typological groupings. Its focus is on how specific typological contrasts affect language practice. Applying linguistic typology in different contexts of use will further our knowledge not only about motion and other domains of experience but also about the impact of language on our increasingly multilingual personal and professional lives.

Acknowledgment

The preparation of this paper was financially supported by grants FFI2010-14903 and FFI2013-45553-C3-1-P from the Spanish Ministry of Economy and Competitiveness (MovEs project) and we are grateful for their generous support.

6 References

Akita, Kimi and Yo Matsumoto (Ms.): Manner salience revisited: Evidence from two Japanese-English contrastive experiments. Osaka University and Kobe University.
Aske, Jon (1989): Path predicates in English and Spanish: A closer look. *Proceedings of the Fifteenth Annual Meeting of the Berkeley Linguistics Society* 15: 1–14.
Beavers, John, Beth Levin, and Shiao-Wei Tham (2010): The typology of motion expressions revisited. *Journal of Linguistics* 44: 183–316.
Berman, Ruth and Dan I. Slobin (eds.) (1994): *Relating Events in Narrative. A Cross Linguistic Developmental Study*. Hillsdale: Lawrence Erlbaum.
Berthele, Raphael (2006): *Ort und Weg. Eine vergleichende Untersuchung der sprachlichen Raumreferenz in Varietäten des Deutschen, Rätorromanischen und Französichen*. Berlin: Mouton de Gruyter.

Bohnemeyer, Jürgen (2003): The unique vector constraint. In: E. van der Zee and J. Slack (eds.), *Representing Direction in Language and Space*, 86–110. Oxford: Oxford University Press.

Bohnemeyer, Jürgen, Nick Enfield, James Essegbey, Iraide Ibarretxe-Antuñano, Sotaro Kita, Friederike Lüpke, and Felix K. Ameka (2007): Principles of event segmentation in language: The case of motion events. *Language* 83(3): 495–532.

Bowerman, Melissa and Soonja Choi (2003): Space under construction: Language-specific spatial categorization in first language acquisition. In: D. Gentner and S. Goldin-Meadow (eds.), *Language in Mind: Advances in the Study of Language and Thought*, 387–427. Cambridge: MIT Press.

Brown, Amanda and Marianne Gullberg (2008): Bidirectional crosslinguistic influence in L1-L2 encoding of manner in speech and gesture: A study of Japanese speakers of English. *Studies in Second Language Acquisition* 30: 225–251.

Brugman, Claudia (1988): *The Story of Over: Polysemy, Semantics, and the Structure of the Lexicon*. New York: Garland.

Caballero, Rosario and Iraide Ibarretxe-Antuñano (forthcoming): *And yet they DON'T move: A genre approach to metaphorical motion*. Berlin/New York: Mouton de Gruyter.

Cadierno, Teresa (2004): Expressing motion events in a second language: A cognitive typological perspective. In: M. Achard and S. Niemeier (eds.), *Cognitive Linguistics, Second Language Acquisition, and Foreign Language Teaching*, 13–49. Berlin: Mouton de Gruyter.

Cadierno, Teresa (2008): Learning to talk about motion in a foreign language. In: P. Robinson and N. C. Ellis (eds.), *Handbook of Cognitive Linguistics and Second Language Acquisition*, 239–275. New York/London: Routledge.

Cadierno, Teresa (2017): Thinking for speaking about motion in a second language: Looking back and forword. In: I. Ibarretxe-Antuñano (ed.), *Motion and Space across Languages and Applications*. Amsterdam: John Benjamins.

Cardini, Filippo-Enrico (2008): Manner of motion saliency: An inquiry into Italian. *Cognitive Linguistics* 19(4): 533–569.

Choi, Soonja and Melissa Bowerman (1991): Learning to express motion events in English and Korean: The influence of language-specific lexicalization patterns. *Cognition* 41: 83–121.

Choi, Soojung and James P. Lantolf (2008): Representation and embodiment of meaning in L2 communication: Motion Events in the Speech and Gesture of Advanced L2 Korean and L2 English Speakers. *Studies in Second Language Acquisition* 30(2): 191–224.

Cifuentes-Férez, Paula (2010): The semantics of the English and the Spanish motion verb lexicons. *Review of Cognitive Linguistics* 8(2): 233–271.

Croft, William, Jóhanna Barðdal, Willem Hollmann, Violeta Sotirova, and Chiaki Taoka (2010): Revising Talmy's typological classification of complex constructions. In: H. C. Boas (ed.), *Contrastive Studies in Construction Grammar*, 201–236. Amsterdam: John Benjamins.

Ellis, Nick C. and Teresa Cadierno (eds.) (2009): Constructing a second language. Special section of *Annual Review of Cognitive Linguistics* 7.

Fausey, Caitlin M. and Lera Boroditsky (2011): Who dunnit? Cross-linguistic differences in eye-witness memory. *Psychonomic Bulletin and Review* 18(1): 150–157.

Ferrari, Giacomo and Monica Mosca (2010): Some constructions of path: From Italian to some Classical languages. In: G. Marotta, A. Lenci, L. Meini and F. Roval (eds.), *Space in Language*, 317–338. Florence: Edizioni ETS.

Filipović, Luna (2007a): *Talking about Motion: A Crosslinguistic Investigation of Lexicalization Patterns*. Amsterdam: John Benjamins.
Filipović, Luna (2007b): Language as a witness: Insights from cognitive linguistics. *International Journal of Speech, Language and the Law* 14(2): 245–267.
Filipović, Luna (2010): Thinking and speaking about motion: Universal vs. language-specific effects. In: G. Marotta, A. Lenci, L. Meini and F. Roval (eds.), *Space in Language*, 235–248. Florence: Edizioni ETS.
Filipović, Luna (2011): Speaking and remembering in one or two languages: Bilingual vs. monolingual lexicalization and memory for motion events. *International Journal of Bilingualism* 15(4): 466–485.
Filipović, Luna (2013): Constructing causation in language and memory: implications for access to justice in multilingual interactions. *International Journal of Speech, Language and the Law* 20(1): 1–19.
Filipović, Luna (2017): Applied language typology: Practical applications of research on typological contrasts between languages. In: I. Ibarretxe-Antuñano (ed.), *Motion and Space across Languages and Applications*. Amsterdam: John Benjamins.
Filipović, Luna and Sharon Geva (2012): Language-specific effects on lexicalization and memory of motion events. In: L. Filipović and K. M. Jaszczolt (eds.), *Space and Time across Languages and Cultures: Language Culture and Cognition*, 269–282. Amsterdam: John Benjamins.
Filipović, Luna and Martin Pütz (eds.) (2014): *Multilingual Cognition and Language Use: Processing and Typological Perspectives*. Amsterdam/Philadelphia: Benjamins.
Filipović, Luna and Ivana Vidaković (2010): *Typology in the L2 classroom: Second language acquisition from a typological perspective* In: M. Pütz and L. Sicola (eds.), *Cognitive Processing in Second Language Acquisition. Inside the Learner's Mind*, 269–291. Amsterdam: John Benjamins.
Finkbeiner, Matthew, Janet Nicol, Delia Greth, and Kumiko Nakamura (2002): The role of language in memory for actions. *Journal of Psycholinguistic Research* 31: 447–457.
Gennari, Silvia P., Steven A. Sloman, Barbara C. Malt, and W. Tecumseh Fitch (2002): Motion events in language and cognition. *Cognition* 83(1): 49–79.
Gentner, Deidre and Lera Boroditsky (2001): Individualism, relativity, and early word learning. In: M. Bowerman and S. C. Levinson (eds.), *Language Acquisition and Conceptual Development*, 215–256. Cambridge: Cambridge University Press.
Gibbs, Raymond W. (volume 1): Metaphor. Berlin/Boston: De Gruyter Mouton.
Göksun, Tilbe, Kathy Hirsh-Pasek, and Roberta M. Golinkoff (2010): Trading spaces: Carving up events for language learning. *Perspectives on Psychological Science* 5: 33–42.
Goschler, Julianna and Anatol Stefanowitsch (eds.) (2013): *Variation and Change in the Encoding of Motion Events*. Amsterdam/Philadelphia: John Benjamins.
Grinevald, Colette (2011): On constructing a working typology of the expression of *path*. *Cahiers de Faits de Langue* 3: 43–70.
Han, Zhao-Hong and Teresa Cadierno (eds.) (2010): *Linguistic Relativity in SLA: Thinking for Speaking*. Clevedon: Multilingual Matters.
Hart, Christopher (volume 2): Discourse. Berlin/Boston: De Gruyter Mouton.
Hasko, Victoria (2009): The locus of difficulties in the acquisition of Russian verbs of motion by highly proficient learners. *Slavic and East European Journal* 53(3): 360–385.
Heine, Bernd and Tania Kuteva (2002): *World Lexicon of Grammaticalization*. Cambridge: Cambridge University Press.

Herskovits, Annette (1986): *Language and Spatial Cognition. An Interdisciplinary Study of Prepositions in English*. Cambridge: Cambridge University Press.

Hickmann, Maya and Henriëtte Hendriks (2010): Typological constraints on the acquisition of spatial language. *Cognitive Linguistics* 21(2): 189–215.

Hijazo-Gascón, Alberto (2018): Acquisition of motion events in L2 Spanish by German, French and Italian speakers. *The Language Learning Journal* 46(3): 241-262.

Hijazo-Gascón, Alberto and Iraide Ibarretxe-Antuñano (2010): Tipología, lexicalización y dialectología aragonesa. *Archivo de Filología Aragonesa* 66: 181–215.

Hijazo-Gascón, Alberto and Iraide Ibarretxe-Antuñano (2013): Las lenguas románicas y la tipología de los eventos de movimiento. *Romanische Forschungen* 125: 467–494.

Huang, Shuanfan and Michael Tanangkingsing (2005): Reference to motion events in six western Austronesian languages: Toward a semantic typology. *Oceanic Linguistics* 44(2): 307–340.

Ibarretxe-Antuñano, Iraide (2004): Language typologies in our language use: the case of Basque motion events in adult oral narratives. *Cognitive Linguistics* 15(3): 317–349.

Ibarretxe-Antuñano, Iraide (2006): *Sound Symbolism and Motion in Basque*. Munich: Lincom Europa.

Ibarretxe-Antuñano, Iraide (2009a): Lexicalization patterns and sound symbolism in Basque. In: J. Valenzuela, A. Rojo and C. Soriano (eds.), *Trends in Cognitive Linguistics: Theoretical and Applied Models*, 239–254. Hamburg: Peter Lang.

Ibarretxe-Antuñano, Iraide (2009b): Path salience in motion events. In: J. Guo, E. Lieven, N. Budwig, S. Ervin-Tripp, K. Nakamura and S. Özçalışkan (eds.), *Crosslinguistic Approaches to the Psychology of Language: Research in the Tradition of Dan Isaac Slobin*, 403–414. New York: Psychology Press.

Ibarretxe-Antuñano, Iraide and Luna Filipović (2013): Lexicalization patterns and translation. In: A. Rojo and I. Ibarretxe-Antuñano (eds.), *Cognitive Linguistics and Translation: Advances in Some Theoretical Models and Applications*, 253–283. Berlin/New York: Mouton de Gruyter.

Ibarretxe-Antuñano, Iraide and Alberto Hijazo-Gascón (2012): Variation in motion events: Theory and applications. In: L. Filipović and K. M. Jaszczolt (eds), *Space and Time across Languages and Cultures*. Volume I: Linguistic Diversity, 349–371. Amsterdam: John Benjamins.

Imai, Mutsumi, Sotaro Kita, Miho Nagumo, and Hiroyuki Okada (2008): Sound symbolism facilitates early verb learning. *Cognition* 109: 5–65.

Iacobini, Claudio and Benjamin Fagard (2011): A diachronic approach to variation and change in the typology of motion event expression. A case study: From Latin to Romance. *Cahiers de Faits de langue* 3: 151–172.

Iacobini, Claudio and Francesca Masini (2007): The emergence of verb-particle constructions in Italian: locative and actional meanings. *Morphology* 16(2): 155–188.

Jackendoff, Ray (1983): *Semantics and Cognition*. Cambridge: MIT Press.

Jarvis, Scott and Aneta Pavlenko (2007): *Crosslinguistic Influence in Language and Cognition*. New York/London: Routledge.

Ji, Yinglin, Henriëtte Hendriks, and Maya Hickmann (2011): How children express caused motion events in Chinese and English: Universal and language-specific influences. *Lingua* 121: 1796–1819.

Kellerman, Eric and Anne-Marie Van Hoof (2003): Manual accents. *International Review of Applied Linguistics* 41: 251–269.

Kita, Sotaro and Aslı Özyürek (2003): What does cross-linguistic variation in semantic coordination of speech and gesture reveal?: Evidence for an interface representation of spatial thinking and speaking. *Journal of Memory and Language* 48: 16–32.

Kopecka, Anetta (2006): The semantic structure of motion verbs in French: Typological perspectives. In: M. Hickmann and S. Robert (eds.), *Space in Languages: Linguistic Systems and Cognitive Categories*, 83–101. Amsterdam: John Benjamins.

Kutscher, Silvia and Daniel A. Werning (eds.) (2013): *On Ancient Grammars of Space. Linguistic Research on the Expression of Spatial Relations and Motion in Ancient Languages*. Berlin: Mouton De Gruyter.

Lai, Vicky Tzuyin, Gabriela Garrido-Rodriguez, and Bhuvana Narasimhan (2013): Thinking for speaking in early and late bilinguals. *Bilingualism: Language and Cognition* 17(1): 139–152.

Landau, Barbara (2010): Paths in language and cognition: Universal asymmetries and their cause. In: G. Marotta, A. Lenci, L. Meini and F. Roval (eds.), *Space in Language*, 73–94. Florence: Edizioni ETS.

Larrañaga, Pilar, Jeanine Treffers-Daller, Françoise Tidball, and Mari-Carmen Gil Ortega (2011): L1 transfer in the acquisition of manner and path in Spanish by native speakers of English. *International Journal of Bilingualism* 16(1): 117–138.

Levinson, Stephen C. (2003): *Space in Language and Cognition*. Cambridge: Cambridge University Press.

Lucy, John and Susan Gaskins (2003): Interaction of language type and referent type in the development of nonverbal classification preferences. In: D. Gentner and S. Goldin-Meadow (eds.), *Language in Mind: Advances in the Study of Language and Thought*, 465–492. Cambridge: MIT Press.

Maguire, Mandy J., Kathy Hirsh-Pasek, Roberta M. Golinkoff, Mutsumi Imai, Etsuko Haryu, Sandra Vengas, Hiroyuki. Okada, Rachel Pulverman, and Brenda Sanchez-Davis (2010): A developmental shift from similar to language specific strategies in verb acquisition: A comparison of English, Spanish, and Japanese. *Cognition* 114(3): 299–319.

Malt, Barbara C., Steven A. Sloman, and Silvia P. Gennari (2003): Speaking versus thinking about objects and actions. In: D. Gentner and S. Goldin-Meadow (eds.), *Language in Mind*, 81–111. Cambridge: MIT Press.

Mandler, Jean M. (2004): *The Foundations of Mind: Origins of Conceptual Thought*. New York: Oxford University Press.

Matlock, Teenie and Till Bergmann (this volume): Fictive motion. Berlin/Boston: De Gruyter Mouton.

Matsumoto, Yo (2003): Typologies of lexicalization patterns and event integration: Clarifications and reformulations. In: S. Chiba et al. (eds.), *Empirical and Theoretical Investigations into Language: A Festschrift for Masaru Kajita*, 403–418. Tokyo: Kaitakusha.

McNeill, David (1992): *Hand and Mind*. Chicago: University of Chicago Press.

McNeill, David (2000): Analogic/analytic representations and cross-linguistic differences in thinking for speaking. *Cognitive Linguistics* 11: 43–60.

McNeill, David (2005): *Gesture and Thought*. Chicago: University of Chicago Press.

Mendoza-Denton, Rodolfo (2010): Are we born racist? Inside the science of stigma, prejudice and intergroup relations. (http://www.psychologytoday.com/blog/are-we-born-racist/201012/linguistic-forensics)

Miller, George A. and Philip N. Johnson-Laird (1976): *Language and Perception*. Cambridge: Belknap Press of Harvard University Press.

Narasimham, Bhuvana (2003): Motion events and the lexicon: a case study of Hindi. *Lingua* 113: 123–160.

Negueruela, Eduardo, James P. Lantolf, Stefanie R. Jordan, and Jaime Gelabert (2004): The "private function" of gesture in second language speaking activity: A study of motion verbs and gesturing in English and Spanish. *International Journal of Applied Linguistics* 14(1): 113–147.

Noonan, Michael (2003): Motion events in Chantyal. In: E. Shay and U. Seibert (eds.), *Motion, Direction and Location in Languages – In Honor of Zygmunt Frajzyngier*, 211–234. Amsterdam: John Benjamins.

Papafragou, Anna, Christine Massey, and Lila Gleitman (2002): Shake, rattle, 'n' roll: The representation of motion in language and cognition. *Cognition* 84(2): 189–219.

Porquier, Rémy (2001): 'Il m'a sauté dessus', 'je lui ai couru après': un cas de postposition en français. *Journal of French Language Studies* 11: 123–134.

Pourcel, Stephanie and Anetta Kopecka (2005): Motion expression in French: Typological diversity. *Durham and Newcastle Working Papers in Linguistics* 11: 139–153.

Pruden, Shannon M., Kathy Hirsh-Pasek, Mandy J. Maguire, and Meredith A. Meyer (2004): Foundations of verb learning: Infants form categories of path and manner in motion events. In: A. Brugos, L. Micciulla, and C. E. Smith (eds.), *Proceedings of the 28th Annual Boston University Conference on Language Development*, 461–472. Somerville: Cascadilla Press.

Pulverman, Rachel, Jennifer L. Sootsman, Roberta M. Golinkoff, and Kathy Hirsh-Pasek (2004): The role of lexical knowledge in nonlinguistic event processing: English-speaking infants' attention to manner and path. In: A. Brugos, L. Micciulla, and C. E. Smith (eds.), *Proceedings of the 28th Annual Boston University Conference on Language Development*, 662–673. Somerville: Cascadilla Press.

Pulverman, Rachel, Roberta M. Golinkoff, Kathy Hirsh-Pasek, and Jennifer Sootsman Buresh (2008): Infants discriminate manners and paths in non-linguistic dynamic events. *Cognition* 108: 825–830.

Özçalışkan, Şeyda (2004): Encoding the manner, path, ground components of a metaphorical motion event. *Annual Review of Cognitive Linguistics* 2: 73–102.

Özçalışkan, Şeyda (2005): Metaphor meets typology: Ways of moving metaphorically in English and Turkish. *Cognitive Linguistics* 16(1): 207–246.

Özyürek, Aslı, Sotaro Kita, and Shanley Allen (2001): *Tomato Man movies:* Stimulus kit designed to elicit manner, path and causal constructions in motion events with regard to speech and gestures [Videotape]. Nijmegen: Max Planck Institute for Psycholinguistics.

Özyürek, Aslı, Sotaro Kita, Shanley Allen, Reyhan Furman, and Amanda Brown (2005): How does linguistic framing of events influence co-speech gestures? Insights from cross-linguistic variations and similarities. *Gesture* 5: 215–237.

Pavlenko, Aneta (eds.) (2011): *Thinking and Speaking in Two Languages*. Bristol: Multilingual Matters.

Ragnarsdóttir, Hrafnhildur and Sven Strömqvist (2004): Time, space, and manner in Swedish and Icelandic narrative construction in two closely related languages. In: S. Strömqvist and L. Verhoeven (eds.), *Relating Events in Narrative: Typological and Contextual Perspectives*, 113–141. Mahwah: Lawrence Erlbaum.

Regier, Terry and Paul Kay (2009): Language, thought, and colour: Whorf was half right. *Trends in Cognitive Sciences* 13: 439–446.

Robinson, Peter and Nick C. Ellis (eds.) (2008): *A Handbook of Cognitive Linguistics and Second Language Acquisition*. London: Routledge.

Schaefer, Ronald P. (2001): Ideophonic adverbs and manner gaps in Emai. In: F. K. Erhard Voeltz and C. Kilian-Hatz (eds.), *Ideophones*, 339–354. Amsterdam/Philadelphia: John Benjamins.

Schwarze, Christoph (1985): Uscire e andare fuori: struttura sintattica e semantica lessicale. In: A. Franchi De Bellis and L. M. Savoia (eds.), *Sintassi e morfologia della lingua italiana d'uso. Teoria ed applicazioni descrittive. SLI XXIV*, 355–371. Rome: Bulzoni.

Sinha, Chris and Tania Kuteva (1995): Distributed spatial semantics. *Nordic Journal of Linguistics* 18: 167–199.

Slobin, Dan I. (1991): Learning to think for speaking: Native language, cognition and rhetorical style. *Pragmatics* 1: 7–26.

Slobin, Dan I. (1996): Two ways to travel: verbs of motion in English and Spanish. In: M. Shibatani and S. A. Thompson (eds.), *Grammatical Constructions: Their Form and Meaning*, 195–220. Oxford: Clarendon Press.

Slobin, Dan I. (2004): The many ways to search for a frog: Linguistic typology and the expression of motion events. In: S. Strömqvist and L. Verhoeven (eds.), *Relating Events in Narrative. Typological and Contextual Perspectives*, 219–257. Mahwah: Lawrence Erlbaum.

Slobin, Dan I. (2005): Relating narrative events in translation. In: D. D. Ravid and H. Bat-Zeev Shyldkrot (eds.), *Perspectives on Language and Language Development: Essays in Honor of Ruth A. Berman*, 115–129. Dordrecht: Kluwer.

Slobin, Dan I. (2006): What makes manner of motion salient? Explorations in linguistic typology, discourse, and cognition. In: M. Hickmann and S. Robert (eds.), *Space in Languages: Linguistic Systems and Cognitive Categories*, 59–81. Philadelphia: John Benjamins.

Slobin, Dan I. (2008): Typology and usage: Explorations of motion events across languages. Ms. University of California Berkeley.

Slobin, Dan I. and Nini Hoiting (1994): Reference to movement in spoken and signed languages: Typological considerations. *Proceedings of the Twentieth Annual Meeting of the Berkeley Linguistics Society*, 487–503.

Slotova, Natalya (2008): From satellite-framed Latin to verb-framed Romance. Late Latin as an intermediary stage. In: R. Wright (ed.), *Latin Vulgaire – Latin Tardif* VIII. *Actes du VIIIe Colloque International sur le Latin Vulgaire et Tardif*, 253–262. Zürich/New York: Olms-Weidmann.

Snell-Hornby, Mary (1983): *Verb-Descriptivity in German and English: A Contrastive Study in Semantic Fields*. Heidelberg: Carl Winter Universitätsverlag.

Soroli, Eva (2012): Variation in spatial language and cognition: Exploring visuo-spatial thinking and speaking cross-linguistically. *Cognitive Processing* 13: 333–337.

Stam, Gale (2006): Thinking for speaking about motion: L1 and L2 speech and gesture. *International Review of Applied Linguistics* 44: 143–169.

Strömqvist, Sven and Ludo Verhoeven (2004): *Relating Events in Narrative: Typological and Contextual Perspectives*. Mahwah: Lawrence Erlbaum.

Sugiyama, Yukiko (2005): Not all verb-framed languages are created equal: The case of Japanese. *Proceedings of the Thirty-First Annual Meeting of the Berkeley Linguistics Society*, 299–310.

Talmy, Leonard (1985): Lexicalization patterns: semantic structure in lexical form. In: T. Shopen (ed.), *Language Typology and Syntactic Description*, Vol. 3: *Grammatical Categories and the Lexicon*, 36–149. Cambridge: Cambridge University Press.

Talmy, Leonard (1991): Path to realization: a typology of event conflation. *Proceedings of the Seventeenth Annual Meeting of the Berkeley Linguistics Society*, 480–520.

Talmy, Leonard (2000): *Toward a Cognitive Semantics* (Vol. 2). Cambridge: MIT Press.

Trueswell, John and Anna Papafragou (2010): Perceiving and remembering events cross-linguistically: Evidence from dual-task paradigms. *Journal of Memory and Language* 63: 64–82.

Vandeloise, Claude (1986): *L'Espace en Français: Sémantique des Prépositions Spatiales*. Paris: Le Seuil.

Verkerk, Annemarie (2014): Diachronic change in Indo-European motion event encoding. *Journal of Historical Linguistics* 4(1): 40–83.

Vinay, Jean Paul and Jean Darbelnet (1958): *Stylistique Comparée du Français et de l'Anglais: Méthode de Traduction*. Paris: Didier.

Vulcanova, Mila and Emile Van der Zee (2013): *Motion Encoding in Language and Space*. Oxford: Oxford University Press.

Wälchli, Bernhard (2001): A typology of displacement (with special reference to Latvian). *Sprachtypologie und Universalienforschung* 54: 298–323.

Teenie Matlock and Till Bergmann
Chapter 6: Fictive motion

1 Introduction

After returning from a road trip down the California coast, a friend asks which part of the drive was your favorite. You think about it for a moment and reply, "Santa Barbara." In formulating your response, you mentally simulate portions of the drive down Highway 1. "Leaving" San Francisco, you "go" south, and "pass" through various coastal communities until you "get to" Los Angeles.[1] Before you embarked on your journey, you read a description of the route you would take:

> Highway 1 runs along the coastline. It goes through Half Moon Bay, Santa Cruz, Monterey, and Carmel, and then enters the Big Sur region. Near Morro Bay, it ambles past the site of a prehistoric Chumash settlement and later it races past the Madonna Inn near San Luis Obispo. After leaving Santa Barbara, it crosses into Ventura County, and then it approaches Los Angeles.

Sentences like these express no information about actual motion, yet they have been argued to include a fleeting, implied sense of motion. They fall under *fictive motion*, a broad conceptual category first characterized by Leonard Talmy (see Talmy 1983, 1996, 2000). The semantics of fictive motion has received much attention over the years, including theoretical and comparative work as well as experimental semantics work.

This chapter provides an overview of cognitive linguistics research on fictive motion. It starts with early foundational work before moving to recent experimental semantics work and ending with future directions.

2 Fictive motion: Where it started

People often use fictive motion expressions, such as *Highway 1 goes through Half Moon Bay* and *A scar runs down his back*. These expressions describe where

---

1 Your mental journey is enabled by your capacity to create, update, and move through imagined spaces. Psychologists have shown that people mentally move through spatial mental

Teenie Matlock, Merced, United States of America
Till Bergmann, Merced, United States of America

objects are, and how they are configured in physical space. Fictive motion expressions occur in many spoken languages, including English (Talmy 1996), Spanish (Rojo and Valenzuela 2003), Hindi (Mishra and Singh 2010), Japanese (Matsumoto 1996a), Thai (Takahashi 2000), Ancient Hebrew (Dewey 2011), Finnish (Huumo 1999, 2005), as well as Serbian (Stosic and Sarda 2009). They are also common in signed languages (Liddell 2003).

Fictive motion sentences have interesting semantic properties that vary according to how the figure, or trajector (hereafter, TR), is conceptualized (Matlock 2004a; Talmy 2000). The TR in these sentences is stationary, for instance, *Highway 1* in *Highway 1 runs along the coastline*. The TR can be linearly extended in various directions, including vertically, as in *The ladder goes up the side of the building*, or horizontally, as in *The freeway runs along the edge of the city*. It can be large or small, as in *The mountain range goes from Mexico to Canada* and *The molecule runs along the hydrocarbon chain that links two benzene rings*. In some cases, the TR is a traversable path, as in *The highway races through the countryside* and *The trail climbs 1,000 meters*, and in others, a relatively long entity that is not ordinarily traversed, as in *The fence runs along the coastline* and *A cable runs underground*. In still other cases, the TR is neither linear nor long, but, rather, it becomes lengthened through dynamic construal, as in *A table runs along the wall*, and *The pond runs along the hillside*.

Fictive motion sentences[2] are also inherently imperfective in that they emphasize the long term or permanent nature of a given situation or state (see Langacker 1987, Matlock 2010). For example, with *Highway 1 runs along the coastline*, it is assumed the highway will retain its position and structural integrity indefinitely. Because of their imperfective character, fictive motion sentences often avoid progressive forms. An exception is when new information about the current condition of the TR Is provided, as in *The highway is (now) running along the coastline*. Another exception is when the progressive is used to emphasize the temporary existence of a TR, as in *A heat rash is running down his leg*. And yet another exception is when the progressive is used to indicate that the conceptualizer is changing position. For instance, imagine you are driving down the road and telling your friend what you are observing moment to moment: *I'm on a road that was going down a long hill, and it's now meandering north* (see Langacker 2005 for discussion of perfective and imperfective versions of fictive motion).

---

models they create from memory and linguistic input (Bower and Morrow 1990; Franklin and Tversky 1990; Morrow et al. 1989; Tversky 1993; Zwaan and Radvansky 1998).

2 The terms "fictive motion expression" and "fictive motion sentence" are used interchangeably.

In his pioneering work on fictive motion, cognitive linguist Leonard Talmy provided a rich taxonomy of fictive motion types, including *co-extension path* fictive motion, the focus of this chapter.[3] He claimed that, despite their static disposition, fictive motion expressions include schematic elements of actual motion. For instance, both *The highway runs along the coastline* and *The athlete runs along the coastline* include physical space and a path (or linear TR) (see Talmy 1975, 1983, 1996). Other cognitive linguists made similar claims, including Ronald Langacker and Yo Matsumoto, who focused on the subjective nature of fictive motion (Langacker 1986, 1987; Matsumoto 1996a, 1996b). Matsumoto also observed interesting differences between Japanese and English. He noted that English fictive motion expressions often have non-traversable TRs (e.g., *The fence goes along the coastline*), but Japanese fictive motion expressions rarely do (see Matsumoto 1996a).[4, 5] Other cognitive linguists, especially George Lakoff and Mark Turner, characterized fictive motion as a type of conceptual metaphor, in particular, FORM IS MOTION (see Lakoff and Turner 1989 for discussion).

Together, this work advanced our knowledge of the fictive motion. It was not until the 21st Century, however, that behavioral studies began testing claims about processing, especially whether they do indeed involve a fleeting sense of motion. Below is a summary of some of behavioral work on fictive motion.

3 Fictive motion: Where it has been lately

In recent years, cognitive linguists have begun using psychological methods to explore fictive motion processing. Much of this research has examined English fictive motion, but other languages are starting to be explored. This constellation of work, beginning with Matlock (2001, 2004b), seeks answers to the following questions: Does fictive motion include simulated motion, and if so, how is this realized? How does fictive motion vary under different conditions? Is it

---

[3] See Talmy (2000) for discussion of types of fictive motion, including co-extension path fictive motion, which is also called *linear path* extension fictive motion (see Talmy 1996).
[4] Ronald Langacker and Yo Matsumoto have referred to the type of fictive motion we are discussing here as "abstract motion" and "subjective motion", respectively (Langacker 1986; Matsumoto 1996a). Langacker has also discussed fictive motion in the context of virtual motion (Langacker 2000, 2005).
[5] Amagawa (1997) also discussed differences between English and Japanese fictive motion, focusing on the motion verb *run* and its counterpart *hashiru*.

similar to actual motion? Methods used include surveys, drawing tasks, narrative understanding tasks, and eye movement tasks.

3.1 Narrative understanding tasks

The experiments reported in Matlock (2004b) explored fictive motion comprehension. Participants, university undergraduates with reported native or near native proficiency, were asked to read passages about motion through a spatial environment (e.g., a man driving through a desert), and then to quickly decide ("yes" or "no" response) whether a fictive motion target sentence (e.g., Road 49 crosses the desert) was related to what they had read. This required people to think about the motion they read about, and to re-experience how it unfolded along a path. Responses were measured in milliseconds and analyzed across participants and items.

In one experiment, people read passages that differed on velocity of travel. In some passages, the protagonist moved slowly, and in others, fast (e.g., driving 25 versus 100 miles per hour across a desert). People read a slow or fast travel passage, and decided whether a subsequent fictive motion sentence was related. In brief, the time it took people to make the decision about the target sentence varied according to travel velocity. On average people were quicker to make decisions about fictive motion target sentences after reading about fast travel than slow travel. In another experiment in Matlock (2004b), people read passages that differed on whether protagonists traveled short or long distances (e.g., 10 versus 100 miles), and then decided whether fictive motion target sentences were related. People made quicker decisions after reading about short distance travel than long distance travel on average. In yet another experiment, people read about travel through cluttered or uncluttered terrains (e.g., bumpy versus smooth). Their responses to fictive motion target sentences were quicker after reading about terrains that were uncluttered than those that were cluttered.

Together, the experiments in Matlock (2004b) showed that people were quicker to process fictive motion sentences in the context of travel with short distances (versus long), fast travel velocity (versus slow), and uncluttered terrains (versus cluttered). Control studies were also conducted using the same passages and target sentences that lacked fictive motion, such as *Road 49 is in the desert*, and no reliable processing differences emerged. Based on these results, it was concluded that fictive motion processing included mentally simulated motion.

3.2 Drawing studies

Drawing studies have also examined the conceptual structure of fictive motion sentences. In one experiment in Matlock (2006), people produced simple line drawings to depict their understanding of sentences that did or did not include fictive motion, for instance, *The highway runs along the coast* and *The highway is next to the coast*. In this experiment, all TRs were inherently long, traversable paths, such as highways, and bike paths. In general, people drew relatively longer TRs in depictions of fictive motion sentences than in depictions of non-fictive motion sentences. In a second drawing experiment in Matlock (2006), people drew pictures of sentences that included TRs that could be construed as either short or long, such as tattoos, as in *The tattoo runs along his spine*, or *The tattoo is next to his spine*. None of these TRs were traversable. Once again, people drew relatively longer TRs in depictions of sentences that included fictive motion than in depictions of sentences that did not. The results were in line with the idea that fictive motion processing involves mentally simulated motion.

3.3 Eye movement studies

In Matlock and Richardson (2004), participants viewed scenes on a computer screen while listening to descriptions of those scenes. Each scene was a line drawing with both a vertical and a horizontal path or object (e.g., a line of trees running vertically, and a road running horizontally). Some sentences included fictive motion, and others did not, for instance, *The cord runs along the wall* and *The cord is on the wall*. While people viewed pictures and listened to sentences, their eye movements were tracked and recorded by an eye-tracking camera.[6] This approach allowed the researchers to pinpoint where and how people directed their visual attention across while processing linguistic information. The results showed that people spent more time viewing the region associated with the relevant path or linear object while listening to sentences with fictive motion. For example, they spent more time looking at the region of the scene that displayed a cord (than other parts of the scene) while listening to *The cord runs along the wall* than they did while listening to *The cord is on the wall*.

---

[6] Eye tracking allows researchers to measure where and when eye fixations occur in the time course of processing visual and linguistic information. For seminal research and comprehensive background, see Tanenhaus and Spivey-Knowlton (1996); Henderson and Ferreira (2004); Richardson and Dale (2005); and Richardson et al. (2007).

A follow-up study by Richardson and Matlock (2007) used similar visual and verbal stimuli. People listened to a sentence that did or did not include fictive motion, such as *The road runs through the valley* or *The road is in the valley*, after listening to a one-sentence terrain description, such as *The valley is covered with dust* or *The valley is covered with ruts*. In each case, the terrain description contained information that implied easy or difficult movement (e.g., *dust* versus *ruts*). Next, they viewed a scene (e.g., a valley). In this experiment, terrain information differentially influenced eye movement patterns with sentences with fictive motion, but not sentences without fictive motion. More visual attention was directed to paths or linear objects (e.g., roads) after listening to information about difficult terrains (e.g., ruts in a valley) than after listening to information about easy terrains (e.g., dust in a valley).

These eye-tracking studies provided evidence to support the hypothesis that fictive motion includes mentally simulated motion. Especially compelling was the second experiment, where terrain information differentially influenced visual attention to the TR with fictive motion sentences only. These findings resonate to how we experience motion in the world; terrain affects how quickly and fluidly we move.

3.4 Time and motion surveys

Some fictive motion research has adapted experimental methods designed to examine the conceptual link between time and space. For decades, linguists and psychologists have argued that temporal reasoning is grounded in everyday thought about space (see, for instance, Clark 1973; Evans 2004, this volume; Lakoff and Johnson 1980; Radden 2011). A series of experiments in Boroditsky and Ramscar (2002) investigated how spatial thinking would influence temporal reasoning (see also McGlone and Harding 1998). People in one experiment were primed to imagine themselves moving toward a physical object, or about a physical object moving toward them, right before answering this question: *Next Wednesday's meeting has been moved forward two days. What day is the meeting now that it has been rescheduled?* A Monday response to this query suggests "moving" the meeting two days further into the past (relative to Wednesday), and a Friday response suggests "moving" two days further into the future. The results showed that the way people conceptualized motion influenced how they responded to the "move-forward" question. They were more likely to provide a Friday response after imagining themselves moving toward an object, and more likely to provide a Monday response after imagining the object moving toward them (see related work and alternative explanations in Núñez et al. 2006; Teuscher et al. 2008; Moore 2006).

Matlock et al. (2005) followed up on this work, and examined whether fictive motion would have a similar effect on temporal reasoning. In one experiment, people read a sentence that did or did not include fictive motion, such as *The bike path runs alongside the creek* or *The bike path is next to the creek*, and drew a picture to represent their understanding of that sentence. Next they answered the "move forward" time question used in Boroditsky and Ramscar (2002), *Next Wednesday's meeting has been moved forward two days. What day is the meeting now that it has been rescheduled?* The results of Matlock et al. (2005) showed that people who had read and depicted a sentence with fictive motion were more likely to provide a Friday response than a Monday response, and people who had read and depicted a sentence with no fictive motion, were no more likely to provide a Friday response than a Monday response. In addition, people were more likely to include motion elements (e.g., people jogging or riding bikes) in fictive motion depictions than in non-fictive motion depictions (see Matlock et al. 2004).

A second experiment in Matlock et al. (2005) further explored fictive motion and temporal reasoning. It investigated how people would conceptualize statements that implied a series of discrete scan points (i.e., a line of trees). Of interest was how fictive motion with increasingly more scan points (i.e., more and more trees along a driveway) would influence how people would respond to the subsequent "move forward" time question. People read about various numbers of trees along a driveway, specifically, *Four pine trees run along the edge of the driveway*, *Eight pine trees run along the edge of the driveway*, *Twenty pine trees run along the edge of the driveway*, or *Over eighty pine trees run along the edge of the driveway*. Next, they drew a picture to represent their understanding of the sentence, and then answered the "move forward" time question. People were more likely to give a Friday response than a Monday response overall, but the proportion of Friday responses varied according to number of pine trees. People were more likely to provide a Friday response with 8 pine trees and 20 pine trees, but not with 4 pine trees or over 80 pine trees. In brief, a "just right" number (i.e., easy to conceptualize as a path) primed people to "move" through time toward Friday. Four trees did not show the same effect because there were not enough trees to scan as a path. Over 80 trees meant too many trees to conceptualize in a linear fashion.[7]

---

[7] Ramscar et al. (2010) did a follow-up study that omitted the drawing task and increased the numbers of scan points in their verbal stimuli, specifically, 10, 11, 12, 19, and 100 pine trees that ran along a driveway. The results were consistent overall with those of Matlock et al. (2005).

A third experiment by Matlock et al. (2005) investigated direction. People read a fictive motion sentence that implied direction toward or away from the body: *The road goes all the way to New York* or *The road comes all the way from New York*. Next, they drew a picture and answered the "move forward" time question. The results revealed more Friday responses with the *goes to* fictive motion sentences, but more Monday responses with *comes from* fictive motion sentences, suggesting that fictive motion direction influenced temporal construal.

Similar effects were obtained in Matlock et al. (2011) in related research on the metaphorical construal of number lines.[8] That work explored the mental connection between number sequences (e.g., *5, 6, 7; 7, 6, 5*) and time. Numerical reasoning is known to be grounded in spatial reasoning, including thought about direction (Dehaene 1997; Lakoff and Núñez 2000). From this, it follows that reasoning about numbers would influence reasoning about time. In one experiment, before answering the "move forward" question, some people were given the numbers 5 and 17 with 11 blanks between, and asked to fill in the blanks. Others were given 17 and 5 with 11 blanks between and asked to fill in the numbers. The logic was that filling in the blanks in canonical counting direction would encourage people to take an ego-moving perspective and move forward through time toward a Friday response, and that counting backwards would not. People were more likely to provide a Friday response with 5 to 17, but not more likely to do so after filling in the blanks from 17 to 5. A second experiment with sequences of letters (e.g., *G, H, I* ... and *J, I, H* ...) led to similar results. These two studies showed that fictive motion need not involve physical space. Simply thinking about the direction of abstract entities in a point by point manner affected temporal reasoning.

Research on how fictive motion would influence time was expanded to include another type of fictive motion, *line of sight paths*, in Matlock (2010). Line of sight paths can use sensory and non-sensory verbs to create a sense of fictively moving, for example, *I slowly looked away from the window* or *I slowly turned my camera towards the door* (Talmy 2000). In the experiment, visual path length was modified in the following sentences: *I can see Fred across the table*, *I can see Fred across the room*, or *I can see Fred across the field* corresponding to short, medium, and long visual paths respectively. People read one of these sentences before answering the "move forward" question. The results revealed a greater likelihood of Friday responses with longer and longer visual paths.

---

[8] Matlock et al. (2011) used the term "abstract motion", but the phenomena are essentially the same.

The results provided further evidence to support the idea that visual paths are conceptually similar to motion paths (see Slobin 2008).

Together, this work contributes behavioral evidence to support the idea that our everyday understanding of language, including non-literal language, is grounded in our embodied experience (Barsalou 1999, 2008; Gibbs 2006; Glenberg 1999, 2010; Pecher and Zwaan 2005; Zwaan et al. 2004). We simulate motion along a path, linear object, or series of entities, including trees, numbers, or letters, and it has consequences for how we think about time in a way that is not unlike thought about actual motion through physical space. This body of work also provides evidence to support the idea that language involves dynamic construal (see Langacker, volume 1).

4 Fictive motion: Where it is going

Many exciting theories about how people mentally "move" through spatial environments have been proposed over the years. Some researchers have argued that motion simulation is similar to engaging in or viewing actual motion (see Barsalou 1999, 2008; Gallese and Lakoff 2005; Gibbs 2006; Glenberg 1999). Such mental simulation is involved in the use and understanding of motion language, including figurative motion language (Bergen 2012; Feldman 2008; Gibbs and Matlock 2008; Matlock 2010; Narayanan 1997), such as discourse about political campaign races (Matlock 2012), romantic relationships (Gibbs 2012), and web use (Maglio and Matlock 1999; Matlock et al. 2014).

Many questions about fictive motion remain, including the following. How does the purported fleeting sense of motion unfold in real time? When do people mentally scan along the TR versus move along it, and is there any difference? Both involve motion. When and how do people extend a TR that is not necessarily long, for instance, while interpreting sentences such as *A table runs along the back wall* or *A scar goes down his back*? What neurological patterns emerge in processing fictive motion sentences, and to what extent do these patterns resemble those involved in processing perceiving or doing actual motion? Careful work is needed to get at processing details, and to clarify how simulation works in different contexts. It is also important to delve more deeply into the subjectivity of fictive motion. Insightful work by Jordan Zlatev and colleagues is beginning to explore this (see Blomberg and Zlatev 2014).

Neuroscientists have begun to study fictive motion processing. They have discovered that brain areas associated with processing actual motion are also activated when viewing scenes that merely suggest motion. In Kourtzi and Kanwisher (2000), people viewed static images that implied motion, for instance, a picture of a man about to hurl a discus. Their results showed that areas of the brain associated with motion perception were activated even though no actual motion was being perceived (see also Kourtzi 2004; Winawer et al. 2007). Such research provides strong evidence that we are biased to conceptualize or infer motion even at the mere suggestion of movement.

Saygin et al. (2010) used fMRI (functional magnetic resonance imaging) to investigate patterns of brain activation in fictive motion processing. People in their study were placed in the fMRI scanner and presented with three types of verbal stimuli: sentences with actual motion, such as *I drove from Modesto to Fresno*; sentences with no motion, such as *Modesto and Fresno are in California*; and sentences with fictive motion, such as *The highway runs from Modesto to Fresno*. The results showed that actual motion sentences activated brain areas associated with the processing of visual motion much more than did no-motion sentences did, and that fictive motion sentences elicited more activation than no-motion sentences (but less than actual motion sentences). These results suggested that fictive motion includes mentally simulated motion that mirrors actual motion. Similar results were obtained by Wallentin et al. (2005) in a study on the neurolinguistic processing of Danish fictive motion sentences. More work in this area is needed to gain a better understanding the dynamics of fictive motion processing.

Much research on fictive motion has focused on coextension path fictive motion. Other types include *access paths* (*The bakery is across the street from the bank*), in which fictive motion is expressed by path prepositions, and *demonstrative paths* (*The arrow on the signpost pointed towards the town*), in which the TR creates a line of sight path (see also Takahashi 2001). These fictive motion constructions do not use motion verbs, so the implicit sense of motion may be less salient than fictive motion constructions that do include motion verbs, but we will not know until this is empirically tested. Closer examination of a wide range of fictive motion sentences may lead to new insights about how spatial language is processed in general. For example, *The road leads to the north* may be processed quite differently from *The road goes to the north*.

It could be informative to apply some of the behavioral methods discussed in this chapter to linguistic constructions that have conceptual overlap with fictive motion, for example, instances of *fictive change* (Sweetser 1997), as in *His girlfriend gets taller every year* and *The windows keep getting cleaner as you walk towards the Bay*. This type of construction might elicit a similar fictive motion effect, with mental scanning proceeding from one window to another, or from one height to another. It might also be worthwhile to extend fictive motion behavioral research to cognitive linguistic work on other forms of spatial language associated with stasis, for instance, verbs of standing, sitting, and lying (see Newman 2002).

Though much behavioral work on fictive motion has focused on English, some experiments have examined other languages, including Spanish (Rojo and Valenzuela 2003), Hindi (Mishra and Singh 2010), and Danish (Wallentin et al. 2005). Large-scale cross-linguistic behavioral study on fictive motion processing would yield new insights about which aspects of fictive motion generalize, and provide valuable information about figurative language. Recent, careful cross-linguistic work has used behavioral methods to compare the interpretation of motion-emotion metaphors in Thai, Bulgarian, English, and Swedish (Zlatev et al. 2012). This approach could inform the design of future experiments that compare fictive motion processing across languages.

In this same vein, more behavioral work could examine manner of motion (see Filipovic and Ibarretxe's chapter on motion in this volume) in figurative language understanding. In English, manner verbs are not uncommon in fictive motion sentences that emphasize unusual or special properties of the TR, as seen in *The hiking trail zigzags up the side of the mountain* and *A bike path cruises through the park*. In some languages, such as English, manner is encoded in the motion verb itself. In other languages, including Spanish, manner is encoded with the help of additional lexical items. For example, to report that a boat rapidly entered a cave, an English speaker could use the manner verb *dart*, as in *The boat darted into the cave*. The verb *dart* would simultaneously express translational motion and speed. In contrast, a Spanish speaker could describe the situation by using a motion verb that conveys no speed along with an adjunct that does convey speed, as in *El barco entró en la cueva como una fleche*, literally *The boat entered the cave like an arrow*. So far, only one experiment (Matlock 2006) has explored people's conceptions of manner in fictive motion sentences. In a drawing study, people drew longer, straighter, and thinner lines while depicting fictive motion paths described with fast manner verbs (e.g., *race*) than those with slow manner verbs (e.g., *crawl*). Studying how manner is realized in various spatial descriptions across languages could shed some light on the issue of linguistic relativity. It is common, for instance, for speakers of Greek and Spanish to ignore or downplay manner information in language, at least in literal motion sentences (see Papafragou et al. 2002). What impact might this have on how they view linearly extended layouts?

It would be fruitful to look closely at grammatical aspect in processing fictive motion language. As mentioned earlier in this chapter, fictive motion has an imperfective quality, and therefore, it often appears without imperfective aspect. Studying when and how fictive motion interacts with progressive and non-progressive forms could tell us more about the role of aspect in language processing, especially in spatial descriptions and in figurative language (e.g., *The highway runs along the coastline*, *The highway is running along the coastline*).

Some psychological work has begun to explore the role of aspect in language understanding and reasoning. Choice of aspect is known, for instance, to affect the inferences people make about magnitude of situations and states, including whether a political candidate seems suitable for office (Fausey and Matlock 2011).

Research on fictive motion in natural discourse would fill an important gap. It would tell us more about fictive motion use. Analyses of gestures in natural discourse, especially fictive motion depictions in face-to-face interactions, could also be informative. Gestures often occur in conversations about spatial configurations, for instance, route descriptions (see Bergmann and Matlock 2014). It would also be useful to investigate when and how children start producing fictive motion sentences in natural speech. We know that spatial relations play an important role in linguistic development (see Mandler 2012), but we do not know what role fictive motion plays.

Research on the explanatory power of fictive motion would be informative for learning abstract scientific concepts. Mathematics is rife with fictive motion (Lakoff and Núñez 2000; Núñez 2008). When discussing limits in calculus, for instance, people often use fictive motion expressions that imply motion and a limit, as in *The sum approaches 7 as n goes to infinity*. According to Núñez (2006), fictive motion (and other figurative language) facilitates the understanding of mathematical concepts (see also Keane 2007). Manual gestures also often occur while people are discussing mathematics, sometimes with fictive motion descriptions. In illustrating a rapidly increasing function, for instance, a person makes a quick, rightward manual gesture (Marghetis and Núñez 2013; Wittmann et al. 2012). Manual gestures are also useful for learning abstract geological concepts, such as relative sea level (see Herrera and Riggs 2013). Metaphorical motion language, including fictive motion language, is also common in learning physics (see Pulaczewska 1999). Much work has yet to be done on when and how fictive motion could be used to enhance learning abstract scientific material.

Finally, motion is a productive source domain in many basic, conceptual metaphors in human languages, such as TIME IS MOTION (Clark 1973; Radden 1996), LIFE IS A JOURNEY (Lakoff and Johnson 1980), RELATIONSHIPS ARE JOURNEYS (Gibbs 2012), and POLITICAL CAMPAIGNS ARE RACES (Matlock 2012), all of which are part of EVENT STRUCTURE (see Lakoff and Johnson 1999). Research on the dynamics of processing non-literal motion language, including how it interacts with grammatical systems, such as aspect, how it is used in everyday conversation, how it interacts with gesture, and how it varies across languages and situations, will help cognitive linguists come to a better understanding how figurative language and more generally, spatial language is processed. Until then, what we have learned about fictive motion research over the past 30 years will continue to take us in the right direction in the years to come.

5 Conclusion

This chapter reviewed cognitive linguistics research on fictive motion, including early theoretical and behavioral work. In sum, it appears that early claims about fictive motion processing were indeed correct: Fictive motion does involve a fleeting sense of motion. Like real motion, it can be modulated by environmental factors, such as how cluttered or uncluttered a terrain is. Like real motion, fictive motion also has magnitude and direction, and can thus influence how people metaphorically reason about time. More generally, the behavioral studies reported here provide good evidence to support claims that language representation and use is grounded in our embodied experience with motion in the physical world.

6 References

Amagawa, Toyoko (1997): Subjective motion in English and Japanese: A case study of *run* and *hashiru*. *Tsukuba English Studies* 16: 33–50.

Barsalou, Lawrence W. (1999): Perceptual symbol systems. *Behavioral and Brain Sciences* 22: 577–660.

Barsalou, Lawrence W. (2008): Grounded cognition. *Annual Review of Psychology* 59: 617–645.

Bergmann, Till and Teenie Matlock (2014): Fictive motion and gestures: Real discourse from the TV news archive. Presented at the 6th Annual Conference of the International Society for Gesture Studies. La Jolla, USA.

Bergen, Benjamin K. (2012): *Louder Than Words: The New Science of How the Mind Makes Meaning*. New York: Basic Books.

Blomberg, Johan and Jordan Zlatev (2014): Actual and non-actual motion: Why experientialist semantics needs phenomenology (and vice versa). *Phenomenology and the Cognitive Sciences* 13(3): 395–418.

Boroditsky, Lera and Michael Ramscar (2002): The roles of body and mind in abstract thought. *Psychological Science* 13: 185–188.

Bower, Gordon H. and Daniel G. Morrow (1990): Mental models in narrative comprehension. *Science* 247: 44–48.

Clark, Herbert H. (1973): Space, time, semantics, and the child. In: T. E. Moore (ed.), *Cognitive Development and the Acquisition of Language*, 2–63. New York: Academic Press.

Dehaene, Stanislaus (1997): *The Number Sense: How the Mind Creates Mathematics*. New York: Oxford University Press.

Dewey, Ryan (2011): Fictive Motion in Ancient Hebrew Descriptions of Geographical Boundaries. Working Paper: Case Western Reserve University.

Evans, Vyvyan (2004): *The Structure of Time: Language, Meaning and Temporal Cognition*. (Human Cognitive Processing 12.) Amsterdam/Philadelphia: John Benjamins.

Evans, Vyvyan (this volume): Time. Berlin/Boston: De Gruyter Mouton.

Fausey, Caitlin M. and Teenie Matlock (2011): Can grammar win elections? *Political Psychology* 32(4): 563–574.

Feldman, Jerome (2008): *From Molecule to Metaphor: A Neural Theory of Language*. Cambridge: MIT Press.

Filipović, Luna and Iraide Ibarretxe-Antuñano (this volume): Motion: Berlin/Boston: De Gruyter Mouton.

Franklin, Nancy and Barbara Tversky (1990): Searching imagined environments. *Journal of Experimental Psychology: General* 119: 63–76.

Gallese, Vittorio and George Lakoff (2005): The brain's concepts: The role of the sensory-motor system in reason and language. *Cognitive Neuropsychology* 22: 455–479.

Gibbs, Raymond W. (2006): Embodiment and Cognitive Science. New York: Cambridge University Press.

Gibbs, Raymond W. (2012): Walking the walk while thinking about the talk: Embodied interpretation of metaphorical narratives. *Journal of Psycholinguistic Research* 42: 363–378.

Gibbs, Raymond W. and Teenie Matlock (2008): Metaphor, imagination, and simulation: Psycholinguistic evidence. In: R. W. Gibbs (ed.), *Cambridge Handbook of Metaphor and Thought*, 161–176.
New York: Cambridge University Press.

Glenberg, Arthur M. (1999): Why mental models must be embodied. In: G. Rickheit and C. Habel (eds.), *Mental Models in Discourse Processing and Reasoning*, 77–90. New York: Elsevier.

Glenberg, Arthur M. (2010): Embodiment as a unifying perspective for psychology. *Wiley Interdisciplinary Reviews: Cognitive Science* 1: 586–596.

Henderson, John M. and Fernanda Ferreira (2004): Scene perception for psycholinguists. In: J. M. Henderson and F. Ferreira (eds.), *The Interface of Language, Vision, and Action*, 1–58. New York: Psychology Press.

Herrera, Juan S. and Eric M. Riggs (2013): Relating gestures and speech: An analysis of students' conceptions about geological sedimentary processes. *International Journal of Science Education* 35(12): 1979–2003.

Huumo, Tuomas (1999): Path settings, subjective motion, and the Finnish partitive subject. In: S. J. J. Hwang and A. L. Lommel (eds.), *LACUS Forum XXV (The Linguistic Association of Canada and the United States)*, 363–374.

Huumo, Tuomas (2005): How fictive dynamicity motivates aspect marking: The riddle of the Finnish quasi-resultative construction. *Cognitive Linguistics* 16: 113–144.

Keane, Karen A. (2007): A characterization of dynamic reasoning: Reasoning with time as parameter. *Mathematical Reasoning* 26: 230–246.

Kourtzi, Zoe (2004): "But still, it moves." *Trends in Cognitive Sciences* 8(2): 47–49.

Kourtzi, Zoe and Nancy Kanwisher (2000): Activation in human MT/MST by static images with implied motion. *Journal of Cognitive Neuroscience* 12(1): 48–55.

Lakoff, George and Mark Johnson (1980): *Metaphors We Live By*. Chicago: University of Chicago Press.

Lakoff, George and Mark Johnson (1999): *Philosophy in the Flesh: The Embodied Mind and Its Challenge to Western Thought*. New York: Basic Books.
Lakoff, George and Rafael E. Nuñez (2000): *Where Mathematics Comes From*. New York: Basic Books.
Lakoff, George and Mark Turner (1989): *More than Cool Reason: A Field Guide to Poetic Metaphor*. Chicago: University of Chicago Press.
Langacker, Ronald W. (1986): Abstract motion. In: V. Nikiforidou, M. van Clay, M. Niepokuj, and D. Feder (eds.), *Proceedings of the 12th Annual Meeting of the Berkeley Linguistics Society*, 455–471. Berkeley: Berkeley Linguistics Society.
Langacker, Ronald W. (1987): *Foundations of Cognitive Grammar*, Volume 1: *Theoretical Prerequisites*. Stanford: Stanford University Press.
Langacker, Ronald W. (2000): Virtual reality. *Studies in the Linguistic Sciences* 29: 77–103.
Langacker, Ronald W. (2005): Dynamicity, fictivity, and scanning: The imaginative basis of logic and linguisticmeaning. In: D. Pecher, and R. A. Zwaan (eds.), *Grounding Cognition: The Role of Perception and Action in Memory, Language, and Thinking*, 164–197. Cambridge University Press.
Langacker, Ronald W. (volume 1): Construal. Berlin/Boston: De Gruyter Mouton.
Liddell, Scott K. (2003): *Grammar, Gesture, and Meaning in American Sign Language*. New York: Cambridge University Press.
Maglio, Paul P. and Teenie Matlock (1999): The conceptual structure of information spaces. In: A. Munro, D. Benyon, D. Hook and K. Hook (eds.), *Personal and Social Navigation of Information Space*. Berlin: Springer-Verlag.
Mandler, Jean M. (2012): On the spatial foundations of the conceptual system and its enrichment. *Cognitive Science* 36(3): 421–451.
Marghetis, Tyler and Rafael Núñez (2013): The motion behind the symbols: A vital role for dynamism in the conceptualization of limits and continuity in expert mathematics. *Topics in Cognitive Science* 5(2): 299–316.
Matlock, Teenie (2001): How real is fictive motion? PhD dissertation, University of California, Santa Cruz.
Matlock, Teenie (2004a): The conceptual motivation of fictive motion. In: G. Radden and R. Dirven (eds.), *Motivation in Grammar*, 221–248. Amsterdam: John Benjamins.
Matlock, Teenie (2004b): Fictive motion as cognitive simulation. *Memory and Cognition* 32: 1389–1400.
Matlock, Teenie (2006): Depicting fictive motion in drawings. In: J. Luchenbroers (ed.), *Cognitive Linguistics: Investigations Across Languages, Fields and Philosophical Boundaries*, 67–85. Amsterdam: John Benjamins.
Matlock, Teenie (2010): Abstract motion is no longer abstract. *Language and Cognition* 2(2): 243–260.
Matlock, Teenie (2012): Framing political messages with grammar and metaphor. *American Scientist* 100: 478–483.
Matlock, Teenie, Spencer C. Castro, Morgan Fleming, Timothy M. Gann, and Paul P. Maglio (2014): Spatial metaphors in web use. *Spatial Cognition and Computation* 14. doi: 10.1080/13875868.2014.945587.
Matlock, Teenie, Kevin Holmes, Mahesh Srinivasan, and Michael Ramscar (2011): Even abstract motion influences the understanding of time. *Metaphor and Symbol* 26(4): 260–271.
Matlock, Teenie, Michael Ramscar, and Lera Boroditsky (2004): The experiential basis of motion language. In: A. S. da Silva, A. Torres and M. Gonçalves (eds.), *Linguagem, Cultura e Cognicao: Estudo de Linguistica Cognitiva*, 43–57.

Matlock, Teenie, Michael Ramscar, and Lera Boroditsky (2005): The experiential link between spatial and temporal language. *Cognitive Science* 29: 655–664.

Matlock, Teenie and Daniel C. Richardson (2004): Do eye movements go with fictive motion? *Proceedings of the 26th Annual Conference of the Cognitive Science Society* 26: 909–914.

Matsumoto, Yo (1996a): Subjective motion and English and Japanese verbs. *Cognitive Linguistics* 7: 183–226.

Matsumoto, Yo (1996b): How abstract is subjective motion? A comparison of access path expressions and coverage path expressions. In: A. Goldberg (ed.), *Conceptual Structure, Discourse and Language*, 359–373. Stanford: CSLI Publications.

McGlone, Matthew S. and Jennifer L. Harding (1998): Back (or forward?) to the future: The role of perspective in temporal language comprehension. *Journal of Experimental Psychology: Learning Memory and Cognition* 24(5): 1211–1223.

Mishra, Ramesh K. and Niharika Singh (2010): Online fictive motion understanding: An eye-movement study with Hindi. *Metaphor and Symbol* 25(3): 144–161.

Moore, Kevin E. (2006): Space-to-time mappings and temporal concepts. *Cognitive Linguistics* 17: 199–244.

Morrow, Daniel G., Gordon H. Bower, and Stephen L. Greenspan (1989): Updating situation models during narrative comprehension. *Journal of Memory and Language* 28: 292–312.

Narayanan, Srini (1997): Talking the talk is like walking the walk: A computational model of verbal aspect. *Proceedings of the Nineteenth Annual Conference of the Cognitive Science Society*, 548–553. Mahwah: Erlbaum.

Newman, John (2002): *The Linguistics of Sitting, Standing, and Lying*. Amsterdam: John Benjamins.

Núñez, Rafael (2006): Do Real numbers really move? Language, thought, and gesture: The embodied cognitive foundations of mathematics. In: R. Hersh (ed.), *18 Unconventional Essays on the Nature of Mathematics*, 160–181. New York: Springer.

Núñez, Rafael (2008): A fresh look at the foundations of mathematics: Gesture and the psychological reality of conceptual metaphor. In: A. Cienki and C. Müller (eds.), *Metaphor and Gesture*, 93–114. Amsterdam and Philadelphia: John Benjamins.

Núñez, Rafael, Benjamin A. Motz, and Ursina Teuscher (2006): Time after time: The psychological reality of the ego- and time-references-point distinction in metaphorical construals of time. *Metaphor and Symbol* 21: 133–146.

Papafragou, Anna, Christine Massey, and Lila Gleitman (2002): Shake, rattle, 'n' roll: the representation of motion in language and cognition. *Cognition* 84(2): 189–219.

Pecher, Diane and Rolf A. Zwaan (eds.) (2005): *Grounding Cognition: The Role of Perception and Action in Memory, Language and Thinking*. New York: Cambridge University Press.

Pulaczewska, Hanna (1999): *Aspects of Metaphor in Physics: Examples and Case Studies*. Tübingen: Max Niemeyer Verlag.

Radden, Günter (1996): Motion metaphorized: The case of coming and going. In: E. H. Casad (ed.), *Cognitive Linguistics in the Redwoods: The Expansion of a New Paradigm in Linguistics*, 424–458. Berlin/New York: Mouton de Gruyter.

Radden, Günter (2011): Spatial time in the West and the East. In: M. Brdar, M. Omazic, V. P. Takac, T. Erdeljic-Gradecak and G. Bulja (eds.), *Space and Time in Language*, 1–40. Frankfurt: Peter Lang.

Ramscar, Michael, Teenie Matlock, and Melody Dye (2010): Running down the clock: the role of expectation in our understanding of time and motion. *Language and Cognitive Processes* 25: 589–615.

Richardson, Daniel C. and Rick Dale (2005): Looking to understand: The coupling between speakers' and listeners' eye movements and its relationship to discourse comprehension. *Cognitive Science* 29: 39–54.

Richardson, Daniel C., Rick Dale, and Michael J. Spivey (2007): Eye movements in language and cognition. In: M. Gonzalez-Marquez, I. Mittelberg, S. Coulson and M. J. Spivey (eds.), *Empirical Methods in Cognitive Linguistics*, 323–344. Amsterdam/Philadelphia: John Benjamins.

Richardson, Daniel C. and Teenie Matlock (2007): The integration of figurative language and static depictions: an eye movement study of fictive motion. *Cognition* 102(1): 129–138.

Rojo, Ana and Javier Valenzuela (2003): Fictive motion in English and Spanish. *International Journal of English Studies* 3: 123–150.

Saygin, Ayse P., Stephen McCullough, Morana Alac, and Karen Emmorey (2010): Modulation of BOLD response in motion-sensitive lateral temporal cortex by real and fictive motion sentences. *Journal of Cognitive Neuroscience* 22(11): 2480–2490.

Slobin, Dan I. (2008): Relations between Paths of Motion and Paths of Vision: A Cross-linguistic and Developmental Exploration. In: V. C. Mueller Gathercole (ed.), *Routes to Language: Studies in Honor of Melissa Bowerman*, 197–221. Mahwah: Lawrence Erlbaum.

Stosic, Dejan and Laure Sarda (2009): The many ways to be located in French and Serbian: the role of fictive motion in the expression of static location. In: M. Brala-Vukanović and L. Gruić-Grmuša (eds.), *Space and Time in Language and Literature*, 39–59. Newcastle: Cambridge Scholars Publishing.

Sweetser, Eve (1997): Role and individual readings of change predicates. In: Jan Nuyts and E. Pederson (eds.), *Language and Conceptualization*. New York: Cambridge University Press.

Takahashi, Kiyoko (2000): Expressions of emanation fictive motion events in Thai. PhD dissertation, Chulalonkorn University.

Takahashi, Kiyoko (2001): Access path expressions in Thai. In: A. Cienki, B. Luka, and M. Smith (eds.), *Conceptual Structure in Discourse Factors in Linguistic Structure*, 237–252. Stanford: CSLI Publications.

Talmy, Leonard (1975): Semantics and syntax of motion. In: J. P. Kimball (ed.), *Syntax and Semantics*, Volume I: *Conceptual Structuring Systems*, 181–238. New York: Academic Press.

Talmy, Leonard (1983): How language structures space. In: H. L. Pick and L. P. Acredolo (eds.), *Spatial Orientation: Theory, Research, and Application*, 225–282. New York: Plenum.

Talmy, Leonard (1996): Fictive motion in language and "ception." In: P. Bloom, M. A. Peterson, L. Nadel and M. F. Garrett (eds.), *Language and Space*, 211–276. Cambridge: MIT Press.

Talmy, Leonard (2000): *Toward a Cognitive Semantics*. Cambridge: MIT Press.

Tanenhaus, Michael K. and Michael J. Spivey-Knowlton (1996): Eye-tracking. *Language and Cognitive Processes* 11(6): 583–588.

Teuscher, Ursina, Marguerite McQuire, Jennifer Collins, and Seana Coulson (2008): Congruity effects in time and space: behavioral and ERP measures. *Cognitive Science* 32(3): 563–578.

Tversky, Barbara (1993): Cognitive maps, cognitive collages, and spatial mental models. In: A. U. Frank and I. Campari (eds.), *Spatial Information Theory: A Theoretical Basis for GIS*, 14–24. Berlin: Springer-Verlag.

Wallentin, Mikkel, Torben E. Lund, Svend Østergaard, Leif Østergaard, and Andreas Roepstorff (2005): Motion verb sentences activate left posterior middle temporal cortex despite static context. *NeuroReport* 16: 649–652.

Winawer, Jonathan, Alex C. Huk, and Lera Boroditsky (2007): A motion aftereffect from still photographs depicting motion. *Psychological Science* 19: 276–283.

Wittmann, Michael C., Virginia J. Flood, and Katrina E. Black (2012): Algebraic manipulation as motion within a landscape. *Educational Studies in Mathematics* 82(2): 169–181.

Zlatev, Jordan, Johan Blomberg, and Ulf Magnusson (2012): Metaphors and subjective experience: motion-emotion metaphors in English, Swedish, Bulgarian and Thai. In: A. Foolen, U. Lüdtke, T. Racine and J. Zlatev (eds.), *Moving Ourselves – Moving Others: Motion and Emotion in Intersubjectivity, Consciousness, and Language*, 423–450. Amsterdam: John Benjamins.

Zwaan, Rolf A., Carol Madden, Richard H. Yaxley, and Mark Aveyard (2004): Moving words: Dynamic representations in language comprehension. *Cognitive Science* 28: 611–619.

Zwaan, Rolf. A. and Gabriel A. Radvansky (1998): Situation models in language comprehension and memory. *Psychological Bulletin* 123(2): 162–185.

John R. Taylor
Chapter 7: Prototype effects in grammar

Keywords: Prototype, construction, polysemy, fuzziness, idiomaticity

1 Introduction/Overview

This chapter addresses the relevance of the prototype concept to the grammatical description of a language. It turns out that "prototype" is not a unified concept and can be understood in different ways with respect to different kinds of categories (section 2). The notion is, however, supported by a range of empirically founded prototype effects, the topic of section 3. The remainder of the chapter surveys the role of these effects in grammatical description, with a focus on lexical categories (section 5), word structure (section 6), and syntactic constructions (section 7). The latter are considered from the perspectives of their formal and semantic identification, and their productivity.

2 Prototypes and prototype categories

As Geeraerts (1987: 592), following Posner (1986), aptly remarked, prototype is itself a prototype concept. There is, namely, no set of necessary and sufficient conditions which are definitional of a prototype. This should not be surprising, given that prototypes can be understood in different ways according to the kind of category whose members are under discussion, the researcher's theoretical agenda, and the kinds of evidence which lead to the prototype's identification (Ramscar volume 1).

The pioneering work of Eleanor Rosch, in the 1970s, is instructive in this respect. In her earliest work (Heider 1972, Rosch 1973) she addressed the categorization of colour, proposing that colour categories were structured around a focal colour (later to be dubbed the prototype). Colour samples could be called "red" to the extent that they resembled a focal red, with some samples being "better" examples of "red" than others. On this account, a category could be equated with its prototype. To "have" the category "red" is to know, quite sim-

---

John R. Taylor, Christchurch, New Zealand

https://doi.org/10.1515/9783110626438-007

ply, what constitutes a good red. Category membership is constrained only by the existence of neighbouring categories, such as orange, purple, or pink. Category boundaries are fuzzy, with samples near the fuzzy boundaries having ambiguous or uncertain status.

With a few exceptions, the colour model is not readily extendible to other categories. We could not, for example, define the bird category with respect to a good example – a sparrow, let us say – and propose that to have the category "bird" (alternatively, to know the meaning of the word *bird*) involves nothing more than to know what a sparrow is, with things being called birds to the extent that they resemble a sparrow. There are other differences vis-à-vis the colours. For example, the bird category does not gradually merge at its fuzzy boundaries with other categories of living creatures, such as reptiles or mammals. On the contrary, the set of things which are called birds is rather strictly circumscribed. The category does display degrees of representativity, however. Penguins, ostriches, and swans may not be particularly representative examples, but they are still birds, no less so than sparrows and crows.

Colour categories have some special properties which are not shared by categories such as "bird". Foremost amongst these is the fact that a colour sample may be uniquely characterized in terms its location on a number of continuous and independent dimensions, namely hue, brightness, and saturation. The focal colours may be thought of as points in this three-dimensional space. Any colour sample can be categorized as a function of its distance from one or more of these focal colours. Depending on the distance, the sample is considered to be a good, or less good member of the category in question.

For many of the categories named by the words in a language, a dimensional account would not be viable. What, for example, would be the dimensions which characterize "bird", "fruit", "vehicle", or "chair"? Whilst we might certainly refer to the attributes of these categories, the attributes do not constitute smoothly varying dimensions, with focal exemplars occupying distinctive locations on these dimensions. It is largely for this reason that we cannot equate the categories with a single, prototypical exemplar, neither do neighbouring categories gradually merge into each other. Having the category and knowing its boundaries requires familiarity with the range of its possible members.

It is worth mentioning, however, that some phonetic categories, especially those pertaining to vowel sounds and perhaps also the fricatives, do have a dimensional structure not unlike that of the colours. A vowel sound may be specified in terms of the location on a frequency scale of its lower formants, in association with the (again continuously variable) dimension of duration. Just as red merges gradually into orange or pink, we can have a range of vowel qualities ranging from [e] through [ɛ] to [æ]. Accordingly, the vowel categories of a language may be identified with prototypes, akin to the focal colours (Kuhl 1991).

A dimensional approach is of only limited applicability with respect to other linguistic categories (though some possible candidates will be discussed later in this chapter). Take the case of nouns and verbs. Givón (1979: 14) proposed that nouns and verbs are distinguished by the time stability of their referents, with nouns designating time-stable configurations, whilst verbs designate situations of rapid change. Whilst time stability certainly constitutes a smoothly varying dimension, nouns do not gradually shade into verbs. This is because categorization as noun or verb depends crucially on other attributes which are discrete in nature; for example, a word either inflects for past tense, or it does not. Though focussing mainly on their semantic aspects, Langacker (1987) also characterized nouns and verbs in terms of discrete properties, having to do with the nature of the entity that they profile, which in turn rests on notions of temporal scanning, domains, and regions.

Broadening the scope of her research in order to address the prototype structure of natural kinds and other categories, Rosch came to focus on the attributes of category members (Rosch 1978). A crucial notion was that of cue validity. An attribute has high cue validity if presence of the attribute is a good predictor of category membership. Ability to fly is a fairly good predictor of bird status (it is not 100% predictive, since some other kinds of creature can fly). Having a liver, on the other hand, is a very poor predictor. Whilst all birds do have a liver, so too do many other living creatures. The prototype was accordingly characterized as that member which maximized the cue validity of its attributes, the member, in other words, whose attributes, collectively, best predicted membership in the category and excluded membership in neighbouring categories.

In contrast to the category-as-prototype approach (exemplified by the colours), the weighted attribute approach was able to capture the full extent of a category, not just the specifics of its central member (Murphy 2002: 49). The approach was sufficiently flexible to allow for many different kinds of category structure. For one thing, it was consistent with the possibility that different category members might have few diagnostic features in common; all that is required for category membership is that the summed cue validity of the features exceeds some criterial value. Second, the approach allowed for the possibility of "virtual prototypes", not in fact instantiated by any actually occurring entity. Third, it envisaged the possibility that one or more of the attributes might be essential to category membership; in such a case, the boundary of the category will be clear-cut, as determined by the presence/absence of the criterial attribute(s), even though individual members might still display greater or lesser degrees of representativity, in accordance with the presence of other, non-criterial attributes.

Rosch's work had been concerned with the referential possibilities of linguistic terms, pre-eminently nouns which designate natural kinds (*bird*, *fruit*, *tree*) or cultural artefacts and activities (*furniture*, *vehicle*, *sport*). As her work became familiar to linguists (e.g., Lakoff 1987; Taylor 2003, 2008), an extension of the prototype notion saw the term applied to the semantic structure of linguistic items. The focus shifted from the range of entities that a word can designate (an extensional, referential, or onomasiological approach) to the range of senses exhibited by a word (an intensional, or conceptual perspective). An influential example of this shift was the Brugman/Lakoff account of the preposition *over* (Brugman and Lakoff [1988] 2006). It is not simply the fact that *over* can designate many different relations in the world. Rather, the word appears to manifest a cluster of related senses, each of which may constitute a prototype category in the extensional understanding of the term, characterized by a set of attributes of greater or lesser cue validity. A key claim of the intensional approach is that of the different senses, one can be identified as the prototype, that is, a central sense to which others are related in a radial, or network structure.

3 Prototype effects

In her 1978 paper *Principles of categorization*, Rosch was careful to emphasize that her empirical findings on the structure of categories did not constitute a theory of mental representation. What she did claim was that any cognitive theory of categorization had to be able to accommodate the range of prototype effects which she had discovered; these constituted a baseline for the viability of any theory of mental representation.

Prototype effects can be broadly divided into those which pertain to the (structural) centrality of the prototype and to its (cognitive) salience.

3.1 Centrality

The prototype is the "centre" of the category; things are assimilated to the category in accordance with their "distance" from the prototype. The metaphor is particularly apt with respect to colour categories. Centrality is also relevant to research on artificial categories, such as two-dimensional displays of dots, geometrical shapes, or configurations of numbers and letters (e.g., Posner and Keele

1968). The prototype in these studies constitutes a kind of category ideal (invented, of course, by the researchers), and displays can be ranked according to the extent to which they deviate from the ideal, or can be regarded as distortions of it. Although of little relevance to the study of word meanings (the primary focus of Rosch's research and its uptake in lexical semantics) a view of category structure as a function of the degree of distortion of an ideal configuration arguably does play a role in the study of the syntactic configurations of a language, a matter to which we return later in this chapter.

The notion of centrality needs to be understood in a somewhat looser sense with respect to the weighted attribute theory. The prototype constitutes the centre of gravity, as it were, of the category, in that it exhibits the maximum number of attributes which are diagnostic of category membership. The notion of centrality might also be applied to the attributes themselves. An attribute is central to the extent that it (a) has high cue validity, in the limiting case being essential to category membership, and (b) is exhibited by a large number (in the limiting case, by all) of the members of the category and by very few (in the limiting case, by none) of the members of contrasting categories.

Centrality is also at issue in the intensional view of polysemous categories, whereby the different senses of a polysemous word are thought of as radiating out, as it were, from the prototypical sense. A major issue with the intensional approach is methodological. Whereas Rosch's work on the referential aspects of prototype categories was supported by rigorous empirical research, the identification of the central, or "prototypical" sense of a polysemous word – not to mention the identification, enumeration, and characterization of the senses themselves – is largely a matter of introspection and theory-driven speculation. There are, in fact, several ways in which one sense of a polysemous word can be regarded as central, and the different approaches do not always converge on a unique solution.

a) The central sense is taken to be the historically oldest one, the progenitor, as it were, from which the others have been derived by processes of metaphor, metonymy, specialization, or generalization. Accordingly, the "literal" sense of a word is likely to be viewed as more central than its metaphorical uses, while concrete (often spatial) senses are taken as more central than abstract ones.

b) Taking a developmental perspective, the central sense is the one which children first learn and which, as it were, "seeds" the full acquisition of the word. Since children are likely to learn concrete and literal uses before abstract and metaphorical ones, the approach delivers outcomes which are largely consistent with historical development. Especially in the case of the prepositions, however, a fair number of the earliest uses tend to occur in a

range of more or less fixed phrasal locutions (*on TV, over here*); these are uses which would probably be regarded as somewhat peripheral on most radial network accounts (e.g., Hallan 2001; Rice 2003).
c) The central sense is the one which enables semanticists and lexicographers to describe the polysemy most perspicaciously and economically. The central member is the one around which the others cluster, or from which they radiate, like spokes of a wheel.

Attempts have been made to ground network proposals in speakers' subjective estimates of the similarity of different uses of a word (Sandra and Rice 1995). Even so, there is sometimes little consensus on the identity of the central sense, especially with regard to highly polysemous words such as *over*. Brugman/Lakoff consider the central sense of *over* to be "above/across", as in *The bird flew over the field*. Tyler and Evans (2001), on the other hand, regard the "above" sense as central, as in *The bee is hovering over the flower*. Others, yet again, have seen the central sense as involving an up-down arc-like trajectory, as in *The cow jumped over the moon* (Dewell 1994).

3.2 Salience

A category prototype is cognitively more salient than other category members. Research by Rosch and others discovered a number of salience effects, including the following:
a) subjective judgements of goodness of membership. When presented with a category name, subjects are able to grade potential exemplars according to their goodness of membership. Results for a given population tend to be highly reliable, even though individual differences might be quite marked (Barsalou 1987).
b) listing. When presented with a category name, subjects are able to generate lists of exemplars, with more prototypical members being mentioned earlier, faster, and by a larger number of subjects than less central members (Battig and Montague 1969).
c) default member. The prototype is the category member that subjects invoke in the absence of contrary indications. Mention of a "grandmother" is likely to conjure up an image of a good-natured, grey-haired old lady. The default may be overridden once specific information is available about *this* grandmother (Fodor 1980).
d) reasoning. Inferences about a category may be based on the properties of prototypical members, not on properties characteristic of the category as a whole (Rips 1975).

e) asymmetrical similarity judgements. A prototype is a kind of cognitive reference point which tends to "draw in" outlying members, thereby reducing their subjective distance from the prototype. Thus, B (a marginal member) may be judged more similar to A (a more central member) than A is to B (Rips 1975; Rosch 1975).
f) imagability and embodiment. When asked to form a mental image of a category, subjects tend to imagine a prototypical instance. They are able to draw a picture of it, they are able to state its typical parts and their arrangement, and simulate how a person would typically interact with it (Rosch 1978).
g) contrastivity. Rosch's research on colour and the more complex categories studied in her subsequent work, points to the contrastive nature of prototypes. The weighted attributes approach, for example, leads to the identification of a prototype as a category member which is maximally distinct – in terms of its characteristic attributes – from the prototypes of neighbouring categories. The prototypical bird can fly; the prototypical mammal does not.

The salience of more central members is confirmed by other experimental techniques, such as priming and verification tasks. For example, in a lexical decision task, a category name is able to prime the names of more central members more effectively than the names of less central members, while sentences of the form *An A is an X* are judged to be true more quickly if A is a central member of category X than if it is a more marginal member.

3.3 Frequency

Centrality and salience effects need not (though they often do) coincide, and not all of these effects are relevant to all kinds of categories. This is especially true of grammatical categories, as we shall see. In this connection, one further effect needs to be mentioned: frequency.

Frequency – whether of non-linguistic experiences, linguistic forms, linguistic meanings, or form-meaning associations – will likely contribute to cognitive entrenchment, which in turn will map onto cognitive salience and thence onto degrees of prototypicality. We are inclined to suppose that apples, pears, and oranges are good examples of fruit because we encounter them more often than olives, papayas, and pineapples. For speakers of the 1890s the prototypical vehicle was no doubt a horse-drawn carriage, not a new-fangled motor-car. Neither is it surprising that rugby football should be a more salient kind of sport for New Zealanders than it is for North Americans (Marshall and Parr 1996).

Frequency effects are ubiquitous in language (Taylor 2012) and provide crucial input data to usage-based models of grammar and of linguistic knowledge more generally. It is not perhaps surprising that in studies of word usage, and of the interaction of words and the contexts in which they occur, frequency effects are often discussed in terms of prototypicality (e.g., Divjak and Arppe 2013; for a review, see Gries 2014). We need to be wary, however, of uncritically equating relative frequency with degrees of prototypicality, especially when other indications of prototypicality, of the kinds listed in the above sections, are not available or give conflicting results. For example, it is doubtful whether frequency plays a role in the prototype status of focal colours. Do we really encounter a "good red" more frequently than other shades of the colour? Experiments with artificial categories – such as displays of dots or configurations of numbers and letters – have shown that subjects are able to identify a prototype (understood as the configuration from which training exemplars have been derived by distortions of greater or lesser degrees), even though it has never been encountered in training sessions (Posner and Keele 1968).

An appeal to frequency is no doubt useful as a research heuristic, but as a pointer to prototypicality it needs to be supported by other considerations. We should probably not want to regard *be* as the prototypical member of the verb category, even though *be* (and its various forms) turns out to be the most frequent of the English verbs on most word counts. Or take the issue, raised above, of identifying the central sense of a polysemous word. Most linguists, as well as laypersons, I daresay, would want say that the "basic", or "central" uses of *eye*, *hand*, *head*, and *heart* refer to parts of a body, even though metaphorical and metonymic uses are equally frequent, if not more so (Deignan and Potter 2004; Hilpert 2006). Theoretical claims about the derived status of non-literal uses would take precedence over frequency data.

4 Application to grammar

Having looked at some different understandings of the notion of prototype and the range of effects which typically adhere to the prototype, let us now turn to the application of the notion, in its various guises, to the categories of linguistic description.

For some linguistic terms, the application of the prototype notion is (relatively) straightforward. In considering notions such as "dialect", "language", "native speaker", "bilingual speaker", and even "meaning", we can bring to bear the same kinds of considerations that are used to characterize "fruit", "vehicle", and "bird". We might, for example, list the attributes of these categories and assess their cue validity, in this way drawing up a profile of the category prototype. In the case of some terms, we might want to recognize a cluster of related senses, the terms, in other words, would need to be regarded as polysemous. *Meaning* is one such – consider the use of the word in expressions such as *word meaning*, *the meaning of life*, and *the meaning of Halloween*.

Many of the terms used in linguistic description, however, require a more sophisticated approach. This is especially true of those terms which refer to the symbolic resources of a language, that is, units of structure which associate a formal specification with a semantic characterization. At issue are categories such as word classes, patterns of word formation, syntactic constructions, and even such foundational concepts as word, morpheme, clause, and sentence. These categories are subject to both a formal and a semantic specification. The formal specification may refer to the internal make-up of category members, whether phonological, morphological, lexical, or syntactic. The formal specification may also make reference to the distribution of category members in the language, that is, the kinds of structures they are able to occur in and the kinds of items they are likely to co-occur with. Likewise, the semantic characterization may focus on the inherent content of the category as well as on its role in larger semantic structures. All of these aspects are liable to give rise to prototype effects, of one kind of another. Moreover, prototypicality from a formal perspective may not always correspond with semantic prototypicality. From the point of view of its distribution in the language, *explosion* is a pretty good example of the noun category. From the point of view of its semantics, however, it would have to be regarded as somewhat marginal.

5 Lexical categories

The sometimes conflicting results of a formal vs. semantic perspective are nowhere more evident than in the case of the lexical categories ("parts of speech"). Linguistics students learn very early in their career that you cannot identify the nouns in a sentence by looking for the names of persons, places, and things (the essence of the traditional semantic definition). The proper criteria, we teach our students, are distributional. *Explosion* is a noun, even though it seems to refer to an event. This is because the word behaves like a noun and has the internal structure of a noun: it terminates in a noun-forming affix *-ion*; it can pluralize; it can be quantified; it can be modified by an adjective; in combination with a determiner it can be part of a noun phrase, which in turn can function as the subject of a verb, the complement of a preposition, and so on.

These formal characteristics are akin to the attributes of semantic categories such as "bird" or "vehicle", and it is not surprising that they should give rise to similar kinds of representativity effects. *Music* would have to be regarded as a less representative noun than *explosion*, since it does not pluralize; a pluralia tantum noun such as *whereabouts* is even less representative, not only because there is no corresponding singular, but also because the word is virtually restricted to occurring in a possessive environment (*his whereabouts, the whereabouts of the suspect*). *Seem* is a less than prototypical verb because it does not readily occur in progressive and imperative environments, while *beware* is typically restricted to an imperative context or to use as an infinitive. There would, however, be no question about the status of the cited words as, respectively, nouns or verbs. Aarts (2007) discusses such matters in terms of what he calls "subsective gradience", that is, degree of representativity within a category.

The adjective category is notorious for the fact that there do not appear to be any formal attributes which uniquely identify its members. (Adverbs are even more heterogeneous). It is useful here to invoke the notion of cue validity. The fact that (many) adjectives can be used both attributively and predicatively (*a large box, the box is large*) loses some of its diagnostic value in light of the fact that nouns may be similarly distributed (attributive: *an apple pie*; predicative: *Jones is president*). Similarly, prefixation by *un-*, commonly cited as a characteristic of adjective status, has less than optimal cue validity, since quite a few verbs and adverbs can also take the prefix (*to undo, unwillingly*), as can derived nominals (*unimportance, untruth*) and even, occasionally, non-derived nouns (e.g., *unperson*, in Orwell's *1984*). The possibility of modification by an adverb is equally suspect, since verbs also display this property. Practically the only attribute uniquely associated with adjectives is the possibility of gradation (*big, bigger, biggest*), though not all adjectives display this property.

A particularly murky area concerns the differentiation of prepositions, participles, and subordinating conjunctions. We can, to be sure, easily cite prototypical examples of these categories, examples which betray no signs of ambiguous status. As noted earlier, prototypical examples tend to be cognitively salient: they are examples which immediately spring to mind when we are asked to list members of a category and they tend to be maximally contrastive vis-à-vis prototypical examples of neighbouring categories. There can be no question about the prepositional status of *on* in *on the bus*, of the participial status of *thinking* in *Thinking the matter over, I ...*, or about the status of *although* as a subordinating conjunction in *Although it was late, I ...* There are some words, however, which can easily be inserted into each of these three kinds of context; examples include *considering* and *regarding*. These words seem genuinely to blur the distinctiveness of the categories in question.

A notorious case, in English, concerns certain uses of gerundials (the literature is vast: see, however, Hudson 2007: Ch. 4 for a particular innovative solution). What is the lexical category of *saying* in *Without my saying a word*? Being construed with possessive *my*, with the resulting combination being the complement of a preposition, we should want to say that *saying* is a noun (or, more precisely, that *saying a word* has the status of a nominal). Yet *saying* takes a direct object – an unambiguous attribute of a verb. The criteria for classification shift somewhat with respect to the alternative (and semantically equivalent) wording *Without me saying a word*, raising the question whether the categorization of *saying* (and indeed the parsing of the whole expression) also undergoes a shift. And what about *Without her saying a word* – which neutralizes the above distinction?

In the above account of the formal attributes of a lexical category such as "noun", it was necessary to refer to other lexical categories, such as "adjective" and "determiner". How are these categories to be defined, from a formal point of view, if not in terms of their distribution with respect to other lexical categories? A certain degree of circularity enters into the discussion (Smith 2015). If nouns are defined (in part) by their ability to be modified by adjectives, and if adjectives are defined (in part) by their ability to modify nouns, we need some independent means for identifying these categories. One approach is to re-admit a semantic characterization. Prototypical nouns and verbs designate things and events, as per the traditional account and as suggested by the acquisition literature (Clark 2015). Conversely, if a word designates a thing, it will be, with a very high degree of probability, a noun. Semantic considerations thus permit a first and indispensable cut for the classification of word types. Words which do not match the semantic prototypes are then assimilated to the categories largely on the basis of their formal attributes (Taylor 2012). At the same time, the very fact of their membership in the formally defined categories may cause the semantic characteristics of the category prototype to adhere to the words. *Explosion* "reifies" the event, construing it as a thing, such that it can be quantified and can be referred to, and properties can be predicated of it (Langacker 1987).

Another way out of the vicious circle is define the categories with respect to larger containing constructions, themselves subject to both formal and semantic characterizations. Thus, determiners and nouns would be defined by their role in noun phrase constructions, whose semantic import is to refer to entities in the world (or, more generally, in a mental space). We address constructions below.

6 Word structure: derivation, compounding, and blending

Aarts (2007) maintained that between-category, or intersective gradience is virtually absent with respect to lexical categories. The situation is quite different when we turn to the structural aspects of words, namely, their status as morphologically simple vs. their status as derived forms, inflected forms, compounds, or blends.

Once again, one's first inclination is to regard these categories as clearly distinct, and it is not difficult to come up with good examples whose categorization is obvious and unambiguous: *farm* is simplex, *farmer* is a derived nominal, *deer-farm* is a compound, and *brunch* is a blend.

The notion of contrast, implicit in approaches to prototype categories, is also to the forefront when we consider the internal make-up of complex words (or, at least, prototypical examples of derivation, compounding, and blending) (Taylor 2015). The constituent morphemes of a derived word like *farmer* are maximally contrastive on a number of dimensions. The *-er* of *farmer* (a) is semantically schematic (it merely characterizes a person in terms of what they do, the bulk of the semantic content of the word being supplied by the base form *farm*); (b) is phonologically dependent (unlike the stem, *-er* cannot stand alone as an independent form, but must attach to another item); and (c) determines the semantic type of the derived form, namely, as an agentive noun. Compounding is different, in that each component has the status of a phonologically independent and semantically contentful word. Note, however, that properties (a) and (b) are in principle continuous, and may thus be expected to give rise to category fuzziness. This is indeed the case. *Idealism* and *Darwinism* look like standard derivations; however, the fact that one can speak of intellectual *isms* suggests that the words have features of a compound (alternatively, that *ism* has some word-like properties).

Blends are something of an anomaly on standard views of word formation, in that the components are identified solely on the basis of their occurrence in the inputs to the blend and have no symbolic status outside the blend itself; there are, for example, no reasons to propose *br-* and *-unch* as morphemes whose meanings contribute to the meaning of *brunch*. Yet the distinction between blending, compounding, and derivation is fluid. *Infographic, infomercial,* and the like, occupy a space between compounds and blends. *Glitterati* no doubt first made its appearance as a blend (of *glitter* and *literati*); further examples such as *twitterati* suggest the emerging status of *-erati* as a derivational suffix (Kemmer 2003).

Neither is the distinction between compound and phrase immune to category blurring. In principle, the distinction is clear; it is based, amongst other things, on the semantic compositionality of phrases vs. the idiosyncratic meaning of compounds and final stress typical of phrases vs. initial stress characteristic of compounds. Problematic examples are legion (Bauer 1998): *stone wall, London University, High Church*, etc. Pursuing the matter further, we would find that the notion of "word" (namely, as a union of a stable phonologically autonomous form with a stable semantic content, relatively unrestricted in its co-occurrence possibilities) turns out to be less than clear-cut. There may be good reasons, for example, to regard *the* not so much as a word but as a clitic, or at least as a word-like clitic (or as a clitic-like word) (Taylor 2003). Although *the* happens to occupy top position in most frequency counts of English, it is unlikely to spring into people's minds as a good example of a word.

7 Syntactic constructions

As Croft (2001) has argued, the construction is the basic unit of linguistic description. As a matter of fact, there are different ways of defining a construction: as any internally complex form, as an association of a form with a meaning, or even as any linguistic unit (including phonological units) that speakers of a language have internalized (Taylor 2012). For present purposes, however, let us take construction to refer to any structural configuration, whether lexically specified or not, along with its associated semantics.

Given this very broad characterization, the number of constructions in a language is legion (and essentially open-ended). Inevitably, therefore, problems arise when we attempt to identify and enumerate the constructions of a language. Are constructions well-defined entities, clearly demarcated one from another? Or do they exhibit fuzzy boundaries, with some expressions having ambiguous status vis-à-vis more than one construction? Given the topic of this chapter, the question also arises whether constructions have a prototype structure, with some expressions being "better", or more representative instances of the construction than others. If this is the case, on what basis can the construction's prototype be identified?

I address these questions on the basis of a couple of examples. I make no claim that the discussion will be representative of the broad range of constructions in a language. I suspect, however, that many features of the examples will carry over, mutatis mutandis, to the study of other constructions in a language.

a) The middle construction

The middle construction in English (exemplified by *This book sells well*) features a verb which elsewhere in the language is transitive but which in the construction appears as intransitive; the verb takes as its subject a non-agentive, typically a patient entity; middles have a stative interpretation, in that they predicate a stable property of the subject entity (specifically, their propensity to participate in the kind of event designated by the verb) and hence typically appear in the simple present tense; the implied agent of the action may not be mentioned; finally, an adjunct phrase (*well*, *easily*, etc.), specifying the potentiality of the designated property to be manifested, is usually required (Yoshimura and Taylor 2004). It is the co-occurrence of these various features, both syntactic and semantic, which justifies the recognition of the middle as a distinct construction.

Middles contrast with a number of other constructions, which are themselves characterized by a cluster of distinctive semantic and syntactic features. With unaccusatives (*The window broke*, *The door opened*), a normally transitive verb is again used intransitively, with a patient entity as its subject, and again the implied agent remains unspecified. Unlike middles, however, unaccusatives have an event reading and an adjunct phrase is not usually required. Middles also contrast with unergatives, that is, intransitives whose subject performs the named activity (*John cried*).

While prototypical examples of the three constructions can easily be cited – prototypical in the sense that the expressions unambiguously exhibit each of the characteristic features – the violation or blurring of the criteria can lead to host of uncertain examples. *This knife cuts steak easily* would probably still be regarded as a middle, even though the subject is not a patient and the verb takes a direct object. *The door wouldn't open (when I tried to go in)* could refer to a stable property of the door, namely, its "non-open-ability", suggesting the status of the expression as a middle. The expression could also refer to the door's refusal to open on that particular occasion, suggesting its status as an unaccusative. Conceptually, it might be hard to differentiate the two readings; in fact, each seems to entail the other. Take, as another example (sourced from the Internet), *I cry easily over anything*. The verb is intransitive, suggesting the status of an unergative. Yet the sentence also exhibits features of a middle, in that it predicates a stable property of the subject referent in association, moreover, with an adjunct (*easily*) which is often associated with the construction. The three constructions thus exemplify fuzzy boundaries, not unlike the colour categories with which we opened this chapter.

These brief remarks are not intended to cast doubt on the validity of the notion "middle construction" in a grammar of English. They do, however, suggest that the construction is by no means as clearly delineated as many scholars seem to presuppose. A more fruitful approach – one which cannot unfortunately be pursued here – would be to conceptualize the construction as a region in a multi-dimensional "transitivity space", defined by a range of formal and semantic/pragmatic aspects, including such matters as the inherent semantics of the verb, the semantic role of subject nominal, and the referential status of the expression.

b) prenominal possessives
From a formal point of view, prenominal possessives are noun phrases with the internal structure [NP]'s [N], exemplified by *the man's hat*. There is, however, a competing construction, the possessive compound, with the structure [N]'s [N], as exemplified by *(a) children's playground*. The distinction is likely to be blurred whenever the possessor is indefinite or generic, or can be interpreted as such (Rosenbach 2006; Taylor 1996). Consider examples such as *taxpayers' money* and *a man's skull* (in the sense "a human skull"). Possessive compounds, in turn, are in competition with non-possessive compounds, of the kind *passenger seat*. The differentiation is especially problematic in cases where the first component is able to be interpreted as a plural. In principle, orthography should be able to come to the rescue: *students union* vs. *students' union*. The use of the possessive apostrophe, however, is famously unstable, a fact which no doubt reflects the inherent fuzziness of the underlying structural and semantic distinction.

The prenominal possessive is compatible with a wide range of semantic relations between possessor and possessee. The same goes for yet another construction with which the prenominal possessive is in contrast, namely the binomial *of* construction, exemplified by *the woman of the year, a photograph of me, the end of the day*. The two constructions are not always interchangeable; *the year's woman* sounds odd, while *the car of me* is virtually unacceptable. The differences are partly due to the semantic-pragmatic properties of the nominals in a prenominal possessive. The possessor is preferentially high in animacy, has definite reference, and names an entity already introduced into the discourse. The possessed is interpreted as definite and tends to be an entity newly introduced in the discourse; there seems, however, to be no particularly strong constraint against inanimates and even abstracts appearing as possessees.

Interestingly, the semantic relation of possession – the supposedly prototypical value of the construction and the basis for its name – is not all that frequent in running text. The situation, however, is somewhat different for speech directed at infants; here, possession, kinship relations, and body part relations predominate (Stefanowitsch and Gries 2005). There is another reason why these relations might be especially associated with the construction. When it comes to designating a person's material possessions or their kin relations, the prenominal possessive is the default option, much preferred over a binomial *of* expression. In cases where the possessor is non-human or inanimate, however, the two constructions are more likely to be in competition. *By year's end* occurs 414 times in the 450 million words of the Corpus of Contemporary American English (COCA: Davies 2008), as against more than twice as many examples (925) of *by the end of the year*.

By all accounts, *year's end* would have to be regarded as a highly untypical possessive; it may even be disputed whether it is a prenominal possessive or a possessive compound. (It is worth noting, by the way, that even possessive compounds tend to favour, as their first element, nouns towards the top of the animacy scale). What is remarkable, however, is that *by year's end* appears to have something of the status of a fixed expression. While other nouns can replace *year*, they do so with rapidly decreasing frequency: *day* (107), *week* (100), *month* (98), *summer* (52), *season* (51), *war* (35), *decade* (31), *century* (26), and *game* (11). The same is true when we try to replace the preposition: *at year's end* (88 examples), *before* (52), *until* (10), *through* (6), *near* and *to* (4 each), *toward* (3), *till* and *from* (one each; data derived from COCA). When it comes to replacing the final nominal, *end*, we draw a complete blank. In spite of the semantic plausibility of the expressions, there are no examples in the corpus of *by year's start*, *by year's beginning*, *by year's middle*, and only one solitary instance of *at year's start* (vis-à-vis 60 examples of *at the start of the year*).

The prenominal possessive construction is highly productive; it is compatible with a wide range of semantic relations, in association with a wide choice of possessor and possessee nominals. Nevertheless, as we have seen, as expressions deviate from its prototypical values (such as animate and discourse-old possessor, discourse-new possessee) we encounter a certain degree of idiomaticity and some unexpected gaps in usage. The example suggests that the catalogue of prototype effects presented earlier in this chapter needs to be extended to include degree of productivity. As expressions deviate more and more from the prototypical value of a construction, they become increasingly subject to lexical and other kinds of idiosyncratic constraints.

c) For weeks on end

Constructions can be studied with an eye on the lexical items which can occur in them. The interaction has been insightfully studied by Stefanowitsch and Gries (2003) with their notion of collostruction. On the one hand, a construction tends to prefer certain lexical items, or items exhibiting certain semantic/pragmatic properties, in its various slots; on the other hand, a lexical item may

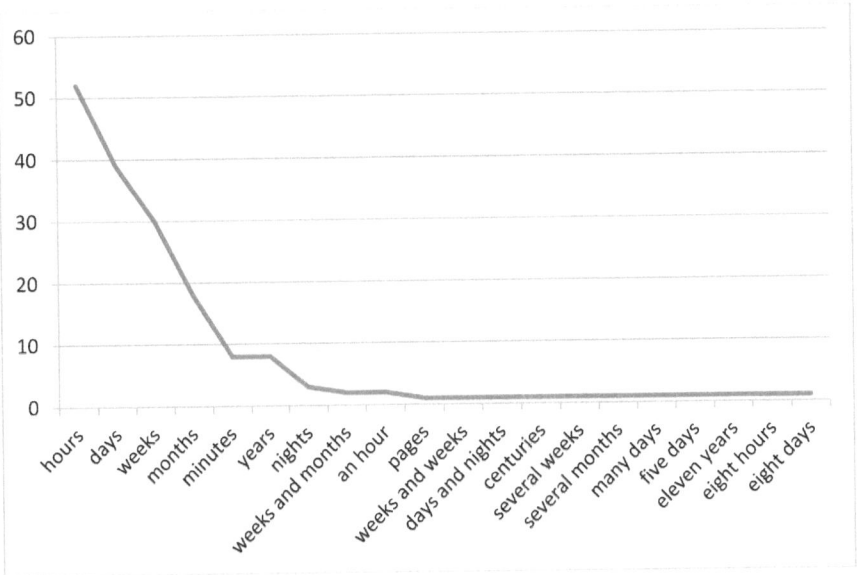

Fig. 7.1: Frequency of expressions of the form [for NP on end] in the BNC.

occur preferentially in a certain construction. Combining the two perspectives makes it possible to identify preferred configurations, which Goldberg (2006) and Gries (2003) have no hesitation in referring to as a construction's prototype.

For my third example I look at one of the myriad phraseological constructions from this perspective. *For [NOUN$_{plural}$] on end* is lexically specified apart from one open slot, which in this case can be filled by a plural noun designating a period of time. Semantically, the construction suggests a subjective experience of the passing of time. It is as if a person is so involved in, or bored by, a situation that she is no longer aware of how many time units have elapsed. The most frequent instantiation in the BNC is *for hours on end*; other nouns, in decreasing order of frequency, which can occur in the construction include *days, weeks, months, minutes,* and *years* (see Fig. 7.1).

Whether we should regard the relative frequency of these nouns as prototype effects is moot. (Should we, for example, say that the prototypical use of the word *unmitigated* is in collocation with *disaster*? Or should we simply say that *unmitigated* typically collocates with *disaster*, and leave it at that?) What is of interest, however, is that we also encounter deviations from the canonical phraseology, albeit with much reduced frequencies. There are occasional examples of repeated and coordinated nominals (*for weeks and weeks on end, for weeks and months on end*), examples with a specific number of time units (*for five days on end*), and even sporadic examples where a single time unit is stated (*for an hour on end*) – the latter usage being somewhat at variance with the proposed semantic value of the construction. It is to be noted, however, that these deviations tend to make use of lexical items selected from the upper frequency range (*hour, month, day*), and in this respect are constrained by what may indeed be regarded as the construction's prototypical instances. *For one century on end* deviates too far from the construction's prototype; there are no corpus examples, and even a Google search failed to return any instances.

The reverse J-shaped distribution in Fig. 7.1 is Zipfian: a small number of types make up the lion's share of the construction's tokens, while a large number of types constitute only a tiny minority of the tokens. In this case, frequency stands out as the principal marker of prototypicality. The long tail of the distribution is largely made up of types which exemplify distortions, of various kinds, from the more prototypical (most frequent) types.

8 Conclusion

In the first part of the chapter I listed the various prototype effects that have been found in relation to the referential categories studied by Rosch and others. These cluster around centrality and salience effects. When the notion of prototype was extended to the study of the semantic structure of polysemous words (*over* being one of the earliest studied examples), a rather different understanding of prototype was needed, one which was based more firmly in the notion of structural centrality. The application of the notion to the grammatical categories of a language (especially those which associate a formal and a semantic specification) raises some further issues, in particular, the need to align prototypicality of form with prototypicality of meaning. Prototypes as the locus of structural and semantic contrast also came into focus. "Good" examples of noun and verb, of word and bound morpheme, of compound and phrase, of middles, unaccusatives, and unergatives, and so on, maximize the distinctiveness of the categories, thereby legitimizing the categories in the linguist's grammar, notwithstanding the plethora of less representative and even ambiguous examples which are easily attested. Indeed, the notion of prototype is valued to the extent that it enables the researcher to bring some order to the inherent messiness and fuzziness of natural language.

Frequency does not always correlate with prototypicality. Nevertheless, frequency does play a crucial role in the study of constructions and the items which are available to fill their various slots. Productivity and idiomaticity also emerge as reflexes of the structure of constructional categories.

9 References

Aarts, Bas (2007): *Syntactic Gradience: The Nature of Grammatical Indeterminacy*. Oxford: Oxford University Press.

Barsalou, Laurence (1987): The instability of graded structure: Implications for the nature of concepts. In: U. Neisser (ed.), *Concepts and Conceptual Development: Ecological and Intellectual Factors in Categorization*, 101–140. Cambridge: Cambridge University Press.

Battig, William F. and William E. Montague (1969): Category norms for verbal items in 56 categories. A replication and extension of the Connecticut category norms. *Journal of Experimental Psychology Monographs* 80: 1–46.

Bauer, Laurie (1998): When is a sequence of two nouns a compound in English? *English Language and Linguistics* 2: 65–86.

Brugman, Claudia and George Lakoff ([1988] 2006): Cognitive topology and lexical networks. In: D. Geeraerts (ed.), *Cognitive Linguistics: Basic Readings*, 109–139. Berlin: Mouton de Gruyter.

Clark, Eve (2015): First words. In: J. R. Taylor (ed.), *The Oxford Handbook of the Word*, 512–535. Oxford: Oxford University Press.

Croft, William (2001): *Radical Construction Grammar: Syntactic Theory in Typological Perspective*. Oxford: Oxford University Press.

Davies, Mark (2008): The Corpus of Contemporary American English (COCA). Available online at http://www.americancorpus.org

Deignan, Alice and L. Potter (2004): A corpus study of metaphors and metonyms in English and Italian. *Journal of Pragmatics* 36: 1231–1252.

Dewell, Robert (1994): *Over* again: Image-schema transformations in semantic analysis. *Cognitive Linguistics* 5: 351–380.

Divjak, Dagmar and Antti Arppe (2013): Extracting prototypes from exemplars: What can corpus data tell us about concept representation? *Cognitive Linguistics* 24: 221–274.

Fodor, Jerry (1980): The present status of the innateness controversy. In: *Representations: Philosophical Essays on the Foundations of Cognitive Science*, 257–316. Cambridge: MIT Press.

Geeraerts, Dirk (1987): Introduction: Prospects and problems of prototype theory. *Linguistics* 27: 587–612.

Givón, Talmy (1979): *On Understanding Grammar*. New York: Academic Press.

Goldberg, Adele (2006): *Constructions at Work*. Oxford: Oxford University Press.

Gries, Stefan Th. (2003): Towards a corpus-based identification of prototypical instances of constructions. *Annual Review of Cognitive Linguistics* 1: 1–27.

Gries, Stefan Th. (2014): Corpus and quantitative methods. In: J. Littlemore and J. Taylor (eds.), *The Bloomsbury Companion to Cognitive Linguistics*, 279–300. London: Bloomsbury.

Hallan, Naomi (2001): Paths to prepositions? A corpus-based study of the acquisition of a lexico-grammatical category. In: J. Bybee and P. Hopper (eds.), *Frequency and the Emergence of Linguistic Structure*, 91–120. Amsterdam: Benjamins.

Heider, Eleanor (1972): Universals in color naming and memory. *Journal of Experimental Psychology* 93: 10–20.

Hilpert, Martin (2006): Keeping an eye on the data? Metonymies and their patterns. In: A. Stefanowitsch and S. Th. Gries (eds.), *Corpus-based Approaches to Metaphor and Metonymy*, 123–152. Berlin: Mouton de Gruyter.

Hudson, Richard (2007): *Language Networks: The New Word Grammar*. Oxford: Oxford University Press.
Kemmer, Suzanne (2003): Schemas and lexical blends. In: H. Cuyckens, Th. Berg, R. Dirven, and K.-U. Panther (eds.), *Motivation in Language*, 69–97. Amsterdam: Benjamins.
Kuhl, Patricia (1991): Human adults and human infants show a "perceptual magnet effect" for prototypes of speech categories, monkeys do not. *Perception and Psychophysics* 50: 93–107.
Lakoff, George (1987): *Women, Fire, and Dangerous Things. What Categories Reveal about the Mind*. Chicago: Chicago University Press.
Langacker, Ronald. W. (1987): Nouns and verbs. *Language* 63: 53–94.
Marshall, Caroline E. and Wendy V. Parr (1996): New Zealand norms for a subset of Battig and Montague's (1969) categories. *New Zealand Journal of Psychology* 25: 24–29.
Murphy, Gregory (2002): *The Big Book of Concepts*. Cambridge: MIT Press.
Posner, Michael (1986): Empirical studies of prototypes. In: C. Craig (ed.), *Noun Classes and Categorization*, 53–61. Amsterdam: Benjamins.
Posner, Michael and Steven W. Keele (1968): On the genesis of abstract ideas. *Journal of Experimental Psychology* 77: 353–363.
Ramscar, Michael (volume 1): Categorization. Berlin/Boston: De Gruyter Mouton.
Rice, Sally (2003): Growth of a lexical network: Nine English prepositions in acquisition. In: H. Cuyckens, R. Dirven, and J. R. Taylor (eds.), *Cognitive Approaches to Lexical Semantics*, 243–280. Berlin: Mouton de Gruyter.
Rips, Lance J. (1975): Inductive judgments about natural categories. *Journal of Verbal Learning and Verbal Behavior* 14: 665–81.
Rosch, Eleanor (1973): On the internal structure of perceptual and semantic categories. In: T. E. Moore (ed.), *Cognitive Development and the Acquisition of Language*, 111–144. New York: Academic Press.
Rosch, Eleanor (1975): Cognitive reference points. *Cognitive Psychology* 7: 532–547.
Rosch, Eleanor (1978): Principles of categorization. In: E. Rosch and B. Lloyd (eds.), *Cognition and Categorization*, 27–48. Hillsdale, NJ: Lawrence Erlbaum.
Rosenbach, Anette (2006): Descriptive genitives in English: a case study on constructional gradience. *English Language and Linguistics* 10: 77–118.
Sandra, Dominiek and Sally Rice (1995): Network analyses of prepositional meaning: mirroring whose mind – the linguist's or the language user's? *Cognitive Linguistics* 6: 89–130.
Smith, Mark (2015): Word categories. In: J. R. Taylor (ed.), *The Oxford Handbook of the Word*, 175–195. Oxford: Oxford University Press.
Stefanowitsch, Anatol and Stefan Th. Gries (2003): Collostructions: Investigating the interaction of words and constructions. *International Journal of Corpus Linguistics* 8: 209–243.
Stefanowitsch, Anatol and Stefan Th. Gries (2005): Covarying collexemes. *Corpus Linguistics and Linguistic Theory* 1: 1–43.
Taylor, John R. (1996): *Possessives in English*. Oxford: Oxford University Press.
Taylor, John R. (2003): *Linguistic Categorization*. Oxford: Oxford University Press.
Taylor, John R. (2008): Prototypes in cognitive linguistics. In: P. Robinson and N. Ellis (eds.), *Handbook of Cognitive Linguistics and Second Language Acquisition*, 39–65. London: Routledge.
Taylor, John R. (2012): *The Mental Corpus: How Language is Represented in the Mind*. Oxford: Oxford University Press.

Taylor, John R. (2015): Word-formation in Cognitive Grammar. To appear in: P. Müller, I. Ohnheiser, S. Olsen, and F. Raine (eds.), *HSK Word-formation*, 158–187. Berlin: de Gruyter.

Tyler, Andrea and Vyvyan Evans (2001): Reconsidering prepositional polysemy networks: The case of over. *Language* 77: 724–765.

Yoshimura, Kimihiro and John R. Taylor (2004): What makes a good middle? The role of qualia in the interpretation and acceptability of middle expressions in English. *English Language and Linguistics* 8: 293–321.

Devin M. Casenhiser and Giulia M. L. Bencini
Chapter 8: Argument structure constructions

1 Introduction

Traditional Generativist (e.g., Chomsky 1957) theory approaches the notion of argument structure by identifying two components that are involved in specifying the meaning and form of an utterance. The first is a set of culturally determined strings (lexical items). The second is a set of universal and innate "linking rules" that map aspects of sentence meaning onto a structural representation of its form (syntax). Central to these approaches is the notion that aspects of sentence meaning, specifically relational meaning ("who does what to whom") as well as sentence form are assumed to be projections of the semantic and syntactic properties of the main verb (we refer to this as the projectionist account of argument structure). General linking rules plus a number of structural principles connect an underlying representation of the utterance to the surface ordering of words. Most traditional generativist theories also assume multi-stratal syntactic levels of representation intervening between meaning and surface structure. In generativist theory, then, the learning issue is simplified since the language learner only has to learn the meaning of lexical items (in particular of verbs), and then select the proper underlying form and linking rules that correspond to the spoken language.

More recently, however, a new approach to argument structure has appeared. This approach, called the constructional approach, eliminates the need for many of the traditional assumptions mentioned above. A number of variations of the constructional approach to argument structure exist (e.g., Birner and Ward 1998; Croft 2001; Fillmore et al. 1988; Lakoff 1987; Langacker 1987; Michaelis and Lambrecht 1996, among others; cf. Goldberg 2013), but these approaches share a set of core assumptions that are sufficient to distinguish them sharply from traditional generative approaches, even when not every single assumption is adopted (Goldberg 2013). Following Goldberg (2013), key tenets of the constructional approach are that 1) knowledge of language consists of learned form-meaning pairings; 2) representations are surface-oriented and non-derivational; 3) constructions exist at different levels of generalization, from the more abstract to the more concrete and lexical.

The specific approach that has been best studied empirically is represented by Goldberg's (1995, 2006) work (though we stress that much of the work is applicable to other constructional approaches). Within a constructional approach to grammar, constructions may be morphemes, words, idioms, phrases or abstract linguistic patterns. Argument structure constructions are learned form-function pairings that are posited to exist independently of the specific verbs in the sentence (see also Diessel volume 2). They are networks of features specifying mappings between syntactic form and semantic-pragmatic function. The patterns are typically specified in terms of semantic and or "functional" levels of processing (as in (1) below), though they may also be specified in terms of word order (as in the NP construction). In addition, constructions may be fully abstract as in the caused-motion construction in (1) or they may be partially lexically filled as in the What's X doing Y construction (Kay and Fillmore 1999) (2).

Example	Construction Name: Pattern
(1) om put the spoon into the drawer.	Caused-Motion Construction: <NP$_{agent}$> <verb$_{motion}$[1]> <NP$_{patient}$> <PP$_{path}$>
(2) What's that fly doing in my soup?	What's X doing Y: What's X doing Y?

Constructions may be combined to form other constructions so long as their specifications do not conflict. The form or meaning of the containing construction, however, is not predictable by the sum of its parts, but is itself unique. Thus, although the caused-motion construction contains an NP and PP construction, its form and meaning are not predictable by the process of stringing NPs and PPs together with a verb.

If argument structure constructions (henceforth *constructions*) themselves are associated directly with relational meaning independent of the meaning of the verb, it should be possible to examine empirically the contribution of the construction to sentence meaning in various sentence comprehension tasks. Likewise, if constructions mediate the mapping between sentence meaning and form, constructions should also be detectable in sentence production tasks. In this chapter we first review evidence from comprehension and production studies that speakers access constructions in language use. Since constructions are *learned* form-meaning pairings, we then move on to examine the evidence that constructions are in fact learned and learnable.

---

[1] The motion may be real or implied.

2 Constructions are associated with meaning independent of the verb

The first study to examine the contribution of constructions to sentence meaning was Bencini and Goldberg (2000). The study compared the semantic contribution of the construction with that of the verb in a categorization task where native speakers of English were asked to sort sentences based on meaning and to provide explanations for their sortings. The stimuli were obtained by crossing four verbs (two semantically light verbs: *get*, *take*, and two semantically rich verbs: *throw*, *slice*) with four different constructions (Transitive: Verb Object, e.g., *Michelle got the book*; Ditransitive: V Object1 Object2, e.g., *Chris threw Linda the pencil*; Resultative: Verb Object Result, e.g., *Nancy sliced the tire open*; Caused Motion: Verb Object Location, e.g., *Kim took the rose into the house*). Participants were instructed to sort the sixteen sentences by "overall sentence meaning" into groups of four. They were told that the purpose of the study was to understand how people sort sentences according to meaning and that there was no right or wrong answer. Non-linguistic categorization research has shown that there is a robust domain-general tendency towards "one-dimensional sorting" even with stimuli and categories that are by design created to induce multidimensional sorting (e.g., Medin et al. 1987). In Bencini and Goldberg's stimuli the one-dimensional sorting bias should be driven by the fact that the sentences shared a common verb. In spite of this bias, results showed that speakers categorized sentences based on overall meaning by taking into account the overall argument structure of sentences in addition to verbs. Participants' explanations for their sorting decisions, as judged by independent judges, showed that they were paying attention to sentence meaning rather than verb tokens. In some cases the explanations corresponded remarkably to the kinds of abstract relational meanings posited for constructions. For example, for a ditransitive sort, one protocol read: "In this pile there were two people, and one person was doing something for the other person" (cf. Ditransitive Meaning: X causes Y to receive Z). For a transitive sort, another protocol read: "In this pile a person is just doing something" (cf. Transitive Meaning: X acts on Y). Bencini and Goldberg took these results to indicate a contribution of sentence structure to sentence meaning, independent of the contribution made by the meaning of the verb. They hypothesized that participants overcame the one-dimensional sorting bias because constructions predict overall sentence meaning better than verbs.

Another series of studies that examined the semantics associated with sentence patterns was conducted by Kako (2006). Participants saw sentences composed of novel words appearing in various constructions, and were asked how likely each was to involve the semantic properties associated with the construction. For example, participants saw the sentence *The rom gorped the blick to the dax* and were asked "How likely is it that gorping involves someone or something changing location?". Results were consistent with the hypothesis that syntactic frames carry meaning independently of the meaning of verbs: likely properties for each construction received significantly higher ratings than did unlikely properties.

Additional comprehension studies that show the importance of constructions in determining aspects of sentence interpretation are the studies by Kaschak and Glenberg (2000) and Goldwater and Markman (2009). Both studies use novel verbs derived from nouns. In Kaschak and Glenberg's study, participants were given short passages that were designed to set up a transfer scenario. They were then asked to paraphrase sentences containing the novel verbs (e.g., *crutch*) and to answer questions related to the semantics of the event. Kaschack and Glenberg found that different constructions influenced speaker's interpretations of the novel verbs. If the verb occurred in the ditransitive construction (e.g., *She crutched him the apple*) they were more likely to say that sentence meant that she used the crutch to transfer him the apple. If the verb appeared in the transitive construction (e.g., *She crutched him*) they interpreted the sentence to mean that she hit him over the head with a crutch.

Goldwater and Markman (2009) used denominal verbs that required a change of state (e.g., the noun *sauce* used as a denominal verb *to sauce* suggesting a process of turning something into a sauce), and presented them either in a passive construction (*The ripe tomatoes were sauced expertly to compliment the pasta at the gala dinner*) or a middle construction (*The ripe tomatoes had sauced expertly to compliment the pasta at the gala dinner*). Speakers should have more difficulty making sense of sentences using the verb *sauce* in the middle construction than sentences in the passive because the event structure associated with the middle construction does not entail agency, while the event structure of the passive *does* entail agency. Indeed, participants judged middle constructions with novel denominal verbs more nonsensical than passive constructions containing the same novel verbs. Critically, agency could not be contributed by the verb because these verbs were novel.

The comprehension studies reviewed so far show that constructions play a role in speaker's interpretations of sentences. The studies, however, leave open the possibility of a strategic or meta-linguistic component to participants' responses. Johnson and Goldberg (2012) addressed this concern with an online study to determine whether abstract semantics is automatically associated with syntactic frames and whether this is also true of constructions instantiated with "Jabberwocky" sentences constructed entirely with nonsense open-class words.

The paradigm was a lexical decision task requiring that participants rapidly decide whether a word presented on the computer screen is a real word or not. Before each lexical decision trial, participants read a Jabberwocky sentence instantiating one of four constructions (Ditransitive: *He daxed her the norp*; Resultative: *She jorped it miggy*; Caused-motion: *He lorped it on the molp*; Removal: *She vakoed it from her*). There were two semantic congruency conditions between the verb and the preceding construction: congruent and incongruent. For example, when *gave* was preceded by the ditransitive construction (e.g., *He jorped him the brap*), it is "congruent;" when *gave* is preceded by the removal construction it is incongruent. Verbs were high frequency associates of the construction or low frequency associates. High frequency associates are verbs that most frequently occur in the construction as determined by corpus studies. For example, *give* is the most frequent verb that occurs in the ditransitive. Low frequency associates are verbs that appear in the construction, but less frequently. For example, *hand* occurs in the ditransitive (e.g., *She handed him something*), but less frequently than *give* does. Results showed that when the construction and the verb were congruent, constructions elicited (*primed*) faster reaction times (RTs) compared to when they were incongruent. Moreover, constructions primed both high associate verbs, that is both verbs with which they regularly occur and verbs with which they occur less frequently. The results suggest that 1) constructions prime verb semantics during sentence comprehension, and 2) that syntactic patterns are associated with semantics even when they contain no open class lexical items.

3 Constructions mediate the mapping from "thought" to "talk" in language production

Evidence for verb-independent constructions as processing units at work in production comes from a particularly powerful experimental technique: structural priming. Structural priming refers to the tendency of speakers to produce previously experienced sentence patterns in their subsequent utterances. The priming logic allows us to draw inferences about the dimensions to which the cognitive architecture is sensitive. If processing of a prime stimulus influences the processing of a subsequent stimulus (the target), we can infer that the cognitive system is sensitive to the overlapping dimensions between the prime and the target. Priming has been used to investigate linguistic representations both in adults (Branigan 1995 et al.; Bencini 2002, 2013; Goldberg 2006) and children (e.g., Bencini and Valian 2008). In the classic implementation by Bock (1986), constructional priming was demonstrated with active vs. passive and double object vs. prepositional dative constructions. Speakers were more likely to describe two-participant transitive events (e.g., a picture of dog chasing a man) with a passive if they previously heard and repeated an unrelated passive sentence with different nouns and verbs (e.g., *The 747 was alerted by the airport control tower*). Whereas these results demonstrate the existence of verb-independent constructional priming in language production, what remains unclear is the nature of the semantic information supporting the priming. There are differences among authors with respect to whether they recognize semantic roles loosely corresponding to traditional thematic/event roles (or abstract relational meaning in constructional terms) such as AGENT, THEME, LOCATION, or whether the generalizations refer to more fine-grained semantic properties such as animacy and concreteness. Evidence against a thematic-role account is that structural priming appears not to depend on the identity of thematic roles in prime and target sentences. Bock and Loebell (1990, Experiment 1) found that prepositional locatives (e.g., *The wealthy widow drove the Mercedes to the church*) primed prepositional dative descriptions to the same degree as prepositional dative primes (e.g., *The wealthy widow gave the Mercedes to the church*). The prepositional locative and the prepositional dative have similar surface structural configurations (NP [V NP [P NP] PP] VP), but they differ in the event roles associated with the prepositional argument. In the prepositional locative, the prepositional phrase encodes the location of the action, while in the dative it encodes the recipient. A second experiment found stronger evidence against a purely thematic-role account of structural repetition (Bock and Loebell 1990, Experiment 2). Locative sentences like *The 747 was landing by the control tower* primed passive descriptions as much as did passives like *The 747 was alerted by the control tower*. The locatives and passives had similar surface structures (NP [AUX V [P NP] PP] VP), but the locatives had agents as subjects, while the passives had patients as subjects. Thematic role overlap per se did not increase structural priming: locatives and passives were equally effective primes for passive descriptions. The authors took these results to suggest that structural priming does not depend on thematic overlap between prime and target sentences. Instead of thematic roles, Bock et al. (1992) proposed that basic semantic features guide language production. Using once again a priming paradigm, they varied the animacy of the subjects of active and passive sentences, and found that an animate subject in the priming sentence increased the tendency to place animate entities as subjects in the target descriptions. Animacy priming was independent of structural priming, i.e., independent of the tendency to reuse the active or passive structure of priming sentences.

One problem in determining whether thematic roles play a role in structural priming is that in English, thematic role variations are typically accompanied by differences in sentence structure (e.g., active, passive) and/or animacy (e.g., ditransitive, prepositional dative). Chang et al. (2003), however, tested thematic-role priming without the confounding influences of animacy or structural changes, using locative constructions (the so called spray-load alternation) in which crucially 1) the order of constituents varies within the same syntactic structures and 2) both arguments are typically inanimate. In the locative alternation the order of the theme (the object that moves) and the location (the place that is moved to) vary within the same surface structure, traditionally NP [V NP [P NP] PP] VP. For example, in *The man sprayed wax on the car*, *wax* is the theme and *car* is its location. The alternative order puts the location before the theme, as in *The man sprayed the car with wax*. Priming of the structural configuration should not differ, but if the order of thematic roles matters, theme-location orders should prime other theme-location orders more than location-theme orders: i.e., *The man sprayed wax on the car* should prime *The workers scuffed dirt across the kitchen floor* more than *The workers scuffed the kitchen floor with dirt*. If thematic roles are not at work in production, no differences are expected between conditions with respect to priming. Consistent with a thematic role account of priming, results showed increased use of the location-theme orders after location-theme orders in the prime, and increased use of theme-location orders after theme-location orders in the prime.

The remaining inconsistent result that supports the notion that priming in production does not depend on thematic role overlap is Bock and Loebell (1990, Experiment 2) showing that Locative sentences like *The 747 was landing by the control tower* prime passives as much as passives like *The 747 was alerted by the control tower*.

We believe that part of the debate arises from the difference between defining constructions as static knowledge representations versus dealing with the processes of language production. The process of language production by definition is meaning driven, in that it starts out with a conceptual representation in the speaker's mind (the *message*) and ends with a grammatically encoded utterance. Therefore finding that at some point during the process of producing a sentence the processor is sensitive to form and less to meaning is not evidence against constructions. Moreover, two important features of the priming experiments using Bock's original paradigm (including Bock and Loebell 1990) are the nature of the priming task, and the nature of the stimuli. Unlike comprehension priming (which measures latencies), production priming examines how people describe pictures in front of them. In Bock and Loebell's Experiment 2, the fact that the surface similarity between locative sentences and passives equally primed participants to describe target pictures using a passive sentence is not surprising on a constructional account. First, construction grammar recognizes that sentences have both form and meaning, and that these are distinct types of information and can be independently accessed by the cognitive system. Second, in the classic production priming paradigm, the semantic support for using a passive is always present in the visual stimuli: target pictures for active/passive priming are events that lend themselves to passive descriptions even without priming. They are pictures of events in which the patient/theme is animate and or salient relative to the agent, e.g., "a bee stinging a man", "a truck hitting a nurse", "lightning striking a church".

The importance of the production priming studies with respect to constructions is that it points to representations that are in all respects "like" constructions in terms of their level of abstraction and in the non-derivational nature of the mapping (Bock et al. 1992). We therefore take the existence of verb-independent priming as strong converging evidence from the psycholinguistics of production for the cognitive reality of constructions.

4 Learning argument structure constructions

An important question and source of debate in acquisition research is whether and when children's early multi-word utterances reflect generalizations over verbs. Until recently, comprehension and production data in child language pointed to a "paradox" in which children appeared to rely on more abstract representations in comprehension than production (see Tomasello 2000, for a review).

Constructions, while being abstract in the sense that they contain open slots and generalizations over classes of words (e.g., verb, noun-phrase) and meanings (e.g., X causes Y to move to Z), are not so abstract that they cannot be learned on the basis of surface patterns in much the same way that other patterns perceived in the environment are learned – that is, through the use of general cognitive abilities. Early research on constructional learning was designed to show that constructions are learned on the basis of input rather than being innate. Like projectionist accounts, this research focused on the central role of the verb, and suggested that constructions are learned on a verb-by-verb basis. That is, while children are able to demonstrate the use of some verbs in a given construction, they are unable to use other verbs in the same construction (cf. Roberts 1983). So a given child might be able to act out *Big Bird tickled Cookie Monster* but be unable to act out *Big Bird hugged Cookie Monster*. Tomasello's (1992) verb island hypothesis makes a similar claim: children initially construct separate verb-specific schemas representing the verb's morphological and syntactic properties (e.g., <tickler> *tickle* <ticklee>). It is only after much exposure to similar patterns with other verbs (<hugger> *hug* <huggee>, and so forth) that the child forms an abstract schema, or construction: <agent> <verb> <patient>.

Subsequent research sought to corroborate this general pattern through experimental, rather than corpus-based results, and to develop a timeline for the shift from item-based constructions to abstract schemas. Akhtar and Tomasello (1997) conducted the first such study in which the authors crucially used novel verbs to eliminate the possibility that children were relying on previously learned verb-specific patterns during testing. The authors tested 2- and 3-year-olds' comprehension (via act-out tasks) and production of reversible transitive sentences. They found that as demonstrated by previous work (e.g., Olguin and Tomasello 1993), children could produce and comprehend the novel verbs with the same patients and agents that children heard during training. However, younger children generally did not produce the verbs in constructions with patients and agents different from the ones they heard the verbs used with during training. It was not until the age of about 3 (2;9–3;8) that children were able to comprehend reversible sentences using the novel verbs and agent/patient combinations different from the ones encountered during training (cf. also Abbot-Smith et al. 2001).

These studies mark an important departure from projectionist accounts. Because the projectionist account posits innate linking rules that dictate the form and meaning of an utterance by mapping syntactic positions on a formal template to the semantic positions of a verb's meaning, the template and linking rules need only be *identified*, not learned. Accordingly, children's productions are not predicted to show a pattern of initially conservative (i.e., verb-specific) usage. This notion has generated some controversy. Gertner et al. (2006), for example, found that children as young as 21 months are able to correctly identify scenes described using novel verbs in transitive sentences. The authors suggest that this is evidence that children's understanding of the transitive pattern is not tied to a particular lexical item, adding that children's performance does not seem to be influenced by their vocabularies since they failed to find any significant correlations between performance and vocabulary size and because 21-month-olds have rather small vocabularies to begin with. Moreover, 21 months is earlier than the age at which the previously mentioned studies suggest schema-based constructions develop. Dittmar and colleagues (Dittmar et al. 2008), however, argue that the results obtained by Gertner and colleagues were due largely to methodology. In particular, they suggest that the preferential looking paradigm used a practice phase (as is common) in which children were primed with several transitive sentences using the same nouns in the same syntactic roles and with the same syntactic marking as in the test sentences. Crucially, Dittmar and colleagues were only able to replicate the results of Gertner and colleagues when they also employed the target practice/training phase. Children, however, failed to show generalization when a more neutral training phase was used to expose children to the materials and methods of the study.

On the other hand, early construction-learning doesn't appear to be an all-or-nothing situation either (although early conservativism in construction use is well-established). Evidence that young children generalize to the level of constructions to some extent comes from structural priming studies similar to the adult language production studies reviewed in section 3. Bencini and Valian (2008) examined priming in young three-year-olds (ages 2;11–3;6) in the absence of verb overlap, and controlling for animacy. During priming, the experimenter described a picture (e.g., *The milk is stirred by the spoon*) and then the child repeated the utterance. This was followed by a "Your Turn" trial, in which the child described a different picture (e.g., a picture of a hammer cracking an egg). The results showed abstract priming of passive sentences, suggesting that 3-year-olds may produce at least some verb-independent constructions.

A crucial tenet of construction grammar is that learners are motivated to abstract to the level of the construction to determine the meanings of the sentences they hear. To examine whether constructional forms are predictive of sentence meaning in the naturally occurring input that children hear, Goldberg et al. (2005) examined a corpus of child directed speech to investigate how consistently the meaning of a construction was encoded by the meaning of the verb used in the construction on the one hand, and the meaning of the construction itself on the other.

The authors looked at two constructions: caused-motion, and ditransitive and examined verbs and constructions in terms of their cue validity and category validity. Cue validity is the probability that an entity belongs to a certain category given the occurrence of a certain cue or feature. Category validity is the inverse: the probability that an entity will have a certain cue or feature given that it is a member of a certain category. In the study, the authors investigated the cue validity of verbs for sentence meaning (e.g., the probability that a sentence [the object] has the meaning of "caused-motion" [the category] given that the verb is *put* [the cue]. Likewise, they investigated the category validity of verbs in sentences (i.e., the probability that a sentence with a caused-motion meaning would contain the verb *put*). Their analyses found that while some verbs had perfect cue validity – that is, they perfectly predicted the constructions that they would appear in (e.g., *put* in the caused-motion construction) – the cue validity of most other verbs was quite low. In fact, they found the cue validity of constructions to be at least as good as the cue validity of individual verbs. In contract, the authors found that constructions have much higher category validity than do verbs. That is, given a caused-motion meaning, for example, a sentence is much more likely to be framed in a caused-motion construction than it is to contain any particular verb (e.g., *put*). This is due to the fact that there is such a large number of different verbs that can appear in a given construction, and since only a few of the verbs – typically those called general purpose or light verbs – encode a meaning the same as the construction, the average category validity of verbs approaches zero as more verbs are considered in the analysis. This leads us to conclude that constructions are at least as useful for determining the meaning of an utterance as are verbs, but they occur with a given meaning more consistently than do verbs in general.

One might also ask whether the learner is able to use the distributional properties of the input to determine what *not* to say. That is, to determine that *She told her the news* is acceptable while *She explained her the news* sounds odd (examples from Goldberg 2011). Several researchers (e.g., Bowerman 1996; Goldberg 2006, 2011; Pinker 1989) have pointed out that the notion of entrenchment – the idea that we choose one way of expressing an idea simply because of the high frequency with which it occurs – is not an entirely sufficient explanation since it doesn't account for why some verbs, which occur with disproportionately high frequency in one argument structure construction are still acceptable when used in a different argument structure construction (i.e., one in which they rarely occur). *Sneeze*, for example, is entrenched in the intransitive construction, yet the utterance *I sneezed the ice cream cone into my lap*, in which *sneeze* occurs in the transitive and caused motion constructions, is acceptable in spite of the rarity of the use of *sneeze* with a direct object. To solve this problem, Goldberg (1993, 1995, 2006, 2011), building on Pinker's (1989) proposal for a preemptability marker in children's grammar, proposed a process of statistical preemption whereby construction A preempts construction B to the extent that a) both constructions ought to be equally appropriate in the given discourse context, and b) construction A occurs rather than construction B. Conducting an analysis of the dative and ditransitive constructions in the 450 million word Corpus of Contemporary American English, Goldberg (2011) shows that in discourse contexts in which the ditransitive might have been expected, the dative was used significantly more than would be expected by chance (83% of the time on average, ranging from .53–1.0).

Experimental evidence also suggests that the notion of statistical preemption is correct. Brooks and Tomasello (1999), for example, modeled the description of a doll swinging a house on a rope by saying *The house is tamming* (intransitive) and *The doll is helping the house tam* (each repeated 44 times). A different group of children heard transitive and causative sentences: *The doll is tamming the house* and *The house is getting tammed*. When children were later asked to describe the scenes, children who heard the intransitive models used *tam* intransitively the vast majority of the time, while children who heard the transitive models had an overwhelming tendency to use it transitively.

Boyd and Goldberg's (2011) investigation of novel a-adjectives produced a similar experimental effect. A-adjectives like *asleep* and *alive* are dispreferred prenominally (*The asleep boy, The alive plant*). When adults were presented with two novel a-adjectives in relative clauses (e.g., *The fox that's adax*) just three times each, speakers treated those two novel a-adjectives in the same way as they treated known a-adjectives, producing them in relative clauses rather than in prenominal position. In fact, even when given two additional a-adjectives that they had not seem previously, participants still treated them as they did the known a-adjectives. Unlike these novel a-adjectives, novel adjectives not beginning with *a-* were freely used prenominally. Boyd and Goldberg's results suggest not only that statistical preemption is at work, but also that statistical preemption may be generalized across categories.

Children's ability to learn argument structure constructions themselves, that is to map novel constructional forms to novel meanings without being influenced (for better or worse) by patterns of language that the child already knows was recently investigated by Goldberg and colleagues in a number of studies that have produced evidence that children are in fact able to assign a novel meaning to a novel construction (e.g., Goldberg et al. 2005; Casenhiser and Goldberg 2005; Boyd et al. 2009).

The general paradigm used in each of the studies to date is reminiscent of the preferential looking paradigm used to test children's understanding of linguistic constructions (e.g., Fisher 1996; Naigles 1990). In it, a novel construction was employed whose meaning indicated that an NP theme appeared in an NP location in the manner specified by a nonsense verb. The form was as follows:

NP_{theme} $NP_{location}$ nonsense verb

The utterances generated with this construction were then paired with videotaped scenes depicting their meaning. For example, *the spot the king moopoed* indicated that the spot (NP_{theme}) appeared on the king ($NP_{location}$) in the manner indicated by the verb (in this case, "fading into existence"). The paradigm is rounded out by using a training phase in which participants are exposed to the utterances paired with the videotaped examples of the utterance's meaning. The intent is to simulate in a controlled manner the sorts of pairings between scenes and utterances that a learner would experience when exposed to a novel construction (cf. Hauser et al. 2002). In the testing phase of the experiment, two minimally different scenes are placed side-by-side while an utterance is played. The child is instructed to touch the scene that corresponds to the utterance. In this paradigm, only the meaning of the noun phrases is known. Thus participants had to determine from context, the meaning of the verb, the meaning of the construction, and the form of the construction. In fact, they also had to determine that the word order did in fact have a meaning rather than being haphazard.

The studies have demonstrated that children can generalize beyond the input they receive to distinguish between a simple transitive scene using transitive syntax (<agent> <verb> <patient>) and a scene of appearance using the novel appearance construction (with novel verbs), and that participants are able to use such newly acquired constructions productively – even when mappings run counter to specifications which are claimed to be universal (Pinker 1989).

4.1 Construction learning as category learning

Other work has investigated construction learning as an instance of category learning that is subject to the same sorts of facilitative and inhibitory effects as other types of category learning (see also Ramscar volume 1). Goldberg and colleagues (Goldberg et al. 2007) present evidence that parallels evidence derived from non-linguistic category learning (Gentner and Medina 1998; Markman and Gentner 1993), suggesting that early presentation of stimuli with shared concrete similarity facilitates construction learning. Other work has demonstrated a facilitative effect on construction learning when exemplars follow a so-called Zipfian distribution (Zipf 1935) in which the frequency with which a verb occurs in a given construction accounts for the lion's share of tokens encountered by learners (Casenhiser and Goldberg 2005; Goldberg et al. 2004). A number of corpus-based studies (e.g., Gries et al. 2005; Gries and Wulff 2005; Cameron-Faulkner et al. 2003), have suggested that natural language input tends to mirror this effect (see also Divjak and Caldwell-Harris volume 1 for a discussion of frequency effects), and evidence from non-linguistic category learning (Elio and Anderson 1984) has shown a facilitative effect for such an input distribution.

This particular effect, however, is not to be overstated since the importance of type frequency (the frequency of occurrence of a pattern or category) in generalization may overshadow the effects of Zipfian distributions. In ESL studies (see also Ellis and Wulff volume 2), McDonough and Kim (2009) found a facilitative effect of greater type frequency in priming *wh*-questions, and Collins and colleagues (Collins et al. 2009) also found type frequency (along with perceptual salience) to reliably distinguish early-learned L2 constructions from those that are learned later. Indeed, the facilitative effect of skewed input appears somewhat fragile and may well be limited to early learning, or may become washed out by extended training. In teaching the English ditransitive construction to Korean speakers, for example, Year and Gordon (2009) trained participants for a total of 200 minutes. Though participants did learn the construction, corroborating earlier results, the authors failed to find a facilitative effect for skewed input.

4.2 Neurolinguistic research on construction learning

Nonetheless, the notion of construction learning as an instance of category learning is an important one that suggests the learnability of syntax in the absence of innate categories. Moreover, there is now emerging neurophysiological evidence supporting the notion. Johnson and colleagues (volume 1) investigated the neural correlates of construction learning by presenting participants with the appearance construction used in Goldberg and colleagues' previous experiments. They compared fMRI activation during this condition with activation during a random condition in which participants encountered the same scenes, but the words were presented in random order (i.e., consistent meaning with no consistent constructional form). They found activation in neural areas related to statistical learning (specifically the left ventral striatum) during the patterned construction learning condition, but not during the condition in which participants were presented with scrambled words (i.e., when they were not learning a construction). This result presents the first evidence of the neurophysiological reality of construction learning. But more to the point of construction learning as an instance of category learning, they also found that the patterned condition showed increasing activation in areas associated with non-linguistic pattern learning (i.e., the posterior precuneus) over the course of the experiment, while no such activation was evident in the random condition. This pattern of activation suggests a neurocognitive kinship between construction learning and non-linguistic category learning.

In the only other neurolinguistic study of construction-learning, Allen and colleagues (2012) conducted an fMRI experiment designed to distinguish regions of neural activation during processing of the ditransitive (*Jessica sold Mike a hotdog*) and dative (*Jessica sold a hotdog to Mike*) constructions. Traditional projectionist theories suggest that such pairs of constructions have equivalent semantics owing to the premise that they are derived from the same underlying representation (e.g., Baker 1996; Hale et al. 1997). Others have argued that the two constructions have subtle but different meanings (e.g., Goldberg 2002) wherein the ditransitive connotes intended transfer and the dative indicates caused motion. Accordingly, if the two constructions are represented and/or processed differently by the brain, neurological differences ought to be able to be detected. This is, in fact, what Allen and colleagues found. Specifically, they found differences in processing for the two constructions with greater activation localized to the left anterior portion of Broadmann Area 22, which has been associated with the understanding and generation of words, and left Broadmann Area 47, which has been implicated in syntactic processing. This result holds in spite of the fact the lexical items in the sentences were identical (excepting the addition of *to* in the dative construction). Moreover, no such differences were found in controls in which the lexical items were presented in scrambled order.

5 Conclusion

In this chapter we have reviewed evidence for a constructional account of argument structure grounded in the empirical evidence for this approach in language use (comprehension and production) and language acquisition. We have reviewed evidence demonstrating that verb independent mappings from sentence level relational meanings to sentence forms are used by speakers to compute sentence meanings alongside verbs, that these mappings are learnable, and that they are at work in the process of language production both in adults and in children. Evidence for a constructional approach to argument structure within linguistics is now solidly convergent with evidence from disparate fields, making construction type units particularly useful to capture linguistic behaviors beyond the classic linguistic data.

6 References

Abbot-Smith, Kirsten, Elena Lieven, and Michael Tomasello (2001): What preschool children do and do not do with ungrammatical word orders. *Cognitive Development* 16(2): 679–692.

Akhtar, Nameera, and Michael Tomasello (1997): Young children's productivity with word order and verb morphology. *Developmental Psychology* 33(6): 952–965.

Allen, Kachina, Francisco Pereira, Matthew Botvinick, and Adele E. Goldberg (2012): Distinguishing grammatical constructions with fMRI pattern analysis. *Brain and Language* 123: 174–182.

Baker, Mark (1996): On the structural positions of themes and goals. In: L. Zaring and J. Rooryck (eds.), *Phrase Structure and the Lexicon*, 7–34. Dordrecht: Kluwert.

Bencini Giulia M. L. (2002): The representation and processing of argument structure constructions. PhD Dissertation. University of Illinois.

Bencini Giulia M. L. (2013): Psycholinguistics. In: T. Hoffmann and G. Trousdale (eds.) *The Oxford Handbook of Construction Grammar* 379–398. Oxford: Oxford University Press.

Bencini, Giulia M. L. and Adele E. Goldberg (2000): The contribution of argument structure constructions to sentence meaning. *Journal of Memory and Language* 43(4): 640–651.

Bencini, Giulia M. L. and Virginia Valian (2008): Abstract sentence representations in 3-year-olds: Evidence from comprehension and production. *Journal of Memory and Language* 59: 97–113.

Birner, Betty and Gregory Ward (1998): *Information Status and Noncanonical Word Order in English*. Philadelphia: John Benjamins.

Bock, Kathryn (1986): Syntactic persistence in language production. *Cognitive Psychology* 18: 355–87.

Bock, Kathryn and Helga Loebell (1990): Framing sentences. *Cognition* 35: 1–39.

Bock, Kathryn J., Helga Loebell, and Randel Morey (1992): From conceptual roles to structural relations: Bridging the syntactic cleft. *Psychological Review* 99: 150–171.

Bowerman, Melissa (1996): Argument structure and learnability: Is a solution in sight? *Proceedings of the Annual Meeting of the Berkeley Linguistics Society* 22(1): 454–468.

Boyd, Jeremy K. and Adele E. Goldberg (2011): Learning what not to say: categorization and preemption in a-adjective production. *Language* 81(1): 1–29.

Boyd, Jeremy K., Emily A. Gottschalk, and Adele E. Goldberg (2009): Linking rule acquisition in novel phrasal constructions. *Lingua* 59(Supplement 1): 64–89.

Branigan, Holly P., Martin J. Pickering, Simon P. Liversedge, Andrew J. Stewart, and Thomas P. Urbach (1995): Syntactic priming: Investigating the mental representation of language. *Journal of Psycholinguistic Research* 24(6): 489–506.

Brooks, Patricia J. and Michael Tomasello (1999): How children constrain their argument structure constructions. *Language* 75(4): 720–738.

Cameron-Faulkner, Thea, Elena Lieven, and Michael Tomasello (2003): A construction based analysis of child directed speech. *Cognitive Science* 27(6): 843–873.

Casenhiser, Devin M. and Adele E. Goldberg (2005): Fast mapping between a phrasal form and meaning. *Developmental Science* 8(6): 500–508.

Chang, Franklin, Kay Bock, and Adele E. Goldberg (2003): Do thematic roles leave traces in their places? *Cognition* 90(1): 29–49.

Chomsky, Noam (1957): *Syntactic Structures*. The Hague: Mouton.

Collins, Laura, Pavel, Trofimovich, Joanna White, Walcir Cardoso, and Marlise Horst (2009): Some input on the easy/difficult grammar question: An empirical study. *The Modern Language Journal* 93(3): 336–353.

Croft, William (2001): *Radical Construction Grammar*. Oxford: Oxford University Press.

Diessel, Holger (volume 2): Usage-based Construction Grammar. Berlin/Boston: De Gruyter Mouton.

Dittmar, Miriam, Kirsten Abbot-Smith, Elena Lieven, and Michael Tomasello (2008): Young German children's early syntactic competence: A preferential looking study. *Developmental Science* 11(4): 575–582.

Divjak, Dagmar and Catherine Caldwell-Harris (volume 1): Frequency and entrenchment. Berlin/Boston: De Gruyter Mouton.

Elio, Renee and John R. Anderson (1984): The effects of information order and learning mode on schema abstraction. *Memory and Cognition* 12(5): 20–30.

Ellis, Nick C. and Stefanie Wulff (volume 1): Second language acquisition. Berlin/Boston: De Gruyter Mouton.

Fillmore, Charles J., Paul Kay, Laura Michaelis, and Ivan Sag (1988): *Construction Grammar.* Stanford: CSLI.

Fisher, Cynthia (1996): Structural limits on verb mapping: The role of analogy in children's interpretations of sentences. *Cognitive Psychology* 31(1): 41–81.

Gertner, Yael, Cynthia Fisher, and Julie Eisengart (2006): Learning words and rules: Abstract knowledge of word order in early sentence comprehension. *Psychological Science* 17(8): 684–691.

Gentner, Dedre and Jose Medina (1998): Similarity and the development of rules. *International Journal of Bilingualism* 65: 263–297.

Goldberg, Adele E. (1993): Another look at some learnability paradoxes. *Proceedings of the 25th Annual Stanford Child Language Research Forum.* Stanford: CSLI Publications.

Goldberg, Adele E. (1995): *Constructions: A Construction Grammar Approach to Argument Structure.* Chicago: Chicago University Press.

Goldberg, Adele E. (2002): Surface generalizations: An alternative to alternations. *Cognitive Linguistics* 13(4): 327–356.

Goldberg, Adele E. (2006): *Constructions at Work: The Nature of Generalization in Language.* Oxford: Oxford University Press.

Goldberg, Adele E. (2011): Corpus evidence of the viability of statistical preemption. *Cognitive Linguistics* 22(1): 131–154.

Goldberg, Adele E. (2013): Constructional approaches. In: T. Hoffmann and G. Trousdale (eds.) *The Oxford Handbook of Construction Grammar* 15–31. Oxford: Oxford University Press.

Goldberg, Adele E., Devin M. Casenhiser, and Niya Sethuraman (2004): Learning argument structure generalizations. *Cognitive Linguistics* 15(3): 289–316.

Goldberg, Adele E., Devin M. Casenhiser, and Niya Sethuraman (2005): The role of prediction in construction-learning. *Journal of Child Language* 32(02): 407–426.

Goldberg, Adele E., Devin M. Casenhiser, and Tiffany R. White (2007): Constructions as categories of language. *New Ideas in Psychology* 25(2): 70–86.

Goldwater, Micah B. and Arthur B. Markman (2009): Constructional sources of implicit agents in sentence comprehension. *Cognitive Linguistics* 20(4): 675–702.

Gries, Stefan Th., Beatte Hampe, and Doris Schönefeld (2005): Converging evidence: Bringing together experimental and corpus data on the association of verbs and constructions. *Cognitive Linguistics* 16(4): 635–676.

Gries, Stefan Th. and Stefanie Wulff (2005): Do foreign language learners also have constructions? Evidence from priming, sorting and corpora. *Annual Review of Cognitive Linguistics* 3: 182–200.

Hale, Kenneth, Jay Keyser, Miriam Butt, and Wilhelm Geuder (1997): On the complex nature of simple predicators. In: M. Butt and W. Geuder (eds.) *The Projection of Arguments.* Stanford, CA: CSLI.

Hauser, Marc D., Noam Chomsky, and W. Tecumseh Fitch (2002): The faculty of language: What is it, who has it, and how did it evolve? *Science* 298(5598): 1569–1579.

Johnson, Matthew A. and Adele E. Goldberg (2012): Evidence that constructional meaning is accessed automatically: Jabberwocky sentences prime associated verbs. *Language and Cognitive Processes* 28(10): 1439–1452.

Johnson, Matt A., Nick Turk-Browne, and Adele E. Goldberg, In press, Prediction is essential to language processing and development. Comment on Pickering and Garrod. *Brain and Behavioral Science.*

Kako, Edward (2006): The semantics of syntactic frames. *Language and Cognitive Processes* 21(5): 562–575.

Kaschak, Michael P. and Arthur M. Glenberg (2000): Constructing meaning: The role of affordances and grammatical constructions in sentence comprehension. *Journal of Memory and Language* 43: 508–529.

Kay, Paul. and Charles J. Fillmore (1999): Grammatical constructions and linguistic generalizations: The What's X doing Y? construction. *Language* 75: 1–34.

Lakoff, George (1987): *Women, Fire, and Dangerous Things: What Categories Reveal about the Mind*. Chicago: University of Chicago Press.

Langacker, Ronald (1987): *Foundations of Cognitive Grammar* Volumes 1 and 2. Stanford: Stanford University Press.

Markman, Arthur B. and Dedre Gentner (1993): Structural alignment during similarity comparisons. *Cognitive Psychology* 25(4): 431–467.

McDonough, Kim M. and Youjin Kim (2009): Syntactic priming, type frequency, and EFL learners' production of wh-questions. *The Modern Language Journal* 93(3): 386–398.

Medin, Douglas L. and William D. Wattenmaker, and Sarah E. Hampson (1987): Family resemblance conceptual cohesiveness, and category construction. *Cognitive Psychology* 12: 242–279.

Michaelis, Laura A. and Knud Lambrecht (1996): Toward a construction-based model of language function: The case of nominal extraposition. *Language* 72: 215–247.

Naigles, Letitia (1990): Children use syntax to learn verb meanings. *Journal of Child Language* 17(2): 357–374.

Olguin, Rachel and Michael Tomasello (1993): Twenty-five-month-old children do not have a grammatical category of verb. *Cognitive Development* 8(3): 245–272.

Pinker, Stephen (1989): *Learnability and Cognition: The Acquisition of Argument Structure*. Cambridge: MIT Press/Bradford Books.

Ramscar, Michael (volume 1): Categorization. Berlin/Boston: De Gruyter Mouton.

Roberts, Kenneth. (1983): Comprehension and production of word order in stage I. *Child Development* 54(2): 443–449.

Tomasello, Michael (1992): *First Verbs: A Case Study of Early Grammatical Development*. Cambridge: Cambridge University Press.

Tomasello, Michael (2000): Do young children have adult syntactic competence? *Cognition* 74: 209–253.

Year, Jungeun and Peter Gordon (2009): Korean speakers. *Modern Language Journal* 93(3): 19.

Zipf, George K. (1935): *The Psycho-Biology of Language*. Boston: Houghton Mifflin.

Rachel Giora
Chapter 9: Default nonliteral interpretations. The case of negation as a low-salience marker

1 Introduction

This chapter looks into some emerging negative constructions in Hebrew.[1] It argues that such infrequent utterances convey *novel* nonliteral (e.g., metaphorical, sarcastic) interpretations by default. *Default nonliteral utterance-level interpretation* is a new notion, not yet (sufficiently) discussed in cognitive linguistics. It focuses both on "defaultness" and "nonliteralness", but importantly, also on the notion of "utterance-level *interpretation*" and the cognitive representations involved in the process. *Default* utterance-level interpretations are singled out in that they differ from conventionalized coded meanings of lexicalized items (meanings listed in the mental lexicon) and from interpretations based on these coded (i.e., salient) meanings, termed here "salience-based interpretations" (Giora et al. 2007). Whereas coded meanings of words and collocations (whether sub- or supra-sentential) are retrieved directly from the mental lexicon (Giora 1997, 1999, 2003), utterance-level interpretations are novel, noncoded, and have to be construed on the fly (Gibbs 2002).

Novel noncoded interpretations are low on salience (Giora 1997, 2003). Albeit nonsalient, the novel nonliteral utterance interpretations to be discussed here are privileged in that they are favored over and processed faster than their noncoded but salience-based, here, literal alternatives. Such findings, attesting to the temporal priority of *nonsalient* nonliteral interpretations over their relatively available *salience-based* literal ones, cannot be accounted for by any contemporary processing model, including the Graded Salience Hypothesis (Giora 1997, 1999, 2003).

The aim of this chapter is to demonstrate, instead, that negation – a marker prompting low-salience interpretations by default – can account for the priority of nonsalient nonliteral interpretations over salience-based, literal ones (Giora 2006; Giora et al. 2005, 2010, 2013, 2015; Givoni et al. 2013). To allow an insight

---

[1] On emerging constructions in cognitive linguistics and construction grammar, see e.g., Bybee (2006); Divjak and Caldwell-Harris (volume 1); Israel (2011).

Rachel Giora, Tel Aviv, Israel

into the notion of default nonliteral interpretations induced by negation, consider the following natural examples (target utterances in bold, interpretations in italics):

(1) **I am not your wife, I am not your maid,** *I'm not someone that you can lay your demands [on] all of [the] time. I'm sick of this it's going to stop!* (Blige 2007).

(2) I will not use the word "*hater*" but **supportive she is not.** (Lady 2013).

(3) *Tom's wait is currently 3 years*, more-or-less. **Punctuality is not his forte** (Marzluf, 2011).

(4) sorry, my **French is not my best attribute**, in fact it is *awful!!* (Anonymous 2010).

In (1), the target constructions (*I am not your wife, I am not your maid*) are of the form "X is not Y". They convey a low-salience metaphorical interpretation (*I'm not someone that you can lay your demands [on] all of [the] time*), while rendering literal, defining features (*married*, *hired*) pragmatically irrelevant.[2] This interpretation is highlighted via the rejection of the concepts (*your wife, your maid*) by means of the negation marker. In (2), the target construction (*Supportive she is not*) is of the form "X s/he is not". It conveys a low-salience sarcastic interpretation which is brought to the fore via the rejection of the concept (*supportive*) within the scope of negation. It thus suggests a contrastive reading (similar to *hater*) of what is negated. In (3), the target construction (*Punctuality is not his forte*) is of the form "X is not his/her forte". It too conveys a low-salience sarcastic interpretation, suggesting the opposite of the negated concept (indicating a long delay of *3 years*, which makes the protagonist very late rather than punctual). In (4), the target construction (*French is not my best attribute*) is of the form "X is not his/her best attribute". It conveys a low-salience sarcastic interpretation by suggesting the opposite (*awful*) of what is negated (*best attribute*). As will be shown here, such nonliteral interpretations, albeit low on salience, are the preferred, default interpretations of such utterances.

Recall that the nonliteral interpretations of these emerging constructions are not lexicalized but need to be construed. No wonder they are often made explicit by their users. For instance, *I am not your wife* in (1) is used differently

---

[2] The view of metaphor adopted here is similar to Glucksberg and Keysar's (1990) and to Carston's (1997, 2012) "broadening" and "narrowing" processes involved in metaphor interpretation.

in (5). While metaphorical too, here, in (5), it is a protest, leveled by a wife against her husband who *didn't treat her with respect like one should treat one's wife* but instead shamed her by *cheating on her, deceiving her*, etc. Here too, negation invites low-salience features of "wife" (*should be treated with respect*), while rendering literal, defining features (*married*) pragmatically irrelevant (Giora et al. 2013):

(5) **"I am not your wife.** *You cheated me; you deceived me. You did not tell me that you were involved with Pakistanis. You did not tell me what were you up to,"* she said loudly (Singh 2002).

The notions of default, preferred, or privileged utterance-interpretation prevalent in the field are either agnostic with regard to degree of (non)literalness, or assume a literalness-based interpretation. Thus, the classical view (Aristotle 350 BCE; Beardsley 1958; Black 1954, 1962, 1979; Richards 1936), promoted by the Standard Pragmatic Model (Grice 1975; Searle 1979; see also Levinson 2000), assumes that an utterance default interpretation is literal, which, for the most part, is context independent. Literal utterance-level interpretations are, therefore, activated first, regardless of contextual information to the contrary (see discussions in Gibbs 1994, 2002; Hamblin and Gibbs 2003; Gibbs and Moise 1997; Récanati 1989, 1995).

The Graded Salience Hypothesis (Giora 1997, 1999, 2003) also assumes a context independent view of default utterance-interpretation, which, however, is not necessarily literal, but salience-based. A salience-based interpretation is an utterance-interpretation, based on the salient meanings of the utterance components. Salient meanings of linguistic (and nonlinguistic) components are coded in the mental lexicon, and enjoy prominence due to a number of factors, regardless of degree of (non)literalness. Factors contributing to salience might be cognitive, such as degree of prototypicality, or related to amount of exposure, such as degree of frequency, conventionality, and experiential familiarity (even if private, or related to the unspoken/unsaid that is often on our mind).

Given that utterance components might have either literal and/or nonliteral meanings high in salience, salience-based interpretations are agnostic with regard to degree of (non)literalness. Less-salient meanings – meanings low on prototypicality or degree of exposure – are also coded in the mental lexicon, regardless of degree of (non)literalness. However, they are low on prominence and might take a while to reach a threshold even in a supportive context. In contrast, novel, nonsalient meanings or interpretations are not coded, and are not considered default interpretations. Rather, they have to be learnt or constructed, often on the basis of contextual information. They can, however, be both, literal or nonliteral.

According to the Graded Salience Hypothesis, then, salience-based interpretations are default interpretations. They are, therefore, expected to be activated initially, regardless of contextual information. On the other hand, nonsalient meanings and interpretations are not derived by default and may therefore lag behind, even when contextual support is strong (Fein et al. 2015; Giora 2003, 2011; Giora et al. 2007; but see Peleg, Giora and Fein 2001 for the effects of predictive contexts).

In contrast to the Standard Pragmatic Model and the Graded Salience Hypothesis, most of the views of default utterance-interpretations postulate richer notions of defaultness, varying with respect to degree of context dependency. Some are more constrained such as "explicatures" (Carston 2002, 2012; Sperber and Wilson 1986/1995), and some are more flexible such as "privileged interactional interpretations" (Ariel 2002), or "primary meanings" (Jaszczolt 2005a, 2005b, 2009, 2010). However, these default interpretations too are indifferent to degree of nonliteralness (Ariel 2002, 2008, 2010; Bach 1994; Carston 2002; Gibbs and Moise 1997; Hamblin and Gibbs 2003; Jaszczolt 2005a, 2005b, 2009, 2010, 2011; Récanati 1989, 2001, 2004, 2005; Sperber and Wilson 1986/1995). This chapter, however, focuses on nonliteralness. It outlines the conditions for a novel notion termed here "default nonliteral utterance-interpretation".

2 Default nonliteral utterance-interpretation

The view of default nonliteral utterance-interpretation has been proposed, developed, and tested in our recent experimental studies, using contrived Hebrew stimuli, based, however, on natural instances, and read by native speakers of Hebrew. In addition, native speakers of Hebrew, English, German, and Russian were involved in corpora-based studies, which are not reported here (but see Giora 2006; Giora et al. 2010, 2013; Giora et al. 2014). In these studies we outlined the conditions for default nonliteral interpretations (specified in 6 below), which require that utterances be a priori potentially ambiguous between literal and nonliteral interpretations. These conditions, then, stipulate that cues, known to prompt nonliteralness, whether utterance external or internal, should be excluded, so that one interpretation may be favored over another *by default*:

(6) Conditions for default nonliteral interpretations
   a. Constituents (words, phrases, utterances) have to be *unfamiliar* so as to exclude salient/coded nonliteral *meanings* of expressions and collocations. For instance, salient nonliteral meanings of familiar idiomatic

(*spill the beans*), metaphorical (*backseat*), sarcastic[3] (*you don't say*), or any conventional formulaic expressions (Bybee 2006; Fillmore et al. 1988; Gibbs 1980, 1981; Giora 2003), as well as prefabs (Erman and Warren 2000), or conventionalized, ritualistic utterances, (Kecskés 1999, 2000) should be excluded. If negative utterances are considered, they should not be negative polarity items (NPIs), but should, instead, have an acceptable affirmative counterpart, so that conventionality is avoided.[4]

b. *Semantic anomaly* (known to invite metaphoricalness, see Beardsley 1958) or any kind of opposition between the elements of a phrase or proposition (known to trigger a sarcastic reading, see Barbe 1993; Partington 2011) should be avoided so that both literal and nonliteral interpretations may be allowed. For this reason, "epitomizations" – negative object-subject-verb (OSV) constructions ("X s/he is not") – in which the fronted constituent is a proper noun, (*Einstein he is not*) – must be excluded. Such constructions are also metaphorical, not least in their affirmative version (Birner and Ward 1998; Ward 1983; Ward and Birner 2006; see also Prince 1981).

c. Specific and informative *contextual information* should not be involved so that pragmatic incongruity – a breach of pragmatic maxims or contextual misfit (Grice 1975) – on the one hand, and supportive biasing information, on the other, (Gibbs 1981, 1986a, 1986b, 1994, 2002; Katz 2009; Katz et al. 2004) may not invite or disinvite a nonliteral or a literal interpretation. Contextual or pragmatic cues such as *metaphorically speaking, sarcastically speaking, literally, pun intended* (see Givoni et al. 2013; Katz and Ferretti 2003), marked intonation/prosodic cues, whether nonliteral, such as sarcastic, effective even outside of a specific context (Bryant and Fox Tree 2002; Rockwell 2007; Voyer and Techentin 2010), corrective, such as assigned to metalinguistic negation (Carston 1996; Chapman 1996; Horn 1985, 1989), or nonverbal, such as gestures or facial expressions (Caucci and Kreuz 2012), should be avoided so that nonliteralness would neither be invited nor blocked.

The view of default nonliteral interpretation predicts that certain constructions, complying with the conditions for default nonliteral interpretations, will be per-

---

3 "Sarcasm" also relates to "sarcastic irony" and "verbal irony".
4 On NPIs exhibiting asymmetric behavior in minimal pairs of negative and affirmative sentences whereby, as a result of conventionalization, affirmatives are almost nonexistent (see Horn 1989; Israel 2006).

ceived as such compared to an equivalent alternative (a) when presented outside of a specific context, (b) regardless of degree of structural markedness. Consequently, when embedded in a strongly biasing context, they (c) will be processed nonliterally initially, regardless of contextual information to the contrary. Given the preference and temporal priority of their nonliteral interpretation, (d) such utterances will convey a nonliteral interpretation when used by speakers and therefore (e) their contextual environment will resonate with and reflect this nonliteral albeit nonsalient interpretation. (For corpus-based evidence supporting predictions d–e, see Giora et al. 2010, 2013; Giora et al. 2014).

In the studies reported here, we tested predictions (a–c) using both offline and online measures (Giora 2006; Giora et al. 2010, 2013, 2015). We showed that negation is an operator generating novel nonliteral utterance-interpretation by default. Below I review our findings with regard to negative constructions such as "X is not Y" (*This is not Memorial Day*) which are primarily metaphorical (section 2.1), and "X s/he is not" (*Punctual he is not*), "X is not her/his forte" (*Punctuality is not her forte*), and "X is not her/his best feature" (*Punctuality is not her best feature*), which are primarily sarcastic (section 2.2).

2.1 Default metaphorical utterance-interpretation: X is not Y constructions

Consider the following natural instances, exemplary of the kind of construction discussed in this section (target utterances in boldface, interpretations in italics):

(7) *I've heard about your needs/wants/desires/witnesses/mother's health a thousand times* ... **I am not your social worker**/*psychologist/person you vent to*. I am your lawyer. So, if I don't *speak to you every other day about your 'feelings'* ... (Seddiq, N. A., retrieved on August 28, 2012)

(8) My name is Mary K. Hill. *I am a Licensed Independent Social Worker.* **I am your Social Worker** at Hmong International Academy. (Hill 2012)

(9) There is such a *racket* going on downstairs, between *doors slamming and dogs barking*. – Makes me want to open the door and scream **"THIS IS NOT A DISCOTHEQUE!"** (Gordon 2011).

(10) Located in Walking Street up on the right hand side from Beach Road, upstairs from Candy Shop and opposite Soi Diamond, just find as it lights up Walking Street with a laser sign. **This is a Discotheque** *with live band,*

the music is House/Techno/Blip Blip. Closed in Spring 2009. (http://www.pattayabarreview.com/tag/live-band/) [Accessed 28 August 2012].

In (7), the negative target utterance *I am not your social worker* is used metaphorically, getting across some non-defining features of the concept (*social worker*) via rejecting them (e.g., *heard about your needs/wants/desires/witnesses/ mother's health, you vent to*, or *speak to you every other day about your 'feelings'*). This metaphor is further reinforced by similar figures of speech, such as *I am not your ... psychologist/person you vent to*. In contrast, in (8), the affirmative counterpart, *I am your Social Worker* gets across some defining features of the concept, such as "I am a Licensed Independent Social Worker". In (9), the target utterance *THIS IS NOT A DISCOTHEQUE!* focuses on a metaphorical nondefining feature of the negated concept *discotheque*, which here refers to disturbing noise (*racket, doors slamming and dogs barking*). Its affirmative counterpart in (10), however, highlights its defining features (*live band, the music is House/Techno/Blip Blip*).

Will such negative utterances be perceived as metaphorical, compared to their affirmative alternatives, when presented in isolation (section 2.1.1)? Will they be processed faster when embedded in metaphorically than in literally biasing context, as predicted by the view of negation as an operator inducing nonliteral interpretations by default (section 2.1.2)?

2.1.1 Evidence from offline measures

Our previous studies (Giora et al. 2010) show that some novel negative utterances (e.g., 7, 9), involving no semantic anomaly, were perceived as more metaphorical compared to their equally novel affirmative counterparts (e.g., 8, 10), when presented in isolation. Items were followed by a 7-point metaphoricalness scale, which (randomly) instantiated either a literal or a metaphorical interpretation at the scale's end. Participants were asked to indicate the proximity of the utterance interpretation to any of those instantiations at the scale's ends (or otherwise propose an alternative).

Results showed that the metaphorical interpretation, albeit nonsalient, was the preferred interpretation of the novel negative items, scoring high on metaphoricalness ($M = 5.50$ $SD = 0.96$). In contrast, the preferred interpretation of their equally novel affirmative counterparts was the salience-based, literal one, scoring significantly lower on metaphoricalness ($M = 3.48$ $SD = 1.27$), $t1(47) = 10.17, p < .0001; t2(14) = 4.36, p < .0005$ (Giora et al. 2010).

2.1.2 Evidence from online measures

Given their preference for metaphoricalness, the view of negation as inducing nonliteral interpretations by default predicts that such negative utterances (as discussed in section 2.1.1) will be read faster when embedded in a context biasing them toward their metaphorical than toward their (equally strongly biased) literal interpretation. In Giora et al. (2013), we tested this prediction with regard to the utterances tested offline in Giora et al. (2010). Utterances were embedded in contexts controlled for equal strength of literal/nonliteral bias. They were followed by a two-word spillover segment, which allows testing whether difficulties in processing a target utterance spill over to the next utterance. The target utterances, followed by the spillover segment, were presented in context non-final position (to avoid wrap-up effects).

Participants were asked to read short paragraphs, which they advanced segment by segment by pressing a key, and answer the question that followed. Reading times of the target utterances and the spillover segments were measured by the computer. Results showed that, as predicted, the negative utterances were read faster when embedded in a context strongly biasing them toward their nonsalient metaphorical interpretation than toward their (equally strongly biased) salience-based literal interpretation, $t1(37) = 2.57, p < .01; t2(11) = 1.51, p = .08$ (see Figure 9.1). There were no spillover effects.

Such results support the view that negation generates nonliteral interpretations by default.

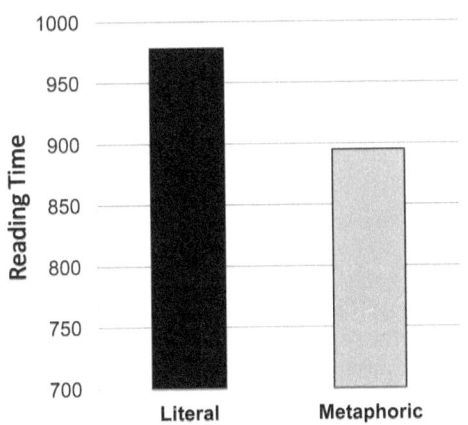

Fig. 9.1: Mean reading times (in ms) of metaphorically and literally biased targets.

2.2 Default sarcastic utterance-interpretation: "X s/he is not" constructions

Consider the following natural instances, exemplary of the kind of constructions discussed in this section (target utterances in boldface, interpretations in italics):

(11) Katherine may be courageous, *but* **smart she is not**. *In fact, I wonder whether she has ever rubbed more than three brain cells together.* (http://www.drphil.com/messageboard/topic/2873/55/) [Accessed 16 October 2012]

(12) Meg is a *smart* girl, maybe she's not pretty, but **smart she is**" says Scott. (http://m.fanfiction.net/s/5142465/7/) [Accessed 16 October 2012]

(13) **Smart he is not** ... *Let it be said at once that Sharon may be as sharp as a whip, as cunning and elusive as an eel, but* – *as the Nahal Brigade troupe used to sing* – *"he's not so smart." Certainly not so smart as many, himself included, may think.* (Rosenblum 2004).

The negative utterance in (11) (*smart she is not*) is used sarcastically, suggesting that the person in question is far from being smart and is in fact stupid, as the context clarifies (*wonder whether she has ever rubbed more than three brain cells together*). The alternative affirmative (*smart she is*) in (12) conveys a literal interpretation of the same concept (Meg is a *smart* girl). In (13), the negative construction (*Smart he is not*), does not convey the opposite of what is said but allows, instead, a mitigated version of the negated concept (Certainly *not so smart* as many, himself included, may think), which is a case of the construction being used literally.

Will such negative utterances be perceived as sarcastic compared to affirmative alternatives when presented in isolation (section 2.2.1)? Will they be processed faster when embedded in sarcastically than in literally biasing contexts (section 2.2.2)?

2.2.1 Evidence from offline measures

Our previous studies (Giora et al. 2013) show that some novel negative utterances of the form "X s/he is not" (*Ambitious she is not*; *Mesmerizing he is not*), involving no semantic anomaly or any internal incongruity, were interpreted sarcastically when presented in isolation. Items, controlled for novelty, were followed by a 7-point scale, instantiating either a literal or a sarcastic interpretation (randomly) displayed at the scale's ends. Participants were asked to indicate the proximity of the utterance interpretation to any of those instantiations at the scale's ends (or otherwise propose an alternative).

Results showed that the sarcastic interpretation, albeit nonsalient, was the preferred interpretation of the novel negative items, scoring high on sarcasm, (M = 5.59, SD = 0.87), significantly higher than 5 on a 7-point sarcasm scale, $t1(18) = 2.99, p < .005; t2(17) = 4.65, p < .0005$.

To verify that the interpretations of the negative items were indeed perceived as sarcastic (rather than only as the opposite of what is said), sarcasm ratings were collected. Participants were asked to rate degree of sarcasm of the negative items and their affirmative counterparts (all of similar novelty controlled for by a pretest). Items, presented in isolation, were followed by a 7-point sarcasm scale, ranging between 1 (not sarcastic at all) and 7 (highly sarcastic). No interpretations were provided.

Results showed that the negative items (*Ambitious she is not*) were significantly more sarcastic (M = 5.92, SD = 0.94) than their novel affirmative counterparts (*Ambitious she is yes*[5]) (M = 2.67, SD = 1.33); $t1(42) = 11.53; p < .0001; t2(17) = 45.55, p < .0001$.

2.2.2 Evidence from online measures

Given their default sarcastic interpretation, the view of negation as inducing nonliteral interpretations by default predicts that such negative utterance as discussed in section 2.2.1 will be read faster when embedded in a context biasing them toward their nonsalient sarcastic interpretation than toward their (equally strongly biased) salience-based literal interpretation. In Giora et al. (2013), such utterances were embedded in contexts controlled for equal strength of literal vs. nonliteral bias. They were followed by a two-word spillover segment. The target utterances, followed by the spillover segment, were presented in context non-final position and were followed by a Yes/No comprehension question.

As before, participants were asked to read the short paragraphs which they advanced segment by segment and answer a comprehension question. Reading times of the target utterances and the spillover segments were measured by the computer. Results showed that, as predicted, the negative utterances were read faster when embedded in a context strongly biasing them toward their nonsalient sarcastic interpretation than toward their (equally strongly biased) salience-based literal interpretation (see Figure 9.2), $t1(43) = 1.75, p < .05; t2(17) = 1.20, p = .12$. There were no spillover effects.

---

[5] In Hebrew the affirmative version is obligatorily marked for affirmation by an explicit marker.

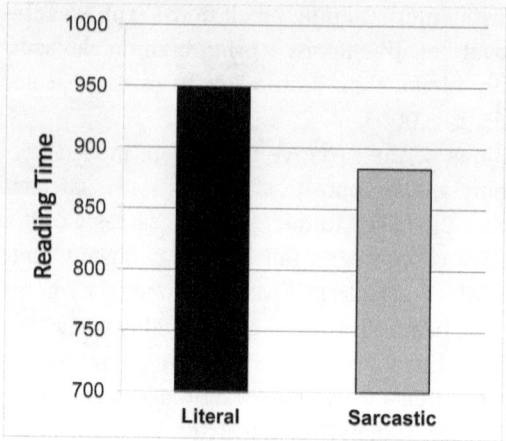

Fig. 9.2: Mean reading times (in ms) of sarcastically and literally biased targets.

Such results support the view of negation as a low-salience marker generating novel nonliteral interpretations by default.

2.3 Default sarcastic utterance-interpretation: "X is not her forte" constructions

Consider the following natural instances, exemplary of the kind of constructions discussed in this section (target utterances in boldface, interpretations in italics):

(14) **Moderation is usually** not my forte – *I'm more of an all-or-none person.* (http://www.letsrun.com/forum/flat_read.php?thread=3020834andpage=4) [Accessed 27 July 2014]

(15) **Maintaining quality is our forte**, *so we ensure that every kind of business functions are monitored on each stage with best co-operation and co-ordination among various departments by a galaxy of supremely qualified and dedicated quality analysts ... The stringent quality control measures are strictly being implemented at each step* ... (http://www.phoenixbiologicals.net/company-information.html) [Accessed 25 October 2012]

(16) Piolo Pascual has admitted to having had *a bit of difficulty doing comedy*, acknowledging that **the genre is not his "forte"**. ... The 35-year old actor-singer maintained that the movie is quite *the change of pace for him* considering that his body of work consists mostly of romantic dramas ... the actor

believes that people will find the movie quite *entertaining* since it's "more *relaxing*, hindi siya nakaka-pressure." (RAMOS 2012).

The negative utterance in (14) (*Moderation is usually not my forte*) is used sarcastically, suggesting that the speaker is far from being moderate but is, instead a person of extremes (*an all-or-none person*). The affirmative construction (*Maintaining quality is our forte*) in (15) conveys a literal interpretation (*The stringent quality control measures are strictly being implemented at each step ...*). In (16), however, the negative construction (*the genre [comedy] is not his "forte"*) is a case in which such utterances convey a mitigated, literal interpretation (the actor believes that people will find the movie quite entertaining) rather than the opposite of what is said.

Will such negative utterances (as in 14) be perceived as sarcastic when presented in isolation (section 2.3.1)? Will they be processed faster when embedded in sarcastically than in literally biasing contexts (section 2.3.2)?

2.3.1 Evidence from offline measures

Our recent studies (Giora et al. 2015) show that some novel negative utterances of the form "X is not her/his forte" (*Alertness is not his forte*), involving no semantic anomaly or any internal incongruity, were interpreted sarcastically when presented in isolation. Items, controlled for novelty, were followed by a 7-point scale, instantiating either a literal or a sarcastic interpretation, (randomly) displayed at the scale's ends. Participants were asked to indicate the proximity of the utterance interpretation to any of those instantiations at the scale's ends (or otherwise propose an alternative).

Results showed that the sarcastic interpretation, albeit nonsalient, was the preferred interpretation of the novel negative items, scoring high on sarcasm ($M = 5.51$, $SD = 0.35$), significantly higher than 5 on a 7-point sarcasm scale, $t(13) = 5.44$, $p < .0001$.

To verify that the interpretations of the negative items were perceived as sarcastic (rather than only as the opposite of what is said), sarcasm ratings were collected. Participants were asked to rate degree of sarcasm of the negative items and their affirmative counterparts (all controlled for novelty by a pretest). Items, presented in isolation, were followed by a 7-point sarcasm scale, ranging between 1 (not sarcastic at all) and 7 (highly sarcastic).

Results replicated previous findings, showing that the negative items (*Alertness is not his forte*) were significantly more sarcastic ($M = 6.02$, $SD = 0.78$) than their novel affirmative counterparts (*Alertness is his forte*) ($M = 2.67$, $SD = 1.01$), $t1(39) = 15.43$, $p < .0001$; $t2(13) = 22.07$, $p < .0001$.

Will these novel negative utterances be interpreted faster when embedded in contexts biasing them toward their nonsalient sarcastic interpretation than toward their salience-based literal interpretation?

2.3.2 Evidence from online measures

Given their preferred sarcastic interpretation, the view of negation as inducing nonsalient nonliteral interpretations by default predicts that such negative utterance, as discussed in section 2.3.1, will be read faster when embedded in a context biasing them toward their nonsalient sarcastic interpretation than toward their (equally strongly biased) salience-based literal interpretation. In Giora et al. (2015), we tested this prediction. Utterances were embedded in contexts controlled for equal strength of literal vs. nonliteral bias. They were presented in context non-final position and followed by a two-word spillover segment. Contexts were followed by a Yes/No comprehension question.

Participants were asked to read the short paragraphs which they advanced segment by segment and answer a comprehension question. Reading times of the target utterances and the spillover segments were measured by the computer. Results showed that, as predicted, the negative utterances were read faster when embedded in contexts strongly biasing them toward their nonsalient sarcastic interpretation ($M = 1349$ ms, $SD = 401$) than toward their (equally strongly biased) salience-based literal interpretation ($M = 1790$ ms, $SD = 579$), $t1(43) = 4.69$, $p < .0001$, $t2(13) = 4.48$, $p < .0005$ (see Figure 9.3). Additionally, there

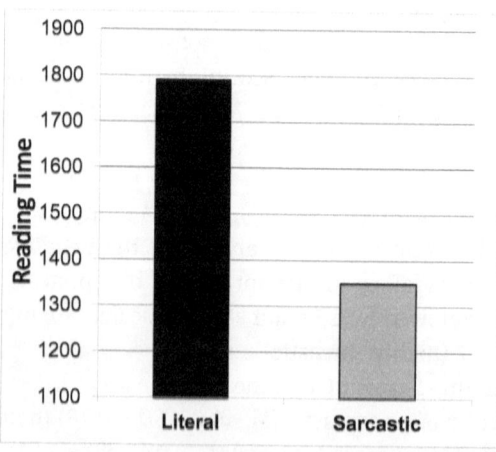

Fig. 9.3: Mean reading times (in ms) of sarcastically and literally biased targets.

were spillover effects showing that, as predicted, following sarcastically biased targets, reading times of spillover segments were faster than those following literally biased targets, $t1(43) = 2.90$, $p < .0005$; $t2(13) = 1.94$, $p < .05$, suggesting processing difficulties in the literal but not in the sarcastic condition.

Such results support the view that negation is a low-salience marker, generating novel nonliteral interpretations by default.

2.4 Default sarcastic utterance-interpretation: "X is not her strong point" constructions

In this section we look at similar constructions to those studied in section 2.3, only short of their semantics (*not her/his **forte***), which, despite their proven novelty, might already be associated with sarcasm. To replicate previous findings, the utterances tested here employ equivalent alternatives but keep the construction constant (*not her/his most distinctive feature, not her/his area of expertise/not what she excels at*). The following natural instances are exemplary of the kind of constructions discussed here (target utterances in boldface, interpretations in italics):

(17) The Baron of Hartlepool, Lord Mandelson, **humility is not his strong point**? This morning on The Andrew Marr show whilst being interviewed showed his inability to admit his wrongs and the *sheer arrogance* of his lordship(lol) was breathtaking to watch (Johnny D. 2008).

(18) ... **his deliverance of the stories is his strong point**. *His prose has been polished to the point that it sparkles and contains more than a good deal of poetry* (Voegele N. A.).

(19) ... if he is played in the lam/cam role on a consistent basis, he can arguably become *the best Asian player in football*. With the possible addition of RVP, I hope we see him used in the lam role rather than the central midfield role or benched in favor of a rooney /RVP partnership. Even without RVP, I hope SAF knows *he is capable of playing in this role*, and wide players are capable of playing more centrally. However, I doubt that as ... erh ... **tactics is not his strong point**. (http://community.manutd.com/forums/p/244135/2145052.aspx) [Accessed 26 October 2012]

In (17), the negative construction (*humility is not his strong point*), is used sarcastically, conveying the opposite of what is said ("*sheer arrogance*"). In contrast, the affirmative version in (18) (*his deliverance of the stories is his strong point*) conveys a literal interpretation ("*His prose has been polished to the point that it sparkles ...*"). However, (in 19), the negative construction (*tactics is not his strong point*) conveys a mitigated, literal interpretation, given that he is good at other things (*the best Asian player in football; I hope we see him used in the lam role rather than the central midfield role or benched in favor of a rooney /RVP partnership. Even without RVP, I hope SAF knows he is capable of playing in this role*), rather than the opposite of what is said.

Will such negative utterances (as in 17) be perceived as sarcastic, compared to affirmative alternatives (19), when presented in isolation (section 2.4.1)? Will they be processed faster when embedded in sarcastically than in literally biasing context (section 2.4.2)?

2.4.1 Evidence from offline measures

Our recent studies (Giora et al. 2015) show that some novel negative utterances of the form "X is not her/his best attribute" (*Alertness is not her most pronounced characteristic*), involving no semantic anomaly or any internal incongruity, were interpreted sarcastically when presented in isolation. As before, items, controlled for novelty, were followed by a 7-point scale, instantiating either a literal or a sarcastic interpretation (randomly) displayed at the scale's ends.

Results showed that sarcastic interpretations, albeit nonsalient, were the preferred interpretation of the novel negative items, scoring high on sarcasm ($M = 5.55$, $SD = 0.29$), significantly higher than 5 on a 7-point sarcasm scale, $t(11) = 5.52$, $p < .0001$.

To verify that the interpretations of the negative items were perceived as sarcastic (rather than only as the opposite of what is said), sarcasm ratings were collected. Participants were asked to rate degree of sarcasm of the negative items and their affirmative counterparts, all controlled for novelty. Items, presented in isolation, were followed by a 7-point sarcasm scale, ranging between 1 (not sarcastic at all) and 7 (highly sarcastic). No interpretations were provided.

Results replicated previous findings, showing that the negative items (*Alertness is not her most pronounced characteristic*) were significantly more sarcastic ($M = 5.96$, $SD = 0.76$) than their novel affirmative counterparts (*Alertness is her most pronounced characteristic*) ($M = 3.29$, $SD = 1.06$), $t1(39) = 12.72$, $p < .0001$, $t2(11) = 13.95$, $p < .0001$.

2.4.2 Evidence from online measures

Given their preferred sarcastic interpretation, the view of negation as a low-salience marker, inducing novel nonliteral interpretations by default, predicts

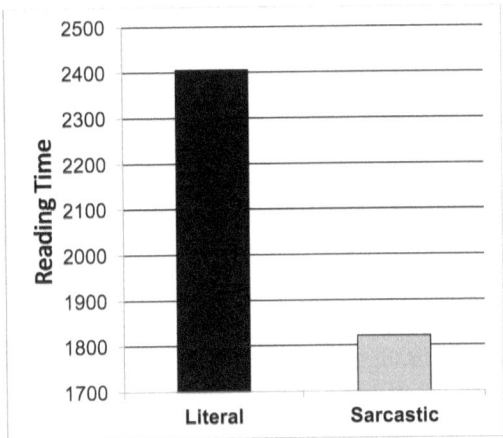

Fig. 9.4: Mean reading times (in ms) of sarcastically and literally biased targets.

that such negative utterances (as discussed in section 2.4.1) will be read faster when embedded in a context biasing them toward their nonsalient sarcastic interpretation than toward their (equally strongly biased) salience-based literal interpretation. In Giora et al. (2015), we tested this prediction. Utterances, presented in context non-final position, followed by a two-word spillover segment, were embedded in contexts controlled for equal strength of literal vs. nonliteral bias.

As before, participants were asked to read the short paragraphs, which they advanced segment by segment, and answer a question that followed. Results showed that, as predicted, the negative utterances were read faster when embedded in a context strongly biasing them toward their nonsalient sarcastic interpretation (M = 1821 ms, SD = 588) than toward their (equally strongly biased) salience-based literal interpretation (M = 2405 ms, SD = 833), $t1(51) = 6.19$, $p < .0001$; $t2(11) = 2.93$, $p < .01$ (see Figure 9.4). Additionally, there were marginal spillover effects showing that, as predicted, following sarcastically biased targets, reading times of spillover segments were somewhat faster (M = 690 ms, SD = 208) than those following literally biased targets (M = 726 ms, SD = 275), disclosing processing difficulties in the latter condition, $t1(51) = 1.48$, $p = .07$; $t2(11) = < 1$, n.s.

Such results support the view that negation is a low-salience marker generating novel nonliteral interpretations by default.

2.5 Default sarcastic utterance-interpretation: negation vs. structural markedness

Recall that the view of negation as inducing default nonliteral interpretation predicts that certain negative constructions, complying with the conditions for default nonliteral interpretations, will be perceived as nonliteral, regardless of degree of structural markedness (prediction b, section 2). Given that the sarcastic utterances tested here are structurally marked, involving a fronted constituent, it is necessary to tease apart negation from markedness effects. Which of the two plays a primary role in affecting nonliteralness by default?

Already at this stage, some of our findings argue against the markedness hypothesis. Recall that the constructions at hand are structurally marked both in the negative and the affirmative. In addition, some of them are also obligatorily marked (in Hebrew) for affirmation (*Ambitious she is **yes***). Regardless, results showed that, whereas the negative constructions were interpreted sarcastically by default, the affirmative counterparts were not, which renders the markedness hypothesis suspicious. Still, negation vs. markedness effects should be examined directly.

To weigh degree of negation (not/yes) against degree of markedness (+/− fronting) in a more systematic way, we ran 2 experiments. In one, we looked at "X s/he is not/yes" constructions (*Ambitious she is not/yes*) (Giora et al. 2013); in the other, we looked at "X is not/yes her/his forte/most prominent feature" constructions (*Alertness is not/yes his forte//most prominent feature*[6]) (Giora et al. 2015). We compared them with structurally unmarked alternatives differing only in negation vs. affirmation (*She is not/yes Ambitious*; *His forte//most prominent feature is not/yes alertness*). We predicted that the negative versions of the utterances will always be more sarcastic than their affirmative counterparts, regardless of degree of structural markedness. Structural markedness, however, may have an additive value.

In each experiment participants were presented 2 different constructions – marked and unmarked (20–23; 24–27), varying between whether they included a negative (not) or an affirmative (yes) marker. There were also 24 filler items, varying between sarcastic, literal, and metaphorical utterances. Four booklets were prepared so that participants saw only one version of a concept; the constructions were counterbalanced. In addition to the 24 filler items, each booklet then contained 8 structurally marked constructions, half negative and half affirmative, and 8 structurally unmarked constructions, half negative and half affirmative:

---

[6] In Hebrew, such utterances may also be marked for the affirmative ("yes").

(20) Ambitious she is not

(21) Ambitious she is yes

(22) She is not ambitious

(23) She is yes ambitious

(24) Alertness is not her forte/most prominent feature

(25) Alertness is yes her forte/most prominent feature

(26) Her forte/most prominent feature is not alertness

(27) Her forte/most prominent feature is yes alertness

Participants were asked to rate the degree of sarcasm of each utterance on a 7-point sarcasm scale (where 1 = not sarcastic at all and 7 = highly sarcastic). Results for the first construction (*Ambitious she is not*) and its variations showed that the negative versions were always rated as more sarcastic than their affirmative counterparts. Markedness also played a role. However, as demonstrated by Figure 9.5, although the difference in sarcasm between negative and affirmative utterances was larger in the marked condition, it was significant in both the Marked ($F1(1, 47) = 26.22, p < .0001; F2(1, 15) = 55.07, p < .0001$) and Unmarked conditions ($F1(1, 47) = 4.25, p < .05; F2(1, 15) = 13.77, p < .005$):

Results for the second construction (*Alertness is not her forte/most prominent feature*) and its variations showed that markedness did not play any role

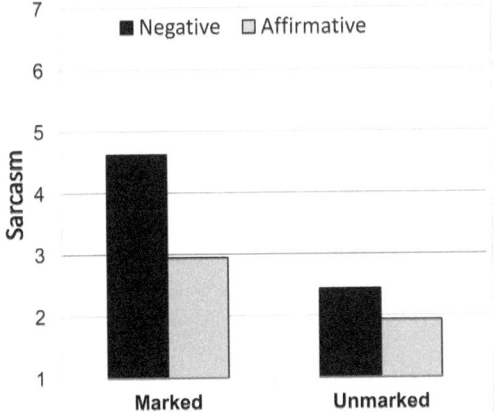

Fig. 9.5: Mean sarcasm ratings for affirmative and negative utterances.

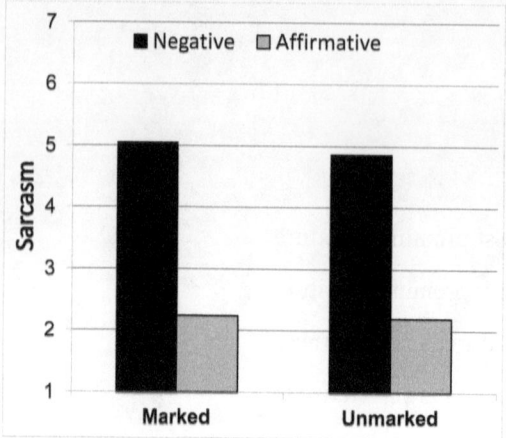

Fig. 9.6: Mean sarcasm ratings for affirmative and negative utterances.

in affecting sarcasm. Instead, it was only negation that played a crucial role in inducing sarcasm by default ($F_1(1,59) = 128.87$, $p < .0001$; $F_2(1,15) = 799.72$, $p < .0001$), as demonstrated by Figure 9.6:

These results support the view that negation, rather than structural markedness, plays a critical role in affecting novel nonliteralness by default.

3 General discussion

Findings in Giora et al. (2010, 2013, 2015) show that negation is an operator eliciting novel metaphorical and sarcastic utterance-interpretation by default. For an utterance to be interpreted nonliterally by default, it has to meet the conditions for default nonliteral interpretation. These conditions guarantee that utterances are *prima facie* ambiguous between literal and nonliteral interpretations. They should therefore be free of utterance external and internal hints known to prompt nonliteralness. Utterances should therefore be:
- *unfamiliar* so that salient/coded nonliteral *meanings* of expressions and collocations will not be involved;
- free of *semantic anomaly* or any kind of internal incongruency (known to trigger nonliteralness), so that both literal and nonliteral interpretations be permissible;

and

– presented outside of biasing *contextual information* so that any pragmatic incongruity or supportive information may neither invoke nor block a specific interpretation.

In this article, the focus is on a certain set of negative constructions, which, under such conditions, generated nonsalient nonliteral interpretations by default. Negative (metaphorical) utterances of the form "X is not Y" (*This is not a bus*) and negative (sarcastic) utterances of the form "X s/he/it is not" (*Supportive she is not*), "X is not her forte" (*Punctuality is not her forte*), "X is not her most distinctive attribute" (*Alertness is her most distinctive feature*), were found to be rated and interpreted as nonliteral compared to their affirmative counterparts when presented in isolation, regardless of degree of structural markedness. When embedded in contexts, they were processed faster when strongly biased toward their nonsalient nonliteral interpretation than toward their (equally strongly biased) salience-based literal interpretation (Giora et al. 2010, 2013, 2015). (For corroborating corpus-based evidence, see Giora et al. 2010, 2013; Giora et al. 2014).

Our studies use a variety of methodologies, whether offline, online, or corpus-based measures. They adduce robust support for the view of negation as an operator inducing low-salience nonliteralness by default.

These results are unprecedented and cannot be accounted for by existing processing models of nonliteral interpretations. For instance, the priority of nonsalient nonliteral interpretation cannot be explained by salience (Giora 1997, 1999, 2003); recall that according to the Graded Salience Hypothesis, nonsalient interpretations of utterances are not expected to be activated prior to their salience-based interpretations. Nor can semantic anomaly (Beardsley 1958), internal incongruity (Partington 2011), or pragmatic incongruity (Grice 1975) explain these results, given that these factors were excluded. Neither can contextual information (Campbell and Katz 2012; Gibbs 1986a, 1986b, 1994; Ortony et al. 1978; Katz 2009; Katz and Ferretti 2003) account for these findings, given that, when employed, contexts were equally strongly supportive of both the literal and nonliteral interpretations of the negative items.

Would construction grammar theories account for the results? Given that the interpretations of our stimuli, both in their negative and affirmative versions, are not coded, but have, instead, to be constructed (hence they are often spelled out or strengthened by similar examples, see examples 1, 5, 7), they might not be considered grammaticized. They might therefore be hard to account for by e.g., Bybee's (2006), Fillmore et al.'s (1988), or Goldberg's (1995) views, according to which pairings of form and meaning are conventionalized in a way that is similar to the conventionalization of lexical items (Croft 2007).

However, given that the items considered here show a strong association between specific negative constructions and nonliteral interpretations and specific affirmative constructions and literal interpretations (of whatever sort), this may be explained by Ariel's (2008) concept of "salient discourse profile". Salient discourse profile represents stored correlations between specific forms and their discourse functions. Such associations demonstrate a strong, though not necessarily coded, form/function association.

Given our focus here on the interpretations of novel negative constructions, we further propose that the view of negation as a low-salience marker may account for these results. As a low-salience marker, highlighting nonsalient interpretations via rejecting them, negation may account for the priority of novel nonliteral interpretations. (On negation and other low-salience markers bringing to the fore low-salience meanings and interpretations, see Giora et al. 2010, 2013, 2015; Givoni et al. 2013; On negation inducing sarcastic interpretation via rendering utterances into understatements or litotes, see Giora et al. 2005). And although a detailed analysis of the constraints of such negative constructions should await further research, the priority of nonsalient over salience-based interpretations challenges contemporary models of processing and interpretation.

Acknowledgement

This research was supported by THE ISRAEL SCIENCE FOUNDATION (grant no. 436/12).

4 References

Anonymous, 18. August, Default meanings, salient meanings, and automatic processing 2010, http://anitasayer-hicksonsbrainpan.blogspot.co.il/2010/08/what-makes-good-father.html [Accessed 9 July 2012].
Ariel, Mira (2002): Privileged interactional interpretations. *Journal of Pragmatics* 34(8): 1003–1044.
Ariel, Mira (2008): *Pragmatics and grammar*. Cambridge: Cambridge University Press.
Ariel, Mira (2010): *Defining Pragmatics*. Cambridge: Cambridge University Press.
Aristotle (350 BCE): Poetics. Translated by Butcher S. H. The internet classic archive. http://classics.mit.edu/Aristotle/poetics.1.1.html
Bach, Kent (1994): Conversational impliciture. *Mind and Language* 9: 124–162.
Barbe, Katharina (1993): "Isn't it ironic that ...?": Explicit irony markers. *Journal of Pragmatics* 20: 578–590.
Beardsley, Monroe C. (1958): *Aesthetics*. New York: Harcourt, Brace and World.
Birner, Betty J. and Gregory Ward (1998): *Information Status and Noncanonical Word Order in English*. Amsterdam: John Benjamins.

Black, Max (1954): Metaphor. *Proceedings of the Aristotelian Society* 55: 27.
Black, Max (1962): *Models and Metaphors: Studies in Language and Philosophy*. Ithaca: Cornell University Press.
Black, Max (1979): More about metaphor. In: A. Ortony (ed.), *Metaphor and Thought*, 19–43. Cambridge: Cambridge University Press.
Blige, Nellie (2007): http://www.streetpoetry.net/id12.html [Accessed 3 May 2008].
Bryant, Greg A. and Jean E. Fox Tree (2002): Recognizing verbal irony in spontaneous speech. *Metaphor and Symbol* 17: 99–117.
Bybee, Joan (2006): From usage to grammar: The mind's response to repetition. *Language* 82(4): 711–733.
Campbell, John D. and Albert N. Katz (2012): Are there necessary conditions for inducing a sense of sarcastic irony? *Discourse Processes* 49: 459–480.
Carston, Robyn (1996): Metalinguistic negation and echoic use. *Journal of Pragmatics* 25(3): 309–330.
Carston, Robyn (1997): Enrichment and loosening: Complementary processes in deriving the proposition expressed? *Linguistische Berichte* 8: 103–127.
Carston, Robyn (2002): *Thoughts and Utterances: The Pragmatics of Explicit Communication*. Oxford: Blackwell.
Carston, Robyn (2012): Metaphor and the literal-nonliteral distinction. In: K. Allan and K. Jaszczolt (eds.), *Cambridge Handbook of Pragmatics*, 469–492. Cambridge: Cambridge University Press.
Caucci, Gina M., and Roger J. Kreuz. (2012): Social and paralinguistic cues to sarcasm. *Humor* 25: 1–22.
Chapman, Siobhan (1996): Some observations on metalinguistic negation. *Journal of Linguistics* 32: 387–402.
Croft, William (2007): Construction grammar. In: D. Geeraerts and H. Cuyckens (eds.), *The Oxford Handbook of Cognitive Linguistics*, 463–508. Oxford: Oxford University Press.
Divjak, Dagmar and Catherine Caldwell-Harris (volume 1): Frequency and entrenchment. Berlin/Boston: De Gruyter Mouton.
Erman, Britt and Beatrice Warren (2000): The idiom principle and the open choice principle. *Text* 20: 29–62.
Fein, Ofer, Menahem Yeari, and Rachel Giora (2015): On the priority of salience-based interpretations: The case of irony. *Intercultural Pragmatics* 12(1): 1–32.
Fillmore, C. J., Paul Kay, and Mary C. O'Connor (1988): Regularity and idiomaticity in grammatical constructions: The case of let alone. *Language* 64(3): 501–538.
Gibbs, Raymond W. Jr. (1980): Spilling the beans on understanding and memory for idioms in conversation. *Memory and Cognition* 8: 449–456.
Gibbs, Raymond W. Jr. (1981): Your wish is my command: Convention and context in interpreting indirect requests. *Journal of Verbal Learning and Verbal Behavior* 20: 431–444.
Gibbs, Raymond W. Jr. (1986a): Comprehension and memory for nonliteral utterances: The problem of sarcastic indirect requests. *Acta Psychologica* 62: 41–57.
Gibbs, Raymond W. Jr. (1986b): On the psycholinguistics of sarcasm. *Journal of Experimental Psychology: General* 115: 3–15.
Gibbs, Raymond W. Jr. (1994): *The Poetics of Mind: Figurative Thought, Language, and Understanding*. New York: Cambridge University Press.

Gibbs, Raymond W. Jr. (2002): A new look at literal meaning in understanding what is said and implicated. *Journal of Pragmatics* 34: 457–486.

Gibbs, Raymond W. Jr. and Jessica F. Moise (1997): Pragmatics in understanding what is said. *Cognition* 62: 51–74.

Giora, Rachel (1997): Understanding figurative and literal language: The graded salience hypothesis. *Cognitive Linguistics* 7: 183–206.

Giora, Rachel (1999): On the priority of salient meanings: Studies of literal and figurative language. *Journal of Pragmatics* 31: 919–929.

Giora, Rachel (2003): *On our Mind: Salience, Context, and Figurative Language*. New York: Oxford University Press.

Giora, Rachel (2006): Anything negatives can do affirmatives can do just as well, except for some metaphors. *Journal of Pragmatics* 38: 981–1014.

Giora, Rachel (2011): Will anticipating irony facilitate it immediately? In: M. Dynel (ed.), *The Pragmatics of Humour across Discourse Domains*, 19–31. Amsterdam: John Benjamins.

Giora, Rachel, Ari Drucker, and Ofer Fein (2014): Resonating with default nonsalient interpretations: A corpus-based study of negative sarcasm. *Belgian Journal of Linguistics* 28: 3–18.

Giora, Rachel, Ari Drucker, Ofer Fein, and Itamar Mendelson (2015): Negation generates sarcastic interpretations by default: Nonsalient vs. salience-based interpretations. *Discourse Processes* 52.

Giora, Rachel, Ofer Fein, Jonathan Ganzi, Natalie Alkeslassy Levi, and Hadas Sabah (2005): On negation as mitigation: The case of irony. *Discourse Processes* 39: 81–100.

Giora, Rachel, Ofer Fein, Dafna Laadan, Joe Wolfson, Michal Zeituny, Ran Kidron, Ronie Kaufman, and Ronit Shaham (2007): Expecting irony: Context vs. salience-based effects. *Metaphor and Symbol* 22(2): 119–146.

Giora, Rachel, Ofer Fein, Nili Metuki, and Pnina Stern (2010): Negation as a metaphor-inducing operator. In: Laurence Horn (ed.), *The Expression of Negation*, 225–256. Berlin/New York: Mouton de Gruyter.

Giora, Rachel, Elad Livnat, Ofer Fein, Anat Barnea, Rakefet Zeiman, and Ido Berger (2013): Negation generates nonliteral interpretations by default. *Metaphor and Symbol* 28: 89–15.

Givoni, Shir, Rachel Giora, and Dafna Bergerbest (2013): How speakers alert addressees to multiple meanings. *Journal of Pragmatics* 48(1): 29–40.

Glucksberg, Sam and Boaz Keysar (1990): Understanding metaphorical comparisons: Beyond similarity. *Psychological Review* 97: 3–18.

Goldberg, Adele E. (1995): *Constructions: A Construction Grammar Approach to Argument Structure*. Chicago: University of Chicago Press.

Gordon, David (2011): David Gordon's Tumblr. http://mrdavidgordon.tumblr.com/post/12160981523/theres-such-a-racket-going-on-downstairs-between [Accessed 28 August 2012].

Grice, H. Paul (1975): Logic and conversation. In: P. Cole and J. Morgan (eds.), *Speech Acts: Syntax and Semantics*, Volume 3, 41–58. New York: Academic Press.

Hamblin, Jennifer L. and Raymond W. Gibbs Jr. (2003): Processing the meanings of what speakers say and implicate. *Discourse Processes* 35: 59–80.

Hill, Mary (2012): http://hia.mpls.k12.mn.us/hill_mary [Accessed 28 August 2012].

Horn, Laurence R. (1985): Metalinguistic negation and pragmatic ambiguity. *Language* 61(1): 121–174.

Horn, Laurence R. (1989/2001): *A Natural History of Negation*. Chicago: University of Chicago Press.
Israel, Michael (2006): The pragmatics of polarity. In: L. Horn and G. Ward (eds.), *Handbook of Pragmatics*, 701–723. Oxford: Blackwell.
Israel, Michael (2011): *The Grammar of Polarity: Pragmatics, Sensitivity, and the Logic of Scales*. Cambridge: Cambridge University Press.
Jaszczolt, Kasia M. (2005a): *Semantics: Foundations of a Compositional Theory of Acts of Communication*. Oxford: Oxford University Press.
Jaszczolt, Kasia M. (2005b): Prolegomena to default semantics. In: S. Marmaridou, K. Nikiforidou and E. Antonopoulou (eds.), *Reviewing Linguistic Thought: Converging Trends for the 21st Century*, 107–142. Berlin/New York: Mouton de Gruyter.
Jaszczolt, Kasia M. (2009): Cancellability and the primary/secondary meaning distinction. *Intercultural Pragmatics* 6: 259–289.
Jaszczolt, Kasia M. (2010): Default semantics. In: B. Heine and H. Narrog (eds). *The Oxford Handbook of Linguistic Analysis*, 193–221. Oxford: Oxford University Press.
Jaszczolt, Kasia M. (2011): Default meanings, salient meanings, and automatic processing. In: K. M. Jaszczolt and K. Allan (eds.), *Salience and Defaults in Utterance Processing*, 11–34. Berlin/New York: Mouton de Gruyter.
Johnny D. (2008): The Baron of Hartlepool, Lord Mandelson, humility is not his strong point? http://uk.answers.yahoo.com/question/index?qid=20081019102454AAhMnSA [Accessed 25 October 25].
Katz, Albert (2009): Commentary on "Does an ironic situation favor an ironic interpretation". In: G. Brône and J. Vandaele (eds.), *Cognitive Poetics: Goals, Gains and Gaps*, 401–406. Berlin/New York: Mouton de Gruyter.
Katz, Albert, Dawn G. Blasko, and Victoria A. Kazmerski (2004): Saying what you don't mean: Social influences on sarcastic language processing. *Current Directions in Psychological Science* 13: 186–189.
Katz, Albert and Todd R. Ferretti (2003): Reading proverbs in context: The role of explicit markers. *Discourse Processes* 36(1): 19–46.
Kecskés, István (1999): The use of situation-bound utterances from an interlanguage perspective. In: J. Verscheuren (ed.), *Pragmatics in 1998: Selected Papers from the 6th International Pragmatics Conference*, Volume 2, 299–310. Antwerp: International Pragmatics Association.
Kecskés, István (2000): A cognitive-pragmatic approach to situation-bound utterances. *Journal of Pragmatics* 32: 605–625.
Lady (2013): http://necolebitchie.com/2013/05/sneak-peek-tionna-smalls-lands-new-reality-show-girl-get-your-mind-right/ [Accessed 17 July 2014].
Levinson, Stephen C. (2000): *Presumptive Meanings: The Theory of Generalized Conversational Implicature*. Cambridge: MIT Press.
Marzluf, Jonathan (2011): http://test.woodwind.org/oboe/BBoard/read.html?f=10andi=18736andt=18711 [Accessed 9 July 2012].
Ortony, Andrew, Diane L. Schallert, Ralph E. Reynolds, and Stephen J. Antos (1978): Interpreting metaphors and idioms: Some effects of context on comprehension. *Journal of Verbal Learning and Verbal Behavior* 17: 465–478.
Partington, Alan (2011): Phrasal irony: Its form, function and exploitation. *Journal of Pragmatics* 43(6): 1786–1800.
Peleg, Orna, Rachel Giora, and Ofer Fein (2001): Salience and context effects: Two are better than one. *Metaphor and Symbol* 16: 173–192.

Prince, Ellen F. (1981): Topicalization, focus-movement, and Yiddish-movement: A pragmatic differentiation. *Berkeley Linguistics Society* 7: 249–264.

RAMOS (2012): Piolo Pascual admits comedy is not his forte http://mb.com.ph/node/358973/piolo-pa#.UIIeJMXR7-A [Accessed 25 October 2012].

Récanati, François (1989): The pragmatics of what is said. *Mind and Behavior* 4: 295–329.

Récanati, François (1995): The alleged priority of literal meaning. *Cognitive Science* 19: 207–232.

Récanati, François (2001): What is said. *Synthese* 128: 75–91.

Récanati, François (2004): *Literal Meaning*. Cambridge: Cambridge University Press.

Récanati, François (2005): Literalism and contextualism: Some varieties. In: G. Preyer and G. Peter (eds.), *Contextualism in Philosophy: Knowledge, Meaning, and Truth*, 171–196. Oxford: Oxford University Press.

Richards, Ivor Armstrong (1936): *The Philosophy of Rhetoric*. Oxford: Oxford University Press.

Rockwell, Patricia (2007): Vocal features of conversational sarcasm: A comparison of methods. *Journal of Psycholinguistic Research* 36: 361–369.

Rosenblum, Doron (2004): Smart he is not. http://www.haaretz.com/print-edition/opinion/smart-he-is-not-1.115908

Searle, John (1979): *Expression and Meaning*. Cambridge: Cambridge University Press.

Seddiq, Mirriam (N. A.): Why I don't want to talk to you. http://notguiltynoway.com/2004/09/why-i-dont-want-to-talk-to-you.html

Singh, Onkar (2002): Parliament attack convicts fight in court. http://www.rediff.com/news/2002/dec/17parl2.htm [Accessed 24 July 2013].

Sperber, Dan and Deirdre Wilson (1986/1995): *Relevance: Communication and Cognition*. Oxford: Blackwell.

Voegele, Jason (N. A.): http://www.jvoegele.com/literarysf/cyberpunk.html

Voyer, Daniel and Cheryl Techentin (2010): Subjective acoustic features of sarcasm: Lower, slower, and more. *Metaphor and Symbol* 25: 1–16.

Ward, Gregory (1983): A pragmatic analysis of epitomization. *Papers in Linguistics* 17: 145–161.

Ward, Gregory and Betty J. Birner (2006): Information structure. In: B. Aarts and A. McMahon (eds.), *Handbook of English Linguistics*, 291–317. Oxford: Basil Blackwell.

Laura A. Janda
Chapter 10: Tense, aspect and mood

1 Introduction

In the framework of cognitive linguistics we approach the grammatical categories of tense, aspect, and mood from the perspective of general cognitive strategies. Like most linguistic categories, the three grammatical categories of verbs discussed here display polysemy. The cognitive strategies relevant for polysemy are metaphor and metonymy, which help to structure radial categories by motivating extension from prototypical meanings (Lakoff 1987). Therefore metaphor and metonymy play an important role in the structure of tense, aspect, and mood categories. For verbal categories, reference to extralinguistic knowledge from domains like reasoning, probability, and hypothesis are particularly important, as are considerations of pragmatics. As a result, the same situation can be encoded differently in terms of tense, aspect, and mood in accordance with the speaker's construal of the situation. Cross-linguistically the categories of tense, aspect, and mood vary, though prototypes tend to be similar across languages.

The structure of grammatical categories of tense, aspect, and mood is motivated by a number of phenomena that are treated in more detail in other chapters in these three volumes. I refer in particular to Gries' chapter on Polysemy, Gibbs' chapter on Metaphor, Barcelona's chapter on Metonymy, and Taylor's chapter on Prototype effects. Although all three categories are dependent on how human beings conceptualize time, the topic of Evans' chapter in this volume, none of them merely encode parameters of reality, but instead are subject to the forces of construal, which is the topic of Langacker's chapter.

Tense reflects the speaker's experience of the sequencing of events. This alignment is inherently metaphorical, since tenses are conceived of in terms of regions along a timeline, which can be oriented and structured differently in different languages. In other words, tense is a metaphorical location of events with respect to a point of reference. Past and present are primary in that they are both available to the speaker; the past is relatively distant with respect to the present, while the future is both distant and unavailable. Tense is not rigidly defined by event time: many types of metaphoric shift are possible, as in (1), where present tense refers to a future event.

(1) *I am flying to DC next week.*

Aspect is the grammatical expression of the experience of change (perfective) or lack thereof (imperfective), evaluated through the cognitive process of mental scanning. The speaker views the situation either in a summary fashion (perfective), or as a relationship that is extended in time (imperfective), and can construe the same situation differently in accordance with narrative and pragmatic intents. Aspect additionally includes the progressive and various types of Aktionsart (referring to modifications of the internal temporal constituency of an event). Verbs can have inherent (lexical) aspect, since some verbs, like *give*, are inherently more punctual or completive than others, like *love*. In addition, the arguments of the verb can contribute to the aspectual interpretation of an event, as we see in (2a) (with a definite subject, a singular object, and a perfective interpretation) vs. (2b) (with an indefinite subject, plural object, and an imperfective interpretation).

(2) a. *The writer wrote a book.*
    b. *A writer writes books.*

Mood (and more generally modality) expresses the speaker's attitude toward the situation, most often in terms of force dynamics, where we see a force opposition between an agonist and an antagonist. Modal expressions are subjectively construed (offstage) grounding elements that refer to (potential) events beyond the bounds of the speaker's conceptualization of reality. While root (deontic) meanings of modals are motivated by the concrete experience of opposing forces (an embodied experience, cf. Bergen's chapter in volume 1) and their extension to the domain of authority and permission as in (3a), modals are further metaphorically extended in epistemic uses to other domains such as reasoning as in (3b). The expression of modality is not limited to modal verbs, but includes imperatives, conditionals, subjunctives, counterfactuals, and a variety of impersonal constructions.

(3) a. *You must be home by midnight.*
    b. *That must be John.*

This chapter first describes how core concepts of cognitive linguistics have shaped the analysis of tense, aspect, and mood, and then turns to interactions between the three categories. Sections 2 and 3 of this chapter take a thematic approach, exploring how studies in cognitive linguistics have used metaphor and construal to frame analyses of tense, aspect, and mood. Section 4 presents some studies of how tense, aspect, and mood interact with each other.

This chapter presents only selected highlights from the study of tense, aspect, and mood from the perspective of cognitive linguistics. It does not discuss human conceptualization of time in any detail beyond that necessary to address tense, aspect, and mood. The reader is referred instead to Evans' chapter on Time in this volume. References to work on tense, aspect, and mood outside of cognitive linguistics are sparse and no attempt is made to compare achievements across linguistic traditions. This chapter also does not present a typological overview of tense, aspect, and mood phenomena in the world's languages, since such information can be found in other sources (e.g., Dahl 1985; Binnick 2012; Narrog 2012).

I follow Croft (2012: 34) in using the term "event" to refer to all kinds of situations described by verbs. Following this tradition, I also use capitalized terms to refer to language-specific grammatical categories (like the Russian Perfective and the English Progressive), and lower-case terms to refer to categories in a more general sense (like perfective, progressive).

2 Metaphor: EVENTS ARE (PHYSICAL) OBJECTS

Implicitly or explicitly, tense, aspect, and mood rely upon a metaphorical understanding of events as "objects" in the domain of time. Thus reified, the situations described by verbs are placed in time, their properties are observed, and their relationship to reality is evaluated. The EVENTS ARE OBJECTS metaphor that underlies both the use of tense, aspect, and mood by speakers and its investigation by linguists is motivated as a special instance of the TIME IS SPACE conceptual metaphor that is probably universal in languages, although its concrete realizations are language-specific (Haspelmath 1997). Dahl (2013) takes a somewhat different perspective on the relationship between the domain of time and its "objects". He argues that it is our human ability to reify events as objects that makes it possible to understand not only their relationship to time, but time itself: telic transitions between states are the cognitive constructs that themselves create the temporal dimension. One can thus view the timeline either as accompanied by a succession of events or as constituted by those events.

The comparison of events with objects makes it possible to treat verbs and nouns as parts of a single continuum. This continuum overlaps formally, of course, in the existence of deverbal nouns (such as *a look*) and noun-to-verb derivation or conversion (such as *to calve*). More importantly, this continuum reflects shared strategies in terms of the types of concepts that can be expressed grammatically, such as relative location, boundedness, multiplicity, definiteness, and force-dynamics.

The role of the EVENTS ARE OBJECTS metaphor in both language use and linguistic analysis is unsurprising because the mapping operation of metaphor is among the basic human cognitive mechanisms that motivate language and other cognitive behaviors. In this section, events are referred to as "event-objects" in order to highlight the metaphor that gives coherence to the various parallels observed in connection with the expression of tense, aspect, and mood.

2.1 Tense: event-objects in a timeline

The use of a timeline as a metaphorical "space" for locating event-objects relative to the moment of speech antedates cognitive linguistics (Reichenbach 1947; Comrie 1985). The presence of a mental timeline accounts for correlations between deictic spatial adverbials that can refer to proximal and distal locations and tenses with a similar range of distinctions. However, as Botne and Kershner (2008) show on the basis of Bantu data, the timeline itself can be quite complicated, including distinctions based on Moving Time vs. Moving Ego conceptualizations as well as various conceptual domains.

Time, grammatically realized as tense, is the most basic and first dimension in the linguistic system that connects tense, aspect, and mood. Aspect can be modeled as a second dimension orthogonal to time, dubbed the "qualitative state dimension" in which the contours of event-objects develop (Croft 2012; cf. Talmy 2000 v. II: 67–78; see 3.2 below). Some of the studies described in section 4 (Croft and Poole 2008; Croft 2012: 127–165; Eckhoff and Janda 2014) have yielded quantitative models in which tense and aspect emerge precisely as perpendicular axes in a two-dimensional space. A third dimension, also partly orthogonal to time, is mood, where event-objects directly experienced in the timeline serve to ground reality, against which the non-reality of possible and potential event-objects is judged as a deviation from the basic dimension of time (Langacker 2008: 300–302).

2.2 Aspect: observing the properties of event-objects

Whereas tense can be thought of as a system for investigating *where* event-objects are located on the timeline, aspect can be thought of as a system for investigating *what kinds of* event-objects there are. One can think of physical reality as comprised of two kinds of objects, often grammaticalized as the types of objects that are countable and the types that are not. The analogy between the count vs. mass distinction for nouns and the perfective vs. imperfective distinction for verbs has been observed often (Dahl 1985: 76). Janda (2004) works out this analogy in detail in an account of Russian aspect, with an inventory of fourteen properties of discrete solid objects as opposed to fluid substances that correlate to differences in aspectual usage. For example, discrete solid objects have inherent boundaries but fluid substances do not, and Perfective event-objects have temporal boundaries that Imperfective ones lack. Solid objects can exist as thin slices but fluid substances cannot, paralleled by the fact that punctual events are limited to Perfectives but Imperfectives require some duration. Fluid substances can be mixed together, whereas solid objects can only be adjacent to each other, though they can be embedded in fluid substances and these properties correspond to the various uses of aspect to express simultaneity and sequencing.

Huumo (2005, 2009) explores the properties of event-objects that are relevant for Finnish, which marks aspect by means of case in noun phrases instead of on its verbs. With transitive verbs there is a choice between Restrictive and Partitive case marking on the object. Restrictive case is associated with single, unique objects and with telic aspect. Partitive case is associated with mass nouns, plurals, and with atelic aspect. A conflict arises in so-called "quasi-resultative" sentences where verbs of position, sensory perception, and maintenance of a state, which would be expected to use the Partitive case, use instead the Restrictive case, thus representing the situation as the result of a change rather than as a neutral state (Huumo 2005). Another kind of interaction can arise with the case marking of predicate noun phrases with intransitive verbs. The general rule is that the Nominative case is associated with singular count nouns and represents the subject holistically, whereas the Partitive is associated with mass nouns or plurals and represents the subject incrementally. The aspectual interpretation of deverbal nouns, however, is directly affected by the case usage. Thus (4a) with the Nominative has a holistic interpretation, but (4b) with the Partitive has an atelic incremental interpretation (Huumo 2009).

(4) a. *Tanssi   oli   kaunis.*
    Dance-NOM was beautiful-NOM
    'The dancing [a specific performance] was beautiful.'

   b. *Tanssi   oli   kaunista.*
    Dance-NOM was beautiful-PRT
    'The dancing [ongoing activity] was beautiful.'

Different languages will of course engage the event-object metaphor in their aspect systems in different ways. Even the closely related Slavic languages show differences in how their aspectual systems are focused. Dickey (2000) observes that two different versions of the event-object metaphor are relevant across the Slavic languages. In the west, Czech, Slovak, and Slovene focus on totality as the interpretation of Perfective as bounded and Gestalt-like. In the east, Russian, Ukrainian, and Bulgarian focus on definiteness as the relevant interpretation; Serbo-Croatian and Polish form transitional zones in this continuum. The distinction between totality in the west and definiteness in the east accounts for a number of differences in the use of aspect, most of which involve more use of the Perfective in the west, where Perfective can mark any action that is completed (including actions that are repeated or coincide with Present tense), whereas such contexts conflict with temporal definiteness in the east and are thus expressed with the Imperfective.

McGregor (2002) offers another perspective on the event-object metaphor by pointing out that in addition to having nominal classifiers, languages can also have verb classifiers. The most relevant type of nominal classifier system is that of numeral classifiers, where the nouns of a language refer to substances and classifiers serve to "unitize" the nouns into discrete objects, sorting the nouns into groups, usually according to the typical shapes of the objects they form. The use of such classifiers is associated with quantifiers and definiteness. McGregor's analogy links nouns to verbs, and quantifiers to aspect, and although he focuses on Australian languages, he argues that verb classifier systems are probably widespread among the world's languages, but have been overlooked because they have not been included in the inventory of features that typologists look for. Janda et al. (2013) present a series of statistical studies to support the hypothesis that Russian aspectual prefixes constitute a verb classifier system, which is likely valid for other Slavic languages as well. In addition to the connection between quantifiers and aspect, the verb classifier hypothesis examines distributional criteria and parallels between noun and verb classifier systems. Russian Imperfective verbs refer to unbounded states and activities (like the unformed substances referenced by nouns in numeral classifier languages), which are shaped into discrete Perfective events by aspectual prefixes, which also sort the verbal lexicon into different (though somewhat overlapping) groups. For example, Russian verbs that signal an APART meaning, like *bit'* 'break' and *krošit'* 'crumble' perfectivize with the prefix *raz-*, whereas verbs with an ARRIVE meaning like *blizit'sja* 'approach' and *celit'sja* 'aim at' perfectivize with the prefix *pri-*.

In addition to simple distinctions such as perfective, imperfective, and progressive, other types of event-objects can be identified, and a more detailed inventory is presented in section 3.2.

2.3 Mood and modality: force-dynamics of event-objects beyond reality

Langacker's model of modality emerges from the conception of reality, its subjective construal, and how these are reflected in the grounding of an event-object. Regardless of whether time is accompanied or constituted by the succession of event-objects, this succession yields a situation in which the past is defined, the present is being defined, and the future is yet to be defined. The human conceptualizer "C" has thus a personal history of experiences that make up immediate reality (along C's personal timeline), plus what is known to belong to reality but has not been directly experienced (parallel to C's immediate reality). Beyond reality lies non-reality, where we find event-objects that are suspected or hypothesized. Whereas mood can be thought of as a dimension that runs perpendicular to time in the past and present, both of which belong to reality, the distinction between mood and tense is less clear beyond that, and this is reflected in languages like English that have grammaticalized a modal verb such as *will* to mark future tense.

Modal elements like English modal verbs shift the grounding of the profiled event-object from the basic timeline of tense, such that it is offstage and subjectively construed. In other words, the force of the modal does not bear directly on the event-object itself, but on how it is viewed (in terms of its potential) from the perspective of the ground (Langacker 2008: 300–309). This model, with spaces corresponding to reality and non-reality, is of course a type of mental space model (Fauconnier 1985), in which modal elements serve to set up and structure the mental space that constitutes non-reality.

Mortelmans (2000) and Achard (2002) apply Langacker's model to verbal categories expressing mood, namely the German Past Subjunctive and the French Conditional respectively. These two grammatical categories are used to make a prediction about an event-object that is construed as alternative to reality. Based on knowledge of the structure of reality and its momentum, the speaker assumes that the event-object will not take place, as in (5) (Mortelmans 2007: 880–882).

(5) *Wenn ich sie kennen würde, würde ich gleich zu ihr gehen*   German
und mit ihr reden.
Si je la connaissais, j'irais lui parler tout de suite.   French
'If I knew her, I would go and talk to her right away.'

Talmy has investigated the role of force-dynamics in language, which are grammaticalized in the case of modals. An Agonist is an element that exerts a force, an Antagonist is an element that resists a force, and there are various force tendencies and results depending upon whether the force is directed from rest to action or the reverse. Modals like English *must, may* express grammatically similar situations of force or blockage that are also expressed lexically in verbs like *make (X happen), let (X happen)*. However, the force tendencies of modals are contingent rather than intrinsic. In modal sentences like (6a) and (7a), the force is connected with the Agonist. Non-modal verbs present parallel situations in (6b) and (7b), where the force is connected instead to the Antagonist, which in this case removes a barrier. This model is elaborated to account for modal verbs, their negation, and also understanding of causation (Talmy 2000 v. I: 409–549).

(6) a. *A flyball can sail out of the stadium.*
    b. *The lack of a dome makes it possible for a flyball to sail out of the stadium.*

(7) a. *You may go to the playground.*
    b. *I permit you to go to the playground.*

Modal verbs tend to have peculiar syntax, as we see in (7a), where we have what looks like a collapsed two-clause structure. Pelyvás (2011) extends the force-dynamic model of modality to include counterforces and roles that motivate this trend. The "doer" (*you*) has a dual role, as both the passive obligee and the agentive of the potential action. The "imposer" (the speaker) is analyzed as a reference point, which is backgrounded, and this explains why it is unexpressed.

Takahashi (2012) offers a quantitative measure for force exertion according to six parameters (DESIRE, CAPABILITY, POWER, COST, BENEFIT, OBLIGATION) and demonstrates how this measure corresponds to prototypicality for English and Japanese imperatives, since a prototypical imperative like (8a) receives a high score, whereas (8b) receives a low one. A second factor in prototypicality is the subject of the imperative, which is individuated and agentive in a prototypical example, but generic (8c) or non-agentive (8d) in less prototypical uses.

(8) a. *Do you have a problem? Tell me about it.*
    b. *So you find Tokyo expensive? Tell me about it! A cup of coffee can cost $10.*
    c. *Shake before using.*
    d. *Get well soon.*

3 Polysemy, construal, profiling, and coercion

Whereas the purpose of section 2 was to set up the basic framework for understanding tense, aspect, and mood, this section focuses on how the basic distinctions in each category are further elaborated. As we know, grammatical categories are typically polysemous, and the relations among the meanings of a category are usually motivated by extensions via metaphor and metonymy. In addition, we recognize the fact that language does not merely report the parameters of reality. The speaker selectively observes and construes both reality and non-reality, and this yields many more options than a mere report would allow. Construal is most often effected by means of differential profiling of event-objects. In addition, it is possible for conflicts between inherent and contextual values to extend the range of use of a category via coercion.

3.1 Tense: present as immediate vs. past as distal

Both the present and the past tense can be used to refer to event-objects that do not belong to the corresponding times. This is generally the result of construal or of coercion presenting a conflict between the tense and the context. Of course different languages conventionalize different construals of the timeline.

The present tense can be used to report event-objects that are associated with past, present, and future times. The historical present is a device that maps past event-objects to the present so that they can be metaphorically re-experienced as if they were immediate as in (9a). Langacker (2008: 303) attributes the use of the present tense in a statement lacking any real time reference like (9b) or to express a proximate future like (9c) to the fact that the speaker is reporting on things that are relevant for immediate reality. The proximate future is primarily used to describe event-objects that are scheduled to occur, so even though they are in the future, they are available to the speaker at the present. Gnomic statements about the inherent nature of the world are likewise available to the speaker at present, and can thus be reported as such. In both cases, the event-objects are construed as part of present experience.

(9) a. *Yesterday I met Sam. He says to me: What's up? I say: Not much. Then we go to lunch at our usual restaurant ...*
    b. *The earth revolves around the sun.*
    c. *We're flying home tomorrow.*

The past tense is also often found to have the capacity to express event-objects that did not take place in the past. Usually the result involves some kind of modal interpretation. In the case of (10a), *knew* does not refer to a past event-object, but rather to a hypothetical situation removed from immediate reality (Langacker 2008: 303). A similar effect is found in Dutch in (10b) (Janssen 1994: 122). The speaker exerts a modal force in both English (10c) and Russian (10d), trying to bring about a situation in the (near) future.

(10) a. *If I knew her, I would go and talk to her right away.* English

    b. *Nou, maar ik vertrok morgen!* Dutch
       Well but I left   tomorrow
       'Well, but I was supposed to leave tomorrow!'

    c. *It's high time we left.* English

    d. *Pošli!* Russian
       Left-PAST-PLURAL
       'Let's go!'

Janssen (2002) invokes the deixis of demonstratives to account for these extensions of the present and past tenses. According to his analysis, the present tense signals 'THIS-context', which can include anything that the speaker has immediate access to. By contrast, the past tense signals 'THAT-context', which is more distal, making it amenable to interpretation as hypothetical, counterfactual, or even future.

3.2 Aspect

The standard baseline for aspectual distinctions are Vendler's (1967) four categories of lexical aspect (further elaborated below):
- States: *be hot, love*
- Activities: *walk, play*
- Achievements: *realize, reach the summit*
- Accomplishments: *write a letter, drown*

These lexical categories have typically been understood to correspond to grammatical aspect in that imperfective refers to states and activities, whereas perfective refers to achievements and accomplishments. Various tests for these categories have been proposed (cf. Mourelatos 1981), invoking features such as dynamicity, punctuality, and boundedness. However, neither the tests nor the categories themselves have proved adequate, largely due to the effects of construal and coercion. Indeed, most verbs can be shown to have multiple possible construals. The range of possibilities has been explored in detail by Talmy (2000 v. II) and Croft (2012) and are represented here in brief.

Croft recognizes four types of states: transitory states, acquired permanent states, inherent permanent states, and point states. A given state can be distinguished according to whether it presupposes a prior state (as in 11a–b), is irreversible (as in 11b–c), or is construed as a point (as in 11d).

(11) a. transitory state   *The door is open.*
     b. acquired permanent state   *Princess Diana is dead.*
     c. inherent permanent state   *Nicolas Sarkozy is French.*
     d. point state   *It is five o'clock.*

Croft distinguishes two types of activities. Directed activities (cf. "gradient verbs" Talmy 2000 v. II: 68) like (12a) involve an incremental change, with continuous progress along a scale. Undirected activities (cf. Talmy's "multiplex verbs") like (12b) do not involve an incremental change and can often be construed as a series of cycles, like in the case of *chant*.

(12) a. directed activity   *The soup cooled.*
     b. undirected activity   *The girls chanted.*

Croft recognizes four types of achievements, plus a class of accomplishments. The first three types of achievements have the same contours as the corresponding states, differing only in profiling. Whereas the state is profiled for the former group, for the achievements, it is only the transition to the relevant state that is profiled. A reversible achievement (cf. Talmy's "one-way resettable") is (13a). An irreversible achievement (cf. Talmy's "one-way nonresettable") is (13b). Both reversible and irreversible achievements are directed changes, but a cyclic achievement (cf. Talmy's "full-cycle") like (13c), when interpreted to signal a single flash, is undirected. This is a common construal for verbs like *sneeze*, *wave*, *flash* which denote repeatable paired transitions between rest and action and the reverse. A runup achievement like (13d) includes an undirected activity (the presentation of various arguments which may or may not convince me), followed by a transition to the final phase (in which I believe Joe). The runup achievement type serves as a transition to accomplishments since it can also be understood as a nonincremental accomplishment, as opposed to a (neutral) accomplishment, which is incremental as in (13e).

(13) a. reversible achievement   *The door opened.*
     b. irreversible achievement   *Princess Diana died.*

c. cyclic achievement   *The light flashed.*
d. runup achievement   *Joe convinced me he was right.*
e. accomplishment   *I wrote a letter.*

Croft observes that construal makes it possible for many verbs to have multiple aspectual interpretations. *Remember* signals a transitory state in (14a), but a directed achievement in (14b). Here different phases of the contour are profiled (the final state vs. the transition to it), and this can be understood as a metonymic relationship since different parts of the whole are selected. An utterance like (13c) can have different interpretations: if the light flashed once, it is a cyclic achievement; if it flashed for a while, it is an undirected activity. This is accounted for by Talmy's full-cycle vs. multiplex types. Croft invokes scalar adjustment for fine-grained (14c) vs. coarse-grained (14d) construals.

(14) a. *I remember how to do this.*
     b. *I remembered the answer.*
     c. *The bridge is collapsing.*
     d. *The bridge collapsed at 9:15 am.*

Croft (2012: 91–92) suggests that a usage-based approach would ideally treat the issues of default vs. alternative construals as an empirical question and investigate the relative frequencies and factors involved rather than making a priori assumptions about which construals exist and which ones are prototypical.

In support of his categories Croft presents a comparative study of English Present, Progressive, and Past constructions with Japanese Present, *te-iru*, and Past constructions. A multi-dimensional scaling analysis of this data yields a circular continuum of verbs, with clusters that correspond to transitory states (*be ill, be president*), directed achievements (*split, die*), directed activities (*cover, shrink*), undirected activities (*dance, run*), cyclic achievements (*scratch, wave*), and inactive actions (*touch, stand*). Thus the behavior of verbs (in terms of the constructions they appear in) supports Croft's categories for lexical aspect.

While Croft claims that his revision of the Vendlerian categories is universally applicable, the most valuable contribution of his model may be at a more abstract level. The combination of profiling and construal gives us a highly nuanced model and the use of aspectual contours makes it possible to visualize different aspectual types. Specific revisions and additions may be necessary in order to accommodate the facts of a given language (see Janda 2015, concerning adjustments needed for Russian), but this is possible if we accept the model as a flexible complex of components rather than as a fixed set of options.

3.3 Mood: root, epistemic, and speech-act modality

Whereas modals in their root (deontic) use refer to obligation, compulsion, and permission and belong primarily to the psychosocial domain, many of the same elements can be used to express epistemic modality. Instead of exposing an event-object to modal force outside the realm of reality, an epistemic modal assesses the likelihood that an event-object belongs to reality. Epistemic modals thus belong to the domain of knowledge and reasoning. A root modal is focused on realizing an event-object, but an epistemic modal, instead of influencing the realization of the event-object, focuses on deciding whether the event-object is likely to be realized. In (15a), *may* represents a root use and influences the outcome of the event-object *leave*, making it more likely to occur. The same modal in (15b) represents an epistemic use: it has no influence on the likelihood of rain, but instead reports the speaker's attitude toward the probability it will rain (Langacker 2008: 304–307). In addition to root and epistemic use, we observe speech-act modality in sentences like (15c). Here the modal is focused on the domain of conversation: *may* removes a barrier to accepting a statement (that John is a rocket scientist). In other words, the import of the modal is: "I accept the assertion that John is a rocket scientist and should be smart, but ..." Here modality applies to the conversational interaction rather than to any effect on an event-object or its evaluation as likely (Sweetser 1990: 69–73).

(15) a. root   *You may leave now.*
     b. epistemic   *It may rain this afternoon.*
     c. speech-act   *John may be a rocket scientist, but he sure is dumb.*

There is some controversy over the relationship between the types of modality, particularly between root and epistemic modality (see overview in Mortelmans 2007). Given that these different uses of modals pertain to different domains (reality vs. nonreality, reasoning, conversation), it is reasonable to interpret their relationship as a kind of mapping from the source domain of the root modals. It is not clear whether this mapping is metaphorical (Sweetser 1990) or metonymic (Bybee et al. 1994); additionally it has been suggested that epistemic uses result from increased subjectification (Traugott 1989). It is important to be aware that while Traugott and Langacker speak of subjectification and subjectivity in ways that may seem superficially similar, their notions differ; Mortelmans (2004) and Narrog (2012) explore these differences in detail. An alternative is to consider deontic and epistemic modality as equipollent components of modality rather than considering either one to be primary (Plungian 2011: 427). Narrog (2012) departs from the use of force dynamics and subjectivity in describing various types of modal expressions, relying instead on the parameters of speech-act orientation and volitivity. According to Narrog, modality refers primarily to a situation in which the factual status of a proposition is underdetermined.

4 Interactions of tense, aspect, and mood

In a previous overview article, Boogaart and Janssen (2007: 820–821) stated that it would be fruitful to explore interactions between the three categories of tense, aspect, and mood, but noted that such studies were sparse or lacking at the time. While there is still ample room for more research into such interactions, cognitive linguists have made considerable headway in filling this gap. Increasingly this involves empirical studies, usually of corpus data, to discover patterns of interaction. Most relevant studies focus on the interaction of only two of the categories, so the three logical pairings and recent studies pertaining to each are examined in turn.

4.1 Tense and aspect

Five studies are cited here to represent the current state of research on how tense and aspect interact. Langacker gives an analysis of how tense and lexical aspect can conflict in English. Croft and Poole present a major typological study, shedding new light on earlier data. The remaining studies focus on corpus analysis of data for Slavic languages, which are famous for their Perfective vs. Imperfective verbs: Russian (Janda and Lyashevskaya), Old Church Slavonic (Eckhoff and Janda), Croatian (Stanojević and Geld).

In an apparent paradox, Langacker (2011) asserts that despite the fact that the English Present cannot be used for present-time events, it does indicate coincidence with time of speaking. According to Langacker, an expression like (16a) is ungrammatical if used to express an ongoing action due a conflict between tense and aspect in English.

(16) a. *He mows the lawn.
 b. I order you to leave.

If one presumes that English has a distinction between perfectives like *mow the lawn* vs. imperfectives like *know Italian*, one can state this restriction as a rule: English does not (usually) allow the use of the Present tense with perfectives.

The conflict arises because in order to identify a perfective, one must observe the entire event-object, and usually this is not possible in the present, since a bounded event-object (a perfective) usually lasts longer than the present moment. Performatives like (16b) are a notable exception to this rule since they appear in the unusual situation in which a bounded event-object (ordering someone to leave) precisely coincides with the present moment (the utterance of the order). The performatives are the exceptions that prove the rule and solve the paradox, along with uses of the English Present for the historical present and proximate future with scheduled events (see 3.1 above): all of these represent event-objects that are available in their entirety at the present moment.

Croft and Poole (2008; see also Croft 2012) undertake a multi-dimensional scaling analysis for Dahl's (1985) data on the coding of tense-aspect markers in 250 contexts across 64 languages. The result is a two-dimensional map showing how various tense-aspect markers cluster; in other words, what kinds of groupings are attested cross-linguistically. The findings confirm the traditional division between tense and aspect, which emerge as perpendicular axes in the map. There is a central cluster consisting of hypothetical and gnomic situations as opposed to another cluster lying toward the future end of the continuum representing planned or expected future events. The separation between these two clusters is located in the future dimension, precisely where Langacker would predict an interaction between tense and mood (see 2.3 above). In terms of Croft's categories for lexical aspect, the contexts that fall on the imperfective end of the aspectual axis are all states or activities, but whereas the majority of contexts on the perfective end are achievements, we also find accomplishments, semelfactives, and even some activities and states. Although this result is not clear-cut, we acknowledge that construal can package activity and state verbs as bounded and therefore perfective event-objects (see 3.2 above).

Janda and Lyashevskaya (2011) present a corpus study of Russian verb forms across four subparadigms: Non-past, Past, Infinitive, and Imperative. The difference in distribution of these forms for Perfective vs. Imperfective verbs is statistically significant with a robust effect size. Furthermore, the difference in distribution between Perfective and Imperfective is the same regardless of whether it is marked by prefixes or suffixes, which shows that the aspectual categories have a consistent grammatical identity at a more abstract level. Janda and Lyashevskaya explore the verbs that are most attracted to various tense and aspect combinations. Despite the fact that grammars of Russian ascribe durative ongoing processes or repeated processes to the Imperfective Non-past, the verbs it attracts most all refer to gnomic event-objects, such as *javljaetsja* 'be' as in (17a). Perfective Non-past is associated in grammars with unique event-objects expected to be completed in the future. This study indeed finds verbs that signal promises (*upravitsja* 'will manage'), threats (*razterzaet* 'will tear to pieces'), and predictions (*vyzdoroveet* 'will get well'), but also performatives (*procitiruju* 'I quote'), and fixed expressions like (17b). Only among Imperfectives do we find verbs that are strongly attracted to the Past tense (the distribution for Perfective verbs is very wide), and these are associated with evidentials (*slyxal* 'heard'), habituals (*proxaživalsja* 'went for strolls'), and the narration of observations (*belel* 'showed white').

(17) a. *Koška   javljaetsja   mlekopitajuščim.*
       Cat-NOM is-3Sg-NONPAST mammal-INST
       'A cat is a mammal'

   b. *vragu   ne poželaeš'*
      enemy-DAT not wish-2Sg-NONPAST
      'I wouldn't wish it on my worst enemy'

Ever since Dostál (1954) published his inventory of the aspectual types of Old Church Slavonic verbs, there has been controversy over whether the Perfective vs. Imperfective distinction was already in effect at that early stage of Slavic history. Eckhoff and Janda (2014) use corpus data to run a study similar to Janda and Lyashevskaya, but in reverse: with the distribution of verb forms as input, two different statistical models (correspondence analysis and divisive-clustering) test the structure of the data. The models do indeed separate the data according to aspect, with results that concur with Dostál's designations for 97% of verbs. Remarkably, while the first dimension that emerges from the correspondence analysis clearly aligns with Perfective vs. Imperfective aspect, the second dimension aligns with tense, yielding perpendicular aspect and tense axes similar to those found by Croft and Poole.

Stanojević and Geld (2011) examine the Croatian Aorist on the basis of both corpus and experimental data. The Croatian Aorist is a past tense formed only from Perfective verbs. Although standard grammars of Croatian state that the primary use of the Aorist is to mark past and often sequenced events, Stanojević and Geld observe that the Aorist is often used to signal recent past events with current relevance, as well as future events that are conceived of as (nearly) certain, as in (18a–b). Furthermore, as in these examples, the Aorist occurs predominantly in the first person singular form. As a Perfective form, the Aorist excludes the Present tense because it must view the event-object in its totality (cf. Langacker's analysis of the English Present above). Stanojević and Geld argue that the Aorist is epistemically immediate (as opposed to the Perfect which is epistemically distant), and this explains its reference to both immediate past and immediate future, as well as its association with the subjective experience of the speaker (first person).

(18) a. *Ljudi,   pogiboh!*
       People-NOM died-1Sg-AORIST
       'People, I'm dying!' (a call for help)

   b. *odoh   i   ja   sutra ...*
      left-1Sg-AORIST and I-NOM tomorrow
      'although I am leaving tomorrow ...'

4.2 Tense and mood

In the future, tense and mood overlap, since future events are necessarily beyond the established realm of reality (see 2.3 above). Additionally, Langacker (2008: 300–302) observes that the tensed forms of English modal verbs serve to indicate epistemic rather than temporal distance. For example, Present tense *can* refers to a potential in relation to reality, whereas Past tense *could* is usually interpreted not as potential, but counterfactual and thus even farther removed from reality. Patard (2011) takes a similar approach to the English Past and French Imperfect, and asserts that both express modality in utterances like (19a–b). In both types of examples, the past tense serves to mark epistemic distance, making such statements counterfactual.

(19) a. *If only I was rich.*   English
     b. *Si j'étais riche.*   French

4.3 Aspect and mood

There appears to be an association between aspect and modality in examples like (20a–b). Whereas the perfective in (20a) facilitates a deontic reading, exerting a force on the event-object itself, the imperfective in (20b) facilitates an epistemic reading, expressing an assessment of the likelihood that John is reading the book. Boogaart and Trnavac (2011) examine this connection across Germanic, Romance, and Slavic languages. They conclude that the motivation for this association is given by a more general connection between imperfective aspect and subjective information, however it seems that this option is exploited only in Germanic and Romance, but not in Slavic languages.

(20) a. *John must read that book.*
    b. *John must be reading that book.*

Russian lacks modal verbs (the only possible candidate being *moč'* 'be able'), but uses constructions containing modal words like *nado* 'have to' and *nel'zja* 'not allowed to' with Infinitives instead. In a quantitative study, Divjak (2009) showed that in such constructions Imperfectives are preferred to refer to generic obligations and possibilities, whereas Perfectives are preferred for specific event-objects. Janda and Lyashevskaya's (2011) results conformed with those in Divjak's study. In addition to aspect and tense (see 4.1), Janda and Lyashevskaya explore Russian verbs strongly attracted to Imperatives and Infinitives. In the Imperative mood it has traditionally been asserted that Imperfectives mark polite uses (21a) as opposed to Perfectives which mark rude uses (21b). However, Imperfective Imperatives are also associated with insistence (which can be rude), and there are many contexts in which a Perfective Imperative is neutral or polite.

(21) a. Imperfective   *Sadites'*
                      Sit-2Pl-IMPERATIVE
                      'Please sit down'

    b. Perfective   *Sjad'te*
                      Sit-2Pl-IMPERATIVE
                      'Sit!'

Šatunovskij (2009) suggests that the difference in aspect has to do with whether the hearer understands what is expected. If the hearer does understand what to do, the Imperfective is preferred (probably because it is gentler, like a fluid substance, cf. 2.2 above), whereas if the hearer needs to receive instructions, the Perfective is preferred (since the hearer needs access to the entire event-object that is expected). Note that Šatunovskij's model accounts for the complexity observed since in a polite situation usually the hearer knows what to do, and the Imperative just acknowledges when the action is to take place, but if the hearer is expected to do something and hesitates, the Imperative can express the speaker's frustration when the hearer fails when s/he should know better. Janda and Lyashevskaya's data confirm Šatunovskij's model, but also turn up some outliers that cannot be motivated, such as Imperfective requests for assistance (*vyručajte* 'help') and kind wishes (*vyzdoravlivajte* 'get well').

5 Conclusion

Despite a diversity of specific topics and languages, recent research on tense, aspect, and mood from a cognitive perspective presents a coherent story. Events are understood linguistically as objects and evaluated according to their location, properties, and relationship to reality or probability. Tense, aspect, and mood are confirmed both inductively and empirically as intersecting axes. All three grammatical categories can be manipulated to express speaker's construal, extending their scope beyond what would be needed to report on the objective reality of time. These three categories overlap and interact with each other in ways that we are only beginning to understand. In recent years, cognitive linguists have increasingly applied corpus-based empirical approaches to the study of these verbal categories. Future usage-based studies will hopefully expand our knowledge about the uses and patterns of tense, aspect, and mood both within given languages and cross-linguistically.

6 References

Achard, Michel (2002): The meaning and distribution of French mood inflections. In: Frank Brisard (ed.), *Grounding: The Epistemic Footing of Deixis and Reference*, 197–249. Berlin: Mouton de Gruyter.

Binnick, Robert I. (ed.) (2012): *The Oxford Handbook of Tense and Aspect*. Oxford: Oxford University Press.

Boogaart, Ronny and Theo Janssen (2007): Tense and aspect. In: D. Geeraerts and H. Cuyckens (eds.), *The Oxford Handbook of Cognitive Linguistics*, 803–828. Oxford: Oxford University Press.

Botne, Robert and Tiffany L. Kershner (2008): Tense and cognitive space: On the organization of tense/aspect systems in Bantu languages and beyond. *Cognitive Linguistics* 19: 145–218.

Bybee, Joan L., Revere D. Perkins, and William Pagliuca (1994): *The Evolution of Grammar: Tense, Aspect and Modality in the Languages of the World*. Chicago: University of Chicago Press.

Comrie, Bernard (1985): *Tense*. Cambridge: Cambridge University Press.

Croft, William (2012): *Verbs: Aspect and Causal Structure*. Oxford: Oxford University Press.

Croft, William and Keith T. Poole (2008): Inferring universals from grammatical variation: Multidimensional scaling for typological analysis. *Theoretical Linguistics* 34: 1–37.

Dahl, Östen (1985): *Tense and Aspect Systems*. Oxford: Basil Blackwell.

Dahl, Östen (2013): How telicity creates time. *Journal of Slavic Linguistics* 21(1) (a special issue entitled *Aspect in Slavic: Creating Time, Creating Grammar*, ed. by Laura A. Janda): 45–76.

Dickey, Stephen M. (2000): *Parameters of Slavic Aspect: A Cognitive Approach*. Stanford, CA: CSLI Publications.

Divjak, Dagmar (2009): Mapping between domains: The aspect-modality interaction in Russian. *Russian Linguistics* 33: 249–269.

Dostál, Antonín (1954): *Studie o vidovém systému v staroslověnštině* [A Study of the Aspectual System of Old Church Slavonic]. Prague: Státní pedagogické nakladatelství.

Eckhoff, Hanne M. and Laura A. Janda (2014): Grammatical profiles and aspect in Old Church Slavonic. *Transactions of the Philological Society* 112, 231–258.

Fauconnier, Gilles (1985): *Mental Spaces*. Cambridge: MIT Press.

Haspelmath, Martin (1997): *From Space to Time: Temporal Adverbials in the World's Languages*. Munich: LINCOM Europa.

Huumo, Tuomas (2005): How fictive dynamicity motivates aspect marking: The Riddle of the Finnish Quasi-resultative construction. *Cognitive Linguistics* 16: 113–144.

Huumo, Tuomas (2009): Fictive dynamicity, nominal aspect, and the Finnish copulative construction. *Cognitive Linguistics* 20: 43–70.

Janda, Laura A. (2004): A metaphor in search of a source domain: The categories of Slavic aspect. *Cognitive Linguistics* 15: 471–527.

Janda, Laura A. (2015): Russian Aspectual Types: Croft's Typology Revised. In: M. Shrager, G. Fowler, E. Andrews and S. Franks (eds.), *Festschrift for Ronald Feldstein*, 147–167. Bloomington: Slavica Publishers.

Janda, Laura A. and Olga Lyashevskaya (2011): Grammatical profiles and the interaction of the lexicon with aspect, tense, and mood in Russian. *Cognitive Linguistics* 22: 719–763.

Janda, Laura A., Anna Endresen, Julia Kuznetsova, Olga Lyashevskaya, Anastasia Makarova, Tore Nesset, and Svetlana Sokolova (2013): *Why Russian Aspectual Prefixes aren't Empty: Prefixes as Verb Classifiers*. Bloomington: Slavica Publishers.

Janssen, Theo A. J. M. (1994): Preterit and perfect in Dutch. In: C. Vet and C. Vetters (eds.), *Tense and Aspect in Discourse*, 115–146. Berlin: Mouton de Gruyter.

Janssen, Theo A. J. M. (2002): Deictic principles of pronominals, demonstratives and tenses. In: Frank Brisard (ed.), *Grounding: The Epistemic Footing of Deixis and Reference*, 151–193. Berlin: Mouton de Gruyter.

Lakoff, George. (1987): *Women, Fire, and Dangerous Things*. Chicago: University of Chicago Press.

Langacker, Ronald W. (2008): *Cognitive Grammar: A Basic Introduction*. Oxford: Oxford University Press.

Langacker, Ronald W. (2011): The English present: Temporal coincidence vs. epistemic immediacy. In: A. Patard and F. Brisard (eds.) *Cognitive Approaches to Tense, Aspect, and Epistemic Modality*, 45–86. Amsterdam/Philadelphia: John Benjamins.

McGregor, William B. (2002): *Verb Classification in Australian Languages*. Berlin: Mouton de Gruyter.

Mortelmans, Tanja (2000): Konjunktiv II and epistemic modals in German: A division of labour. In: A. Foolen and F. van der Leek (eds.), *Constructions in Cognitive Linguistics*, 191–215. Amsterdam: John Benjamins.

Mortelmans, Tanja (2004): Grammatikalisierung und Subjecktivierung: Traugott und Langacker revisited. *Zeitschrift für germanistische Linguistik* 2: 188–209.

Mortelmans, Tanja (2007): Modality in Cognitive Linguistics. In: D. Geeraerts and H. Cuyckens (eds.), *The Oxford Handbook of Cognitive Linguistics*, 869–889. Oxford: Oxford University Press.

Mourelatos, Alexander P. D. (1981): Events, processes and states. In: P. Tedeschi and A. Zaenen (eds.), *Tense and Aspect*. (Syntax and Semantics 14.), 191–212. New York: Academic Press.

Narrog, Heiko (2012): *Modality, Subjectivity, and Semantic Change: A Cross-Linguistic Perspective*. Oxford: Oxford University Press.
Patard, Adeline (2011): The epistemic uses of the English simple past and the French imparfait: When temporality conveys modality. In: A. Patard and F. Brisard (eds.), *Cognitive Approaches to Tense, Aspect, and Epistemic Modality*, 279–310. Amsterdam/Philadelphia: John Benjamins.
Pelyvás, Péter (2011): Motivation in English *must* and Hungarian *kell*. In: K. Panther and G. Radden (eds.), *Motivation in Grammar and the Lexicon*, 171–190. Amsterdam: John Benjamins.
Plungian, Vladimir A. (2011): *Vvedenie v grammatičeskuju semantiku: grammatičeskie značenija i grammatičeskie sistemy jazykov mira* [Introduction to the Semantics of Grammar: Grammatical Meanings and the Grammatical Systems of the World's Languages]. Moscow: RGGU.
Reichenbach, Hans (1947): *Elements of Symbolic Logic*. New York: The Free Press.
Šatunovskij, Il'ja B. (2009): *Problemy russkogo vida* [Problems of Russian Aspect]. Moscow: Jazyki slavjanskix kul'tur.
Stanojević, Mateusz-Milan and Renata Geld (2011): New current relevance in Croatian: Epistemic immediacy and the aorist. In: A. Patard and F. Brisard (eds.), *Cognitive Approaches to Tense, Aspect, and Epistemic Modality*, 159–180. Amsterdam/Philadelphia: John Benjamins.
Sweetser, Eve (1990): *From Etymology to Pragmatics: Metaphorical and Cultural Aspects of Semantic Structure*. Cambridge: Cambridge University Press.
Takahashi, Hidemitsu (2012): *A Cognitive Linguistic Analysis of the English Imperative: With Special Reference to Japanese Imperatives*. Amsterdam: John Benjamins.
Talmy, Leonard (2000): *Toward a Cognitive Semantics*. Cambridge: MIT Press.
Traugott, Elizabeth C. (1989): On the rise of epistemic meanings in English: An example of subjectification in semantic change. *Language* 65: 31–55.
Vendler, Zeno (1967): Verbs and times. In: Z. Vendler (ed.), *Linguistics in Philosophy* 97–121. Ithaca: Cornell University Press.

Johan van der Auwera, Daniël Van Olmen, and Denies Du Mon
Chapter 11: Grammaticalization

1 Introduction

This chapter first provides a brief historical perspective on grammaticalization, in section 2: it gives a general definition of the process, examines the origin of both the term and the idea and describes how it rose to prominence in the 80s and has been problematized more and more since the late 90s. Some of the reasons for this recent development are raised in the next two sections, which look at the link between grammaticalization and cognitive linguistics from two different angles. Section 3, on the one hand, discusses what cognition – in the broadest sense of the word – there is in current grammaticalization work. The following issues in particular are addressed, though they are not necessarily unique to grammaticalization: language acquisition as the locus of change; grammatical innovation as the result of the principles of clarity and economy, the desire to be expressive or the ubiquitous variation in the construal of situations; the effects of frequency in grammaticalization and their cognitive basis; the role of reanalysis versus analogy; and, finally, the mechanisms underlying the semantic changes in grammaticalization. Section 4, on the other hand, looks at what grammaticalization there is in current cognitive approaches to grammar. The focus is on Construction Grammar and Cognitive Grammar, two theories whose original orientation was predominantly synchronic. It is discussed how the former's notion of (grammatical) constructionalization involves a drastic widening of the scope of investigation as compared to the linguistic phenomena traditionally subsumed under grammaticalization and how subjectification is central to the grammaticalization work within the latter framework. Section 5 is the conclusion.

2 Grammaticalization – 100 years and more

In general terms, grammaticalization is the process that creates grammar. Most of the work on grammaticalization has focused on the development of morphosyntactic categories such as 'perfect' and 'number', involving function words

---

Johan van der Auwera, Antwerp, Belgium
Daniël Van Olmen, Lancaster, United Kingdom
Denies Du Mon, Antwerp, Belgium

such as articles, auxiliaries, conjunctions and particles, and derivational and inflectional morphemes, out of lexical items or (multiword) constructions. Thus the English modal verb *ought* 'grammaticalized' from a verb that meant 'to owe', the French negative particle *pas* meaning 'not' derives from a noun meaning 'step', the Italian derivational adverb marker *-mente* (as in *rigorosamente* 'rigorously') comes from the noun *mens* 'mind', and the English dental preterite *-ed* as in *danced* probably originates from an ancestor of the verb *do*. It is taken for granted that grammaticalization is not a process affecting individual words only. Thus it is not really the word *pas* itself that grammaticalized from 'step' to 'not', but a specific construction containing *pas* as well as the negative particle *ne* also meaning 'not'. Outside of this kind of context *pas* retained its 'step' meaning. Another assumption is that the change from lexicon to grammar is gradual and that even within the realm of grammar formations can be more or less 'grammatical', with e.g. inflection being more grammatical than derivation. Furthermore, grammar is more than a system of function words, a crucial component being word order. If in any language the word order is strict, this strictness will have developed out of discourse habits, and this rigidification also constitutes grammaticalization.

It would thus seem that grammaticalization is central to the understanding of language. Nevertheless, at least the term if not also the concept of grammaticalization have been claimed to have outlived its usefulness. One recent 'death penalty' was pronounced in 2012, the very year of its one hundredth anniversary. The year of birth is 1912 and the place of birth is a frequently cited but much less frequently read[1] short French article, which appeared in an Italian journal with a Latin Italian name (*Scientia – Rivista di Scienza*), but which became more easily accessible through its inclusion in a 1921 edition of collected papers. The single parent is Antoine Meillet. To the extent that we can see, the term was indeed new, but the idea was not. Meillet was very explicit on this: he considered grammaticalization phenomena to be "well known, even by people that have never studied linguistics and everybody has the opportunity to study them or at least observe them" (Meillet 1912: 384, our translation). Meillet, did not, however, name any predecessors. Christian Lehmann (1995: 1) traces the study of *avant la lettre* grammaticalization back to the French philosopher Condillac

---

[1] A telling illustration of the way Meillet (1912) was not read with sufficient care comes from the study of negation. One of Meillet's illustrations of grammaticalization is the diachrony of negation as with French *ne* going to *ne pas* and then *pas*. The process became well known under the term 'Jespersen cycle', with reference to Jespersen (1917). Jespersen (1917), however, came later than Meillet (1912), and Jespersen did not himself use the term 'cycle', whereas Meillet did use a 'cycle' type concept, viz. 'spiral' in good Gabelentzian tradition (von der Gabelentz 1891: 251; see van der Auwera 2009).

(*Essai sur l'origine des connaissances humaines*, 1746) and Lehmann further assigns major roles to Wilhelm von Humboldt, Franz Bopp, and Georg von der Gabelentz and, in more general terms, to 19th century typology and Indo-European historical linguistics. In their introduction to a handbook on grammaticalization, Heiko Narrog and Bernd Heine (2011: 1) even say that the study of grammaticalization is "almost as old as linguistics".

Despite this longevity, however, the days of grammaticalization might be numbered. At a conference on 'Refining Grammaticalization', organized in February 2012 by Ferdinand von Mengden and Horst Simon, Graeme Trousdale claimed that at least the term was no longer useful (see section 4 for his plea for 'constructionalization'). If we are allowed to read this as a death announcement, we could, of course, in good European royal tradition continue with the phrase 'Long live grammaticalization' and in a way Trousdale did exactly that, by organizing a conference on 'New perspectives on grammaticalization' in July in Edinburgh. Its goal was the same as the one in Berlin, viz. to refine current thinking on the topic. We can conclude that just like grammaticalization was not really born in 1912, it did not really die in 2012 either. Yet the existence of a concept of grammaticalization *avant la lettre* and the fact that even after a century *après la lettre* specialists are still in need of refining the concept show that grammaticalization is a problematic notion.

In the first seventy years following 1912, the topic was treated off and on but typically without using the term, e.g. Jespersen (1922: 367–395), Benveniste (1968), and Givón (1979) – one exception is Kuryłowicz (1965). At least a partial reason for the lack of interest in the topic was the synchronic preoccupation of both North American and European linguistics. This changed from 1982 on with the catalyst work by Christian Lehmann (1982), Elizabeth Closs Traugott (1982), and Bernd Heine and Mechtild Reh (1984), the latter two interacting with Lehmann at the University of Cologne. From the nineties on there was a veritable explosion of studies, important ones involving the ground breakers of the previous decade (e.g. Traugott and Heine 1991; Hopper and Traugott 2003; Heine et al. 1991). It is true that some linguists who entered the debate found the concept dubious or at least some of the by then standard assumptions about it, see especially Newmeyer (1998: 225–295) and a special issue of *Language Sciences* (Campbell 2001). It is also true that for the diachronic study of grammar other notions were proposed and increasingly more so. Of some it was claimed – and also contested – that they were more important, e.g. reanalysis (Roberts 1993 vs. Haspelmath 1998) or constructionalization (see section 4). Other notions referred to processes that were claimed to compete with grammaticalization, viz. analogical change (already in Meillet 1912), lexicalization (Lehmann 2002; Brinton and Traugott 2005; but already in Kuryłowicz 1965), degrammaticalization (Norde 2009; but already in Lehmann 1982), regrammaticalization (Greenberg 1991), exaptation (Lass 1990), pragmaticalization (special issue of *Linguistics* – Degand and Simon-Vandenbergen 2011; but already in Traugott 1982), and subjectification and intersubjectification (van der Auwera and Nuyts 2012). Meanwhile, 'grammaticalization' has seen contenders in 'auxilation' (Benveniste 1968), 'grammaticization' (Bybee, Perkins and Pagliuca 1994) and 'grammation' (Andersen 2006). In the literature confronting the various *-ation* terms, it is often difficult to decide to what extent the debate concerns important conceptual issues or only terminology. Hence the organizers of both the 2012 Berlin and Edinburgh conferences were correct: current thinking still needs refinement ... and this is also the case for the cognitive aspects of grammaticalization.

3 Cognition in grammaticalization theory

The question of which mental processes are at work in grammaticalization has been central to much of the work in the field of cognitive or functionalist linguistics. But generative linguists too have made certain claims about cognition in grammaticalization – especially with respect to the first of the two steps that Croft (2000: 4–5) distinguishes in language change, i.e., 'innovation' (the second one being 'propagation'). In their view, grammaticalization takes place during language acquisition (e.g. Roberts and Roussou 2003: 33–34). In essence, change is regarded as reanalysis by the learner of the language. Children are assumed to possess an innate set of principles (valid for all languages) and parameters (to be set), which allows the ambiguous output of an adult grammar to receive a representation in their grammars that differs from the 'original' one. The actual change is caused by considerations of least effort or economy within the linguistic system. According to Van Gelderen (2004), for instance, learners tend to posit a head rather than a phrase and to assume a position higher up in the tree in cases of ambiguity. In the minimalist framework, both tendencies can be argued to reduce the computational load: "full phrases have more features (to check) and they are more likely to be interpreted" and "the lower ... element in the tree has more semantic features whereas the grammatical/functional elements has uninterpretable features" (Van Gelderen 2011: 372).

Despite the increase in generative grammaticalization studies in the 21st century (e.g. Simpson and Wu 2002; Abraham 2004; and Fuß 2005), the model is problematic in at least two respects. Acquisition does not appear to be the primary locus of language change (see Croft 2000: 57–59 and Bybee 2010: 114–119). Moreover, it is highly doubtful from a typological as well as from an evolutionary perspective (see Croft 2001 and Christiansen and Chater 2008 respectively) that humans are born with a set of linguistic principles and parameters in any case. From a cognitive perspective (see Tomasello 2006) this assumption is unnecessary.

The dominant view, which is characteristic of the functionalist paradigm, is that grammaticalization does not happen during acquisition or is at least not restricted to it (see Bruyn 1995 on creoles and Singleton and Newport 2004 on sign language). Croft (2010: 6) distinguishes two models for the beginning of change in adult language. In the first model, innovation is triggered by the interaction of the conflicting principles of economy and clarity: first, economy motivates the formal reduction of grammatical items, then the desire to be clear prompts speakers to develop more substantial, typically periphrastic alternatives and the new forms may eventually be reduced as well. One of the exponents of this model is Langacker (1977: 128): "Language change reflects the pressure to achieve linguistic optimality". This goal subsumes the opposite tendencies toward simplicity on the one hand and perceptual optimality and transparency on the other hand (see also von der Gabelentz 1891 on *Bequemlichkeit* 'ease' and *Deutlichkeit* 'clearness').

The view that reduction comes first has been criticized by, among others, Haspelmath (1999, 2000), and this brings us to the second model. One of the arguments is that the first model "cannot explain why erosion does not stop at the point where it would threaten intelligibility" (Haspelmath 2000: 791). In Haspelmath's opinion, innovation is motivated by the desire to be expressive or, in his words, "extravagant". In an attempt to be noticed and achieve social success, speakers violate the so-called maxim of conformity and – within reason – draw on the lexicon to produce more 'creative' expressions. Lehmann (1985: 315) puts it as follows: "They do not want to express themselves the same way they did yesterday, and in particular not the same way as somebody else did yesterday. To some extent, language is comparable to fashion". The new forms then catch on, conventionalize and tend to become subject to formal reduction. This model is not unproblematic either, however. Croft (2010) is right in pointing to the pervasive nature of variation in speech. If new or different ways of saying things constitute expressiveness, every speaker can be said to be expressive almost all the time and no speaker will ever really be noticed. He argues that variation (and thus innovation) is inherent to ordinary speech and that it is cognitively motivated. As speakers experience and construe the same situation in various ways, it is only normal that their verbalizations differ too. According to Croft (2010: 42), who observes that the synchronic diversity of forms often reflects potential paths of grammaticalization, it is "this ubiquitous variation" on which "selection mechanisms [of a social type] operate" in language change (see Waltereit 2011: 415–416 for cursory criticism).

Most of the explanations discussed in the preceding paragraph are partially cognitive but primarily communicative in nature. But there are other factors. Frequency, for instance, has been shown to have a huge impact on the manner in which linguistic items are stored in the brain and, as such, on the manner in which they develop (see Bybee 2003, 2006 and Divjak and Caldwell-Harris, volume 1). The fact that speaking is neuromotoric and that repetition correlates with increasing fluency accounts for the aforementioned phonetic erosion of high frequency (grammaticalizing) items. More significantly perhaps, the more a particular word sequence or construction occurs, the more it is 'saved' and uttered as a unit. As a consequence, it can disassociate itself from its components. At the formal level, this autonomy combines with repetition to result in fusion (e.g. *going to* turning into *gonna*). It also renders the word sequence or construction less analyzable and allows it to lose its internal structure and change categories (e.g. *be going to* becoming an auxiliary). At the functional level, autonomy makes it possible for a unit to get a new meaning (through repeated inferences, see below), which may not be reducible to the semantic sum of its subparts (e.g. *be going to* turning into a marker of futurity). On the whole, repetition can be regarded as an important driving force behind grammaticalization (but see e.g. Hundt 2001 on the low frequency of the *get*-passive). It is not the whole cognitive story, though.

One hotly debated issue is what happens mentally when, say, *be going to* develops into an auxiliary. The usual answer is reanalysis or a "change in the structure of an expression or class of expressions that does not involve any immediate or intrinsic modification of its surface structure" (Langacker 1977: 58) (see also Hopper and Traugott 2003: 50–63). In other words, speakers are said to restructure the sequence [*be* + *going*]$_{MainVerbPhrase}$ + [*to* + X]$_{Purpose}$ as [*be* + *going* + *to*]$_{Auxiliary}$ + [X]$_{MainVerb}$. Still, the role or even the existence of reanalysis has been called into question by some linguists (e.g. Haspelmath 1998). Fischer (2009: 7–8), for example, claims that "the very first time a historical speaker-listener identified *going-to* as an auxiliary, therefore, did not constitute an actual reanalysis of *going*(full verb)+*to*-infinitive but a category mistake that he could make because the *going-to* form fitted both the V-*to*-V as well as the Aux-V pattern". More fundamentally, reanalysis has been argued to be logically impossible: it suggests that new categories can come into being as the result of some structural ambiguity while this ambiguity "exists only in retrospect – that is, after the change has taken place" (De Smet 2009: 1729).

The alternative that most of the critics of reanalysis propose is analogy. In much of late 20th century and early 2000s work (e.g. Hopper and Traugott 2003: 63–68), analogy is regarded as interacting with reanalysis. The latter is responsible for rule changes and for creating forms, the former for widening a new rule's scope and for extending a new form's contexts of use (e.g. from activity verbs after *be going to* to all verbs). But especially in recent work within the usage-based framework which takes Antilla's (2003: 438) statement that "humans are simply analogical animals" to heart (e.g. Fischer 2008), analogy has taken center stage. Language – with no fundamental distinction between grammar and lexicon – is argued to be shaped by analogical connections in form and function between individual items or tokens, groups of tokens and/or types. In this model, analogy is considered not only a mechanism but also a cause for change. The grammaticalization of *a lot of* into a quantifier, for instance, can be said to be motivated by its similarity to the older construction *a heap of* (see Brems 2012).

It is not entirely clear, however, how strong an analogical link has to be to trigger change. The aforementioned 'match' between *be going to* and the Aux-V pattern can serve as an example: the auxiliaries followed by a *to*-infinitive that existed at the time of the change did not contain an *-ing* form (see Traugott 2011: 26). Relatedly, scholars have raised the question how the first auxiliary (or any new category) ever came into existence given the lack of a pattern to model it on. One tentative answer is that "the [first] 'auxiliary' would have been an under-analysed and grammatically isolated chunk" and that "only when another such chunk developed, language users could perceive a similarity between the two", at which "point a category 'auxiliary' arises" (De Smet 2009: 1751).

Another important question is how grammaticalizing items evolve semantically. Heine et al. (1991) look at the issue from a typological perspective and observe considerable similarities in the source and target meanings between languages. They argue that speakers "conceptualize abstract domains of cognition in terms of concrete domains" (Heine et al. 1991: 31) and try to capture this process of metaphorical extension in the following hierarchy: person > object > activity > space > time > quality. The semantic evolution of *be going to* can thus be said to involve the metaphor 'time is space'. One crucial aspect of the hierarchy is that the sources are typically anthropocentric (e.g. body parts, 'basic' activities such as 'say' and 'go') or, put differently, rooted in human experience. The metaphor approach has been criticized, however, for not explaining the gradual nature of the semantic evolution in grammaticalization. *Be going to* does not change from a marker of movement into one of futurity in one step but via a number of intermediate, metonymic steps – which, for clarity's sake, Heine et al. (1991) do acknowledge.

Several proposals have been made to account for these gradual changes (e.g. Nicolle 1998 within the framework of relevance theory), the most influential one being the invited inference theory by Traugott and Dasher (2002). The idea is that a form used by the speaker in a particular context (see Diewald 2002 and Heine 2002 on critical and bridging contexts respectively) encourages the addressee to draw a specific inference or, in other words, to see the conversational implicature as part of the message (but see Ariel 2002 on the role of explicatures in grammaticalization). Through repetition, this inference may generalize – i.e., it becomes typical but is still cancellable – and eventually conventionalize as the form's new meaning. According to Bybee, Perkins and Pagliuca (1994: 268), markers of futurity such as *be going to* involve (at least) the following contiguous steps:

> The temporal meaning ... is already present as an inference from the spatial meaning. When one moves along a path toward a goal in space, one also moves in time ... The function of expressing intention comes into play. When a speaker announces that s/he is going somewhere to do something, s/he is also announcing the intention to do that thing ... The only change necessary is the generalization to contexts in which an intention is expressed, but the subject is not moving spatially to fulfill that intention.

On the whole, the metonymy of pragmatic inferencing seems to describe the semantic evolution of grammaticalizing items better than the metaphorical account, though the former could be argued to be motivated by the latter (see also Heine et al. 1991: 96).

Obviously, the mechanisms discussed in the present section are not restricted to grammaticalization. Analogy, inferences and the like belong to the general human mental faculty and also play a role in other processes of language change (see Hilpert, volume 2) such as lexicalization as well as, if one accepts that it exists, pragmaticalization.

In the next section, we will turn things around. We will look at existing cognitive theories and describe how they deal with grammaticalization.

4 Grammaticalization in cognitive linguistic theory

Within the edifice of cognitive linguistics, several positions have been taken with regards to grammaticalization. This section deals with how two main strands in cognitive linguistics, viz. Cognitive Grammar (Langacker 1999, 2005, 2006, 2007, 2010) and (Diachronic) 'Construction Grammar' (Croft 2001; Noël 2007; Trousdale 2010; Hilpert, volume 2).[2] Even though Construction Grammar

---

[2] The Traugott/Trousdale approach, which we will focus on below, is not strictly speaking a kind of (Diachronic) Construction Grammar, but since constructions and diachrony are crucial to them, we include it under this heading.

(henceforth CxG) and Cognitive Grammar (henceforth CG) are very similar in that they are both usage-based, cognitive approaches, operating on the principle that language is built up of conventionalized form-meaning pairings ('symbolic units') that represent all grammatical knowledge, there are some important differences between the two. Exactly those differences have led to differing takes on grammaticalization.

CG and CxG conceive of the 'form' component of a construction differently. In CG, form solely refers to the phonological form (Langacker 2005: 104–107), whereas in CxG, form also captures grammatical form. The CG and CxG views on meaning are similar, but for CG meaning is the more important component and grammaticalization is seen as a primarily semantic phenomenon, to be described in terms of what is called 'construal' and 'profiling'. For CxG, grammaticalization concerns pairings of both meaning and form, i.e., the 'constructions', which come in different types and are related to each other in taxonomic networks. Traugott (2008a: 236) introduces a specific nomenclature to refer to four different types of constructions which can be distinguished in these networks (although in some cases more or fewer levels can be distinguished (see also Hilpert 2013: 5). These types range from the lowest level or 'construct'-level, which are individual instantiations of language use. Higher up we find 'micro-constructions' or individual construction types. More abstract are 'meso-constructions', which represent sets of constructions. The highest level of abstraction are 'macro-constructions'; "meaning-form pairings that are defined by structure and function, e.g., Partitive, or Degree ModifierConstructions" (Traugott 2008a: 236).

4.1 (Diachronic) Construction Grammar

The CxG view on grammaticalization is different from that of CG, but there are in fact even different CxG views. Undoubtedly partly due to the characterization of grammaticalization as "the creation of constructions", it seems just one step away from conflating the term 'grammaticalization' with the framework-specific term 'constructionalization' or even with 'constructional change' (Wiemer and Bisang 2004: 4). There have been strong arguments, however, to maintain that 'grammaticalization' and 'constructionalization' should be kept apart (Noël 2007). Noël (2007: 195–196) argues that grammaticalization should still exist in diachronic construction grammar as a more advanced step in change, distinguishing it from constructionalization as an initial establishment of form-meaning pairings (see also Gisborne and Patten 2010). As a result, the term 'grammatical constructionalization' – as opposed to 'lexical constructionalization' – has found its way into the literature with only the former doing the grammaticalization work (Traugott 2008b; Trousdale 2008; Traugott and Trousdale 2010, 2013). However, grammatical constructionalization may still not be the same as grammaticalization. A true construction grammarian will adhere to a very wide conception of what is grammar, because all constructions are conceived of as the building blocks of grammar (e.g. Wiemer and Bisang 2004). Consequently, grammatical constructionalization may incorporate more conventionalized form-meaning pairings than traditional grammaticalization theorists will see apt in grammaticalization. In the following, we will go deeper into grammatical and lexical constructionalization as developed by both Traugott and Trousdale (individually or jointly).

For Traugott and Trousdale (Traugott 2008b; Trousdale 2008, 2010; Traugott and Trousdale 2010), constructionalization is the emergence of constructions at any level in the constructional taxonomy. Through conventionalization, it can result in what is traditionally known as the grammaticalization of a construction, now called "grammatical constructionalization" and also in what is traditionally known as the lexicalization of a construction. Put simply, through repeated language use grammaticalizing constructions emerge at an increasingly schematic level whereby they become more general, and whereby their schema becomes increasingly productive (Trousdale 2010: 52). Lexicalizing constructions, however, exhibit a smaller degree of schematicity and next to no syntactic productivity (Gisborne and Patten 2010: 102). Hilpert (2013: 18–19), amongst others, argues against the no productivity statement (giving the example of productive *-hood* and *-ness* words), and also Traugott and Trousdale (2013) take a new stance on this. Croft and Cruse (2004: 309) further explain that productivity, schematization and frequency are interdependent: the productivity of a construction is proportionate to the number of instances at any level of schematicity. Key features (or even prerequisites) for the gradual process of grammatical constructionalization at every level are an increase in productivity, semantic generality and non-compositionality (Langacker 2005; Gisborne and Patten 2010; Trousdale 2008). Compare, for instance, the lexical construction (or idiom) *kick the bucket*, which has no syntactic productivity nor semantic reduction to the extent that its internal components may be replaced by new ones (* *hit the bucket*, * *kick the pot*) and the grammatical aspectual construction (*GIVE N a V-ing*), exemplified by *he gave the dog a kicking*, which has become syntactically productive and semantically applicable to items previously not accepted in the constructional schema (*He gave her a thorough seeing to* > *He gave the shirt a good ironing*). In both processes features are not acquired in an abrupt fashion, rather the constructions undergo micro-steps towards constructionalization higher up the taxonomy.

Central to grammatical constructionalization (GCzn) accounts are two collaborating, yet seemingly opposite, forces. On the one hand, the GCzn of a construction/construct implies a bottom-up movement upward in the constructional taxonomy (Hudson 2007: 49). Change is only possible through language use. Construct-level ambiguity, supported by inherited schema knowledge[3] (or default inheritance, see below) is the first step towards change (see also Croft 2001: 126–129). Repeated use of related constructs may lead to the formation of a micro-construction. When this micro-construction becomes entrenched, a meso-construction may be formed on a higher level of abstraction. Through the ongoing, gradual conventionalization, the meso-construction can in turn affect new constructs and coerce them into forming a new micro-construction (Gisborne and Patten 2010: 103; Noël 2007: 184). This constitutes a feedback loop whereby a meso-construction becomes entrenched and more schematic and whereby it can, in itself, start to function as an analogical template for future innovations.

On the other hand, GCzn relies on the 'default inheritance' of constructional (idiosyncratic) properties from more schematic, higher-level constructions onto lower-level constructs. Default inheritance, here, represents all individual linguistic knowledge in a speaker. It also presents the basic mechanism of change in CxG accounts through which novel constructions may emerge. The macro- and meso-constructional schemas serve as templates with linguistically successful (conventional and productive) properties which may recruit new constructs and consequently project their internal properties onto them; this is a process of innovation by analogy. Gisborne and Patten (2010: 103) see these constructional schemas as coercion environments. In a way, then, we could say that language change is an innovation through coercion. This does not mean, however, that an emerging construction needs to inherit all the properties of the higher-level construction (see also Hudson 2007); otherwise it is not a newly recruited construction. Take for instance a subtype of the Composite Predicate Construction (Trousdale 2008) (1), which inherits from the Ditransitive Give Construction (*to give N to N*).

(1) *He gave his employee a good grilling.*

The second noun in the Composite Predicate Construction is not retained but replaced by a verbal noun. In summary, the grammatical development of a construction should be seen in relation to the constructional taxonomy from which it inherits. If a chronological order needs to be assigned, this would happen after repeated use of a construct. The bidirectional construction strengthening

---

[3] It must be kept in mind that it is the schema (or construction *pattern*) that carries meaning, and that this meaningful pattern recruits new elements into it through analogy.

can eventually lead to further entrenchment and abstraction as a macro-construction.

Even though the framework-specific term roughly captures the same changes traditionally associated with grammaticalization, it is considered better because it allows for a coherent account of the processes making up grammaticalization (Gisborne and Patten 2010; Trousdale 2010: 52, 55). In being able to map the specific steps inherent to constructionalization, grammatical change is unidirectional in a "non-trivial way" (Trousdale 2010: 55). Specifically, it tackles the seemingly contradictory accounts which have been appearing over the last three decades, where one conceives of the restriction and reduction of elements (in paradigmaticization, univerbation, semantic bleaching, etc.; Lehmann 1982) as well as of their expansion (semantic scope, complementation, etc.; Brinton 2006; Traugott 2010). The constructionalist approach mediates between these two initially contradictory views by allowing for both movements. A grammaticalizing construction shows stronger internal dependencies – restrictions and reductions such as morpho-phonological univerbation – and a scope flexibility of its environment (expansion).

All in all, we see the same processes in GCzn as we see in traditional grammaticalization theory, with the exception that they apply to more units than traditionally assumed. Also, subjectification can be part of GCzn (Trousdale 2008, 2010), but not to the extent that it defines the change, as in Cognitive Grammar.

4.2 Cognitive Grammar

If CxG can be referred to as the cognitive linguistic approach to syntax (Croft and Cruse 2004: 225), then CG – albeit "a kind of construction grammar" (Langacker 2010: 79) – could be referred to as the cognitive linguistic approach to semantics or meaning. With all grammatical items being meaningful and meaning being identified with conceptualization, it is taken as self-evident in CG that grammaticalization is primarily characterized in conceptual semantics. CG holds that the process of subjectification (which, as defined by Langacker, deals with construal and perspectivization) is central to grammaticalization. Grammaticalization itself is defined – quite simply – as "the evolution of grammatical elements from lexical sources" (Langacker 1999: 297). Grammatical status lies in the secondary, supplementing function of items to lexical, descriptive items. This secondary status (see Boye and Harder 2012) can be exhibited by conjunctions or case markers indicating how conceptual chunks fit together, they can be aspect or voice markers imposing a perspective for the object and they can point at external factors in the subjective realm through illocutionary force and deixis. Like most accounts, CG sees grammaticalization as a composite change with interrelated, mutually reinforcing aspects – although formal aspects are tended to more as a consequence of conceptual change (Langacker 2010: 83, 89; see also Trousdale and Norde 2013).

In the conceptual semantics advocated by CG, it is assumed that there is an 'object' and a 'subject' of conception. The object of conception is the content of the expression; the subject of conception is the conceptualizer, i.e., the speaker (and secondarily the hearer). Maximally objective is an expression with an implicit or 'off-stage' subject. When the subject is 'on-stage', it is objectified, i.e., in the object of conception as both the subject and object of conception, for example, by means of a subject pronoun *I*, *we*, *you*, ... The 'profile' is what most attention is directed at in the object of conception and is highly objectively construed. 'Construal' is the subject's particular selection of what is in the (profile of the) object of conception (Langacker 2006: 18, 2010: 80; see also Nuyts 2012: 67–69). Being in the object of conception means that an item is 'on-stage' and thus objectively construed. Construal always manifests itself 'on-stage'. Subjective construal is immanent in expressions, so most expressions have both subjectively and objectively construed elements, which can both only be 'on-stage' because they have been construed (Evans and Green 2006: 728).

The driving force behind grammatical change and grammaticalization in CG is subjectification (Evans and Green 2006: 728; Langacker 1999: 314). The term should not be confused with Traugott's use of this term, which refers to the subjective content of an entire expression (Langacker 2006: 17). In CG, subjectification is more complex. Subjectification as the main process moving just a single item on the continuum from lexical to grammatical is an umbrella term for a set of (reductive) changes affecting this item. It is the movement of an item from the objective to the subjective construal realm or, in other words, the attenuation of objectivity of an item whereby it goes from maximally specific to maximally schematic – schematization (Langacker 2006: 21; 2010: 81). In highly grammaticalized cases, this attenuation leads to transparency. The attenuation is characterized by at least four conceptual processes (Langacker 1999: 301–302): we can see a shift in the *locus of activity* or *potency* (from objectively construed (on-stage) to subjectively construed (off-stage), e.g. the English modals, see below), *status* (from actual to potential or from specific to generic) (e.g. the construction 'thing', see below), *focus* (from profiled to unprofiled), and *domain* (from physical interaction to a social or experiential one) of the item (e.g. the English modals). Additionally, grammaticalization and, by association, subjectification, is accompanied by other processes of attenuation, viz. phonological (i.e., formal) attenuation (*going to* > *gonna* > *gon/onna* > *a*) and a shift in salience from primary (lexical, i.e., descriptive) to secondary (grammatical, i.e., supplementary) *function*. See Figure 11.1.

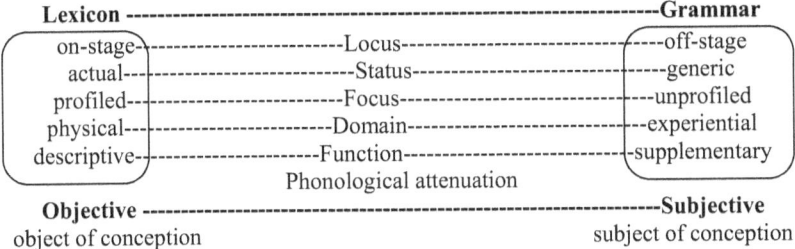

Fig. 11.1: Processes involved in subjectification.

As such, grammaticalization is seen as a mainly reductive process. However, it can initially be seen as expansive when an item's reference starts to broaden from actual to generic, through which its meaning will be applicable to any content. This is what drives schematization and gradual loss of analyzability leading to the erosion of the original motivation for its spread (Langacker 2010: 83).

By means of illustration, a look at the word *thing* may be revealing. In its most specific meaning (2), it denotes an inanimate physical object. In its most schematic meaning (4), it can occur in the pronoun *something*, where it merely designates any product of grouping and reification (Langacker 2010: 81). An intermediate stage (3) shows that *thing* has abstract (discourse) reference.

(2) What is that thing over there?

(3) Who said those awful things?

(4) You moaning is something I could really do without right now.

In (4), the construction *thing* shows signatures of grammaticalization (and schematization) in the following ways: Being schematic, it has been subject to objective attenuation (i.e., subjectification). It is no longer profiled, and thus it can also occur in the pronoun *something*. It has moved from an actual to a generic domain, denoting any content labeled by a noun, any abstract or concrete product of grouping and reification. Another illustration (although highly simplified) is given by the present-day epistemic modal verbs, which have developed from objective (lexical) verbs to subjective (grammatical) markers of likelihood located in the subjective domain. As such, they have also become increasingly unprofiled, generic, experiential and even off-stage in that the likelihood is located in the subject's vantage point rather than in a grammatical subject or in the object of conception.

5 Conclusion

What does this overview teach us and what does it tell us about the future? First, we think that the sketch tells us that it does not matter too much what label one chooses to describe the phenomena at hand: grammaticalization by any other name would smell as sweet. Second, any term one settles for has to be defined or described as clearly as possible, and placed within a larger framework, where its role is to be delineated in relation to other factors and processes, cognitive, communicative and other. We briefly outlined two such frameworks, CcG and CG. Neither was originally designed for diachrony and both are coping with grammaticalization in promising ways.

6 References

Abraham, Werner (2004): The grammaticalization of the infinitival preposition: Toward a theory of 'grammaticalizing reanalysis'. *Journal of Comparative Germanic Linguistics* 7: 111–170.

Andersen, Henning (2006): Grammation, regrammation, and degrammation: Tense loss in Russian. *Diachronica* 23: 231–258.

Antilla, Raimo (2003): Analogy: The warp and woof of cognition. In: B. D. Joseph and R. D. Janda (eds.), *The Handbook of Historical Linguistics*, 425–440. Oxford: Oxford University Press.

Ariel, Mira (2002): Privileged interactional interpretations. *Journal of Pragmatics* 34: 1003–1044.

Benveniste, Émile (1968): Mutations of linguistic categories. In: W. P. Lehmann and Y. Malkiel (eds.), *Directions for Historical Linguistics. A Symposium*, 85–94. Austin: University of Texas Press.

Boye, Kasper and Peter Harder (2012): A usage-based theory of grammatical status and grammaticalization *Language* 88: 1–44.

Brems, Lieselotte (2012): The establishment of quantifier constructions for size nouns: A diachronic study of heap(s) and lot(s). *Journal of Historical Pragmatics* 13: 202–231.

Brinton, Laurel J. (2006): Pathways in the development of pragmatic markers in English. In: A. van Kemenade and B. Los (eds.), *The Handbook of the History of English*, 307–334. London: Blackwell.

Brinton, Laurel J. and Elizabeth C. Traugott (2005): *Lexicalization and Language Change*. Cambridge: Cambridge University Press.

Bruyn, Adrienne (1995): *Grammaticalization in Creoles: The Development of Determiners and Relative Clauses in Sranan*. Amsterdam: University of Amsterdam.

Bybee, Joan L. (2003): Cognitive processes in grammaticalization. In: M. Tomasello (ed.), *The New Psychology of Language: Cognitive and Functional Approaches to Language Structure*, Volume 1, 145–167. Mahwah: Lawrence Erlbaum Associates.

Bybee, Joan L. (2006): From usage to grammar: The mind's response to repetition. *Language* 82: 711–733.

Bybee, Joan L. (2010): *Language, Usage and Cognition*. Cambridge: Cambridge University Press.

Bybee, Joan, Revere Perkins, and William Pagliuca (1994): *The Evolution of Grammar: Tense, Aspect and Modality in the Languages of the World*. Chicago: University of Chicago.

Campbell, Lyle (ed.) (2001): *Grammaticalization: A Critical Assessment*, Special issue (2/3) *Language Sciences* 23.

Christiansen, Morten H. and Nick Chater (2008): Language as shaped by the brain. *Behavioral and Brain Sciences* 31: 489–509.

Croft, William (2000): *Explaining Language Change: An Evolutionary Approach*. London: Longman.

Croft, William (2001): *Radical Construction Grammar: Syntactic Theory in Typological Perspective*. Oxford: Oxford University Press.

Croft, William (2010): The origins of grammaticalization in the verbalization of experience. *Linguistics* 48: 1–48.

Croft, William and Alan Cruse (2004): *Cognitive Linguistics*. Cambridge: Cambridge University Press.

de Condillac, Étienne Bonnot (1746): *Essai sur l'Origine des Connaissances Humaines* [Essay on the Origin of Human Knowledges]. Paris.

Degand, Liesbeth and Anne-Marie Simon-Vandenbergen (2011): *Grammaticalization, Pragmaticalization, and (Inter)Subjectification: Methodological Issues in the Study of Discourse Markers*. Special issue (3) *Linguistics* 49.

De Smet, Hendrik (2009): Analysing reanalysis. *Lingua* 119: 1728–1755.

Diewald, Gabriele (2002): A model for relevant types of contexts in grammaticalization. In: I. Wischer and G. Diewald (eds.), *New Reflections on Grammaticalization*, 103–120. Amsterdam: John Benjamins.

Divjak, Dagmar and Catherine Caldwell-Harris (volume 1): Frequency and entrenchment. Berlin/Boston: De Gruyter Mouton.

Evans, Vyvyan and Melanie Green (2006): Cognitive Linguistics: An Introduction. Edinburgh: Edinburgh University Press.

Fischer, Olga (2008): On analogy as the motivation for grammaticalization. *Studies in Language* 32: 336–382.

Fischer, Olga (2009): Grammaticalization as analogically driven change? *Vienna English Working Papers* 18: 3–23.

Fuß, Eric (2005): *The Rise of Agreement: A Formal Approach to the Syntax and Grammaticalization of Verbal Inflection*. Amsterdam: John Benjamins.

Gisborne, Nikolas and Amanda Patten (2010): Construction grammar and grammaticalization. In: H. Narrog and B. Heine (eds.), *The Oxford Handbook of Grammaticalization*, 92–104. Oxford: Oxford University Press.

Givón, Talmy (1979): From discourse to syntax: Grammar as a processing strategy. In: T. Givón (ed.), *Syntax and Semantics*, Volume 12: *Discourse and Syntax*, 81–112. New York: Academic Press.

Greenberg, Joseph H. (1991): The last stages of grammatical elements: Contractive and expansive desemanticization. In: E. C. Traugott and B. Heine (eds.), *Approaches to Grammaticalization*, Volume 1, 301–314. Amsterdam: John Benjamins.

Haspelmath, Martin (1998): Does grammaticalization need reanalysis? *Studies in Language* 22: 315–351.

Haspelmath, Martin (1999): Why is grammaticalization irreversible? *Linguistics* 37: 1043–1068.

Haspelmath, Martin (2000): The relevance of extravagance: A reply to Bart Geurts. *Linguistics* 38: 789–798.

Heine, Bernd (2002): On the role of context in grammaticalization. In: I. Wischer and G. Diewald (eds.), *New Reflections on Grammaticalization*, 83–101. Amsterdam: John Benjamins.

Heine, Bernd, Ulrike Claudi, and Friederike Hünnemeyer (1991): *Grammaticalization: A Conceptual Framework*. Chicago: University of Chicago Press.

Heine, Bernd and Mechtild Reh (1984): *Grammaticalization and Reanalysis in African Languages*. Hamburg: Buske.

Hilpert, Martin (volume 2): Historical Linguistics. Berlin/Boston: De Gruyter Mouton.

Hilpert, Martin (2013): *Constructional Change in English: Developments in Allomorphy, Word Formation, and Syntax*. Cambridge: Cambridge University Press.

Hopper, Paul J. and Elizabeth C. Traugott (2003): *Grammaticalization*. Cambridge: Cambridge University Press.

Hudson, Richard (2007): *Language Networks: The New Word Grammar*. Oxford: Oxford University Press.

Hundt, Marianne (2001): What corpora tell us about the grammaticalization of voice in *get*-constructions. *Studies in Language* 25: 49–88.

Jespersen, Otto (1917): *Negation in English and Other Languages*. Copenhagen: A. F. Høst & Søn.

Jespersen, Otto (1922): *Language: Its Nature, Development and Origin*. London: Georg Allen & Unwin.

Kuryłowicz, Jerzy (1965): The evolution of grammatical categories. *Diogenes* 51: 55–71. [Reprinted in Kurylowiz, Jerzy. 1975. *Esquisses linguistiques II* [Linguistic Sketches II], 38–54. Munich: Wilhelm Fink].

Lass, Roger (1990): How to do things with junk: Exaptation in language evolution. *Journal of Linguistics* 26: 79–102.

Langacker, Ronald W. (1977): Syntactic reanalysis. In: C. N. Li (ed.), *Mechanisms of Syntactic Change*, 57–139 Austin: University of Texas Press.

Langacker, Ronald W. (1999): Grammar and Conceptualization. Berlin: Mouton de Gruyter.

Langacker, Ronald W. (2005): Construction grammars: Cognitive, radical, and less so. In: F. J. Ruiz de Mendoza Ibáñez and S. Peña Cervel (eds.), *Cognitive Linguistics: Internal Dynamics and Interdisciplinary Interaction*, 101–159. Berlin: Mouton de Gruyter.

Langacker, Ronald W. (2006): Subjectification, grammaticization, and conceptual archetypes. In: A. Athanasiadou, C. Canakis and B. Cornillie (eds.), *Subjectification: Various Paths to Subjectivity*, 17–40. Berlin: Mouton de Gruyter.

Langacker, Ronald W. (2007): Cognitive Grammar. In: D. Geeraerts and H. Cuyckens (eds.), *The Oxford Handbook of Cognitive Linguistics*, 421–462. Oxford: Oxford University Press.

Langacker, Ronald W. (2010): Grammaticalization and Cognitive Grammar. In: H. Narrog and B. Heine (eds.), *The Oxford Handbook of Grammaticalization*, 79–91. Oxford: Oxford University Press.

Lehmann, Christian (1982): *Thoughts on Grammaticalization: A Programmatic Sketch*, Volume 1. Cologne: Institut für Sprachwissenschaft der Universität. (Revised in 1995 Munich: LINCOM EUROPA).

Lehmann, Christian (1985): Grammaticalization: Synchronic variation and diachronic change. *Lingua e Stile* 20: 303–318.

Lehmann, Christian (2002): New reflections on grammaticalization and lexicalization. In: I. Wischer and G. Diewald (eds.), *New Reflections on Grammaticalizations*, 1–18. Amsterdam: John Benjamins.

Meillet, Antoine (1912): L'évolution des formes grammaticales [The evolution of grammatical forms]. *Scienti – Rivista di Scienza* 12: 384–400. [Reprinted in Meillet, Antoine. 1926. *Linguistique Historique et Linguistique Générale [Historical Linguistics and General Linguistics*, 130–148. Paris: H. Champion].

Narrog, Heiko and Bernd Heine (2011): Introduction. In: H. Narrog and Bernd Heine (eds.), *The Oxford Handbook of Grammaticalization*, 1–16. Oxford: Oxford University Press.

Newmeyer, Frederick J. (1998): *Language Form and Language Function*. Cambridge: MIT Press.

Nicolle, Steve (1998): A relevance theory perspective on grammaticalization. *Cognitive Linguistics* 9: 1–35.

Noël, Dirk (2007): Diachronic construction grammar and grammaticalization theory. *Functions of Language* 14: 177–202.

Norde, Muriel (2009): *Degrammaticalization*. Oxford: Oxford University Press.

Nuyts, Jan (2012): Notions of (inter)subjectivity. *English Text Construction* 5: 53–76.

Roberts, Ian (1993): A formal account of grammaticalisation in the history of Romance futures. *Folia Linguistica Historica* 13: 219–251.

Roberts, Ian and Anna Roussou (2003): *Syntactic Change: A Minimalist Approach to Grammaticalization*. Cambridge: Cambridge University Press.

Simpson, Andrew and Xiu-Zhi Zoe Wu (2002): Agreement shells and focus. *Language* 78: 287–313.

Singleton, Jenny L. and Elissa L. Newport (2004): When learners surpass their models: The acquisition of American Sign Language from inconsistent input. *Cognitive Psychology* 49: 370–407.

Tomasello, Michael (2006): Construction grammar for kids. *Constructions*, Special issue 1. [http://elanguage.net/journals/constructions/article/view/26].

Traugott, Elizabeth C. (1982): From propositional to textual to expressive meanings: Some semantic-pragmatic aspects of grammaticalization. In: W. P. Lehmann and Y. Malkiel (eds.), *Perspectives in Historical Linguistics*, 245–271. Amsterdam: John Benjamins.

Traugott, Elizabeth C. (2008a): Grammaticalization, constructions and the incremental development of language: Suggestions from the development of degree modifiers in English. In: R. Eckardt, G. Jäger and T. Veenstra (eds.), *Variation, Selection, Development: Probing the Evolutionary Model of Language Change*, 219–250. Berlin: Mouton de Gruyter.

Traugott, Elizabeth C. (2008b): The grammaticalization of NP of NP constructions. In: A. Bergs and G. Diewald (eds.), *Constructions and Language Change*, 23–45. Berlin: Mouton de Gruyter.

Traugott, Elizabeth C. (2010): Grammaticalization. In: S. Luraghi and V. Bubenik (eds.), *A Companion to Historical Linguistics*, 269–283. London: Continuum Press.

Traugott, Elizabeth C. (2011): Grammaticalization and mechanisms of change. In: H. Narrog and B. Heine (eds.), *The Handbook of Grammaticalization*, 19–30. Oxford: Oxford University Press.

Traugott, Elizabeth C. and Richard B. Dasher (2002): *Regularity in Semantic Change*. Cambridge: Cambridge University Press.

Traugott, Elizabeth C. and Bernd Heine (1991): *Approaches to Grammaticalization*, Volume 2. Amsterdam: John Benjamins.

Traugott, Elizabeth C. and Graeme Trousdale (2010): *Gradience, Gradualness and Grammaticalization*. Amsterdam: John Benjamins.

Traugott, Elizabeth C. and Graeme Trousdale (2013): *Constructionalization and Constructional Changes*. Oxford: Oxford University Press.
Trousdale, Graeme (2008): Constructions in grammaticalization and lexicalization: Evidence from the history of a composite predicate construction in English. In: N. Gisborne and G. Trousdale (eds.), *Constructional Approaches to English Grammar*, 33–67. Berlin: Mouton de Gruyter.
Trousdale, Graeme (2010): Issues in constructional approaches to grammaticalization in English. In: K. Stathi, E. Gehweiler and E. König (eds.), *Grammaticalization: Current Views and Issues*, 51–71. Amsterdam: John Benjamins.
Trousdale, Graeme and Muriel Norde. (2013): Degrammaticalization and constructionalization: Two case studies. Language Sciences 36: 32–46.
van der Auwera, Johan (2009): The Jespersen cycles. In: E. van Gelderen (ed.), *Cyclical Change*, 35–71. Amsterdam: John Benjamins.
van der Auwera, Johan and Jan Nuyt (eds.) (2012): *Grammaticalization and (Inter)Subjectification*. Brussels: Koninklijke Vlaamse Academie van België voor Wetenschappen en Kunsten.
van Gelderen, Elly (2004): *Grammaticalization as Economy*. Amsterdam: John Benjamins.
van Gelderen, Elly (2011): *The Linguistic Cycle: Language Change and the Language Faculty*. Oxford: Oxford University Press.
von der Gabelentz, Georg (1891): *Die Sprachwissenschaft. Ihre Aufgaben, Methoden und bisherigen Ergebnisse [Linguistics: Its Duties, Methods and Current Results]*. Leipzig: Weigel.
Waltereit, Richard (2011): Grammaticalization and discourse. In: H. Narrog and B. Heine (eds.), *The Handbook of Grammaticalization*, 409–423. Oxford: Oxford University Press.
Wiemer, Björn and Walter Bisang (2004): What makes grammaticalization? An appraisal of its components and fringes. In: W. Bisang, N. Himmelmann and B. Wiemer (eds.), *What Makes Grammaticalization? A Look From its Fringes and Its Components*, 3–20. Berlin: Mouton de Gruyter.

Ewa Dąbrowska
Chapter 12: Individual differences in grammatical knowledge

1 Introduction

According to usage-based models, linguistic knowledge is built up from experience using domain-general cognitive abilities. Since speakers differ in general cognitive abilities and in their linguistic experience, we would expect considerable differences in their mental grammars as well. It is widely acknowledged that there are large differences between children in the rate and manner that they acquire language (Bates et al. 1988; Dąbrowska 2004; Peters and Menn 1993; Richards 1990) and between adult speakers in areas such as lexical knowledge, fluency, and processing speed (Clark 1997; Farmer et al. 2012; Mulder and Hulstijn 2011). Yet for several decades, generative linguists have confidently asserted (without providing any evidence) that " ... children in the same linguistic community all learn the same grammar" (Crain and Lillo-Martin 1999: 9; see also Bley-Vroman 2009: 179; Chomsky 1965: 11, 1975: 11; Crain et al. 2009: 124; Herschensohn 2009: 264; Lidz and Williams 2009: 177; Montrul 2008: 4; Nowak et al. 2001: 114; Smith 1999: 41), and this view continues to be widely espoused, even by cognitive and functional linguists.[1]

This chapter will show that the claim that all learners converge on the same grammar is a myth. It reviews a number of studies which demonstrate that speakers of the same language sometimes represent "the same" knowledge differently, and that some basic grammatical structures are not fully mastered by all native speakers. It will also explore some of reasons for individual differences in grammatical knowledge, and discuss their implications for linguistic theory.

---

[1] There were, however, some dissenting voices: see, for example, Seuren (1982). It is also widely acknowledged that speakers of different dialects have different grammars; the discussion in this chapter concerns differences that are not attributable to systematic differences between linguistic communities or subcommunities.

Ewa Dąbrowska, Northumbria University, United Kingdom

2 Irregular morphology: The Polish genitive singular

As a first example, let us consider the Polish genitive. The genitive is the second most frequent case after the nominative, and the most frequent case in written language. It has several very general functions, including marking the possessor and the direct object of negated verbs, and is also used to mark the object of a number of frequent verbs and prepositions. The genitive of masculine nouns is signalled by two inflectional endings, -*a* and -*u*, whose distribution is determined by several factors (see Buttler et al. 1973: 158–172; Westfal 1956). Some of these are semantic: for instance, nearly all animate nouns, and a substantial majority of nouns designating body parts and small easily manipulable objects, take -*a*, while nouns designating substances, locations, collections of objects and abstract concepts usually take -*u*. Others are morphological and phonological: some derivational affixes and stem-final consonants or consonant clusters are associated with -*a*, others with -*u*. However, there are many exceptions to these tendencies, and they are sometimes in conflict. Thus, it is not clear what the 'correct' generalization, or generalizations, would be.

Dąbrowska (2008a) describes a nonce word inflection experiment designed to reveal the generalizations underlying speakers' use of the two affixes with inanimate nouns.[2] Adult native speakers of Polish were taught nonce nouns referring to various unfamiliar objects and substances and asked to use them in grammatical contexts requiring the genitive. The results indicated that about 12 % of the participants had a strong preference for -*a*, the most frequent ending overall: they used it with over 80 % of inanimate referents. This suggests that they had acquired a simple general rule ("add -*a* to the stem if the noun is masculine") with a large number of exceptions. About 46 % of the participants had a clear preference for -*u* (which is used with most inanimate nouns), also choosing it over 80 % of time; these participants appear to have learned a somewhat more complex rule with fewer exceptions ("add -*a* if the noun is masculine and animate and -*u* if the noun is masculine and inanimate"). A further 8 % had a narrow semantic rule and consistently used -*a* with nouns referring to objects and -*u* with nouns referring to substances. The remaining speakers either relied on phonological criteria or used the two endings more or less interchangeably. Thus, different speakers had extracted different rules from the input they had been exposed to.

---

[2] Dąbrowska and Szczerbiński (2006) have shown that speakers consistently use -*a* with animate nouns.

3 Regular morphology: The Polish dative

The regularities found in the distribution of genitive endings are only partial and rather complex; it is not surprising, therefore, that different learners end up with different generalizations. The next example that we will consider, the Polish dative, is very different in that it is highly regular, with only a few exceptions, but rather infrequent with full nouns. There are four dative endings: *-owi* for masculines (with a few exceptions for high frequency nouns), *-u* for neuters, and *-e* and *-i/y* for feminines; the distribution of the feminine endings is determined by phonological properties of the last consonant of the stem.

Dąbrowska (2008b) investigated Polish speakers' productivity with dative endings. Adult native speakers of Polish were presented with nonce words in the nominative and asked to use them in grammatical contexts requiring the dative. It was hypothesized that speakers may rely on low-level schemas that apply to clusters of phonologically similar nouns rather than general rules which apply "across the board"; in order to determine whether this was the case, half of the nonce nouns came from densely populated phonological neighbourhoods (i.e., they resembled many real nouns) and half from sparsely populated neighbourhoods.

Mean scores on the task ranged from 38 % target for low-density neuter neighbourhoods to 95 % for high-density feminine neighbourhoods, with an overall mean of 74 %. However, these figures hide vast individual differences. Individual scores ranged from 29 % to 100 %, and for words from low-density neuter neighbourhoods, from 0 % to 100 %. Interestingly, performance on the inflection task was strongly correlated ($r = 0.72$) with the number of years spent in formal education.

Why should we see such a correlation? Since all participants reliably supplied the dative forms of some nouns, e.g. feminine nouns from densely populated neighbourhoods, we can rule out relatively uninteresting explanations such as failure to understand the experimental task, lack of familiarity with the testing situation, or unwillingness to cooperate. Follow-up studies revealed that even the less educated participants reliably inflected real nouns in the dative contexts used in the experiment and reliably selected the gender-appropriate form of a demonstrative adjective used in construction with the nonce nouns, showing that their failure to provide the correct dative inflection could not be attributed to lack of lexical knowledge about which verbs or prepositions require the dative case or problems with identifying the gender of the nonce noun. Thus their relatively low scores on the inflection task must be due to problems with the inflections themselves.

As argued in Dąbrowska (2008b), the education-related differences observed in the experiment can be most plausibly attributed to asymmetries in the distribution of dative nouns in spoken and written discourse, and differences in the amount of exposure to written discourse. In spoken language, the dative case is predominantly used to mark semantic functions such as experiencer, addressee and beneficiary, and the nouns used in these functions tend to be kinship terms, personal names or nicknames, and nouns referring to various occupations. Consequently, datives in spoken language occur with a fairly restricted range of nouns, resulting in relatively low type frequencies of the individual endings. In written language, the dative also occurs in a number of lexically-governed environments which allow a wider variety of nouns, including inanimate nouns. This can be seen by comparing the proportion of inanimate nouns used in the dative in various genres: 1.4% in child-directed speech, 14% in adult-directed speech, and 62% in written texts. Since more educated speakers have more experience with formal written language, they encounter a larger number of noun types in the dative, and since high type frequency leads to greater productivity, more educated speakers become more productive with dative inflections.

4 Complex syntax: Subordination

Both of the examples discussed so far involved knowledge of inflectional morphology. We now turn to studies examining adult native speakers' knowledge of syntax. Dąbrowska (1997) tested comprehension of four types of complex sentences in English, all based on examples from *Linguistic Inquiry*: complex NP sentences, which contained a subordinate clause with a noun complement clause in the subject position (e.g. *Paul noticed that the fact that the room was tidy surprised Shona*), 'tough movement' sentences (e.g. *John will be hard to get his wife to vouch for*), and two types of sentences with parasitic gaps (e.g. *It was King Louis who the general convinced that this slave might speak to*), as well as some sentences which slightly longer, but syntactically simpler; these served as control sentences. The participants (unskilled workers, undergraduates, postgraduates, and university lecturers) were asked simple questions about the sentences (e.g., *What did Paul notice?, Who will vouch?*).

The experiment revealed both individual and group differences in comprehension of the experimental sentences. As anticipated, the lecturers achieved the highest scores (mean 89% correct), followed by postgraduates (68%), undergraduates (59%), and unskilled workers (42%); all group differences were highly significant. Individual performance ranged from 0% to 100% on complex NP and tough movement sentences and from 25% to 100% on sentences with parasitic gaps. Performance on control sentences, in contrast, was much better: mean 91% correct in the unskilled group and 100% correct in the other groups (range 75–100%).

The obvious question that arises at this point is whether the differences observed in the experiment are attributable to differences in linguistic knowledge, or whether they are due to linguistically irrelevant factors such as working memory limitations or failure to engage with the task. It should be noted that the participants were tested under ideal conditions: the sentences were presented to them in both spoken and written form, and they could re-read them, or have them repeated, as many times as they needed. Thus, there is a real sense in which some participants' inability to respond correctly can be regarded as a problem with linguistic knowledge, i.e. competence, rather than the ability to access that knowledge. On the other hand, it cannot be denied that the test sentences placed heavy demands on the processing system, and hence a performance explanation cannot be dismissed out of hand.

This issue was addressed by Chipere (2001), who conducted a more in-depth study of one of the structures used in the Dąbrowska (1997) study, namely, complex NP sentences. Chipere tested two groups of eighteen-year-olds from the same school. One group – the High Academic Attainment, or HAA group – obtained A's in at least 5 GCSE subjects, including English. The Low Academic Attainment (LAA) participants, in contrast, got a D or below in GCSE English. Chipere's participants were given two tasks: a comprehension task similar to that used in the Dąbrowska study, and recall task in which participants first read sentences and then had to recall them verbatim. The HAA group performed much better on both tasks. This finding is compatible with both explanations mentioned above, since both comprehension and recall would be affected if the participants had not acquired the construction (or its subcomponents) but also if they were unable to hold such complex sentences in working memory. To distinguish between these two interpretations, Chipere conducted a follow-up training experiment with the LAA participants only. The participants were randomly assigned to one of two training conditions: memory training, which involved learning to repeat complex NP sentences, and comprehension training, which involved a brief explanation of the target structure followed by practice with feedback. Both groups were trained on the pre-test sentences and then tested with a new set of complex NP sentences. The results were unequivocal. Memory training resulted in improved performance on the memory task, but had no effect on the comprehension task. Comprehension training, in contrast, improved performance on both tasks: the comprehension-trained LAA participants performed as well as the HAA group on the recall task, and even better than the HAA group on the comprehension task. Thus, it is clear that the low academic attainment participants' difficulties on the pre-test were attributable to lack of linguistic knowledge rather than limited working memory capacity.

5 Simpler syntax: Quantifiers

While Chipere's study provides strong evidence against explanations of individual differences in the comprehension of complex sentences that appeal only to processing capacity, there is no doubt that the structures tested in the studies described in the preceding section place heavy demands on working memory. Could comparable differences in performance be observed on simpler structures? Brooks and Sekerina's (2005/2006, 2006) work on comprehension of sentences with quantifiers shows that knowledge about quantifier scope is acquired late in the course of acquisition, and that even adults sometimes misinterpret sentences such as (1) and (2).[3]

(1) *Every rabbit is in a hat.*

(2) *Every hat has a rabbit in it.*

Brooks and Sekerina tested comprehension of sentences with quantifiers using a picture selection task (where participants heard one of the above sentences and had to select the matching picture from an array of two (see Figure 12.1) and a picture verification task (where the participants were shown one of the pictures and heard one of the sentences and had to decide whether the picture and the sentence matched). Their participants (undergraduate students) supplied the correct answer 79 % of the time on the picture selection task and 87 % of the time on the picture verification task. Although this is well above chance (50 %), their performance was far from perfect, and many individuals in both studies were in fact performing at chance.

To determine whether the individual differences observed in these studies were related to educational attainment, Street and Dąbrowska (2010) compared the performance of high and low academic achievement participants (postgraduate students and unskilled workers respectively) using a picture-selection task similar to that employed by Brooks and Sekerina. The experiment also tested

---

[3] Note that these sentences, and the pictures in Figure 12.1, come from a later study by Street and Dąbrowska (2010); however, the pictures and sentences used by Brooks and Sekerina were similar.

Fig. 12.1: Examples of pictures used by Street and Dąbrowska (2010) to test comprehension of sentences with the universal quantifier *every*.

comprehension of passive sentences (discussed in the next section) and actives, which were used as a control condition. As expected, all HAA participants performed at ceiling (100% correct) in all conditions. The LAA participants performed very well (97% correct) on actives, but had problems with the quantifier sentences, scoring 78% on simple locatives with *every* such as (1), and 43% (i.e., at chance) on *have*-locatives such as (2). Individual scores in the LAA group ranged from 0 to 100% on both types of quantifier sentences, with the majority of participants performing at or even below chance.

In a second experiment, LAA participants were pretested on comprehension of the same structures. The results were very similar to those obtained in the first study. Those participants who scored no more than 4 out of 6 in each of the experimental conditions (the two types of quantifier sentences and passives) were randomly assigned to either a quantifier training condition or a passive training condition. In both cases, training involved a short explanation of the kind that one might give to second language learners followed by practice with feedback using the sentences from the pre-test; the whole training session lasted about 5 minutes. Participants were then given three post-tests, one administered immediately after training, one a week later, and the last one twelve weeks later. Finally, all participants, including those who did not participate in the training phase, were given a questionnaire investigating their reading habits and the short version of the need for cognition questionnaire (Cacioppo et al. 1984), which measures how much people enjoy effortful cognitive activities.

The results for the quantifier training group are shown in Figure 12.2. As can be seen from the figure, training resulted in a dramatic increase in per-

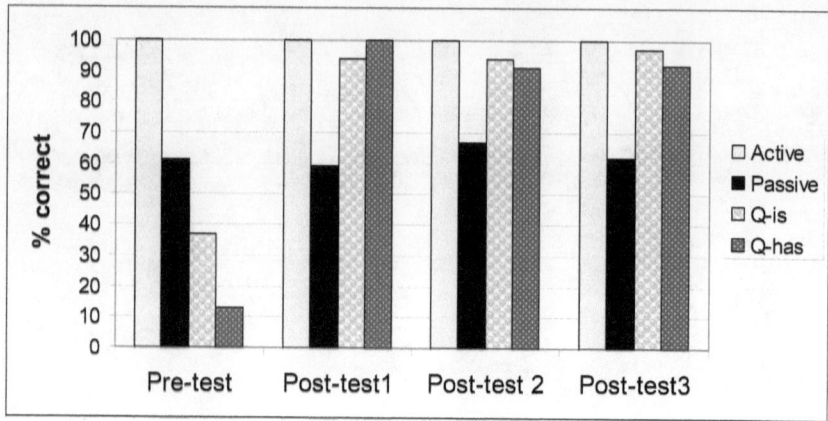

Fig. 12.2: Quantifier training group results (Street and Dąbrowska 2010, Experiment 2).

formance on the trained construction (i.e., quantifiers). Moreover, the improvement was long-lasting: even 12 weeks after training, the LAA participants performed close to ceiling. Performance on the passive (the untrained construction), on the other hand, remained unchanged. Thus, participants were clearly able to perform the task, and able to learn the construction with a minimal amount of exposure (and hence were not language impaired).

6 Simpler syntax: Passives

Three studies (Dąbrowska and Street 2006; Street and Dąbrowska 2010, 2014) examined individual and education-related differences in the comprehension of another relatively simple structure, namely passives. Earlier research by Ferreira (2003) demonstrated that even university students sometimes misinterpreted passive sentences, particularly semantically implausible ones. Since passives occur predominantly in formal written texts, one would predict that less educated speakers, who typically have relatively little exposure to such texts, will make even more errors.

Dąbrowska and Street (2006) tested comprehension of plausible and implausible passives (*The man was bitten by the dog* v. *The dog was bitten by the man*); the corresponding actives were used as controls. The task was to identify the "do-er" (i.e., the agent) in each sentence. As in the studies discussed earlier, two groups of participants were tested: a high academic attainment group (postgraduate students) and a low academic attainment group (manual workers who had no more than secondary-school education). The HAA group performed at ceiling on all sentence types. The LAA group were at ceiling on plausible sentences, 64 % correct on implausible actives, and 36 % correct on implausible passives. The high error rates on active sentences suggest that some of the LAA participants may have misunderstood the task, perhaps thinking that they were being asked what a person who uttered a sentence like *The dog was bitten by the man* probably meant, rather than what the sentence meant, and thus chose the more plausible (though syntactically impossible) interpretation. However, such pragmatic normalization cannot explain all the results, since performance on implausible passives was much worse than on the corresponding actives. Thus, in addition to a possible problem with the task itself, the LAA participants also had difficulty with the passive construction.

This was confirmed by a second study (Street and Dąbrowska 2010), which tested unbiased passives such as *The boy kissed the girl* using a different methodology, namely, picture selection – a less demanding task which can be used even with very young children. In this study, the HAA participants were again at ceiling, while the LAA group scored 88 % correct (range: 33–100 %) in experiment 1 and 79 % (range: 17–100 %) on the pre-test in experiment 2. In spite of the relatively low group averages, a significant proportion of the LAA participants (59 % in experiment 1 and 43 % in experiment 2) performed at ceiling.

As indicated earlier, the second experiment described in Street and Dąbrowska (2010) was a training study. The results for the passive training group are presented in Figure 12.3, and mirror those for the quantifier training group: there was a substantial improvement in performance on the trained construction, but not on the other sentences, and the effects were long-lasting.

Note that in the last two experiments, which used unbiased passives, the LAA participants' performance, though relatively poor, was still above chance, suggesting that they had some knowledge. The last study that will be discussed here, Street and Dąbrowska (2014), examined the nature of their knowledge in more detail. The study was designed to explore two possible explanations for this above-chance-but-below-ceiling pattern of performance.

Usage-based models of language acquisition claim that early in development, learners acquire lexically specific templates which are gradually generalized to more abstract schemas as they experience type variation in various positions in the construction (see Matthews and Krajewski volume 2). If this is the case, then it is possible that speakers who don't read very much never progress beyond lexically specific templates for constructions which are relatively infrequent in spoken language – such as the passive: in other words, such speakers may acquire lexically specific passive templates such as *NP1 BE injured by NP2*, containing verbs that frequently occur in the passive, but not a fully general

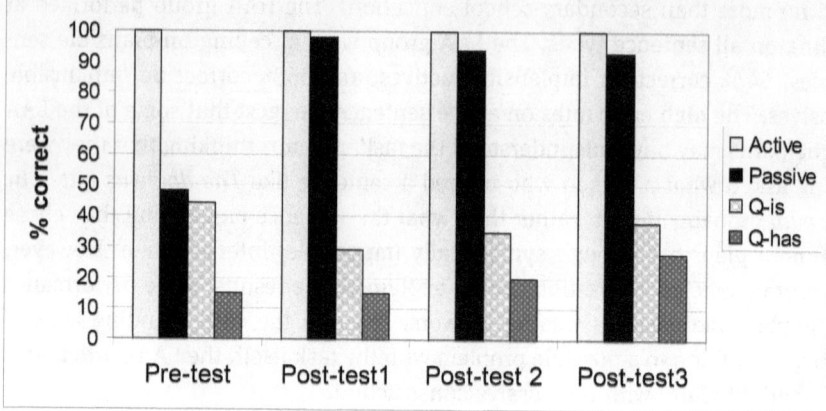

Fig. 12.3: Passive training group results (Street and Dąbrowska 2010).

passive construction (*NP1 BE VERB-ed by NP2*). Such speakers would perform relatively well on verbs that occur frequently in the passive voice, but would be at chance on verbs which are used predominantly in the active.

Ferreira (2003) offers a different explanation for the less-then-perfect performance on passives that she observed in her experiment. She adopts a two-stage model of processing, according to which speakers first perform a "quick and dirty" parse which relies on simple processing heuristics (such as NVN = Agent-Verb-Patient) to arrive at a preliminary interpretation of a sentence, which is then verified through a full parse. Processing heuristics are faster and less effortful than a full syntactic analysis, and the representations they produce are 'good enough' for most everyday purposes; consequently, speakers don't always complete the full parse, particularly when they are under time pressure, or when their processing resources are limited. Ferreira's approach could explain the education-related differences observed in the studies discussed here if we assume that LAA participants' processing resources are more limited, and hence they are more likely to abandon processing after the first stage. If this were the case, we would expect a negative relationship between passive processing speed and accuracy: in other words, participants who responded quickly (after the first stage of processing) would make more errors on passives.

To test these hypotheses, Street and Dąbrowska (2014) presented HAA and LAA participants with active and passive sentences and asked them to decide whether a particular person mentioned in the sentence was the "do-er", i.e., agent, or the "acted-on", i.e., patient. Half of the sentences contained 'passive-attracting' verbs such as *injure* and *attach*, i.e., verbs which are relatively frequent in the passive; the other half contained 'active-attracting' verbs like *touch* or *shake*. All the sentences used in the study were semantically reversible. The dependent variables were decision accuracy and reaction time.

The experiment confirmed earlier findings on individual and education-related differences in comprehension of passive sentences. The HAA participants were at ceiling on both constructions. The LAA participants were also at ceiling on actives (98% correct), but performed significantly worse on passives (only 86% correct). Moreover, there were considerable individual differences within the LAA group: while 31% of the participants were at ceiling (100% correct), 22% were at chance, and one participant performed significantly *below* chance;[4] the remaining participants were above chance but below ceiling.

The results are broadly compatible with usage-based models. Participants were faster and more accurate with active sentences than with passives, which is likely to be an entrenchment effect; and they processed passives with passive-attracting verbs faster than passives with active-attracting verbs, suggesting that they have lexical templates for verbs which frequently occur in the passive. However, there was no difference in accuracy on passives with the two verb types, and the reaction time data indicated that both groups showed the same advantage for passives with passive-attracting verbs: in other words, there was no interaction between verb type and group for either accuracy or reaction time. Thus, the group differences cannot be attributed to the LAA participants relying more on lexical templates.

The results also do not support a processing heuristics account of individual differences, which predicts a positive correlation between speed and accuracy (speakers who do not conduct a full parse should respond faster but less accurately). Instead, the results revealed a moderately significant *negative* correlation between reaction time and accuracy ($r = .-41$ for LAA group; $r = .-42$ for all participants): in other words, participants who responded faster were also more accurate. The most plausible interpretation of these findings is that all of the HAA, and the majority of the LAA participants, had lexical templates *as well as* a more general passive construction, but for the LAA group, these were less well entrenched, presumably because they had less experience with written texts. Moreover, a small but significant minority of the LAA group showed no evidence of having mastered the passive.

---

[4] This participant reliably supplied the target answer with active sentences, suggesting that s/he consistently applied the first NP = Agent strategy.

7 Reasons for individual differences

The research described in this chapter indicates that there are individual differences in performance on tasks tapping knowledge of various linguistic constructions, including case marking, "tough movement", various types of subordination, quantifiers, and passives. These differences cannot be explained by appealing to working memory capacity, test-taking skills, or willingness to cooperate with the experimenter (see Dąbrowska 2012). How do these differences come about? Logically, they could be attributed to individual differences in language learning abilities, cognitive style, etc., to differences in language experience, or, most likely, to some combination of the two.

There is some evidence that underlying cognitive differences play a significant role. It is well known that individual differences in sentence processing skill correlate with working memory capacity (Daneman and Menkle 1996; Farmer et al. 2012; Just and Carpenter 1992). There are also moderately strong relationships between grammatical comprehension and nonverbal IQ and need for cognition, i.e., the extent to which people enjoy, and hence seek, effortful cognitive activities (Brooks and Sekerina 2006; Street and Dąbrowska 2010). More recent research (Dąbrowska 2018) suggests a close link between grammatical comprehension and metalinguistic awareness. Of course, correlation is not the same as causation, so we must be careful in interpreting these results; however, given that there are substantial individual differences in almost every area of human cognition (Gruszka et al. 2010) and that language development depends on general cognitive abilities, there are good theoretical grounds for postulating a causal link.

It is also likely that differences in linguistic knowledge are at least partially attributable to differences in experience. The linguistic experience of individual speakers varies considerably both in amount and quality, and these differences are correlated with education and occupational status. University students and professionals rely on language more in their daily lives than individuals who do menial jobs, in that most of their working day is spent in some kind of linguistic activity. They also tend to read more, and are more likely to be skilled readers. This means that they are exposed to more language (since skilled readers absorb more words per unit of time than skilled conversationalists – see Dąbrowska 2004: 19) and also more varied language (since many complex constructions are considerably more frequent in written language than in speech – see Biber 1986; Miller 1994; Roland et al. 2007). Highly educated speakers will also have experienced more complex language in various educational settings. Furthermore, they often come from middle class backgrounds, which means that they are likely to have been spoken to (Ginsborg 2006; Hart and Risley

1995, 1999) and read to (Hartas 2011) more as children, and there is some evidence that early childhood experience may be particularly important for ultimate language attainment (Pakulak and Neville 2010). This is yet another example of the accumulation of advantage, or what Stanovich (1986) called the "Matthew effect" (the rich get richer and the poor get poorer, metaphorically speaking: for instance, children who are good readers read more, which makes them even better readers, while poor readers usually read less, which causes them to fall even further behind their peers.) Note, however, that exposure to reading has an effect on performance that is independent of educational experience: Street and Dąbrowska (2010) found a significant correlation between amount of reading and grammatical comprehension in a group of LAA speakers of very similar educational backgrounds.

Perhaps the most convincing evidence that differences in grammatical attainment are at least partly attributable to differences in linguistic experience comes from the two training studies discussed earlier (Chipere 2001; Street and Dąbrowska 2010). As we have seen, Chipere demonstrated that additional experience with a construction improves comprehension as well as memory for that construction, while Street and Dąbrowska found that training results in improvement on the trained construction (but not the untrained one), and, moreover, that the effects are long lasting. In both studies, the number of exemplars presented during training was quite small (10 the Chipere experiment and just 6 in Street and Dąbrowska's study). This raises an interesting question: if such a minimal amount of exposure is enough for learning to occur, why hadn't the participants acquired the construction earlier? After all, they are likely to have experienced much more than 10 exemplars of the trained constructions prior to their participation in the experiment, and yet they had not acquired the relevant knowledge.

The training provided during the two studies differs from normal experience in two ways: the participants were presented with a number of exemplars in a very short time (whereas in normal experience, individual exemplars are usually more spaced), and it involved explicit explanation and feedback as well as exposure to relevant data. Research on learning in general, and construction learning in particular, suggests that 'spaced' exposure, where individual learning episodes are distributed over a number of sessions, is more effective than 'massed' exposure, where the same number of learning opportunities is presented in a single session (Ambridge et al. 2006; Childers and Tomasello 2002; Divjak and Cardwell-Harris volume 1). This suggests that the fact that the training session provided more intensive exposure is unlikely to be primarily responsible for the dramatic improvement in performance observed in the experiments.

It is important to note that not every instance of exposure to the relevant structure is necessarily a learning episode. In order for construction learning to take place, there must be enough contextual information to allow the learner to infer the meaning of the utterance exemplifying the construction, and the learner must be attending to the linguistic form and the relevant the contextual information. In the training phase of both studies, the experimenter explicitly directed the participants' attention to the relevant aspects of both form and meaning, thus maximising the chances of learning taking place. It is likely that some language learners are not exposed to this kind of input often enough, and as a result, do not acquire these constructions. Importantly, the HAA participants were more likely to have had parents (or teachers) who provided this kind of experience, and hence more opportunities for learning.[5]

The dramatic improvement in performance in the training study raises some interesting questions. One may wonder, for instance, whether the knowledge that the participants acquired during the training session will generalize to ordinary language use outside the lab, and, if it does, whether it is of the same kind as the knowledge possessed by participants who were already performing at ceiling at pre-test. It could be argued that the trained participants' knowledge is likely to be explicit, and hence differs fundamentally from the implicit knowledge of "normal" native speakers, and is more like the kind of knowledge acquired by second language learners. It must be pointed out, however, that it also possible that at least some of those who performed well at pre-test were also relying on explicit knowledge. Clearly, further research will be necessary to answer these questions. In particular, we may need to re-examine the widely-held assumption that first language acquisition is almost entirely implicit. While it is undeniable that implicit learning plays an important role in acquisition, the results reported here suggest that explicit processes, at least at the level of attending to the relevant information, may also be involved (for further discussion, see Dąbrowska 2009).

To sum up: the results summarized here suggest that individual differences in native language attainment are partly attributable to individual cognitive differences and partly to environmental differences. It should be stressed that these factors interact in complex ways. Children of university-educated parents often get more input than their peers (Hart and Risley 1995, 1999), and their

---

[5] I am not suggesting that parents or teachers provide true grammar lessons, i.e., that they actually explain the structure and meaning of the construction, but simply that they ensure that the language learner attends to both structure and meaning at the same time – for instance, by emphasizing particular phrases in the utterance while pointing to the critical elements in the scene, by explicitly contrasting two utterances, etc.

input tends to be of higher quality (e.g., more one-on-one interaction, more book reading, etc.). This leads to better language skills, and better language skills lead to educational success. As a result, they become better readers, and hence read more, and thus get more varied input; they are also more likely to go on to higher education, and so on – the Matthew effect all over. In other words, we have a virtuous circle: better language skills lead to educational success which leads to better language skills, while the opposite often happens in children from less privileged backgrounds (Hoff 2006, 2013).

Finally, it is worth noting that different factors may contribute in different ways to knowledge of different constructions. Street and Dąbrowska (2010) provide some suggestive evidence that this might be the case: in their study, reading was the best predictor of performance on passives, while need for cognition was a better predictor of performance on quantifier constructions. This may be due to the fact that full passives are much more frequent in written texts than in informal spoken discourse; hence, people who read more get more exposure to this construction. Conversely, the relationship between comprehension of sentences with quantifiers and need for cognition may be attributable to the fact that quantifiers play an important role in logical reasoning.

8 Concluding remarks

The existence of individual differences in native language attainment raises some interesting questions. First, if speakers have different grammars, how can they understand each other? This can be partly explained by the fact that the same expressions can be produced using different grammars (see Dąbrowska 2014). Consider, for example, the Polish dative neuter inflection discussed earlier. While some speakers have a fully general rule for the dative neuter, most speakers appear to have a number of low-level schemas, and some may only have memorized a few exemplars. However, the forms that they actually produce are identical. One may also observe that speakers do not need to have exactly the same grammar to be able to communicate. We are very good at reading people's minds (Tomasello 2008), and we are usually able to construct a reasonable approximation of a speakers' communicative intention on the basis of relatively little evidence.

Secondly, if different speakers have different grammars, in what sense can they be said to speak the same language? In one of his famous analogies, Saussure suggests that speakers belonging to a particular speech community have copies of the same dictionary in their heads:

> A language, as a collective phenomenon, takes the form of a totality of imprints in everyone's brain, rather like a dictionary of which each individual has an identical copy ... Thus it is something which is in each individual, but is none the less common to all. (Saussure [1972] 1986: 19)

This is clearly an oversimplification: while some words, such as *head*, *give*, and *good* are presumably shared by all English speakers, others (*mumble*, *haunted*, *declare*) may not be, and some (*cataphoric*, *amygdala*) are known only by a relatively small number of specialists. So different speakers have different dictionaries in their heads – although, of course, there is considerable overlap between them. The same is true of grammar. A linguistic convention, be it a lexical item or a grammatical construction, will survive in the language as long as it is shared by some speakers; it needn't be shared by everyone. As Millikan (2008: 88) argues,

> Speakers and hearers may have quite different sets of linguistic conventions in their repertoires, so long as there is some overlap ... all that is required for a ... convention to survive, to be repeated and passed on, is to succeed in coordinating the interests of speakers and hearers some critical proportion of the time.

Languages belong to communities, not to individual speakers: an individual speaker "owns" only a part of his/her language. However, since speakers approximate each other's behaviour, collective grammars tend to be more systematic than individual grammars (see Dąbrowska 2013; Hurford 2000: 342).

The existence of individual differences also has important methodological implications. We cannot simply assume that what is true of one native speaker of a language will also be true of others: to make general statements about a particular language or language variety, we need to collect data from a range of speakers. Related to this, we need to be aware that data from highly educated participants is not representative: as we have seen earlier, their responses tend to be much more homogenous than those of less educated speakers. This is not surprising, given that their linguistic competence has been shaped by years of schooling in the standard language – which itself was to some extent shaped by language planners (Deumert and Vandenbussche 2003; Garvin 1993).

That variation is ubiquitous in language is widely acknowledged in sociolinguistics (Henry 2002). On the other hand, theoretical linguists steeped in the nativist tradition are committed to the idea that speakers' mental grammars are strongly constrained by a shared Universal Grammar and find it hard to accept that individual grammars differ substantially. This, however, should not come as a surprise to cognitive linguists: after all, there are large individual differences in almost every area of human cognition, and different individuals experience different subsamples of language, so we expect considerable variation. Yet many cognitive linguists implicitly accept the Chomskyan idealization that all speakers in the same community share the same grammar, thus neglecting the study of individual differences in linguistic knowledge.

The research described here shows that differences between speakers run even deeper than the previous sociolinguistic research suggests, in that they involve knowledge of linguistic constructions, i.e. competence, rather than just frequency of use of particular variants. As we have seen, even when two speakers' overt production is identical, the underlying grammatical system may not be: in other words, the differences may be invisible to the naked eye (or rather inaudible to the naked ear) and only revealed by a specially designed experimental procedure (see, for example, the earlier discussion of Polish speakers' ability to produce dative forms of real and nonce nouns).

This is not surprising, given that most aspects of linguistic structure, and virtually all aspects of meaning, are not directly observable, and hence must be inferred by the learner from indirect cues, and hence – as many linguists have pointed out – a given corpus of data is compatible with many descriptions. Thus, grammar viewed as a mental phenomenon is necessarily private, and so to speak, is counterbalanc this fact necessarily leads to variation. This "centrifugal" force, so to speak, is counterbalanced by the fact that in actual language use, speakers tend to align, or accommodate to each other's speech. They do this not just in order to communicate successfully, although communication is obviously an important motive: speaker alignment is also a major mechanism for maintaining social cohesion (Dediu et al. 2013), and acts as a centripetal force which prevents individual grammars from becoming too different. The tension between the centrifugal force of individual grammars and the centripetal norms that evolve in the speech community is a central factor shaping language (Croft 2000), and we cannot hope to understand language in either its individual or its social dimension without considering their interaction (cf. Geeraerts 2010). Let us hope that future research in cognitive linguistics will give this question the attention that it deserves.

9 References

Ambridge, Ben, Anna L. Theakston, Elena Lieven, and Michael Tomasello (2006): The distributed learning effect for children's acquisition of an abstract grammatical construction. *Cognitive Development* 21: 74–193.

Bates, Elizabeth, Inge Bretherton, and Lynn Snyder (1988): *From First Words to Grammar: Individual Differences and Dissociable Mechanisms.* Cambridge: Cambridge University Press.

Biber, Douglas (1986): Spoken and written textual dimensions in English: Resolving the contradictory findings. *Language* 62: 384–414.

Bley-Vroman, Robert (2009): The evolving context of the fundamental difference hypothesis. *Studies in Second Language Acquisition* 31: 175–198.

Brooks, Patricia J. and Irina A. Sekerina (2005/2006): Shortcuts to quantifier interpretation in children and adults. *Language Acquisition* 13: 177–206.

Brooks, Patricia J. and Irina A. Sekerina (2006): Shallow processing of universal quantification: A comparison of monolingual and bilingual adults. In: K. Forbus, D. Gentner and T. Regier (eds.), *Proceedings of the 28th Annual Conference of the Cognitive Science Society*, 2450. Mahwah: Lawrence Erlbaum Associates.

Buttler, Danuta, Halina Kurkowska, and Halina Satkiewicz (1973): *Kultura języka polskiego [A Guide to Polish Usage]*. Warszawa: PWN.

Cacioppo, John T., Richard E. Petty, and Chaun Feng Kao (1984): The efficient assessment of need for cognition. *Journal of Personality Assessment* 48: 306–307.

Childers, Jane B. and Michael Tomasello (2002): Two-year-olds learn novel nouns, verbs and conventional actions from massed or distributed exposures. *Developmental Psychology* 38: 967–978.

Chipere, Ngoni (2001): Native speaker variations in syntactic competence: Implications for first language teaching. *Language Awareness* 10: 107–124.

Chomsky, Noam (1965): *Aspects of the Theory of Syntax*. Cambridge: MIT Press.

Chomsky, Noam (1975): *Reflections on Language*. New York: Pantheon.

Clark, Herbert H. (1997): Communal lexicons. In: K. Malmkjær and J. Williams (eds.), *Context in Language Learning and Language Understanding*, 63–87. Cambridge: Cambridge University Press.

Crain, Stephen, Rosalind Thornton, and Keiko Murasugi (2009): Capturing the evasive passive. *Language Acquisition* 16: 123–133.

Croft, William (2000): *Explaining Language Change: An Evolutionary Approach*. London: Longman.

Dąbrowska, Ewa (1997): The LAD goes to school: A cautionary tale for nativists. *Linguistics* 35: 735–766.

Dąbrowska, Ewa (2004): *Language, Mind and Brain: Some Psychological and Neurological Constraints on Theories of Grammar*. Edinburgh: Edinburgh University Press.

Dąbrowska, Ewa (2008a): The later development of an early-emerging system: The curious case of the Polish genitive. *Linguistics* 46: 629–650.

Dąbrowska, Ewa (2008b): The effects of frequency and neighbourhood density on adult speakers' productivity with Polish case inflections: An empirical test of usage-based approaches to morphology. *Journal of Memory and Language* 58: 931–951.

Dąbrowska, Ewa (2009): Constructing a second language: Some final thoughts. *Annual Review of Cognitive Linguistics* 7: 277–290.

Dąbrowska, Ewa (2012): Different speakers, different grammars: Individual differences in native language attainment. *Linguistic Approaches to Bilingualism* 2: 219–253.

Dąbrowska, Ewa (2013): Functional constraints, usage, and mental grammars: A study of speakers' intuitions about questions with long-distance dependencies. *Cognitive Linguistics* 24: 633–665.

Dąbrowska, Ewa (2018). Experience, aptitude and individual differences in native language ultimate attainment. *Cognition*, 178: 222–235.

Dąbrowska, Ewa (2014): Recycling utterances: A speaker's guide to sentence processing. *Cognitive Linguistics* 25: 617–653.

Dąbrowska, Ewa and James A. Street (2006): Individual differences in language attainment: Comprehension of passive sentences by native and non-native English speakers. *Language Sciences* 28: 604–615.

Dąbrowska, Ewa and Marcin Szczerbiński (2006): Polish children's productivity with case marking: the role of regularity, type frequency, and phonological coherence. *Journal of Child Language* 33: 559–597.

Daneman, Meredith and Philip M. Merikle (1996): Working Memory and Language Comprehension: A Meta-Analysis. *Psychonomic Bulletin and Review* 3: 422–433.

Dediu, Dan, Michael Cysouw, Stephen C. Levinson, Andrea Baronchelli, Morten H. Christiansen, William Croft, Nicholas Evans, Simon Garrod, Russell D. Gray, Anne Kandler, and Elena Lieven (2013): Cultural evolution of language. In: P. J. Richerson and M. H. Christiansen (eds.), *Cultural Evolution: Society, Technology, Language, and Religion*, 303–332. Cambridge: Cambridge University Press.

Deumert, Ana and Wim Vandenbussche (2003): Standard languages: Taxonomies and Histories. In: A. Deumert and W. Vandenbussche (eds.), *Germanic Standardizations: Past and Present*, 1–14. Amsterdam/New York: John Benjamins.

Divjak, Dagmar and Catherine Cardwell-Harris (volume 1): Frequency and entrenchment. Berin/Boston: De Gruyter Mouton.

Farmer, Thomas A., Jennifer B. Misyak, and Morten H. Christiansen (2012): Individual differences in sentence processing. In: M. Spivey, K. McRae and M. Joannisse (eds.), *Cambridge Handbook of Psycholinguistics*, 353–364. Cambridge: Cambridge University Press.

Ferreira, Fernanda (2003): The misinterpretation of noncanonical sentences. *Cognitive Psychology* 47: 164–203.

Garvin, Paul L. (1993): A conceptual framework for the study of language standardization. *International Journal of the Sociology of Language* 100/101: 37–54.

Geeraerts, Dirk (2010): Schmidt redux: How systematic is language if variation is rampant? In: K. Boye and E. Engeberg-Pedersen (eds.), *Language Usage and Language Structure*, 237–262. Berlin/New York: De Gruyter Mouton.

Ginsborg, Jane (2006): The effects of socio-economic status on children's language acquisition and use. In: J. Clegg and J. Ginsborg (eds.), *Language and Social Disadvantage*, 9–27. Chichester: John Wiley and Sons.

Gruszka, Aleksandra, Gerald Matthews, and Błażej Szymura (eds.) (2010): *Handbook of Individual Differences in Cognition: Attention, Memory, and Executive Control*. New York: Springer.

Hart, Betty and Todd R. Risley (1995): *Meaningful Differences in the Everyday Experience of Young American Children*. Baltimore: Paul Brooks.

Hart, Betty and Todd R. Risley (1999): *The Social World of Children Learning to Talk*. Baltimore: Paul Brookes.

Hartas, Dimitra (2011): Families' social backgrounds matter: Socio-economic factors, home learning and young children's language, literacy and social outcomes. *British Educational Research Journal* 37: 893–914.

Henry, Alison (2002): Variation and syntactic theory. In: J. K. Chambers, P. Trudgill and N. Shilling-Estes (eds.), *The Handbook of Language Variation and Change*, 267–282. Oxford: Blackwell.

Herschensohn, Julia (2009): Fundamental and gradient differences in language development. *Studies in Second Language Acquisition* 31: 259–289.

Hoff, Erika (2006): How social contexts support and shape language development. *Developmental Review* 26: 55–88.

Hoff, Erika (2013): Interpreting the early language trajectories of children from low-SES and language minority homes: Implications for closing achievement gaps. *Developmental Psychology* 49: 4–14.

Hurford, James R. (2000): Social transmission favours linguistic generalisation. In: C. Knight, M. Studdert-Kennedy and J. R. Hurford (eds.), *The Evolutionary Emergence of Language: Social Function and the Origins of Linguistic Form*, 324–352. Cambridge: Cambridge University Press.

Just, Marcel A. and Patricia A. Carpenter (1992): A capacity theory of comprehension: Individual differences in working memory. *Psychological Review* 99: 122–149.

Lidz, Jeffrey and Alexander Williams (2009): Constructions on holiday. *Cognitive Linguistics* 20: 177–189.

Matthews, Danielle and Grzegorz Krajewski (volume 2): First language acquisition. Berlin/Boston: De Gruyter Mouton.

Miller, Jim E. (1994): Speech and writing. In: R. E. Asher and J. M. Y. Simpson (eds.), *The Encyclopaedia of Language and Linguistics*, Volume 8, 4301–4306. Oxford: Pergamon Press.

Millikan, Ruth G. (2008): A difference of some consequence between conventions and rules. *Topoi* 27: 87–99.

Montrul, Silvina (2008): *Incomplete Acquisition in Bilingualism: Re-Examining the Age Factor*. Amsterdam: John Benjamins.

Mulder, Kimberley and Jan H. Hulstijn (2011): Linguistic skills of adult native speakers, as a function of age and level of education. *Applied Linguistics* 32: 475–494.

Nowak, Martin A., Natalia Komarova, and Partha Niyogi (2001): Evolution of Universal Grammar. *Science* 291: 114–118.

Pakulak, Eric and Helen Neville (2010): Proficiency differences in syntactic processing of monolingual native speakers indexed by event-related potentials. *Journal of Cognitive Neuroscience* 22: 2728–2744.

Peters, Ann M. and Lise Menn (1993): False starts and filler syllables: Ways to learn grammatical morphemes. *Language* 69: 742–777.

Richards, Brian J. (1990): *Language Development and Individual Differences: A Study of Auxiliary Verb Learning*. Cambridge: Cambridge University Press.

Roland, Douglas, Frederic Dick, and Jeffrey L. Elman (2007): Frequency of basic English grammatical structures: A corpus analysis. *Journal of Memory and Language* 57: 348–379.

Saussure, Ferdinand de ([1972] 1986): *Course in General Linguistics* (R. Harris, Trans.). Peru: Open Court Publishing Company.

Seuren, Pieter (1982): Internal variability in competence. *Linguistische Berichte* 77: 1–31.

Smith, Neil (1999): *Chomsky: Ideas and Ideals*. Cambridge: Cambridge University Press.

Stanovich, Keith E. (1986): Matthew effects in reading: Some consequences of individual differences in the acquisition of literacy. *Reading Research Quarterly* 21: 360–407.

Street, James A. and Ewa Dąbrowska (2010): More individual differences in language attainment: How much do adult native speakers of English know about passives and quantifiers? *Lingua* 120: 2080–2094.

Street, James A. and Ewa Dąbrowska (2014): Lexically specific knowledge and individual differences in adult native speakers' processing of the English passive. *Applied Psycholinguistics* 35: 97–118.

Tomasello, Michael (2008): *Origins of Human Communication*. Cambridge: MIT Press.

Westfal, Stanisław (1956): *A Study in Polish Morphology: The Genitive Singular Masculine*. The Hague: Mouton.

Sherman Wilcox
Chapter 13: Signed languages

1 Introduction

For centuries, signed languages were not considered to be language. Rather, they were regarded as depictive gestures lacking features of language such as phonology, word formation, and syntax. The Roman rhetorician Quintilian made passing reference to the use of gestures by deaf people in his Institutes of Oratory, saying that for them gestures are a substitute for speech. The view that signed languages are merely pantomimic gestures culminated in the debate over the use of speech versus signing in the education of deaf children that took place during the Milan Conference of 1880. Supporters of speech maintained that signed languages lacked any features of language and thus were not suited for developing the minds of deaf children. One of the proponents of speech proclaimed that children who are taught to sign are defiant and corruptible. He attributed this to the disadvantages of signed language, claiming that they cannot convey number, gender, person, time, nouns, verbs, adverbs, adjectives (Lane 1984). Because of this, educators maintained that signed languages cannot elicit reasoning, reflection, generalization, and abstraction. These views persisted into the 20th century, with psychologists, educators, and linguists continuing to deny the linguistic status of signed languages, maintaining that they are harmful for intellectual and educational development.

A similarly contentious picture describes the relation between language and gesture. While some early philosophers believed the origin of language lay in gesture, for the most part gesture was placed in an either/or relation with language. Whorf and Caroll (1956), for example, proposed a dualistic mode of thinking in the Western mind characterized by such either/or thinking: either a word, or, in the absence of adequate vocabulary, a gesture.

Although Pike (1967) offered a unified model of language and gesture, most linguists held views such as Chomsky's (1972: 70), who grouped human gesture with animal communication and considered both to be categorically distinct from human language: "The examples of animal communication that have been examined to date do share many of the properties of human gestural systems, and it might be reasonable to explore the possibility of direct connection in this case. But human language, it appears, is based on entirely different principles."

Sherman Wilcox, University of New Mexico, United States of America

Many scholars however have argued to the contrary, that non-human primate gestural communication is more similar to human language than primate vocalizations (Liebal et al. 2007). It has only been within the last several decades that psycholinguists (Bates and Dick 2002; McNeill 1992, 2005), gesture researchers (Kendon 2004; Müller 2007), neuroscientists (Gentilucci 2006; Husain et al. 2009; Rizzolatti and Arbib 1998) and others (Capirci et al. 2002; Corballis 2003; Skipper et al. 2009; Xu et al. 2009) have discovered cognitive and neural links between language and gesture.

There is a need to establish an overarching framework that can encompass spoken language, signed language, and gesture as a manifestation of the human expressive ability (Wilcox and Xavier 2013). Currently, two approaches attack the problem: an abstractionist solution and an embodied solution. The abstractionist solution accomplishes unification across the distinct modalities in which spoken and signed languages are manifest by viewing language as a system of abstract rules independent of physical manifestation. This solution strips away the performance of language by means of vocal tracts, hands, faces, and the anatomy and musculature that controls these articulators. Likewise, perceptual systems play no part in the cognitive organization of language from this perspective. In more traditional formalist terminology, the abstractionist solution maintains a distinction between competence and performance. The abstractionist solution is best represented by structuralist and formalist approaches (Aronoff et al. 2005; Brentari 1998; Lillo Martin 1986; Neidle et al. 2000; Petronio and Lillo Martin 1997; Pfau and Quer 2003, 2007; Sandler and Lillo Martin 2006; Stokoe 1960).

The embodied solution claims that all language, and indeed all communication, is made possible because we have physical bodies that we move to produce signals (Bergen volume 1; Wilcox 2013). What unites language across different modalities from this perspective is that both spoken and signed languages, and gestures, are the performance of physical systems in actual usage events.

Thus, the abstractionist solution maintains that while the physical embodiment of language may have an impact on production, it has no impact on the cognitive organization of grammar. The embodied solution argues instead that physical embodiment has direct influence on the nature of cognition, which is manifest in all aspects of language.[1]

---

[1] See Thelen and Smith (1994) for a similar claim about two approaches to the development of cognition and action systems. Rączaszek-Leonardi and Kelso (2007) also make the case against what is here called the abstractionist solution and in favor of a more embodied approach, also incorporating dynamic systems theory into their model.

2 Signed language structure

Phonology

The view that signed languages lacked linguistic structure was most powerfully manifest in the claim that they lack duality of patterning, that the meaningful elements of these languages are not formed from a finite set of meaningless elements – that is, that signed languages lack a phonology. Stokoe (1960) dispelled this view with his pioneering description of the phonology of American Sign Language (ASL). Stokoe demonstrated that signs consist of analyzable units of sublexical structure. Stokoe coined the term 'chereme' for these units, the structural equivalent of the phonemes of spoken languages.

Stokoe analyzed the phonology of signs into three major classes: handshape (the configuration that the hand makes when producing the sign), location (the place where the sign is produced, for example on the head, or in the neutral space in front of the signer's body), and movement (the motion made by the signer in producing the sign, for example upward or towards the signer's body). Battison (1978) added a fourth class, orientation (the direction the hand faces when producing the sign). Since Stokoe's discovery, a multitude of phonological theories of signed languages have been proposed (Brentari 1998; Liddell 1984; Padden and Perlmutter 1987; Sandler 1999; Uyechi 1996).

Use of space

One unique characteristic of signed languages is that they are produced in visible space. This "signing space" plays a critical role in the grammar of signed languages. For example the arguments of certain verbs are marked by locations in space (Meier 2002). In ASL, the agent and recipient of GIVE-TO "X gives the book to Y" are indicated by points in the signing space.

Time is often marked by spatial location. The present is in the plane of the signer's body, the future is indicated by the space in front of the signer, and the past is marked by spatial locations behind and over the signer's shoulder. Time may also be indicated by side-to-side spatial locations and movements (Engberg-Pedersen 1993).

Topics may be indicated by location in space as well. For example, if a signer is discussing two competing linguistic theories, she may place one in the signing space on her left, and another on her right. Pointing to these spatial locations, or even orienting her upper torso in the direction of these locations, may be used to direct the addressee's attention to the corresponding topic.

Facial grammar

In addition to the hands, the signer's face, including the eyes, eyebrows, cheeks, and mouth, is an important articulator in signed languages. In many signed languages, the face predominantly functions as grammatical or discourse markers. In ASL, for example, the face may be used to mark polar questions, content questions, topics, and conditionals. The mouth has a variety of functions, marking adverbial meaning (e.g., the distinction between "work carelessly" and "work carefully" is marked in ASL by different mouth gestures), and intensification (Bridges and Metzger 1996).

Eye gaze is another important aspect of facial grammar. It may be used to mark pronominal reference (Metzer 1998) and as a syntactic agreement marker in ASL (Thompson et al. 2006). Eye gaze also marks role shift in narratives; for example, a change from the narrator's perspective to that of a character in the story may be marked by a change in eye gaze.

Lexicalization and grammaticization

Lexicalization is the process by which words (signs) are formed in a language. One common lexicalization process in signed languages is compounding. In ASL, for example, many compounds have become lexicalized: 'bruise' from BLUE_SPOT; 'brother' and 'sister' from BOY_SAME and GIRL_SAME; 'husband' and 'wife' from MAN_MARRY and WOMAN_MARRY. Lexicalization has been described in detail for Australian Sign Language (Johnston and Schembri 2007); British Sign Language (Sutton-Spence and Woll 1999), and American Sign Language (Janzen 2012).

Grammaticization refers to the process by which lexical morphemes, or grammatical morphemes, take on grammatical or more grammatical function (Bybee et al. 1994). Grammaticization operates in signed languages in two ways. In the first, certain lexical morphemes take on grammatical meaning. Janzen (2012) shows that the ASL lexical item FINISH, for example, has developed from a full verb to a more grammatical form used to mark completives and perfectives, eventually forming an affix. Another example from ASL is the lexical verb 'leave', meaning movement in physical space, which takes on grammatical function as a future marker. Janzen (2012) also claims that topic marking has developed along the following grammaticization path:

generalized questioning gesture > yes/no question marking > topic marking

This grammaticization path also demonstrates the second way in which grammaticization appears in signed languages: gestural forms may become incorporated into a signed language, often first as lexical forms, which take on more grammatical function. The future marker described above, which grammaticized from a lexical verb, seems to have originated as a gesture meaning 'leave'. The grammaticization of gesture is described in more detail in the section *Gesture is incorporated into signed languages*.

3 Cognitive linguistics and signed languages

Linguists have found cognitive linguistic theory especially revealing when applied to the study of signed languages. Wilcox and colleagues (Wilcox 2007; Wilcox and Morford 2007; Wilcox and P. Wilcox 2009) have documented the application of cognitive linguistics to signed languages. Janzen and colleagues (Janzen 2006, 2012; Janzen et al. 2001) examined the linguistic use of space, the construal of events, and the cognitive factors at work in lexicalization and grammaticalization in signed languages. Working with Danish Sign Language, Engberg-Pedersen (1993, 1996a, 1996b, 1999) has also contributed to our understanding of the role of space. Shaffer (2002, 2004) applied force dynamics to the study of modality in ASL. Liddell (1995, 1998, 2000, 2003a) pioneered the application of conceptual blending theory to ASL. Expanding on this work, Dudis (2004; Wulf and Dudis 2005) described body partitioning, a construction unique to signed languages, and investigated its role in conceptual blends. In body partitioning, one part of a signer's body is used to represent one character in a story, while another part depicts a second character. For example, in telling about the reaction of a person being punched in the face by another person, the signer's face will represent the person getting hit, and the signer's arm and fist will represent the arm and fist of the person who is hitting.

Metaphor
Wilbur (1987) was one of the first scholars to systematically explore metaphor in ASL. She noted that many ASL signs exhibit spatialization metaphors. The metaphor HAPPY IS UP is exemplified in signs such as HAPPY, CHEERFUL, and LAUGH, which are produced with upward movements. The metaphor NEGATIVE IS DOWN shows up in signs such as LOUSY, IGNORE, and FAIL, which are produced with downward movements.

P. Wilcox (2000) expanded the analysis of metaphor in ASL by demonstrating systematic relationships among the signs used to convey the metaphor IDEAS ARE OBJECTS. P. Wilcox noted that this metaphor is expressed in ASL by distinct lexical signs. IDEAS ARE OBJECTS TO BE GRASPED may be expressed using the S-handshape (Figure 13.1). The S-handshape in ASL is used to express the concept of grasping. It would be used to sign 'grasp a bicycle handlebar' and is seen in ASL signs meaning 'broom' and 'to sweep' where it depicts holding a broom handle. The S-handshape is also used to 'hold' or 'grasp' ideas as metaphorical objects.

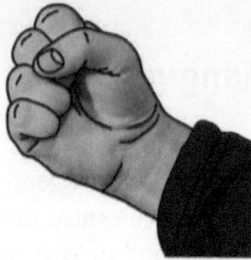

Fig. 13.1: S-handshape.

Handshapes which are used to represent grasping a flat object can also be used metaphorically to represent IDEAS ARE OBJECTS TO BE MANIPULATED (Figure 13.2). This handshape appears in signs used to express the manipulation of objects: moving an object from one location to another (for example, 'to give') or removing a paper from a shelf. When ideas are metaphorically understood to be objects to be manipulated, moved, or placed, this handshape is used. For example, a signer would use this handshape to talk about moving ideas around various locations in her mind to convey the concept of organizing her thoughts.

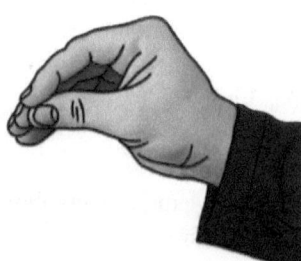

Fig. 13.2: Grasping flat-O handshape.

When an idea is metaphorically discriminated, carefully selected, or extracted from some location, the F-handshape is used (Figure 13.3). This handshape is used in ASL to convey the notion of selecting or picking up small physical objects such as seeds, small buttons, or a sewing needle. When used metaphorically with the concept of ideas, it suggests that the idea is being carefully selected. It also implies limited quantity; whereas the S-handshape may represent the grasping of many ideas, when the F-handshape is used metaphorically in connection with ideas it suggests that only a single idea has been selected.

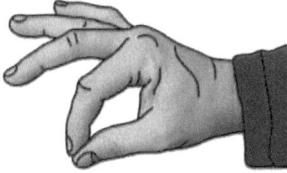
Fig. 13.3: F-handshape.

While the congruent metaphors MIND IS A CONTAINER and IDEAS ARE OBJECTS (that are contained within the mind) are pervasive in signed languages, including ASL, British Sign Language (BSL), Catalan Sign Language (LSC), French Sign Language (LSF), and Italian Sign Language (LIS), they are not universal (P. Wilcox 2007). Signed languages exhibit cultural variability in metaphorical expression. In Japanese Sign language (JSL) the metaphor TORSO IS A CONTAINER interacts with IDEAS ARE OBJECTS and UNDERSTANDING IS CONSUMING FOOD. In JSL, the torso is understood as the container for ideas; the body, the same cavity where food is digested, instead of the forehead, provides a container where understanding takes place. The JSL sign meaning 'to comprehend' is DRINK-QUICK.

Metonymy

Wilcox and colleagues (Wilcox et al. 2003) reported several types of lexical metonymies in ASL and LSC. The metonymy PROTOTYPICAL CHARACTERISTIC FOR WHOLE ENTITY appears in both ASL and LSC, in which the signs for 'bird', 'horse', and 'cow' depict prototypical physical properties of these animals: the beak, the ears, and horns, respectively. In ACTION FOR INSTRUMENT metonymies, the action of the hands in interaction with some object represents the instrument. In the ASL sign TYPEWRITER, for example, the hands and fingers are moved in a way representing the action of typing. In the metonymy PROTOTYPICAL ACTION FOR ACTIVITY the hands and their movement represent prototypical action taken with an object; this in turn may come to metonymically express the general activity. The ASL and LSC signs DRIVE-CAR, EAT, and BATHE exemplify this. The ASL sign DRIVE-CAR, for example, represents the prototypical action of the hands holding onto a car's steering wheel. In LSC, the signs DRINK-BEER, DRINK-BRANDY, DRINK-RUM-AND-COKE use specific handshapes representing interaction with a container of a specific, prototypical shape, as well as movements characteristic of drinking from these containers.

A number of signs in LSC rely on a metonymy in which a salient characteristic of a well-known person is extended to stand for a more general quality. These metonymies also typically involve metonymic chains. The LSC sign CHARLIE-CHAPLIN is a compound that iconically depicts Chaplin's moustache and the movement of holding the cane and moving it in circles as Chaplin did, thus relying on a physical characteristic for person (in this case two characteristics) metonymy. The sign is also used to mean 'person moving fast', which extends the first metonymy to a more abstract characteristic of person for general quality metonymy.

Wilcox and P. Wilcox (2013) describe the role that metaphor and metonymy play in the semantic extension and grammaticization of perception signs. ASL has a family of tactile perception signs related phonologically and semantically. Phonologically, the signs are made with the open-8 handshape (Figure 13.4). Frishberg and Gough ([1973] 2000: 111) described this family of signs:

> The meaning this handshape carries relates to feelings, both sensation and emotion, with some interesting extensions along those lines. Along the chest we find discouraged, depressed, thrilled, excited, sensitive, feel, like, dislike, have-a-hunch, and interesting. In some cases both hands use the configuration and in other cases just one hand does. On the forehead we find sick, sickly ('habitually sick'), differing only in that the second has characteristic slow repetition, which is used quite productively to show habitual, repeated action or plurality. Other signs which use this handshape include delicious, taste (at the mouth), touch (on the back of the hand), favorite (on the chin). glory and shining are variants of one another which both occur on a palm up base hand. brilliant shows the same movement and handshape as shining except that it is made on the forehead, like many other words having to do with thought processes.

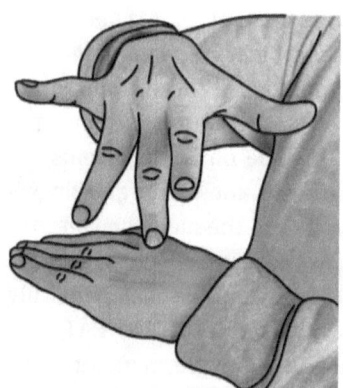

Fig. 13.4: ASL sign TOUCH.

The phonological parameter of location is a source of metaphorical meanings using the TOUCH sign. SHINING is produced in a neutral space in front of the signer, in a location where bright, shining light would most prototypically be viewed. BRILLIANT (in the mental sense) uses the same handshape and movement as SHINING, but it is produced at the forehead, thus evoking a metaphorical connection with the head as the place where cognitive activities take place.

The signs discouraged, depressed, thrilled, excited, sensitive, feel, like, dislike, have-a-hunch, and interesting are produced on the chest, suggesting a metaphorical connection between the heart and emotions or intuitive feelings. delicious, taste, and FAVORITE are produced on the mouth or chin. TOUCH is produced on the back of the hand in citation form, but can be produced on other locations as well to indicate touching some specific location.

In many languages the verb meaning 'feel' in the tactile sense is also used to indicate general sensory perception (Sweetser 1990). Sweetser notes that "the sense of touch is not only linked with general sense perception, but is also closely tied to emotional 'feeling'" (Sweetser 1990: 37). She also points out that there is a metonymic link between touch and emotion: physical pain, for example, makes us unhappy, while physical pleasure makes us cheerful. Metaphor and metonymy play a role in semantic extension and grammaticalization of TOUCH and FEEL forms in ASL (Figures 13.4 and 13.5). A metonymic path of semantic extension leads from TOUCH and FEEL referring to the perception of external sensations, to the perception of internal sensation, to emotion, to emotion tied to cognitive action, and finally to the use of TOUCH/FEEL forms to refer primarily to cognitive activity with little or no emotional content such as planning, considering, or deciding (Wilcox and P. Wilcox 2013).

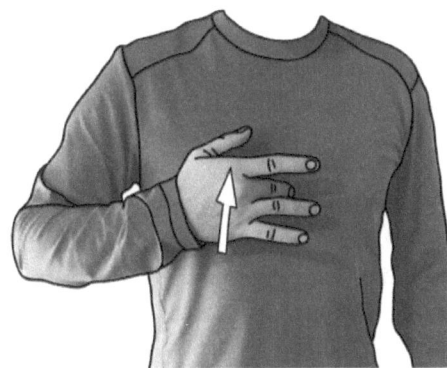

Fig. 13.5: ASL sign FEEL.

Iconicity

Signed languages are particularly intriguing for linguists interested in the study of iconicity. Early on, linguists recognized the pervasive iconicity of signed languages. Stokoe et al. (1965) noted metaphorical, metonymic, and iconic aspects of ASL. Mandel (1977) described several iconic devices that he argued play a role in the grammar of ASL. Following this period of interest in iconicity, linguists began to document constraints on iconicity. Frishberg (1975) studied the erosion of iconicity in historical change. While acknowledging the two faces of signs – the iconic face and the encoded, arbitrary face – Klima and Bellugi (1979: 34) argued that grammatical processes in ASL work to diminish lexical iconicity:

> Grammatical operations that signs undergo can further submerge iconicity. Thus many signs, while having their roots deeply embedded in mimetic representation, have lost their original transparency as they have been constrained more tightly by the linguistic system.

The example they offer is the morphological marking of intensification in ASL, expressed phonologically as an initial hold of the sign's movement followed by sudden, rapid release. When this grammatical marker appears on the ASL root sign SLOW the resulting sign means 'very slow'. Klima and Bellugi pointed out that the sign VERY-SLOW is made with a faster movement than that used in the sign SLOW, and thus they argued that the form of VERY-SLOW is non-iconic with its meaning: VERY-SLOW is articulated very fast. Wilcox (2004a) proposed a metaphorical analysis of the intensification marker on VERY-SLOW as the build up and sudden of release of pressure. Since the sign is produced with an initial hold followed by a sudden release movement, he argued that rather than demonstrating how grammar diminishes iconicity, this example instead is a case of iconicity emerging in grammatical morphology.

Recently, research on iconicity has seen a resurgence, with linguists documenting its role in the grammars of signed languages. Meir and colleagues (Meir et al. 2007) have shown that iconic signs denoting states of affairs manifests an inherent pattern of iconicity in which the signer's body represents one argument of the verb, the subject, and the hands, moving in relation to the body, represent other arguments. Taub (2001) and Meir (2010) have documented the complex relation between iconicity and metaphor. Russo and colleagues explored the role iconicity plays in Italian Sign Language poetry (Russo et al. 2001). Perniss (2007) reported on iconicity in German Sign Language.

Wilcox (2004a) introduced the concept of cognitive iconicity, based on cognitive grammar (Langacker 1987, 2008). In the cognitive grammar framework, semantic and phonological structures reside within conceptual space. Similarities among concepts are regarded as distance relations between structures in conceptual space (Gärdenfors 2000, 2014). Cognitive iconicity builds on these concepts by defining iconicity not as a relation between the form of a sign and its real world referent, but as a distance relation within a multidimensional conceptual space between the phonological and semantic poles of symbolic structures. Greater distance in conceptual space between a symbolic unit's semantic and phonological poles creates arbitrariness. When the phonological and semantic poles of a sign lie more closely together in conceptual space, iconicity is increased.

Cognitive iconicity is a manifestation of the cognitive abilities that structure both the phonological and semantic poles of language. A key claim of cognitive grammar is that grammar and language are structured by an embodied conceptual system with certain basic abilities. One cognitive ability is schematization, "the process of extracting the commonality inherent in multiple experiences to arrive at a conception representing a higher level of abstraction" (Langacker 2008: 17). One class of schemas is conceptual archetypes; examples include "a physical object, an object in a location, an object moving through space, the human face and its parts, a physical container and its contents, seeing something, holding something, handing something to someone, exerting force to effect a desired change, a face-to-face encounter" (Langacker 2008: 33).

Cognitive iconicity captures the fact that conceptual archetypes derive not only from our experience with general events in the world, but also from a distinct class of visible events: hands, faces, and their movements. Hands are arguably the physical objects with which we have the most experience. They are certainly the most common way that we interact with the world. Signing or gesturing hands are located in and move through space. Facial gestures are used in every known signed language. Hands are containers, both for real contents and for metaphorical contents such as ideas or emotions. Hands are visually perceived. Hands exert force on other objects to effect change, making the phonological pole of signs describable in terms of transitivity (Wilcox and P. Wilcox 1995). For signed languages these articulators have rich conceptual import. Hands and faces are not only the means by which semantic structures are phonologically expressed, they are themselves a significant source of our embodied conceptual system. In other words, signing hands have rich semantic properties, a feature described by Stokoe (1991) as semantic phonology.

4 Signed language and gesture

Unburdened by the need to defend the status of signed languages as nothing more than gesture, sign linguists have begun to explore the complex relationship between the two systems. Gesture and sign may co-occur in signer's utterances, either simultaneously or in alternation. Gestures also become incorporated over time into the linguistic systems of signed languages through lexicalization and grammaticalization.

Gesture and sign co-occur

A growing body of research examines how gesture and sign co-occur within an utterance. Vermeergen and Demey (2007) offer a comprehensive review with data from Flemish Sign Language, showing how sign and gesture co-occur in utterances both simultaneously and in alternation. McCleary and Viotti (2009) provide an overview of the interaction of gesture and sign and demonstrate such co-occurrence in Língua Brasileira de Sinais (Libras). Duncan (2005) has suggested that Taiwanese Sign Language signers incorporate manual gestures into signs at the point in narratives where hearing narrators using spoken language also make manual gestures.

One proposal for the interaction of gesture and sign is offered by Liddell (2003a, 2003b), who suggests that sign and gesture co-occur simultaneously in several ways, including aspects of spatialized syntax, pointing or indexical signs, and classifier predicates. Liddell argues that location in pointing signs cannot be morphemic because the number of possible locations is uncountable. He applies the same analysis to classifier signs, arguing that while parts of these signs (e.g., handshape and movement) are linguistic, other parts (locations) are variable, gradient elements and should be classified as gesture (see also Schembri et al. 2005: 287, who suggest that classifier verbs may be analyzed as blends of linguistic and gestural elements).

For example, Liddell (2003b: 212) argues that in ASL constructions such as UPRIGHT-PERSON-WALK-ALONG, meaning 'person walks along (in an unhurried manner and in a normal forward orientation)', the handshape and movement are formally stable and linguistic, but the initial and end locations are gradient and thus gesture. Wilbur (2013) makes a cogent, non-cognitive argument against this analysis.

A cognitive linguistic rebuttal would point out first that what Liddell analyzes as a sign is actually a complex symbolic construction, and, more importantly, that what he characterizes as gestural elements (the initial and end locations) are more appropriately analyzed as schematic components in this complex, composite construction. English constructions can serve as an example. Adjectives such as *moonless* and *hopeless* lead to the abstraction of a schematic template *N+less*, which sanctions *senseless* and *thoughtless* and is itself a component of a more complex construction N_1+less N_2 (Langacker 2008: 24). Parts of this complex construction are more specific (*-less*), and parts are more schematic (N_1 and N_2).

Similarly, signers extract schematic constructional templates from usage events. The ASL expression UPRIGHT-PERSON-WALK-ALONG may lead to the abstraction of a schematic template in which the frequently occurring handshape and movement are more specific (specifying a person walking normally), while the variable initial and end locations are more schematic (until they are actually articulated). In the complex English construction, the more schematic elements will sanction limitless conventional as well as novel instantiations (in Langacker's discussion, even the unlikely novel expression *ireless dwarf* is sanctioned by the schematic assembly N_1+*less* N_2). The same is true for the novel instantiations of the initial and end locations of the ASL construction, which, as Liddell points out, also appear to be uncountable. The mistake we should not make is categorizing the schematic elements as gesture.

Gesture is incorporated into signed languages

Gestures may become lexicalized and grammaticalized into the linguistic system of signed languages (Janzen 2012). Wilcox and Xavier (2013) offer data demonstrating lexicalization of gesture in Libras. The thumb-up gesture performed with one hand is a gestural emblem[2] for Brazilian hearing people (Sherzer 1991), as well as for deaf Brazilian users of Libras. The gesture also appears to be the source for several lexical signs in Libras, which fall along a continuum from more gesture-like (emblems incorporating some Libras morphology) to more linguistic (fully lexicalized signs incorporating Libras morphology).

Once lexicalized, gesture may undergo grammaticalization. Several researchers have documented the process by which lexicalized gestures grammaticalize (Janzen and Shaffer 2002; Pfau and Steinbach 2007; Wilcox 2004b, 2005; Wilcox and P. Wilcox 1995). In general, the process starts with a manually produced gesture which enters a signed language as a lexical morpheme. That lexical sign then acquires grammatical meaning. For example, it has been proposed (Janzen and Shaffer 2002) that a departure gesture used in the Mediterranean region entered French Sign Language (LSF) as the lexical sign PARTIR 'leave'. Because ASL is historically related to French Sign Language (LSF), the sign also appeared in ASL at the turn of the 20th century with the lexical meaning 'to depart'. It also occurs with a more grammatical function marking future.

In addition to manual gestures becoming grammaticalized, a second route leads from gesture to language (Wilcox 2004b, 2005; Wilcox et al. 2010). This route begins as facial gestures or manner of movement gestures. These gestures do not enter the linguistic system as lexical signs; rather, they first appear as prosody or intonation. As they grammaticalize, they take on grammatical function as, for example, markers of interrogatives, topics, conditionals, verb aspect, and intensification.

---

[2] Emblems are conventionalized gestures that have a spoken equivalent, such as the V gesture representing 'victory'.

What is language and what is gesture?

Examining the relation between gesture and language raises the question of how to determine what is gesture and what is language. Distinguishing between gesture and language within the diachronic approach is relatively straightforward: gestures are those behaviors that can be shown to be in use outside of the signed language community. In the example discussed above, the departure gesture used by non-signers that is the source for PARTIR is well-documented by gesture scholars (de Jorio and Kendon [1832] 2001; Morris et al. 1979). Facial gestures that may serve as the non-linguistic source of prosody and intonation have been studied and documented as well (Darwin 1872) and arguably have a language external, biological origin (see also Bolinger 1986). Manner of movement of gesture has a long history of description. According to Aldrete (1999: 36–37), Quintilian taught that "by altering the speed with which a gesture was made and its range of motion, the same gesture could have multiple meanings or purposes."

The proposal that gesture and signed language co-occur poses a more serious problem, since they are both produced with the same articulators. Often, sign linguists who make the claim for the distinction of language and gesture adopt criterial models of language and gesture as classical categories, assuming that linguistic material is categorical, discrete, and conventional, while gestural material is gradient, analog, and idiosyncratic (Liddell 2003a; Sandler 2009).

These assumptions contradict cognitive linguistic research findings in three ways. First, cognitive linguists have soundly rejected criterial and shared properties models in favor of prototype models (Lakoff 1987; Langacker 2008). Second, linguists working within usage-based and cognitive linguistic theories have convincingly demonstrated that gradience pervades language at all levels (Bybee 2010; Langacker 2008). Whereas some sign linguists classify gradience in morphology as non-linguistic gesture, spoken language linguists come to quite a different conclusion. Hay and Baayen (2005: 346) ask whether morphological structure is inherently graded and reply, "The issue is controversial, but the evidence that is currently accumulating in the literature suggests that the answer is yes." This leads them to conclude that gradedness is part and parcel of the grammar (Hay and Baayen 2005).

The third way these assumptions are at odds with usage-based and cognitive linguistic findings is that they implicitly accept the formalist distinction between competence and performance. The formalist approach assumes that linguistic competence consists of "well-defined discrete categories and categorical grammaticality criteria. Performance may be full of fuzziness, gradience, and continua, but linguistic competence is not" (Bod et al. 2003: 1). Fuzziness, gradience, and continua characterize the grammars of spoken language; a cognitive linguistic approach recognizes them as properties of the grammars of signed languages as well.

Looking towards the future of cognitive linguistic research on signed languages, linguists should recognize that language and gesture are not classical categories based on objective properties. A solution to the problem of what is language and what is gesture more compatible with the cognitive linguistic framework would be to recognize that language and gesture are culturally and linguistically constructed prototype categories. As Lakoff (1987: 8) long ago explained, categories are "a matter of both human experience and imagination – of perception, motor activity, and culture on the one hand, and of metaphor, metonymy, and mental imagery on the other." We should expect that deaf and hearing people will have different notions of what is language and what is gesture, if only because they have different perceptual, motor, and cultural experiences. We also should predict that, just as for any category, the boundaries of language and gesture will be fuzzy and gradient, varying by individual, by context, and subject to change over time (see also Bybee 2010 on the nature of categories).

5 Dynamic systems theory

A foundational assumption of cognitive linguistics and the usage-based approach is that language is a dynamic, emergent system (Barlow and Kemmer 2000; Bybee 2000; Langacker 2000; MacWhinney this volume). Dynamic systems theory (DST) strives to account for how emergent systems arise. Looking to the future of cognitive linguistics, a unified framework will require, as one step, the integration of cognitive linguistics with dynamic systems theory.

One of the first applications of dynamic systems theory to language was an approach called articulatory phonology or gestural phonology (Browman and Goldstein 1985). In this model, the basic units of speech are articulatory gestures, where gesture is defined as "a functional unit, an equivalence class of coordinated movements that achieve some end" (Studdert Kennedy 1987: 77). These functionally-defined ends, or tasks, are modeled in terms of task dynamics (Hawkins 1992).

The significance of DST for cognitive linguistics, and for an embodied solution that seeks to unify the relationship between signed language, spoken language, and gesture, is that it applies not only to the production of language as articulatory gesture but to the emergence and cognitive organization of grammar (Bybee 2010). Rather than viewing the units of language – whether they are phonemes, syllables, morphemes, words or formalist structural descriptions – as timeless and non-physical (i.e., mental) units which must be passed to and implemented in a performance system, the dynamic view defines language "in a unitary way across both abstract 'planning' and concrete articulatory 'production' levels" (Kelso et al. 1986: 31). Thus, the distinction between competence and performance, between language as knowledge and language as action, is replaced by a single system described not in the machine vocabulary of mental programs and computational systems, but in terms of a "fluid, organic system with certain thermodynamic properties" (Thelen and Smith 1994: xix).

Several other linguists and cognitive scientists also have explored a dynamic systems approach to language (Elman 1998; Port and van Gelder 1995; Spivey 2007). To date, however, there has been no systematic exploration of how DST can be integrated with cognitive linguistics. Key principles of DST are clearly mirrored in cognitive linguistic theory. One example is entrenchment, the process by which a complex structure becomes automatized through repetition or rehearsal, eventually becoming established as a unit (Divjak and Caldwell-Harris volume 1; Langacker 2008). Entrenchment is the cognitive linguistic equivalent of the DST concept of entrainment, a process by which two or more independent systems become functionally coupled, resulting in a structure with fewer degrees of freedom. In cognitive grammar terminology, the complex structure acquires unit status.

One of the first efforts to apply DST to signed languages was a study of the articulatory phonetics of fingerspelling (Wilcox 1992). Using motion tracking equipment to measure the trajectories of the hand and fingers, Wilcox found that fluent fingerspelling exhibits synchronicity across multiple articulators. In producing letters and letter combinations, the articulators are harnessed to produce task-specific patterns of coordinated motion. This functional entrenchment or entrainment results in a reduction of degrees of freedom characteristic of dynamic systems.

Dynamic systems theory also has been used to analyze signed language production. Tyrone and her colleagues (Tyrone and Mauk 2010; Tyrone et al. 2010) examined prosodic lengthening at phrase boundaries, and sign lowering and phonetic reduction, in ASL. Their findings are consistent with the predictions of a task-dynamic model. Advances in motion tracking technology, and the relative ease with which visible sign articulators can be tracked compared to vocal articulators, makes research on DST approaches to signed language a field ripe for future research.

The application of DST to speech and language suggests a theoretical basis for describing language as a dynamic, real-time, physical process (Bybee 2001; Fowler 2004, 2010; Fowler et al. 1980; Kelso 1995). When we consider the theoretical problems posed in developing an embodied theory of spoken language, signed language, and gesture, it becomes clear that a unified solution will require "compatible dynamics so that perception, action, and cognition can be mutually and flexibly coupled" (Iverson and Thelen 1999: 37) across different perceptual and motor systems.

6 Conclusions

Cognitive linguistics has greatly advanced our understanding of signed languages. In turn, discoveries from the analysis of signed languages challenge linguists to rethink our basic ideas about language and gesture as semiotic systems, and how a modality-free theory may be developed within a usage-based approach in which grammar is directly constructed from experience.

Signed languages presented two problems for linguists. The first problem was to ensure that linguistic theory could account for languages in two modalities. One solution to this problem is offered by formalist or generative theories that posit modality-free grammars independent of physical implementation. In a usage-based theory, grammar emerges from form-meaning pairings of actual utterances. Still, this leaves open the question of how to unify spoken utterances and signed utterances, how to cross the acoustic-optical perceptual divide. The embodied solution, which couples cognitive linguistics with dynamic systems theory, provides an answer.

The second problem was to understand the relationship between language and gesture. This problem was long overlooked by spoken language linguists, who regarded the two as entirely distinct systems. The issue has proved to be challenging for signed language linguists. First, the field had to overcome the widespread perception that signs are nothing more than gestures. Then, unable to apply a simple rubric classifying gestures as behavior that is produced by the hands and face (because signs are produced with the same articulators), sign linguists sought to distinguish the two by viewing them as classical categories definable by objective properties. These proposals, however, contradict two of the most robust findings of cognitive linguistics: that criterial models cannot account for linguistic data, and that gradience pervades language. Relying on criterial models and classical categories to distinguish language from gesture by characterizing language as the domain of the discrete and categorical, and gesture as the realm of gradience and variability, is certain to prove futile. As Bybee (2010: 2) observes, "All types of units proposed by linguists show gradience, in the sense that there is a lot of variation within the domain of the unit (different types of words, morphemes, syllables) and difficulty in setting the boundaries of the unit."

Spoken language, signed language, and gesture are gradient, variable, and emergent systems. The most important contribution that cognitive linguistics can make to future research on signed languages will be to take the usage-based perspective (Bybee 2010; Croft 2001; Langacker 2008) seriously and explore the implications fully. The results of such research are also likely to transform our understanding of language and human communication.

Acknowledgement

Figures designed by Kip Fletcher, Riverlight Studios, Oregon City, OR.

7 References

Aldrete, Gregory S. (1999): *Gestures and Acclamations in Ancient Rome*. Baltimore: Johns Hopkins University Press.
Aronoff, Mark, Irit Meir, and Wendy Sandler (2005): The paradox of sign language morphology. *Language* 81(2): 301–344.
Barlow, Michael and Suzanne Kemmer (2000): *Usage-based models of language*. Stanford: CSLI Publications Center for the Study of Language and Information.
Bates, Elizabeth and Frederic Dick (2002): Language, gesture, and the developing brain. *Developmental Psychobiology* 40(3): 293–310.
Battison, Robbin (1978): *Lexical borrowing in American Sign Language*. Silver Spring: Linkstok Press.
Bergen, Benjamin (volume 1): Embodiment. Berlin/Boston: De Gruyter Mouton.
Bod, Rens, Jennifer Hay, and Stefanie Jannedy (2003): *Probabilistic Linguistics*. Cambridge: MIT Press.
Bolinger, Dwight (1986): *Intonation and its Parts: Melody in Spoken English*. Stanford: Stanford University Press.
Brentari, Diane (1998): *A Prosodic Model of Sign Language Phonology*. Cambridge: MIT Press.
Bridges, Byron and Melanie Metzger (1996): *Deaf Tend Your: Non-Manual Signals in American Sign Language*. Silver Spring: Caliope Press.
Browman, Catherine P. and Louis M. Goldstein (1985): Dynamic modeling of phonetic structure. In: V. A. Fromkin (ed.), *Phonetic Linguistics*. New York: Academic Press.
Bybee, Joan (2000): The phonology of the lexicon: Evidence from lexical diffusion. In: M. Barlow and S. Kemmer (eds.), *Usage-Based Models of Language*, 65–85. Stanford: CSLI.
Bybee, Joan (2001): *Phonology and Language Use*. Cambridge: Cambridge University Press.
Bybee, Joan (2010): *Language, Usage and Cognition*. Cambridge/New York: Cambridge University Press.

Bybee, Joan, Revere Perkins, and William Pagliuca (1994): *The Evolution of Grammar: Tense, Aspect, and Modality in the Languages of the World*. Chicago: University of Chicago Press.

Capirci, Olga, Cristina Caselli, Jana Iverson, Elena Pizzuto, and Virginia Volterra (2002): Gesture and the nature of language in infancy: The role of gesture as a transitional device en route to two-word speech. In: D. F. Armstrong, M. A. Karchmer and J. V. Van Cleve (eds.), *The Study of Signed Languages: Essays in Honor of William C. Stokoe*, 213–246. Washington, DC: Gallaudet University Press.

Chomsky, Noam (1972): *Language and Mind*. New York: Harcourt Brace Jovanovich.

Corballis, Michael C. (2003): From mouth to hand: Gesture, speech, and the evolution of language. *Behavioral and Brain Sciences* 26(2): 199.

Croft, William (2001): *Radical Construction Grammar: Syntactic Theory in Typological Perspective*. Oxford: Oxford University Press.

Darwin, Charles (1872): *The Expression of the Emotions in Man and Animals*. London: J. Murray.

de Jorio, Andrea and Adam Kendon ([1832] 2001): *Gesture in Naples and Gesture in Classical Antiquity: A Translation of La Mimica degli Antichi Investigata nel Gestire Napoletano, Gestural Expression of the Ancients in the Light of Neapolitan Gesturing*. Bloomington: Indiana University Press.

Divjak, Dagmar and Catherine Caldwell-Harris (volume 1): Frequency and entrenchment. Berlin/Boston: De Gruyter Mouton.

Dudis, Paul G. (2004): Body partitioning and real-space blends. *Cognitive Linguistics* 15(2): 223–238.

Duncan, Susan (2005): Gesture in signing: A case study in Taiwan Sign Language. *Language and Linguistics* 6: 279–318.

Elman, Jeffrey L. (1998): Language as a dynamical system. In: R. F. Port and T. van Gelder (eds.), *Mind as Motion: Explorations in the Dynamics of Cognition*, 195–225. Cambridge: MIT Press.

Engberg-Pedersen, Elisabeth (1993): *Space in Danish Sign Language: The Semantics and Morphosyntax of the Use of Space in a Visual Language*. Hamburg: SIGNUM-Verlag.

Engberg-Pedersen, Elisabeth (1996a): Iconic motivations in conflict: Language-specific structure and influence from the medium. In: E. Engberg-Pedersen, M. Fortescue, P. Harder, L. Heltoft, and L. F. Jakobsen (eds.), *Content, Expression and Structure: Studies in Danish Functional Grammar*, 39–64. Amsterdam: John Benjamins Publishing Company.

Engberg-Pedersen, Elisabeth (1996b): Iconicity and arbitrariness. In: E. Engberg-Pedersen, M. Fortescue, P. Harder, L. Heltoft, and L. F. Jakobsen (eds.), *Content, Expression and Structure: Studies in Danish Functional Grammar*, 453–468. Amsterdam: John Benjamins Publishing Company.

Engberg-Pedersen, Elisabeth (1999): Space and time. In: J. Allwood & P. Gärdenfors (eds.), *Cognitive Semantics: Meaning and Cognition*, 131–152. Amsterdam: John Benjamins Publishing Company.

Fowler, Carol A. (2004): Listeners do hear sounds, not tongues. *The Journal of the Acoustical Society of America* 99(3): 1730–1741.

Fowler, Carol A. (2010): Embodied, embedded language use. *Ecological Psychology* 22(4): 286–303.

Fowler, Carol A., Philip Rubin, Richard E. Remez, and Michael Turvey (1980): Implications for speech production of a general theory of action. In: B. Butterworth (ed.), *Language Production*, 373–420. New York: Academic Press.

Frishberg, Nancy (1975): Arbitrariness and iconicity: Historical change in American Sign Language. *Language* 51: 676–710.
Frishberg, Nancy and Bonnie Gough ([1973] 2000): Morphology in American Sign Language. *Sign Language and Linguistics* 3(1): 103–131.
Gärdenfors, Peter (2000): *Conceptual Spaces: The Geometry of Thought*. Cambridge: MIT Press.
Gärdenfors, Peter (2014): *The Geometry of Meaning: Semantics Based on Conceptual Spaces*. Cambridge: MIT Press.
Gentilucci, Maurizio (2006): From manual gesture to speech: A gradual transition. *Neuroscience and Biobehavioral Reviews* 30(7): 949–960.
Hawkins, Sarah (1992): An introduction to task dynamics. *Papers in Laboratory Phonology: Gesture, Segment, Prosody* 2: 9–25.
Hay, Jennifer B. and R. Harald Baayen (2005): Shifting paradigms: gradient structure in morphology. *Trends in Cognitive Science* 9(7): 342–348.
Husain, Fatima T., Debra J. Patkin, Hung Thai-Van, Allen R. Braun, and Barry Horwitz (2009): Distinguishing the processing of gestures from signs in deaf individuals: An FMRI study. *Brain Research* 1276: 140–150.
Iverson, Jana and Esther Thelen (1999): Hand, mouth and brain. The dynamic emergence of speech and gesture. *Journal of Consciousness Studies* 6(11): 19–40.
Janzen, Terry (2006): Visual communication: Signed language and cognition. In: G. Kristiansen, M. Achard, R. Dirven, and F. R. M. de Ibáñez (eds.), *Cognitive Linguistics: Current Applications and Future Perspectives*, 359–377. Berlin/New York: Mouton de Gruyter.
Janzen, Terry (2012): Lexicalization and grammaticalization. In: M. Steinbach, R. Pfau and B. Woll (eds.), *Handbook of Sign Languages*, 1–23. Berlin: Mouton de Gruyter.
Janzen, Terry and Barbara Shaffer (2002): Gesture as the substrate in the process of ASL grammaticization. In: R. Meier, D. Quinto and K. Cormier (eds.), *Modality and Structure in Signed and Spoken Languages*, 199–223. Cambridge: Cambridge University Press.
Janzen, Terry, Barbara O'Dea, and Barbara Shaffer (2001): The construal of events: Passives in American Sign Language. *Sign Language Studies* 1(3): 281–310.
Johnston, Trevor and Adam Schembri (2007): *Australian Sign Language (Auslan): An Introduction to Sign Language Linguistics*. Cambridge: Cambridge University Press.
Kelso, J. A. Scott (1995): *Dynamic Patterns: The Self-Organization of Brain and Behavior*. Cambridge: The MIT Press.
Kelso, J. A. Scott, Elliot Saltzman, and Betty Tuller (1986): The dynamical perspective on speech production: Data and theory. *Journal of Phonetics* 14: 29–59.
Kendon, Adam (2004): *Gesture: Visible Action as Utterance*. Cambridge/New York: Cambridge University Press.
Klima, Edward and Ursula Bellugi (1979): *The Signs of Language*. Cambridge: Harvard University Press.
Lakoff, George (1987): *Women, Fire, and Dangerous Things: What Categories Reveal About the Mind*. Chicago: University of Chicago Press.
Lane, Harlan (1984): *When the Mind Hears: A History of the Deaf*. New York: Random House.
Langacker, Ronald W. (1987): *Foundations of Cognitive Grammar, Volume 1: Theoretical Foundations*. Stanford: Stanford University Press.
Langacker, Ronald W. (2000): A dynamic usage-based model. In: M. Barlow and S. Kemmer (eds.), *Usage-Based Models of Language*, 1–63. Stanford: CSLI Publications Center for the Study of Language and Information.

Langacker, Ronald W. (2008): *Cognitive Grammar: A Basic Introduction*. Oxford: Oxford University Press.
Liddell, Scott K. (1984): Think and believe: Sequentiality in American Sign Language. *Language* 60(2): 372–399.
Liddell, Scott K. (1995): Real, surrogate, and token space: Grammatical consequences in ASL. In: K. Emmorey and J. Riley (eds.), *Language, Gesture, and Space*, 19–41. Hillsdale: Lawrence Erlbaum Associates, Inc.
Liddell, Scott K. (1998): Grounded blends, gestures, and conceptual shifts. *Cognitive Linguistics*, 9(3): 283–314.
Liddell, Scott K. (2000): Blended spaces and deixis in sign language discourse. In: D. McNeill (ed.), *Language and Gesture*, 331–357. Cambridge: Cambridge University Press.
Liddell, Scott K. (2003a): *Grammar, Gesture, and Meaning in American Sign Language*. New York: Cambridge University Press.
Liddell, Scott K. (2003b): Sources of meaning in ASL classifier predicates. In: K. Emmorey (ed.), *Perspectives on Classifier Constructions in Sign Languages*, 199–220. Mahwah: Lawrence Erlbaum Associates.
Liebal, Katja, Cornelia Müller, and Simone Pika (eds.) (2007): *Gestural Communication in Nonhuman and Human Primates*. (Benjamins Current Topics 10.) Amsterdam/ Philadelphia: John Benjamins Publishing.
Lillo Martin, Diane (1986): Two kinds of null arguments in American Sign Language. *Natural Language and Linguistic Theory* 4(4): 415–444.
MacWhinney, Brian (this volume): Emergentism. Berlin/Boston: De Gruyter Mouton.
Mandel, Mark A. (1977): Iconic devices in American Sign Language. In: L. A. Friedman (ed.), *On the Other Hand: New Perspectives on American Sign Language*, 57–108. New York: Academic Press.
McCleary, Leland and Evani Viotti (2009): Sign-gesture symbiosis in Brazilian Sign Language narrative. In: F. Parrill, V. Tobin and M. Turner (eds.), *Meaning, Form, and Body*, 181–201. Stanford: CSLI Publications.
McNeill, David (1992): *Hand and Mind: What Gestures Reveal about Thought*. Chicago: University of Chicago Press.
McNeill, David (2005): *Gesture and Thought*. Chicago: University of Chicago Press.
Meier, Richard (2002): The acquisition of verb agreement: Pointing out arguments for the linguistic status of agreement in signed languages. In: G. Morgan and B. Woll (eds.), *Directions in Sign Language Acquisition*, 115–141. Amsterdam: John Benjamins.
Meir, Irit (2010): Iconicity and metaphor: Constraints on metaphorical extension of iconic forms. *Language* 86(4): 865–896.
Meir, Irit, Carol Padden, Mark Aronoff, and Wendy Sandler (2007): Body as subject. *Journal of Linguistics* 43(03): 531–563.
Metzger, Melanie (1998): Eye gaze and pronominal reference in American Sign Language. In: C. Lucas (ed.), *Pinky Extension and Eye Gaze: Language Use in Deaf Communities*, 170–182. Washington, DC: Gallaudet University Press.
Morris, Desmond, Peter Collett, Peter Marsh, and Marie O'Shaughnessy (1979): *Gestures: Their Origin and Distribution*. New York: Stein and Day.
Müller, Cornelia (2007): A dynamic view of metaphor, gesture, and thought. In: S. D. Duncan, J. Cassell and E. T. Levy (eds.), *Gesture and the Dynamic Dimension of Language. Essays in Honor of David McNeill*, 109–116. Amsterdam/Philadelphia: John Benjamins.

Neidle, Carol, Judy Kegl, Dawn MacLaughlin, Benjamin Bahan, and Robert Lee (2000): *American Sign Language: Functional Categories and Hierarchical Structure*. Cambridge: MIT Press.

Padden, Carol A. and David M. Perlmutter (1987): American Sign Language and the architecture of phonological theory. *Natural Language and Linguistic Theory* 5(3): 335–375.

Perniss, Pamela M. (2007): *Space and Iconicity in German Sign Language (DGS)*. MPI Series in Psycholinguistics 45, Radboud University Nijmegen.

Petronio, Karen and Diane Lillo Martin (1997): Wh-movement and the position of spec-CP: Evidence from American Sign Language. *Language* 73(1): 18–57.

Pfau, Roland and Josep Quer (2003): V-to-neg raising and negative concord in three sign languages. Paper presented at the XXIX Incontro di Grammatica Generativa, Urbino, February.

Pfau, Roland and Josep Quer (2007): On the syntax of negation and modals in Catalan Sign Language and German Sign Language. *Trends in Linguistics Studies and Monographs* 188: 129.

Pfau, Roland and Martin Steinbach (2007): Modality independent and modality specific aspects of grammaticalization in sign languages. *Linguistics in Potsdam* 24: 3–98.

Pike, Kenneth L. (1967): *Language in Relation to a Unified Theory of the Structure of Human Behavior*. The Hague: Mouton.

Port, Robert F. and Timothy van Gelder (1995): *Mind as Motion: Explorations in the Dynamics of Cognition*. Cambridge: The MIT Press.

Rączaszek-Leonardi, Joanna and J. A. Scott Kelso (2008): Reconciling symbolic and dynamic aspects of language: Toward a dynamic psycholinguistics. *New Ideas in Psychology* 26(2): 193–207.

Rizzolatti, Giacomo and Michael A. Arbib (1998): Language within our grasp. *Trends in Neurosciences* 21(5): 188–194.

Russo, Tommaso, Rosaria Giurana, and Elena Pizzuto (2001): Italian Sign Language (LIS) poetry: Iconic properties and structural regularities. *Sign Language Studies* 2(1): 85–112.

Sandler, Wendy (1999): A prosodic model of sign language phonology. *Phonology* 16(3): 443–447.

Sandler, Wendy (2009): Symbiotic symbolization by hand and mouth in sign language. *Semiotica* 2009(174): 241–275.

Sandler, Wendy and Diane Lillo Martin (2006): *Sign Language and Linguistic Universals*. Cambridge: Cambridge University Press.

Schembri, Adam, Caroline Jones, and Denis Burnham (2005): Comparing action gestures and classifier verbs of motion: Evidence from Australian Sign Language, Taiwan Sign Language, and nonsigners' gestures without speech. *Journal of Deaf Studies and Deaf Education* 10(3): 272–290.

Shaffer, Barbara (2002): CAN'T: The negation of modal notions in ASL. *Sign Language Studies*, 3(1): 34–53.

Shaffer, Barbara (2004): Information ordering and speaker subjectivity: Modality in ASL. *Cognitive Linguistics* 15(2): 175–195.

Sherzer, Joel (1991): The Brazilian thumbs-up gesture. *Journal of Linguistic Anthropology* 1(2): 189–197.

Skipper, Jeremy I., Susan Goldin-Meadow, Howard C. Nusbaum, and Steven L. Small (2009): Gestures orchestrate brain networks for language understanding. *Current Biology* 19(8): 661–667.

Spivey, Michael (2007): *The Continuity of Mind*. Oxford/New York: Oxford University Press.

Stokoe, William C. (1960): Sign language structure. *Studies in Linguistics, Occasional Papers* 8. Buffalo: Department of Anthropology and Linguistics, University of Buffalo.
Stokoe, William C. (1991): Semantic phonology. *Sign Language Studies* 71: 107–114.
Stokoe, William C., Dorothy Casterline, and Carl Croneberg (1965): *A Dictionary of American Sign Language on Linguistic Principles*. Washington, DC: Gallaudet College Press.
Studdert-Kennedy, Michael (1987): The phoneme as a perceptuomotor structure. In: D. Allport (ed.), *Language Perception and Production: Relationships between Listening, Speaking, Reading, and Writing*, 67–84. London: Academic Press.
Sutton-Spence, Rachel and Bencie Woll (1999): *The Linguistics of British Sign Language: An Introduction*. Cambridge: Cambridge University Press.
Sweetser, Eve E. (1990): *From Etymology to Pragmatics: Metaphorical and Cultural Aspects of Semantic Structure*. Cambridge: Cambridge University Press.
Taub, Sarah (2001): *Language from the Body: Iconicity and Metaphor in American Sign Language*. Cambridge: Cambridge University Press.
Thelen, Esther and Linda B. Smith (1994): *A Dynamic Systems Approach to the Development of Cognition and Action*. Cambridge: The MIT Press.
Thompson, Robin, Karen Emmorey, and Robert Kluender (2006): The relationship between eye gaze and verb agreement in American Sign Language: An eye-tracking study. *Natural Language & Linguistic Theory* 24(2): 571–604.
Tyrone, Martha E. and Claude Mauk (2010): Sign lowering and phonetic reduction in American Sign Language. *Journal of Phonetics* 38(2): 317–328.
Tyrone, Martha E., Housung Nam, Elliot Saltzman, Gaurav Mathur, and Louis M. Goldstein (2010): Prosody and movement in American Sign Language: A task-dynamics approach. *Speech Prosody*, 100957: 1–4.
Uyechi, Linda (1996): *The Geometry of Visual Phonology*. Stanford: CSLI Publications Center for the Study of Language and Information.
Vermeerbergen, Miriam and Eline Demey (2007): Sign + gesture = speech + gesture? In: M. Vermeerbergen, L. Leeson and O. Crasborn (eds.), *Simultaneity in Signed Languages: Form and Function*, 257–282. Amsterdam/Philadelphia: John Benjamins Publishing Company.
Whorf, Benjamin L. and John B. Caroll (1956): *Language, Thought, and Reality*. Cambridge: MIT Press.
Wilbur, Ronnie B. (1987): *American Sign Language: Linguistic and Applied Dimensions*. Boston: College-Hill Press.
Wilbur, Ronnie B. (2013): The point of agreement: Changing how we think about sign language, gesture, and agreement. *Sign Language and Linguistics* 16(2): 221–258.
Wilcox, Phyllis Perrin (2000): *Metaphor in American Sign Language*. Washington, D. C.: Gallaudet University Press.
Wilcox, Phyllis Perrin (2007): Constructs of the mind: Cross-linguistic contrast of metaphor in verbal and signed languages. In: E. Pizzuto, P. Pietrandrea and R. Simone (eds.), *Verbal and Signed Languages: Comparing Structures, Constructs and Methodologies*, 251–274. Berlin/New York: Mouton de Gruyter.
Wilcox, Sherman (1992): *The Phonetics of Fingerspelling*. Amsterdam/Philadelphia: John Benjamins Publishing Company.
Wilcox, Sherman (2004a): Cognitive iconicity: Conceptual spaces, meaning, and gesture in signed language. *Cognitive Linguistics* 15(2): 119–147.
Wilcox, Sherman (2004b): Gesture and language: Cross-linguistic and historical data from signed languages. *Gesture* 4(1): 43–75.

Wilcox, Sherman (2005): Routes from gesture to language. *Revista Da ABRALIN – Associação Brasileira De Lingüística* 4(1/2): 11–45.
Wilcox, Sherman (2007): Signed languages. In: D. Geeraerts and H. Cuyckens (eds.), *The Oxford Handbook of Cognitive Linguistics*, 1113–1136. Oxford: Oxford University Press.
Wilcox, Sherman (2013): Language in motion: A framework for unifying spoken language, signed language, and gesture. *Anuari de Filologia Estudis de Lingüística* 2: 49–57.
Wilcox, Sherman and Jill P. Morford (2007): Empirical methods in signed language research. In: M. Gonzalez-Marquez, S. Coulson, M. Spivey and I. Mittelberg (eds.), *Methods in Cognitive Linguistics*, 171–200. Amsterdam: John Benjamins Publishing Company.
Wilcox, Sherman, Paulo Rossini, and Elena Antinoro Pizzuto (2010): Grammaticalization in sign languages. In: D. Brentari (ed.), *Sign Languages*, 332–354. Cambridge: Cambridge University Press.
Wilcox, Sherman and Phyllis Perrin Wilcox (1995): The gestural expression of modality in American Sign Language. In: J. Bybee and S. Fleischman (eds.), *Modality in Grammar and Discourse*, 135–162. Amsterdam: John Benjamins Publishing Company.
Wilcox, Sherman and Phyllis Perrin Wilcox (2009): The analysis of signed languages. In: B. Heine and H. Narrog (eds.), *The Oxford Handbook of Linguistic Analysis*, 739–760. Oxford: Oxford University Press.
Wilcox, Sherman and Phyllis Perrin Wilcox (2013): Cognitive linguistics and signed languages. *International Journal of Cognitive Linguistics* 3(2): 127–151.
Wilcox, Sherman, Phyllis Perrin Wilcox, and Maria Josep Jarque (2003): Mappings in conceptual space: Metonymy, metaphor, and iconicity in two signed languages. *Jezikoslovlje* 4(1): 139–156.
Wilcox, Sherman and André Xavier (2013): A framework for unifying spoken language, signed language, and gesture. *Revista Todas as Letras* 15(1): 88–110.
Wulf, Alyssa and Paul Dudis (2005): Body partitioning in ASL metaphorical blends. *Sign Language Studies* 5(3): 317–332.
Xu, Jiang, Patrick J. Gannon, Karen Emmorey, Jason F. Smith, and Allen R. Braun (2009): Symbolic gestures and spoken language are processed by a common neural system. *Proceedings of the National Academy of Sciences* 106(49): 20664–20669.

Brian MacWhinney
Chapter 14: Emergentism

The modern study of language can be viewed as the tale of two competing paradigms: Universal Grammar (UG) and Emergentism. These two paradigms assume fundamentally different positions on ten core issues: the scope of language, the uniqueness of recursion, rules vs. cues, the relevance of E-Language, the suddenness of the evolution of language, the genetic control of language, the idea that speech is special, critical periods for language learning, neurological modules for language, and the poverty of the stimulus during the language learning.

UG analyses emphasize explanations of language structure grounded on inborn principles specific to human language (Hauser et al. 2002), as expressed in recursive function theory (Chomsky 1963, 1976, 2010). In contrast, emergentist analyses are grounded on three core frameworks deriving from adaptive systems theory. The first is the Darwinian theory of evolution based on proliferation, competition, and selection. The second is the analysis of complex systems as structured hierarchically into levels, such that higher levels of complexity emerge from lower levels in ways not fully predictable from lower level properties. The third is the theory of timeframes that holds that processes on different levels are linked to very different timescales that mesh together through competition in the present. These three frameworks are not unique to linguistic analysis. In fact, they are fundamental to scientific investigation of all physical, biological, and social processes. In this paper, we will first describe how these frameworks apply to the study of language. Second, we will consider the relation between Emergentism and more specific linguistic frameworks, such as functionalism, cognitive linguistics, connectionism, embodied cognition, usage-based linguistics, and competition theory. Third, we will examine some of the specific mechanisms and structures involved in emergentist models. Fourth, we will survey the methods required for elaborating the theory of language emergence. Finally, we will contrast the Emergentist Program with the Minimalist Program of Universal Grammar in terms of their positions on the ten core issues mentioned above.

Brian MacWhinney, Carnegie Mellon University, United States of America

https://doi.org/10.1515/9783110626438-014

1 The three frameworks supporting Emergentism

In this section we will explain and illustrate the ways in which Emergentism relies on the theories of natural selection, complexity, and timeframes.

1.1 Natural selection and competition

Competition is fundamental to biological processes. Darwin (1859) showed how the evolution of the species emerges from the competition between organisms for survival and reproduction. The three basic principles Darwin identified are proliferation, competition, and selection. Proliferation generates variation through mutation and sexual recombination. Organisms with different compositions then compete for resources or rewards such as food, shelter, and the opportunity to reproduce. The outcome of competition is selection through which more adaptive organisms survive and less adaptive ones disappear.

The emergence of structures from proliferation, competition, and selection represents the basic source of change in all biological and social systems, including language. Economic analysis (Friedman 1953) has shown that free markets generate a wide variety of products, sellers, and buyers who then compete and cooperate to achieve optimal pricing and efficiency. In social systems, we can characterize the emergence and spread of new fashions, trends, and ideas through the theory of memetics (Mesoudi et al. 2006), which is closely modelled on evolutionary theory (D. Campbell 1960). In multicellular organisms, the immune system proliferates a multitude of antigens to compete with and defeat invading antibodies. Those antigens that match actual threats are replicated and those that do not are winnowed out. In all of these systems, from economics to the brain, development emerges from the mindless interaction of proliferation and competition without relying on any external master plan.

Emergentist approaches to language (MacWhinney 1999) also view language shape and language change as arising from the processes of proliferation and competition. For the organism as a whole, the fundamental functional pressure is to reproduce. For language, the overall functional pressure is to communicate. However, just as the genes are the basic units of biological proliferation and competition, the actual units of linguistic competition are the constructions, which are mappings between forms and functions. Functions include motives as diverse as identifying a referent (Silverstein 1976), expressing politeness (Helmbrecht 2013), expressing derision through imitation (Haiman 2014), setting a temporal reference point (Smith 1991), coding exclusive disjunction (Ariel 2014), placing presentational focus (Francis and Michaelis 2014), shifting agential perspective (MacWhinney 2008c), inserting parenthetical material (Kaltenboeck and Heine, 2014), and scores of others. All of these many functions are mapped onto forms using overlapping vocal, gestural, and prosodic constructions in a process of continual competition (MacWhinney 1987) during language use, learning, and change.

As MacWhinney et al. (1984: 128) noted, "the forms of natural languages are created, governed, constrained, acquired and used in the service of communicative functions". Bates and MacWhinney (1982) noted that this functionalist position can be dissected into three separate claims. The first is that language change across generations is determined by communicative function; the second is that language acquisition in the child is shaped by communicative function; and the third is that language form in real time conversations is controlled by communicative function. On all three levels, the facilitation of communicative function is viewed as depending on the availability of supporting neural mechanisms.

The handmaiden of competition is cooperation. As Bates and MacWhinney (1982) noted, humans have a great many ideas that they would love to express all at once. But language only allows us to say one thing at a time. One way in which language addresses this problem is by allowing motives to form coalitions. Bates and MacWhinney (1982) analysed the possible solutions to competition as: (1) peaceful coexistence, (2) divide-the-spoils, and (3) winner-take-all.

We can illustrate these solutions by looking at subject marking in English. In the unmarked active transitive clause, such as *the car hit the pole*, the subject (*the car*) expresses a coalition of motives including agency, perspective, givenness, and topicality. This construction represents peaceful coexistence or coalition between the motives, because they all point in the same direction. In the vast majority of cases, these motives do in fact co-occur yielding the active clause as the dominant form for transitive verbs. Peaceful coexistence depends on natural patterns of co-occurence in the real world. For example, the properties of solidity, boundary, and firmness tend to co-occur for objects. Similarly, in animals, properties such agency, movement, warmth, and directed attention all tend to cooccur.

When speakers of a language choose to emphasize one of the features in a peaceful coalition over others, the coalition can break down, precipitating a divide-the-spoils solution. For example, English uses the passive construction, as in *the pole was hit by a car*, as a way of dividing the spoils between the topic/perspective (*the pole*) and the agent (*a car*). In this case, the topic receives the prizes of subject position and agreement and the agent receives the "consolation prize" of placement in a by-clause. An alternative to this divide-the-spoils approach is the winner-take-all solution in which one motivation overrides the others. For English transitive verbs, this solution gives rise to the truncated passive, as in *the pole was hit*. In that solution, the agent is not expressed at all.

1.2 Complexity

Complexity arises from the hierarchical recombination of small parts into larger structures. For biological evolution, the parts are the genes. For the brain, the parts are neuronal structures working to generate competing ideas (D. Campbell 1960). For language, the parts are articulatory gestures. In a seminal article entitled *The Architecture of Complexity,* Simon (1962) analyzed higher-level cognitive processes as hierarchically-structured combinations of elementary information processes or modules into which they could be partially decomposed. The basic principles involved can be illustrated by the four levels of structure that emerge during protein folding (N. A. Campbell et al. 1999). In this process, the primary structure of the protein is determined by the sequence of amino acids in the chain of RNA used by the ribosome as the template for protein synthesis. This chain then folds into a secondary structure of coils and folds created by hydrogen bonding across the amino acid chain. These forces can only impact the geometry of the protein once the primary structure is released from the ribosome and begins to contract. Next, a tertiary structure emerges from hydrophobic reactions and disulfide bridges across the folds and coils of the secondary structures. Finally, the quaternary structure derives from the aggregation of polypeptide subunits based on the ternary structures. It is this final structure that allows each protein to serve its unique role, be it oxygen transport for hemoglobin or antigen detection for antibodies. In this partially decomposable emergent system, each level involves a configuration of components from lower levels, but the physical and biochemical constraints operative on each level are unique to that level and only operate once that level has emerged during the process of folding. If a given protein operates successfully, it promotes the adaptation of the whole organism, eventually leading to positive evolutionary selection for the DNA sequence from which it derives. This can be viewed as a type of backwards or downwards causality between levels (Andersen et al. 2000). These principles of partial decomposability, level-specific constraints, and backwards causality apply with even greater force to the study of language, where the interactions between levels and timeframes are so intense. For language studies, the level of analysis achieved in the study of proteomics is clearly not yet possible. However, we can use these principles is to guide our analysis of linguistic levels, cue strength, and the ways in which levels mesh (Labov 1972).

1.3 Timeframes

To understand how cues combine in real time, we must examine inputs from processes that are sensitive to inputs across very different timeframes. This integration is particularly important for understanding the connections between psycholinguistic processes and historical change. The usual assumption here is that adaptive changes in the moment lead to long-term typological shifts (Bybee 2010). However, to elaborate these models we will need rich longitudinal corpora that can allow us to study changing patterns over time. In the area of child language acquisition, the CHILDES corpus (MacWhinney 1991) has begun to fill this need. However, the fields of second language acquisition, sociolinguistics, neurolinguistics, or language typology will need much greater amounts of publically available longitudinal data to understand the details of timeframe linkages.

Integration across levels occurs at the moment of speaking as we activate patterns in motor cortex that then lead to articulatory gestures and phonation. Before this final volley of excitation, our brains have integrated competing information from a wide variety of stored lexical, prosodic, constructional, and conceptual patterns. Although these patterns reveal their interactions in the moment, their relative strength and scope has been shaped by hours, days, or even decades of usage. Across these various timescales, patterns have come to adjust their input to the ways in which they can be expressed in the moment. For example, the WXDY construction found in *what is this fly doing in my soup* (Kay and Fillmore 1999) only surfaces rarely. When it occurs, it expresses a unique configuration of shock or pretended shock regarding some untoward condition, and either enough social solidarity to withstand the intended irony or else a power differential that allows for expression of some level of approbation or even accusation. These various sociolinguistic and affective assignments depend on the computation of the status of personal relations as they have developed across days, months, and years. These computations must then be linked to more immediate practical judgments regarding the unexpected nature of the condition (i.e., the fly in the soup). If the relevant preconditions are not fulfilled, we may select a more neutral statement, such as *Oh goodness, there is a fly in my soup.*

In order to understand how the brain links such inputs across diverse timeframes, it will help to take a detour into the simpler world of the honeybee. Menzel (1999) explains how honeybee cognition relies on five memory phases, each involving different cellular processes, different timeframes, and different environmental challenges. The first phase is early short-term memory (eSTM). When foraging within a single patch of flowers of the same type, bees are able to concentrate on a pollen source by resonant activation of a particular neural ensemble (Edelman 1987; Pulvermüller 2003). In the second phase of late short-term memory (lSTM), synthesis of the PKA protein kinase begins to solidify the currently active circuit. The third phase of middle-term memory (MTM) spans a timeframe of hours and involves the formation of covalent modifications in the synapses between neurons. During these first three timeframes, bees have not yet returned to the hive, but are still processing flowers encountered during a single foraging bout. The fourth phase of memory consolidation relies on the formation of early long-term memories (eLTM) through the action of nitrous oxide (NO) and PKC1. This type of consolidation is important, because it allows the bee to return to remembered pollen sources even after a trip back to the hive. The fifth phase of consolidation in late long-term memory (lLTM) operates across a timeframe of over three days, using PKC2 protein synthesis for even more permanent memories. Thus, each of the five phases of memory consolidation is responsive to the nature of the memory that must be retained to allow the bee to continue successful foraging.

When the bee is trying to decide where to fly, her decision is impacted by an array of wheels that mesh in the current moment. Some of the wheels derive from the memories for pollen sources described above. Others derive from activities in the hive, including the dances of other bees. Still others relate to the season, the need to defend the hive, and so on. Bees have an neural module for evaluation that meshes information from all of these sources, much as our language production device serves to evaluate and mesh inputs from all sorts of memories and motives. For both the bee and the human speaker, this meshing of inputs from contrasting timeframes all occurs at the moment of deciding either where to fly or what to say.

This linkage between environmental tasks, timeframes, and neuronal processes is not unique to bees. However, these relations are particularly transparent in the honeybee, because of the way in which the distribution of flowers structures the bee's environment. We find the same five memory mechanisms operating across these timeframes in humans. However, for humans, there are additional mechanisms that support even more complex consolidation over longer timeframes for integrating increasingly complex memories. Many of these additional mechanisms rely on links between the hippocampus and the cortex (McClelland et al. 1995; Wittenberg et al. 2002), including episodic storage in the medial temporal lobes (Daselaar et al. 2004). In addition, the frontal lobes provide a hierarchical system of executive control involving increasingly complex and longer-term structures as one moves from the posterior to anterior frontal areas (Koechlin and Summerfield 2007).

For both bees and humans, behavior is often organized into sequences of repetitive actions. Flying in bees and walking and breathing in humans is based on an iterative closed loop that includes methods for monitoring and stabilizing the iterative process (Feldman 2006). In speech, the basic iterative loop involves the repetitive production of syllables lasting about 150 ms each (Massaro 1975). MacNeilage and Davis (1998) argue that the basic syllable gesture has a CV (consonant-vowel) structure that is homologous to the lip-smacking gesture in other primates. In their frame-content theory, the positioning of the jaw and articulatory closures for the consonant constitutes the "frame" and the positioning of the tongue for the vowel constitutes the "content". The generation of these gestures is controlled by the pars opercularis (Bookheimer 2007) which is the segment of the inferior frontal gyrus nearest to the motor area, which places it next to the motor map for the tongue and lips. In a syllable-timed language like Spanish, this circuit produces a clear periodicity of syllabic gestures. We can think of this process as a wheel revolving with a periodicity of 150 milliseconds. The output of this wheel is then further modified by a second wheel that imposes syllabic stress at the slightly longer timeframe of the metrical foot. The imposition of stress on the syllabic chain can be based either on lexical signals or on conversational emphases.

Short-term processes must mesh with long-term processes. Some of these long-term processes reside not just in neural memories, but also in the memes of social symbolism as they spread through the community (Hruschka et al. 2009). Language is essentially a collection of social memes that becomes internalized within group members. The memes controlling conventions for conversational sequencing, alignment, and focusing also mesh with physical systems for maintaining gaze contact, proxemics, and postural alignment. The analysis of meshing across timeframes can help us understand exactly how motivations compete. In this way, we can better evaluate the claims of the strong functionalist position.

Online meshing takes in motives or pressures from across at least ten major functional domains, each sensitive to inputs from different timeframes. These ten domains include: word production, word comprehension, sentence production, sentence comprehension, language acquisition, diachronic change, interactional maintenance, encounter structure, group membership, and phylogenetic change. Example analyses of how meshing occurs can be found in MacWhinney (2014), Toscano and McMurray (2010), Goodwin (2002), and Poplack and Cacoullos (2014).

2 Emergentist approaches

Recent work in linguistics has produced a variety of theoretical frameworks with overlapping goals and assumptions. Among these are functionalism (Givón 1979),

Systemic Functional Grammar (Halliday and Matthiessen 2004), Cognitive Grammar (Langacker 1987), Usage-based Linguistics (Bybee and Hopper 2001), Sociolinguistic Variable Rule Analysis (Kay 1978), the Competition Model (MacWhinney 1987), Construction Grammar (Goldberg 2006), Conceptual Metaphor Theory (Lakoff and Johnson 1980), Blending Theory (Fauconnier and Turner 1996), Optimality Theory (Bresnan et al. 2001; Kager 1999), and the Neural Theory of Language (Feldman 2006). In psychology, theories such as Parallel Distributed Processing (Rumelhart and McClelland 1986), self-organizing maps (Kohonen 2001), Bayesian modeling (Kemp et al. 2007), Information Integration Theory (Massaro 1987), and Dynamic Systems Theory (Thelen and Smith 1994) provide quantifiable predictions regarding the outcomes of competition. In addition, formulations from neurolinguistics such as mirror neurons (Arbib 2010), Embodied Cognition (Pecher and Zwaan 2005), and Common Coding (Schütz-Bosbach and Prinz 2007) link up well with many aspects of functionalist linguistics.

Faced with this embarrassment of theoretical riches, students often ask what is the relation between Emergentism and all these other approaches. The answer is that all of these approaches fall under the general category of Emergentism, because all recognize the importance of the principles of proliferation, competition, selection, and complexity. However, within this general framework, there is a great diversity of contrasting emphases on specific mechanisms of emergence. We will discuss some of these alternative approaches in the next section. It is also true that, although these approaches utilize the basic concepts of competition and complexity, many of them provide no clear role for the processes that mesh inputs across timeframes. There are some exceptions to this. First, there are sociolinguistic analyses, such as those presented by Poplack and Cacoullos (2014) that have succeeded in tracing changes and continuities in grammar and lexicon over centuries, based on indirect accounts from spoken language data. Second, researchers such as Goodwin (2000), Sfard and McClain (2002), and Lemke (2000) have shown how the use of artifacts (tools, maps, books, color chips, computers) during interaction can provide links to long-term timeframes. Third, researchers in child language (Bates and Goodman 1999) and second language (Verspoor et al. 2011) have developed longitudinal corpora to trace the ways in which competing processes interact across several years. MacWhinney (2005a, 2014) provides further analysis of this issue.

3 Mechanisms

Emergentist approaches to language can be characterized most clearly in terms of the emphases they place on alternative mechanisms for language use, learning, and change. In some cases, similar approaches differ only in the detailed computational algorithms they utilize. For example, Parallel Distributed Processing (Rumelhart and McClelland 1986), Self-Organizing Feature Maps (Kohonen 2001), and Dynamic Systems Theory (Thelen and Smith 1994) all represent networks of connections, but differ in the algorithms that operate on these connections. Sometimes there is overlap in terms of both concepts and mechanisms. For example, Construction Grammar (Goldberg 2006) is a direct outgrowth of work in Cognitive Grammar (Langacker 1987), differing largely in terms of the detail with which it analyses competitions between constructions. All emergentist theories recognize the importance of embodied cognition, but they may differ in terms of how they see these effects operating in detail. To understand some of these contrasts, it is helpful to survey some of the most important emergentist mechanisms that have been proposed.

1. Generalization. Many emergentist theories emphasize the basic cognitive mechanism of generalization, often pointing to its basis in neuronal connectivity and spreading activation. Generalization plays a major role as a further support for theories of coercion (MacWhinney 1989), polysemy (Gries volume 2), metaphor (Gibbs volume 1), prototype application (Taylor this volume), constructions (Perfors et al. 2010), and learning (McDonald and MacWhinney 1991).
2. Error correction. Some learning theories emphasize the importance of corrective feedback, although this feedback can also involve failure to match self-imposed targets, as in the DIVA model of phonological learning (Guenther and Perkell 2003).
3. Self-organization. Mechanisms such as the self-organizing feature map (Kohonen 2001) provide alternatives to mechanisms based on error propagation. An important assumption of these models is that the brain prefers to establish connections between local units, rather than between distant units (Jacobs and Jordan 1992).
4. Structure mapping. Theories of metaphor, metonymy, and analogy in Cognitive Linguistics often assume some method of mapping from the structure of a source domain to a target domain (Gentner and Markman 1997). Mechanisms of this type can also be used to account for convergence between cognitive systems (Goldstone et al. 2004).
5. Embodied representations. The representations and schemata used in Cognitive Linguistics align well with neurolinguistic theories of body image (Knoblich 2008), embodied perspective-taking (MacWhinney 2008c), empathy (Meltzoff and Decety 2003), situated spatial processing (Coventry this volume), and motion processing (Filipović this volume). For further discussion of embodiment, see Bergen (volume 1) and Speed et al. (volume 1).

6. Item-based patterns. The theory of item-based patterns (MacWhinney 1975, 1982; Tomasello 2000) provides a solid underpinning for Construction Grammar (Goldberg 2006), as well as a systematic answer to the logical problem of language acquisition (MacWhinney 2004).
7. Composition. All syntactic theories must deal with the ways in which words cluster into phrases. Emergentist models of comprehension such as O'Grady (2005) show how this can be done in an incremental fashion. In this area, the emphasis in UG Minimalism on the Merge process (Chomsky 2007) is compatible with emergentist accounts.
8. Conversational emergence. Linguistic structures adapt to frequent conversational patterns. For example, Du Bois (1987) has argued that ergative marking emerges from the tendency to delete the actor in transitive sentences, because it is already given or known.
9. Perceptual recording. Studies of infant auditory perception have revealed that, even in the first few months, infants apply general-purpose mechanisms to record and learn sequential patterns from both visual and auditory input (Thiessen and Erickson 2014).
10. Imitation. Human children display a strong propensity to imitate gestures (Meltzoff and Decety 2003), actions (Ratner and Bruner 1978), and vocal productions (Whitehurst and Vasta 1975). Imitation in both children and adults is the fundamental mechanism postulated by usage-based linguistics.
11. Plasticity. Children with early left focal lesions are able to recover language function by reorganizing language to the right hemisphere. This plasticity in development is a general mechanism that supports a wide variety of emergent responses to injury or sensory disability (MacWhinney et al. 2000).
12. Physical structures. Phonologists have shown that the shape of the vocal mechanism has a wide-ranging impact on phonological processes (Ohala 1974). Rather than stipulating phonological rules or constraints (Bernhardt and Stemberger 1998), we can view them as emergent responses to these underlying pressures.

This is just a sampling of the many mechanisms and pressures that shape the emergence of language. Understanding how these mechanisms interact to produce language structures is the major task facing emergentist approaches to language.

4 Methods

The growth of emergentist approaches to language has depended heavily on the introduction of new scientific methods and the improvement of old methods through technological advances. In particular, we can point to advances in these six methodologies:

1. Corpora. The development of usage-based linguistics has relied heavily on the creation of web-accessible corpora of language interactions, such as those distributed through the CHILDES (Child Language Data Exchange System at http://childes.talkbank.org), TalkBank (http://talkbank.org), and LDC (Linguistic Data Consortium at http://www.ldc.upenn.edu) systems. These databases include transcripts of learners' written productions, as well as spoken productions linked to audio and/or video. As these databases grow, we are developing increasingly powerful analytic and computational linguistic methods, including automatic part of speech tagging (Parisse and Le Normand 2000), dependency parsing (Sagae et al. 2007), lexical diversity analysis (Malvern et al. 2004), and other analytic routines (MacWhinney 2008b).

2. Multimedia Analysis. The construction of an emergentist account of language usage also requires careful attention to gestural and proxemic aspects of conversational interactions (Goldman et al. 2007). The last few years have seen a rapid proliferation of technology for linking transcripts to video and analysing these transcripts for conversational and linguistic structures (MacWhinney 2007). Longitudinal video corpora are particularly useful for studying the meshing of competing motivations across timeframes.

3. Neural Network Modelling. Neural network modelling has allowed researchers to examine how complex systems can emerge from the processing of input patterns. Increasingly, these systems are linked to benchmark data sets that can be used to compare and test alternative emergentist models (MacWhinney 2010).

4. Neuroimaging. Before the recent period, our understanding of neurolinguistics was dependent primarily on data obtained from brain lesions that produced aphasia. This type of data led researchers to focus on localizing language in specific modules (MacWhinney and Li 2008). However, with the advent of fine-grained localization through fMRI imaging, researchers have been able to formulate emergentist accounts of neural functioning based on the dynamic interactions of functional neural circuits. In addition, it has been possible to use ERP methodology to study competition between lan-

guages in second language and bilingual processing (Tolentino and Tokowicz 2011).
5. Neuroscience. Advances in neuroscience have also begun to extend our understanding of cognitive function down to the level of individual cells and local cell assemblies. Although this level of detail is not yet available for imaging methods such as fMRI, ERP, or MEG, we are learning a great deal from the study of single cell recordings in animals (Rizzolatti et al. 1996) and humans undergoing surgery for epilepsy (Bookheimer 2007). This work has emphasized the ways in which the brain encodes a full map of the body, thereby providing support for the theory of embodied cognition (Klatzky et al. 2008).
6. In vivo learning. Until very recently, it has been difficult to study the learning of second languages in realistic contexts. However, we can now use web-based methods (http://talkbank.org/SLA) to study students' learning of second languages on a trial-by-trial basis as they engage in exercises over the web, providing further tests and elaborations of emergentist theories.

5 Ten core issues

Over the last three decades, the dialog between Emergentism and UG has revolved around ten core issues.
1. What is Language? UG focuses its attention on the recursive application of rules in the modules of the syntactic component. This emphasis leaves large areas of lexicon, phonology, dialog, meaning, and interpretation outside of the domain of the language faculty. In contrast, Emergentism treats all of the components of human language, including those controlling communication, as parts of an interlocking, unified system.
2. E-Language vs I-Language. UG bases limits linguistic inquiry to the study of the internalized I-Language of the ideal speaker-hearer. Emergentism views language as arising dynamically from the ways in which speakers reach conceptual consensus (Goldstone et al. 2004; Wittgenstein 1953).
3. The Uniqueness of Recursion. UG views recursion as the crucial defining feature of human language (Hauser et al. 2002). Emergentism views recursion as emerging in contrasting linguistic structures from the combined activities of memory, lexicon, discourse, and role activation (MacWhinney 2009).
4. Rules vs. Cues. Emergentism holds that linguistic structures are not the deterministic rules of UG, but cue-based patterns that arise from usage, gener-

alization, and self-organization (MacWhinney, Malchukov, and Moravcsik 2014).
5. Evolution. UG holds that language evolved recently as a way of supporting more elaborate cognition. Emergentism views language as deriving from a gradual adaptation of the human species to the niche of upright posture, communication in large social groups, and support for late infant maturation (MacWhinney 2008a).
6. Genetics. UG accounts seek to link the supposed recent emergence of language to specific genetic changes (Fisher and Scharff 2009) in the last 70,000 years. Emergentism views language as grounded on a wide-ranging set of genetic adaptations across millions of years.
7. Speech is special. Generative theory has often been associated with the idea that, "speech is special." Emergentist approaches to speech and phonological development emphasize the role of physiological mechanisms in controlling articulation (Oller 2000). They also view auditory learning as governed by basic aspects of the auditory system and temporal processing constraints (Holt and Lotto 2010).
8. Critical Periods. Many UG formulations hold that there is an expiration date on the Special Gift underlying language learning and use (Lenneberg 1967). Emergentist accounts attribute the gradual decline in language learning abilities to loss of plasticity through entrenchment of the first language, parasitic transfer of first language abilities, and social isolation (MacWhinney 2012).
9. Modularity. UG emphasizes the encapsulated, modular composition of grammar (Fodor 1983). Emergentist accounts emphasize interactivity between permeable, emergent modules (McClelland et al. 2006).
10. Poverty of the stimulus. UG holds that there is insufficient information in the input to the language learner to properly determine the shape of the native language (Piattelli-Palmarini 1980). As a result, language learning is guided by a rich set of innate hypotheses regarding the shape of Universal Grammar. Emergentist accounts emphasize the richness of the input to the learner and the role of item-based learning strategies in achieving effective learning of complex structures (MacWhinney 2005b).

6 Conclusion

This dialog between Emergentism and UG has stimulated three decades of useful empirical and theoretical work. However, Emergentism must now move beyond the confines of this debate. Because Emergentism views language as a meshing of inputs from at least seven structural levels (MacWhinney 2014), these accounts will necessarily be more complex. Fortunately, we can use powerful new methods for qualitative and quantitative analysis of longitudinal multimedia corpora to track the effects of inputs from the many contrasting processes and inputs that shape the totality of human language. Models as diverse as variable rule analysis, dynamic systems theory, and neural networks can be translated into a core language (Farmer 1990) of cue strength and interactive activation. We will need to move ahead on six fronts simultaneously: (1) neurolinguistics and neuroimaging, (2) longitudinal collection of naturalistic and structured corpora, (3) linkage of typology and diachrony to synchronic processes, (4) psycholinguistic experimentation, (5) computational linguistic analysis, and (6) computational modelling. Finally, we must work to interpret the results from each of these six efforts in the context of advances from the other five. We definitely have our work cut out for us.

7 References

Andersen, Peter, Claus Emmeche, Niels Finnemann, and Peder Christiansen (eds.) (2000): *Downward causation: Minds, Bodies, and Matter.* Aarhus: Aarhus University Press.

Arbib, Michael (2010): *Beyond the Mirror: Evolving Language and our Social Selves.* New York: Oxford University Press.

Ariel, Mira (2014): Or-constructions: monosemy versus polysemy. In: B. MacWhinney, A. Malchukov and E. Moravcsik (eds.), *Competing Motivations in Grammar and Usage* 333–347. New York: Oxford University Press.

Bates, Elizabeth and Judith Goodman (1999): On the emergence of grammar from the lexicon. In: B. MacWhinney (ed.), *The Emergence of Language,* 29–80. Mahwah: Lawrence Erlbaum Associates.

Bates, Elizabeth and Brian MacWhinney (1982): Functionalist approaches to grammar. In: E. Wanner and L. Gleitman (eds.), *Language Acquisition: The State of the Art,* 173–218. New York: Cambridge University Press.

Bergen, Benjamin (volume 1): Embodiment. Berlin/Boston: De Gruyter Mouton.

Bernhardt, Barbara and Joseph Stemberger (1998): *Handbook of Phonological Development from the Perspective of Constraint-based Nonlinear Phonology.* San Diego: Academic Press.

Bookheimer, Susan (2007): Pre-surgical language mapping with functional magnetic resonance imaging. *Neuropsychological Review* 17, 145–155.

Bresnan, Joan, Shipra Dingare, and Christopher Manning (2001): Soft constraints mirror hard constraints: Voice and person in English and Lummi. Paper presented at the LFG01, Hong Kong.

Bybee, Joan (2010): *Language, Usage, and Cognition.* New York: Cambridge University Press.

Bybee, Joan and Paul Hopper (2001): *Frequency and the Emergence of Linguistic Structure.* Amsterdam: John Benjamins.

Campbell, Donald (1960): Blind variation and selective retention in creative thought as in other knowledge processes. *Psychological Review* 67, 380–400.

Campbell, Neil A., Jane B. Reece, and Larry G. Mitchell (1999): *Biology* Fifth Edition. Menlo Park: Addison Wesley.
Chomsky, Noam (1963): Formal properties of grammars. In: R. Bush, R. Luce and E. Galanter (eds.), *Handbook of Mathematical Psychology*, Volume 2. New York: Wiley.
Chomsky, Noam (1976): Conditions on rules of grammar. *Linguistic Analysis* 2: 163–210.
Chomsky, Noam (2007): Approaching UG from below. In: U. Sauerland and M. Gaertner (eds.), *Interfaces + Recursion = Language?*, 1–30. New York: Mouton de Gruyter.
Chomsky, Noam (2010): Some simple evo devo theses: How true might they be for language. In: R. Larson, V. Déprez and H. Yamakido (eds.), *The Evolution of Language: Biolinguistic Perspectives*, 45–62. Cambridge: Cambridge University Press.
Coventry, Kenny (this volume): Space. Berlin/Boston: De Gruyter Mouton.
Darwin, Charles (1859): *On the Origin of Species*. London: John Murray.
Daselaar, Sander, Dick Veltman, and Menno Witter (2004): Common pathway in the medial temporal lobe for storage and recovery of words as revealed by event-related functional MRI. *Hippocampus* 14: 163–169.
Davis, Barbara L. and Peter F. MacNeilage (1995): The articulatory basis of babbling. *Journal of Speech and Hearing Research* 38: 1199–1211.
Du Bois, John (1987): The discourse basis of ergativity. *Language*, 63: 805–856.
Edelman, Gerald (1987): *Neural Darwinism: The Theory of Neuronal Group Selection*. New York: Basic Books.
Farmer, J. Doyne (1990): A Rosetta Stone for connectionism. *Physica* 42: 153–187.
Fauconnier, Gilles and Mark Turner (1996): Blending as a central process of grammar. In: A. Goldberg (ed.), *Conceptual Structure, Discourse, and Language*, 113–130. Stanford: CSLI.
Feldman, Jerome (2006): *From Molecule to Metaphor: A Neural Theory of Language*. Cambridge: MIT Press.
Filipović, Luna (this volume): Motion. Berlin/Boston: De Gruyter Mouton.
Fisher, Simon and Constance Scharff (2009): FOXP2 as a molecular window into speech and language. *Trends in Genetics* 25: 166–177.
Francis, Elaine and Laura Michaelis (2014): Why move? How weight and discourse factors combine to predict relative clause extraposition in English. In: B. MacWhinney, A. Malchukov and E. Moravcsik (eds.), *Competing Motivations in Grammar and Usage* 70–87. New York: Oxford University Press.
Friedman, Milton (1953): *Essays in Positive Economics*. Chicago: University of Chicago Press.
Gentner, D. and A. Markman (1997): Structure mapping in analogy and similarity. *American Psychologist* 52: 45–56.
Gibbs Jr., Raymond W. (volume 1): Metaphor. Berlin/Boston: De Gruyter Mouton.
Givón, T. (1979): *On Understanding Grammar*. New York: Academic Press.
Goldberg, Adele (2006): *Constructions at Work: The Nature of Generalization in Language*. Oxford: Oxford University Press.
Goldman, Ricki, Roy Pea, Brigid Barron, and Sharon Derry (eds.) (2007): *Video Research in the Learning Sciences*. Mahwah: Lawrence Erlbaum Associates.
Goldstone, Robert, Ying Feng, and Brian Rogosky (2004): Connecting concepts to each other and the world. In: Rolf Zwaan and Diane Pecher (eds.), *The Grounding of Cognition: The Role of Perception and Action in Memory, Language, and Thinking*. Cambridge: Cambridge University Press.
Goodwin, Charles (2000): Gesture, aphasia, and interaction. In: D. McNeill (ed.), *Language and Gesture*, 84–98. Cambridge: Cambridge University Press.

Goodwin, Charles (2002): Time in action. *Current Anthropology* 43: 19–35.
Gries, Stefan Th. (this volume): Polysemy. Berlin/Boston: De Gruyter Mouton.
Guenther, Frank and Joseph Perkell (2003): A neural model of speech production and its application to studies of the role of auditory feedback in speech. In: B. Maasen, R. D. Kent, H. Peters, P. van Lieshout and W. Hulstijn (eds.), *Speech Motor Control in Normal and Disordered Speech*, 29–50. Oxford: Oxford University Press.
Haiman, John (2014): On competing motives for repetition. In: B. MacWhinney, A. Malchukov and E. Moravcsik (eds.), *Competing Motivations in Grammar and Usage* 348–363. New York: Oxford University Press.
Halliday, Michael and Christian Matthiessen (2004): *An Introduction to Functional Grammar.* 3rd revised edition. London: Hodder Arnold.
Hauser, M., Noam Chomsky, and T. Fitch (2002): The faculty of language: What is it, who has it, and how did it evolve? *Science* 298: 1569–1579.
Helmbrecht, Johannes (2013): Politeness distinctions in personal pronouns – a case study of competing motivations. In: B. MacWhinney, A. Malchukov and E. Moravcsik (eds.), *Competing Motivations in Grammar and Usage*. New York: Oxford University Press.
Holt, Lori and Andrew Lotto (2010): Speech perception as categorization. *Perception and Psychophysics* 72(5): 1218–1227.
Hruschka, Daniel, Morten Christiansen, Richard Blythe, William Croft, Paul Heggarty, Salikoko Mufwene, Janet B. Pierrehumbert, and Shana Poplack (2009): Building social cognitive models of language change. *Trends in Cognitive Sciences* 13: 464–469.
Jacobs, Robert and Michael Jordan (1992): Computational consequences of a bias toward short connections. *Journal of Cognitive Neuroscience* 4: 323–336.
Kager, René (1999): *Optimality Theory*. New York: Cambridge University Press.
Kaltenboeck, Gunther and Bernd Heine (2014): Sentence grammar vs. thetical grammar: two competing domains. In: B. MacWhinney, A. Malchukov and E. Moravcsik (eds.), *Competing Motivations in Grammar and Usage*, 348–363. New York: Oxford University Press.
Kay, Paul (1978): Variable rules, community grammar, and linguistic change. In: D. Sankoff (ed.), *Linguistic Variation: Models and Methods*. New York: Academic Press.
Kay, Paul and Charles Fillmore (1999): Grammatical constructions and linguistic generalization: The "what's X doing Y?" construction. *Language* 75: 1–33.
Kemp, Charles, Amy Perfors, and Joshua Tenenbaum (2007): Learning overhypotheses with hierarchical Bayesian models. *Developmental Science* 10: 307–321.
Klatzky, Roberta, Brian MacWhinney, and Marlene Behrmann (eds.) (2008): *Embodiment, Ego-Space, and Action*. New York: Psychology Press.
Knoblich, Guenther (2008): Bodily and motor contributions to action perception. In: R. Klatzky, B. MacWhinney and M. Behrmann (eds.), *Embodied Cognition*. Mahwah: Lawrence Erlbaum.
Koechlin, Etienne and Christopher Summerfield (2007): An information theoretical approach to prefrontal executive function. *Trends in Cognitive Sciences* 11: 229–235.
Kohonen, Teuvo (2001): *Self-organizing Maps* Third edition. Berlin: Springer.
Labov, William (1972): *Sociolinguistic Patterns*. Philadelphia: University of Pennsylvania Press.
Lakoff, George and Mark Johnson (1980): *Metaphors We Live By*. Chicago: Chicago University Press.
Langacker, Ronald (1987): *Foundations of Cognitive Grammar*: Vol. 1: *Theory*. Stanford: Stanford University Press.

Lemke, Jay (2000): Across the scales of time: Artifacts, activities, and meanings in ecosocial systems. *Mind, Culture, and Activity* 7: 273–290.
Lenneberg, Eric (1967): *Biological Foundations of Language*. New York: Wiley.
MacWhinney, Brian (1975): Pragmatic patterns in child syntax. *Stanford Papers And Reports on Child Language Development* 10: 153–165.
MacWhinney, Brian (1982): Basic syntactic processes. In: S. Kuczaj (ed.), *Language Acquisition*: Vol. 1. *Syntax and Semantics*, 73–136. Hillsdale: Lawrence Erlbaum.
MacWhinney, Brian (1987): The Competition Model. In: B. MacWhinney (ed.), *Mechanisms of Language Acquisition*, 249–308. Hillsdale: Lawrence Erlbaum.
MacWhinney, Brian (1989): Competition and lexical categorization. In: R. Corrigan, F. Eckman and M. Noonan (eds.), *Linguistic Categorization*, 195–242. Philadelphia: Benjamins.
MacWhinney, Brian (1991): *The CHILDES Project: Tools for Analyzing Talk*. Hillsdale: Erlbaum.
MacWhinney, Brian (2004): A multiple process solution to the logical problem of language acquisition. *Journal of Child Language* 31: 883–914.
MacWhinney, Brian (2005a): The emergence of linguistic form in time. *Connection Science* 17: 191–211.
MacWhinney, Brian (2005b): Item-based constructions and the logical problem. *Proceedings of the Workshop on Psychocomputational Models of Human Language Acquisition*, 46–54. Association for Computational Linguistics.
MacWhinney, Brian (2007): A transcript-video database for collaborative commentary in the Learning Sciences. In: R. Goldman, R. Pea, B. Barron and S. Derry (eds.), *Video Research in the Learning Sciences*, 537–546. Mahwah: Lawrence Erlbaum Associates.
MacWhinney, Brian (2008a): Cognitive precursors to language. In: K. Oller and U. Griebel (eds.), *The Evolution of Communicative Flexibility*, 193–214. Cambridge: MIT Press.
MacWhinney, Brian (2008b): Enriching CHILDES for morphosyntactic analysis. In: H. Behrens (ed.), *Trends in Corpus Research: Finding Structure in Data*, 165–198. Amsterdam: John Benjamins.
MacWhinney, Brian (2008c): How mental models encode embodied linguistic perspectives. In: R. Klatzky, B. MacWhinney and M. Behrmann (eds.), *Embodiment, Ego-Space, and Action*, 369–410. Mahwah: Lawrence Erlbaum.
MacWhinney, Brian (2009): The emergence of linguistic complexity. In: T. Givon and M. Shibatani (eds.), *Linguistic Complexity*, 405–432. New York: Benjamins.
MacWhinney, Brian (2010): Computational models of child language learning. *Journal of Child Language* 37: 477–485.
MacWhinney, Brian (2012): The logic of the Unified Model. In: S. Gass and A. Mackey (eds.), *The Routledge Handbook of Second Language Acquisition*, 211–227. New York: Routledge.
MacWhinney, Brian (2014): Competition across time. In: B. MacWhinney, A. Malchukov and E. Moravcsik (eds.), *Competing Motivations in Grammar and Usage*. New York: Oxford University Press.
MacWhinney, Brian (ed.) (1999): *The Emergence of Language*. Mahwah, NJ: Lawrence Erlbaum Associates.
MacWhinney, Brian, Elizabeth Bates, and Reinhold Kliegl (1984): Cue validity and sentence interpretation in English, German, and Italian. *Journal of Verbal Learning and Verbal Behavior* 23: 127–150.
MacWhinney, Brian, Heidi Feldman, Kelly Sacco, and Raul Valdes-Perez (2000): Online measures of basic language skills in children with early focal brain lesions. *Brain and Language* 71: 400–431.

MacWhinney, Brian and Ping Li (2008): Neurolinguistic computational models. In: B. Stemmer and H. Whitaker (eds.), *Handbook of the Neuroscience of Language*, 229–236. Mahwah: Lawrence Erlbaum Associates.

MacWhinney, Brian, Andrej Malchukov, and Edith Moravcsik (eds.) (2014): *Competing Motivations in Grammar and Usage*. New York: Oxford University Press.

Malvern, David, Brian Richards, Ngoni Chipere, and Pilar Purán (2004): *Lexical Diversity and Language Development*. New York: Palgrave Macmillan.

Massaro, Dominic (1987): *Speech Perception by Ear and Eye*. Hillsdale: Lawrence Erlbaum.

Massaro, Dominic (ed.) (1975): *Understanding Language: An Introduction-Processing Analysis of Speech Perception, Reading, and Psycholinguistics*. New York: Academic Press.

McClelland, James L., Bruce McNaughton, and Randy O'Reilly (1995): Why there are complementary learning systems in the hippocampus and neocortex: Insights from the successes and failures of connectionist models of learning and memory. *Psychological Review* 102: 419–457.

McClelland, James, Daniel Mirman, and Lori Holt (2006): Are there interactive processes in speech perception? *Trends in Cognitive Sciences* 10: 363–369.

McDonald, Janet and Brian MacWhinney (1991): Levels of learning: A microdevelopmental study of concept formation. *Journal of Memory and Language* 30: 407–430.

Meltzoff, Andrew and Jean Decety (2003): What imitation tells us about social cognition: A rapprochement between developmental psychology and cognitive neuroscience. *Philosophical Transactions of the Royal Society of London B* 358: 491–500.

Menzel, Randolf (1999): Memory dynamics in the honeybee. *Journal of Comparative Physiology A* 185: 323–340.

Mesoudi, Alex, Andrew Whiten, and Kevin Laland (2006): Towards a unified science of cultural evolution. *Behavioral and Brain Sciences* 29: 329–383.

O'Grady, William (2005): *Syntactic Carpentry*. Mahwah: Lawrence Erlbaum Associates.

Ohala, John (1974): Phonetic explanation in phonology. In: A. Bruck, R. Fox and M. La Galy (eds.), *Papers from the Parassession on Natural Phonology*, 251–274. Chicago: Chicago Linguistic Society.

Oller, D. Kimbrough (2000): *The Emergence of the Speech Capacity*. Mahwah: Lawrence Erlbaum Associates.

Parisse, Christophe and Marie-Thérèse Le Normand (2000): Automatic disambiguation of the morphosyntax in spoken language corpora. *Behavior Research Methods, Instruments, and Computers* 32: 468–481.

Pecher, Diane and Rolf Zwaan (eds.) (2005): *Grounding Cognition*. Cambridge: Cambridge University Press.

Perfors, Amy, Joshua Tenenbaum, and Elizabeth Wonnacott (2010): Variability, negative evidence, and the acquisition of verb argument constructions. *Journal of Child Language* 37: 607–642.

Poplack, Shana and Rena Cacoullos (2014): A variationist paradigm for linguistic emergence. In: B. MacWhinney and W. O'Grady (eds.), *Handbook of Language Emergence*. New York: Wiley.

Pulvermüller, Friedemann (2003): *The Neuroscience of Language*. Cambridge: Cambridge University Press.

Ratner, Nancy and Jerome Bruner (1978): Games, social exchange and the acquisition of language. *Journal of Child Language* 5: 391–401.

Rizzolatti, Giacomo, Luciano Fadiga, Vittorio Gallese, and Leonardi Fogassi (1996): Premotor cortex and the recognition of motor actions. *Cognitive Brain Research* 3: 131–141.

Rumelhart, David and James McClelland (1986): *Parallel Distributed Processing*. Cambridge: MIT Press.
Sagae, Kenji, Eric Davis, Alon Lavie, Brian MacWhinney, and Shuly Wintner (2007): High-accuracy annotation and parsing of CHILDES transcripts *Proceedings of the 45th Meeting of the Association for Computational Linguistics*, 1044–1050. Prague: ACL.
Schütz-Bosbach, Simone and Wolfgang Prinz (2007): Perceptual resonance: Action-induced modulation of perception. *Trends in Cognitive Sciences* 11: 349–355.
Sfard, Anna and Kay McClain (2002): Special Issue: Analyzing tools: Perspective on the role of designed artifacts in mathematics learning. *Journal of the Learning Sciences* 11: 153–388.
Silverstein, Michael (1976): Shifters, linguistic categories and cultural description. In: K. H. Basso and H. A. Selby (eds.), *Meaning in Anthropology* 11–55. Albuquerque: University of New Mexico Press.
Simon, Herbert (1962): The architecture of complexity. *Proceedings of the American Philosophical Society* 106: 467–482.
Smith, Carlota (1991): *The Parameter of Aspect*. Dordrecht: Kluwer.
Speed, Laura, David P. Vinson, and Gabriella Vigliocco (volume 1): Representing meaning. Berlin/Boston: De Gruyter Mouton.
Thelen, Esther and Linda Smith (1994): *A Dynamic Systems Approach to the Development of Cognition and Action*. Cambridge: MIT Press.
Thiessen, Erik and Lucy Erickson (2014): Perceptual development and statistical learning. In: B. MacWhinney and W. O'Grady (eds.), *Handbook of Language Emergence*. New York: Wiley.
Tolentino, Leida and Natasha Tokowicz (2011): Across languages, space, and time: A review of the role of cross-language similarity in L2 (morpho)syntactic processing as revealed by fMRI and ERP. *Studies in Second Language Acquisition* 33: 1–34.
Tomasello, Michael (2000): The item-based nature of children's early syntactic development. *Trends in Cognitive Sciences* 4: 156–163.
Toscano, Joseph C. and Bob McMurray (2010): Cue integration with categories: Weighting acoustic cues in speech using unsupervised learning and distributional statistics. *Cognitive Science* 34: 434–464.
Taylor, John R. (this volume): Prototype effects in grammar. Berlin/Boston: De Gruyter Mouton.
Verspoor, Marjolijn, Kees de Bot, and Wander Lowie (2011): *A Dynamic Approach to Second Language Development*. New York: John Benjamins.
Whitehurst, G. and R. Vasta (1975): Is language acquired through imitation? *Journal of Psycholinguistic Research* 4: 37–59.
Wittenberg, Gayle, Megan Sullivan, and Joe Tsien (2002): Synaptic reentry reinforcement based network model for long-term memory consolidation. *Hippocampus* 12: 637–647.
Wittgenstein, Ludwig (1953): *Philosophical Investigations*. Oxford: Blackwell.

Index

References such as '178–9' indicate (not necessarily continuous) discussion of a topic across a range of pages. Wherever possible in the case of topics with many references, these have either been divided into sub-topics or only the most significant discussions of the topic are listed. Because the entire work is about 'cognitive linguistics', the use of this term (and certain others which occur constantly throughout the book) as an entry point has been minimised. Information will be found under the corresponding detailed topics.

7-point metaphoricalness scale 172
7-point sarcasm scale 174–5, 177, 180, 183

a-adjectives 159
– known 159
– novel 159
Aarts, B. 136, 138
abstract concepts 120, 232
abstract domains 11, 218
abstract motion 111, 116
abstract relational meanings 150, 153
abstract schemas 156, 239
abstraction 66, 220, 223, 251, 262
– levels 155, 222, 261
acceptability 33, 53
– ratings 48, 52
accuracy 97, 100, 240–1
achievements, mental 67, 69, 79–80
acquisition 100, 131, 215–16, 236, 244
– language 95, 100, 212, 215, 239, 277, 281, 284
– motion in 95–6
– process 91
action systems 51, 54, 252
activation 33, 35, 118, 161–2, 279, 283, 288
actual motion 109, 111–12, 117–18
adjectives 35, 135–7, 251, 262
– comparative 53–4
– polysemous 34–5
adpositions, spatial 44–54
adult native speakers 232–4
adult-directed speech 234
adults 48, 152, 159, 162, 236, 284
adverbs 90, 136, 251
affirmation 175, 182
affirmative, alternatives 172, 174, 180
affirmative constructions 177, 186

affirmative counterparts 175, 177, 180, 182–3, 185
– novel 172, 175, 177, 180
age 24, 46, 48, 95, 156–7
agency 14, 151, 277
agents 99, 153, 155–6, 160, 238, 240, 253, 277–8
– implied 140
agonists 192, 197–8
alertness 177, 180, 182–3, 185
alternations 261–2
– locative 154
ambiguity 23, 32–3, 35–6, 215, 217, 222
American Sign Language see ASL
Amondawa 77–8, 80
analogy 36, 99, 195, 212, 217–19, 222, 245, 283
animacy 14, 141, 153–4, 157
– priming 153
anisotropicity 75, 78–9
anomaly, semantic 170, 172, 174, 177, 180, 184–5
antagonists 192, 198
aorist 206–7
appearance constructions 160–1
appropriateness 48–50, 52
argument structure constructions 16, 27, 148–62
– associated with meaning independent of the verb 150–2
– learning 155–62
argument strucure constructions, mediating mapping from thought to talk 152–5
Ariel, M. 169, 186, 219, 276
articulation 287
articulators 252, 261, 264, 266–7
articulatory gestures 265, 278–9

artificial categories 130, 134
ASL (American Sign Language) 253–60, 263, 266
– signs 255–6, 259
aspect 120, 191–6, 199–202, 204–9, 218, 223
– definition 192
– grammatical 119, 200
– imperfective 74, 110, 119, 192, 195–6, 200, 204–8
– lexical 200, 202, 204–5
– metaphors 194–6
– and mood 207–9
– role 119–20
– and tense 204–7
aspectual interpretations 192, 195
association 128, 139–40, 142, 186, 207, 224
assumptions 9, 24, 30, 213, 216, 264, 279, 281
– basic 13, 91
asymmetric organisation 72–3, 75
asymmetrical similarity judgements 133
asymmetries 8, 234
– inherent 75, 79
attention 6, 13–14, 45, 89–90, 94–7, 244, 247, 285–6
– visual 113–14
attenuation, objective 224–5
attributes 25, 128–31, 134, 136, 199
– formal 136–7
– weighted 129, 131, 133
authors 92–4, 153, 156–7, 161
auxiliaries 213, 217–18
awareness 78–9, 81, 97, 100, 242
Aymara 77
Azuma, T. 33, 35

Baayen, R. H. 264
Basque 11, 90, 92, 94, 99
Bates, E. 231, 252, 277, 282
bees 132, 279–80
behavioral work 111, 118–19, 121
Bellugi, U. 260
Benveniste, E. 214–15
Bergen, B. 4, 6, 44, 82, 117, 192, 252, 283
Berlin-Kay paradigm 3
Berthele, R. 93–4
bias, nonliteral 175, 178, 181

biased targets 173, 176, 178–9, 181
biasing, contexts 171–2, 174, 177, 180
bilingual speakers 17, 97, 134
blends 138, 262
– conceptual 255
Bock, K. 152–5
body from different angles 6–8
body temperature 68
Bonato, M. 73–4
Boroditsky, L. 44, 72–3, 81–2, 95, 99, 114–15
boundaries 8, 30, 93, 128–9, 265, 268, 277
– category 14, 128
– fuzzy 14, 128, 139–40
– inherent 195
– temporal 195
Boyd, J. K. 159
brain 37, 73, 78, 81, 276, 278–9, 283, 286
– areas 117–18
British Sign Language (BSL) 254, 257
Brooks, P. J. 158, 236, 242
Brugman, C. 25–6, 45, 88, 130, 132
BSL (British Sign Language) 254, 257
Bybee, J. 166, 170, 215, 217, 219, 264–8, 279, 282

Cacoullos, R. 281–2
Cadierno, T. 91, 96
Caldwell-Harris, C. 160, 166, 217, 266
capacity, memory 37, 236, 242
Carlson-Radvansky, L. A. 51–2
Caroll, J. B. 251
Carston, R. 167, 169–70
Casasanto, D. 44, 73, 81–3
Casasola, M. 46, 60
Catalan Sign Language (LSC) 257
categories 12–14, 23–5, 27, 127–38, 157, 159–60, 199–200, 265
– artificial 130, 134
– classical 264–5, 267
– colour 4, 127–8, 130, 140
– Croft's 202, 205
– grammatical 88, 133, 144, 191, 193, 197, 199, 209
– lexical 14, 37, 127, 135, 137–8, 200
– linguistic 12, 17, 129, 191
– morpho-syntactic 212
– neighbouring 128–9, 133, 136
– non-linguistic 16, 160–1

- ontological 68-9, 77
- polysemous 29, 131
- prototype 127, 130-1, 138, 265
- radial 25-6, 45
- of tense 191, 204
- verbal 191, 197, 209
categorization 2-3, 7, 13-14, 16-17, 24, 127, 129-30, 137-8
- cross-linguistic 8
- non-linguistic 16
category boundaries 14, 128
category learning 160-1
category membership 24, 128-9, 131-3, 135
category prototypes 132, 135, 137
category structures 25, 35, 129, 131
causation 99-100, 198, 242
caused-motion 27, 152, 157
caused-motion construction 149, 157-8
caused-motion meanings 157-8
central members 25, 129, 132-3
central sense 130-2, 134
centrality 130-1, 133, 144
chance 158, 236-7, 239-41, 244
change 79, 87-8, 192, 212-13, 215-20, 222-3, 254, 276-7
- constructional 220
- diachronic 281
- grammatical 223-4
- historical 260, 279
- incremental 201
- language 215-16, 219, 222, 276-7
- of location 87
- of state 88, 151
characterization, semantic 135, 137
Charles, W. G. 30
child language 155, 282
child-directed speech 157, 234
children 17, 48, 95, 131, 155-60, 231, 243, 284
- deaf 251
- young 157, 239
Chipere, N. 235-6, 243
Choi, S. 17, 59, 95-6
choice 17, 45, 48, 89, 195
- demonstrative 56, 58
Chomsky, N. 148, 231, 251, 275, 284
classes 29, 33, 51, 155, 201, 217, 253, 261
- verb 29
- word 2, 135

classical categories 264-5, 267
classifier verbs 262
classifiers, verb 196
cluster analysis 31, 34
clusters 59, 130, 132, 135, 140, 144, 202, 205
coded meanings 166
coercion 199-200, 222, 283
cognition
- embodied 275, 282-3, 286
- extensions to 4-5
cognitive abilities 155, 231, 242, 261
cognitive activities 258-9
- effortful 237, 242
cognitive differences 242, 244
cognitive domains 2, 11, 17, 98, 101
cognitive functions 78, 98, 286
Cognitive Grammar 212, 219-20, 223-5, 260-1, 282-3
Cognitive Linguistics see *Introductory Note*
cognitive semantics 2, 10, 23, 32
collocations 32, 50, 143, 166, 169, 184
colour 3-4, 9, 14, 17, 98, 127-8, 133-4
- categories 4, 127-8, 130, 140
- focal 4, 127-9, 134
communication 14, 100, 247, 252, 286-7
- animal 251
comparative adjectives 53-4
competence 235, 247, 252, 264, 266
- linguistic 246, 264
competition 141-2, 275-7, 282
- and natural selection 276-8
complex constructions 88, 242, 262-3
complex motion events 98-9
complex sentences 234-6
complex structures 94, 266, 287
complexity 31, 68, 93, 208, 275-6, 278, 282
composite predicate construction 222
composition 276, 284
compounds 138-9, 254
- non-possessive 141
- possessive 141-2
comprehension 46-7, 49, 52, 149, 155-6, 162, 234-8, 243
- emergentist models 284
- grammatical 242-3
- of passive sentences 237, 241
- questions 175, 178

- sentence 149, 152, 237, 241, 245, 281
- tasks 235–6
- training 235
computational approaches/methods 30, 32, 285, 288
computers 113, 152, 173, 175, 178, 282
conception 36, 68, 197, 224, 261
- object of 224–5
- subject of 224–5
concepts 12, 67, 79–81, 167, 172, 213–14, 255–6, 260
- abstract 120, 232
- lexical 67, 69–70, 76
- negated 167, 174
- spatial 44, 46, 59, 67
- temporal 67, 69, 78, 80–1
conceptual blends 255
conceptual domains 66, 69, 74, 76, 194
conceptual metaphors 15, 67, 70–1, 77, 80, 111, 120
conceptual semantics 223–4
conceptual space 260–1
conceptualisation 67–70, 72, 80, 89, 115, 118, 218, 223
configurations, structural 139, 153–4
conjunctions 213, 223
- subordinating 136
construal 191, 193, 199–202, 205, 209, 212, 220, 223–4
- dynamic 110, 117
- subjective 197, 224
Construction Grammar 16, 154, 157, 166, 219–20, 282–4
construction learning 243–4
- as category learning 160–1
- neurolinguistic research 161–2
constructional approaches 148–9, 154, 162
constructional change 220
constructional forms 157, 159
constructional priming 153
constructional taxonomy 221–2
constructionalization 212, 214, 220–1, 223
- grammatical 220–1
- lexical 220–1
constructions 29, 139–44, 149–52, 154–62, 170–1, 182, 217–22, 243–5
- affirmative 177, 186
- appearance 160–1

- argument structure see *argument structure constructions*
- associated with meaning independent of the verb 150–2
- caused-motion 149, 157–8
- complex 88, 242, 262–3
- containing 137, 149
- ditransitive 27, 29, 150–2, 154, 157–8, 161, 222
- emerging 166–7, 222
- grammatical 23, 246
- item-based 156
- mediating mapping from thought to talk 152–5
- middle 140–1, 151
- motion 6, 118, 158
- negative 166, 171, 174, 177, 179–80, 182, 185–6
- noun phrase 137, 149
- novel 159, 186, 222
- passive 151, 239–41, 277
- quantifier 245
- syntactic 2, 27, 127, 135, 139
- target 167
- trained 238–9, 243
- verb-independent 152, 157
constructs 44, 80, 96, 193, 220, 222, 245
- geometric 47
- spatial 44, 60
containers 23, 46, 48, 53, 257, 261
containing constructions 137, 149
containment 14, 44, 46–8, 59
context biasing 34, 173, 175, 178, 181
contexts 23–4, 33–4, 100–101, 168, 173–5, 178, 181, 205
- biasing 171–2, 174, 177, 180
- grammatical 232–3
- importance 24, 33
contextual information 168–71, 185, 244
contrast 45, 48, 68, 75, 140–1, 168–9, 172, 235
contrastivity 133, 136, 138, 167
control
- conditions 48, 237
- location 48–50, 60
- motor 78
- sentences 234–5

conventionality 168, 170
conventionalization 170, 185, 199, 216, 219–21
conventions 15, 246, 281
conversation 5, 120, 203
conversational emergence 284
conversational interactions 203, 285
corpora 28, 30, 46, 142, 157, 204, 206, 285
corpus data 29, 31–2, 204, 206
corpus linguistics 23, 30–2, 36, 152, 160, 205
corpus-based evidence 171, 185
correspondence analysis 31, 206
counterparts, affirmative 175, 177, 180, 182–3, 185
Crick, F. 81
criterial models 264, 267
critical periods 275, 287
Croatian 204, 206
Croft, W. 6, 28–9, 193–4, 201–2, 204–6, 215–16, 219, 221–3
Croft's categories 202, 205
cross-linguistic categorization 8
cross-linguistic comparison 1, 11, 13
cross-linguistic differences 3, 8, 17, 56, 59, 97–8
cross-linguistic research 6, 8, 10–11, 13–15, 95, 119
cross-linguistic variation 10, 13–16, 59
cues 73, 157, 169–70, 247, 275, 279, 286
– validity 25, 129–31, 135–6, 157
cultural variability 77, 257
cultures 8–9, 45, 77–8, 80, 82, 265
cyclic achievements 201–2
Cysouw, M. 6, 11–13

Dahl, Ö 193, 195, 205
data, corpus 29, 31–2, 204, 206
dative 153, 158, 161, 233–4, 247
– endings 233
– Icelandic 27
– inflections 234
– Polish 233, 245
– prepositional 153–4
deaf children 251
default inheritance 222
default interpretations 167–9

default metaphorical utterance-interpretation 171–3
– offline measures 172
– online measures 173
default nonliteral interpretations 166–86
– conditions for 169–70, 182, 184
– utterance-interpretation 166, 169–84
default sarcastic utterance-interpretation 174–84
– offline measures 174–5, 177–8, 180
– online measures 175–6, 178–81
defaultness 166, 169
definiteness 194, 196
degrammaticalization 214
deictic gestures 17, 54
demonstrative choice 56, 58
demonstratives 45, 55–8, 200
– spatial 45, 54–5, 57
– systems 55–8
denominal verbs 151
derivation 138, 194, 213
descriptions 26, 50, 55, 57, 90, 101, 109, 113
– linguistic 17, 134–5, 139
– passive 153, 155
descriptive meanings 10, 13
determiners 135, 137
developmental psychology 95
deverbal nouns 194–5
diachronic change 281
diatopic variation 94
dictionaries 11–12, 34, 245–6
Diessel, H. 54–6, 58, 149
dimensionality 74–5
dimensions 14, 50, 74–5, 128, 138, 194, 197, 205
direct objects 137, 140, 158, 232
directed activities 201–2
directedness 74–5
discourse 15, 117, 141, 225, 286
– analysis 88
– written 234
distance 54–6, 58, 72, 128, 130, 260
distortions 131, 134, 144
ditransitive constructions 27, 29, 150–2, 154, 157–8, 161, 222
Dittmar, M. 156
diversity 1, 14, 94, 209, 282
– cross-linguistic 3, 17
– linguistic 1–2, 9, 16

Divjak, D. S. 31, 134, 160, 166, 208, 217, 243, 266
do-ers 238, 240 see also *agents*
domains 11–12, 14, 73–5, 100–101, 191–2, 203, 224–5, 267
– abstract 11, 218
– conceptual 66, 69, 74, 76, 194
– linguistic 2, 5
– semantic 3, 9, 88
– source 71–2, 120, 203, 283
– of space 69–70, 73–4
– target 71–2, 97, 283
– of time 66, 69–70, 73–5, 77, 81, 193
dominant senses 33–4
drawing studies 113
DST see *dynamic systems theory*
Dudis, P. G. 255
duration 74–6, 78–81, 128, 195
– experience of 78, 80
– perception of 67–8
– protracted 68, 76
dynamic construal 110, 117
dynamic systems theory (DST) 252, 265–7, 282–3, 288
– and signed languages 265–7
dynamicity 200
dynamic-kinematic routines 48–50, 53–4
dynamics 118, 120, 255, 267
– force 48, 192, 194, 197–8, 203, 255
– task 265–6

Eckhoff, H. M. 194, 204, 206
education 97, 242, 245, 251
education-related differences 234, 238, 240–1
E-Language 275, 286
Ellis, N. C. 91, 96, 160
embodied experience 80, 117, 121, 192
embodied representations 283
embodied solutions 252, 265, 267
embodiment 3–4, 6, 32, 133, 283
– physical 252
emergence 221, 265, 276, 282, 284
emergent systems 265, 268, 278
Emergentism 275–88
– approaches 281–2
– and complexity 278
– core issues 286–7

– frameworks supporting 276–81
– mechanisms 282–6
– natural selection and competition 276–8
– timeframes 275–6, 278–82
emotions 6–7, 9–10, 15, 17, 44, 258–9, 261
empirical evidence 29–30, 46, 89, 162
English speakers 57, 60, 83, 99, 119, 246
entrenchment 133, 158, 223, 241, 266, 287
epistemic modality 203
epistemic modals 203
errors 28, 238–40, 283
Evans, N. 1–2, 4, 11–13, 27, 29, 47, 80–1, 224
event-objects 194–7, 199, 203, 205–8
events 66–8, 70–2, 75–7, 79–81, 97–9, 137, 191–4, 205–7
– construal 255
– motion see *motion events*
– perception 67, 81
– stimuli 98–9
– structure 120, 151
– succession of 77, 193
– usage 252, 262
evidence 50–3, 152–4, 156–7, 162, 172–5, 177–8, 180, 241–3
– corpus-based 171, 185
– empirical 29–30, 46, 89, 162
– linguistic 28, 69–70, 76
– from offline measures 172, 174, 177, 180
– from online measures 171, 173, 175, 178, 180
evolution 92, 223, 275–6, 278, 287
– biological 278
– semantic 218–19
exemplars 36, 128, 132, 134, 160, 243, 245
experience 66–8, 78–9, 81–2, 100–101, 231, 241–2, 244, 261
– of duration 78, 80
– embodied 80, 117, 121, 192
– linguistic 231, 242–3
– real 67–8, 76
– sensory-motor 67, 80–2
– subjective 67, 143, 207
– temporal 73, 76, 79, 81
– of time see *temporal experience*
– of transience 78
experimental approaches 44–6, 58, 60

experimentation, psycholinguistic 29–30, 288
experimenters 55, 57–8, 157, 242, 244
experiments 57–8, 112–16, 119, 153–4, 161, 233–6, 238–41, 243
expressions 69–70, 72, 97, 135, 137, 139–43, 217, 224
- facial 170
- fictive motion 109–11, 120
- fixed 142, 206
- linguistic 2, 10, 12–13, 100
- modal 192, 204
- salient/coded nonliteral meanings of 169, 184
- spatial 49
extensions 4–5, 9, 27, 37, 55, 74–5, 191–2, 199–200
- metaphorical 4, 218
- semantic 4, 258–9
extreme splitting 26–7
eye movements 34, 91, 112–14
eye tracking 53, 113

facial expressions 170
facial gestures 261, 263–4
feedback 222, 235, 237, 243, 283
feelings 9, 171–2, 258–9
feminine nouns 233
Ferreira, F. 113, 238, 240
F-handshape 256–7
fictive motion 91, 109–21
- drawing studies 113
- expressions 109–11, 120
- eye movement studies 113–14
- future 117–21
- narrative understanding tasks 112
- recent developments 111–17
- start 109–11
- time and motion surveys 114–17
figurative language 117, 119–20
filler items 182
Fillmore, C. J. 24, 148–9, 170, 185, 279
films 11–12
Fischer, O. 217–18
fixed expressions 142, 206
Flaherty, M. G. 67–8, 76
fleeting sense of motion 111, 121
fluid substances 195, 208

focal colours 4, 127–9, 134
force dynamics 48, 192, 194, 197–8, 203, 255
formal attributes 136–7
formalism 252, 264–5, 267
form-function pairings, learned 149
form-meaning pairings 148–9, 220–1, 267
forms
- constructional 157, 159
- grammatical 92, 220, 254
- lexical 77–9, 254
- linguistic 88, 133, 244
- phonological 32, 220
frameworks 16, 87, 212, 218, 226, 275–6
- general 89, 282
- usage-based 89, 218
French Sign Language (LSF) 257, 263
frequency 79, 133–4, 139, 143–4, 160, 212, 217, 221
- effects 134, 160
- high 45, 158, 217
- low 217
- relative 134, 143, 202
Frishberg, N. 258–9
Frisson, S. 34
Frog Story 90, 94–5
function words 37, 212–13
functional pressure 276
functionalism 215, 275, 281–2
functions 50, 52–4, 67–8, 91–2, 218–20, 224–5, 254, 276–7
- cognitive 78, 98, 286
- grammatical 254–5, 263
futurity 217–19
fuzziness 127, 138, 141, 144, 264
fuzzy boundaries 14, 128, 139–40

Galton, A. 74, 76
games 11–12, 25, 76, 142
Garrod, S. C. 45–9
Geld, R. 204, 206
generality, semantic 13, 221
generalizations 7–8, 24–5, 153, 155, 157, 160, 232–3, 283
generative linguists 215, 231
genetics 287
genitive 27, 232–3
genres 91, 176–7, 234

Index

geometric constructs 47
geometric relations 47, 54
geometric routines 47–52
geometry 44, 47–9, 52–3, 278
– manipulations of 48–9
Gertner, Y. 156–7
gestures 17, 82–3, 96, 120, 251–2, 254–5, 261–5, 267–8
– articulatory 265, 278–9
– co-occurrence with signs 262–3
– deictic 17, 54
– facial 261, 263–4
– incorporation into signed languages 263
– and language 251–2, 267
– distinguished 264–5
– and signed languages 261–5
Gibbs, R. W. Jr 25, 31, 33, 117, 120, 166, 168–70, 185
Gisborne, N. 220–3
Glenberg, A. M. 117, 151
Glynn, D. 31
Goldberg, A. 27, 143, 148–52, 157–61, 185, 282–4
Goldwater, M. B. 151
Goodwin, C. 281–2
Graded Salience Hypothesis 166, 168–9, 185
gradience 136, 138, 264, 267
Grady, J. E. 67, 76, 81
grammar 133–5, 139–41, 212–15, 231, 245–7, 259–61, 264–5, 267
– cognitive 212, 219–20, 223, 260–1, 282–3
– collective 246
– individual 246–7
– mental 231, 246
– prototype effects in 127, 129, 131, 133, 135, 137, 139, 141
– of signed languages 253, 260, 265
grammatical categories 88, 133, 144, 191, 193, 197, 199, 209
grammatical change 223–4
grammatical comprehension 242–3
grammatical constructionalization 220–1
grammatical constructions 23, 246
grammatical contexts 232–3
grammatical forms 92, 220, 254
grammatical functions 254–5, 263

grammatical knowledge 220
– individual differences 231–47
– irregular morphoogy 232
– passives 238–41
– quantifiers 236–8
– reasons for individual differences 242–5
– regular morphoogy 233–4
– subordination 234–6
grammatical meanings 254, 263
grammatical morphemes 254
grammatical typology 15
grammaticalization 212–26, 255, 259, 261, 263
– cognition in grammaticalization theory 215–19
– Cognitive Grammar 223–5
– in cognitive linguistic theory 219–26
– Construction Grammar 220–3
– history 212–15
– and lexicalization 255, 261
grammaticalizing items 218–19
grammaticization 215, 254–5, 258
gravitational plane 48, 51
grounded representations 51, 78
group differences 234, 241

HAA (High Academic Attainment) 235, 238, 241
– participants 235–7, 239–41, 244
handshapes 256, 258, 262
Hart, B. 88, 242, 244
Haspelmath, M. 11, 13, 193, 214, 216–17
have-a-hunch 258–9
hearers 44, 208, 224, 246
hearing 4–5, 34
Hebrew 82, 95, 166, 169, 175, 182
– Ancient 110
Heider, F. 3, 81, 127
Heine, B. 87, 214, 218–19, 277
High Academic Attainment see HAA
Hijazo-Gascón, A. 92–4, 96
Hilpert, M. 134, 219–21
historical change 260, 279
homonymous meanings 34–5
homonyms 34–5
– meanings 33–4
homonymy 23, 33

humility 179
Huumo, T. 110, 195

Iacobini, C. 92
iconicity 259–61
identification 79, 131, 133
idiomaticity 127, 142, 144
I-Language 286
imagability 133
image schemata 46–7, 51
imitation 276, 284
immediate reality 197, 199–200
imperfective aspect 74, 110, 119, 192, 195–6, 200, 204–8
imperfective verbs 204–5
implausible passives 238–9
implied agents 140
implied motion 117
in vivo learning 286
inanimate nouns 232, 234
incongruity
– internal 174, 177, 180, 185
– pragmatic 170, 185
infants 46, 95–6, 141, 284
inferences 120, 132, 152, 218–19
infinitives 136, 205, 208
information 17, 81, 90–2, 95, 97–100, 109, 114, 119
– content 90, 98
– contextual 168–71, 185, 244
– manner 97, 119
– supportive 170, 185
– terrain 114
inheritance, default 222
innovation 137, 212, 215–16, 222
inputs 138, 155, 157–8, 160, 244–5, 279, 281, 287–8
– meshing 280, 282, 288
instantiations 14, 172, 174, 177, 263
integration 81, 265, 279
interactions 1, 4, 192, 195, 204–5, 257, 278–9, 282
– conversational 203, 285
interactions of tense aspect, and mood 204–8
internal incongruity 174, 177, 180, 185
internal structures 135, 141, 217

interpretations 166–9, 171, 174–7, 179–80, 185–6, 200, 202, 235
– aspectual 192, 195
– default 167–9
– literal see *literal interpretations*
– low-salience 166–7
– metaphorical 167, 172
– nonliteral see *nonliteral interpretations*
– novel nonliteral 171, 176, 179, 181
– perfective 192, 196
– preferred 172, 175, 177–8, 180
– salience-based 166, 168–9, 185–6
– sarcastic 167, 174–5, 177–8, 180, 186
– utterance 166, 168, 171–2, 174, 177
intertypological variation 93–4
intonation 263–4
intransitive verbs 27, 195
intratypological variation 94
irregular morphology 232
isolation 172, 174–5, 177, 180, 185
– social 287
Israel 166, 170
Italian Sign Language 257, 260
item-based constructions 156
item-based patterns 284

Janzen, T. 254–5, 263
Johnson, M. 4, 6, 44, 46, 66–7, 70, 80, 120
JSL (Japanese Sign language) 257

Kaschak, M. P. 151
Kay, P. 3, 98, 149, 279, 282
Kelso, J. A. S. 252, 266
Klein, D. E. 33, 35
knowledge 101, 197, 203, 209, 234–6, 239, 244–5, 247
– grammatical see *grammatical knowledge*
– linguistic 134, 222, 231, 235–6, 242, 247
known a-adjectives 159
Koch, C. 2, 15–16, 81
Kourtzi, Z. 117–18
Kurylowicz, J. 214
Kuteva, T. 87–8

LAA (Low Academic Attainment) participants 235–41
labels 7, 13, 48, 88, 93, 95, 99, 226

Lakoff, G. 24–7, 44–5, 66–7, 70, 72–3, 80, 116–17, 120
Langacker, R. 110–11, 199–200, 203–5, 216–17, 219–21, 223–5, 260–2, 264–6
language acquisition 95, 100, 212, 215, 239, 277, 281, 284
language and gestures 251–2, 264–5, 267
language change 215–16, 219, 222, 276–7
language processing 98, 100, 119
language production 152–4, 157, 162, 265
language use 100, 149, 162, 194, 220, 222, 277, 282
learned form-function pairings 149
learners 157–60, 215, 231, 233, 244, 247, 285, 287
– second language 237, 244
learning 5, 59, 95, 120, 243–4, 277, 282–3, 286
– argument structure constructions 155–62
– construction 243–4
– episodes 243–4
– phonological 283
– in vivo 286
Lehmann, C. 213–16, 223
letters 116–17, 130, 134, 200, 202
Levinson, S. C. 1, 3, 10, 12, 14, 16–17, 56, 59
lexical aspect 200, 202, 204–5
lexical categories 14, 37, 127, 135, 137–8, 200
– prototype effects 135–7
lexical concepts 67, 69–70, 76
lexical constructionalization 220–1
lexical forms 77–9, 254
lexical items 2, 23–4, 29, 142, 144, 148, 162, 185
– open class 151–2
lexical meanings 12–13, 24, 148, 263
lexical morphemes 254, 263
lexical networks 26, 29, 32
lexical semantics 16, 23, 27, 131
lexical templates 241
lexical typology 2, 13, 15
lexical verbs 254–5
lexicalization 5, 214, 219, 221, 254, 263
– and grammaticalization 255, 261
– motion 96, 98, 100
– patterns 87–94, 96, 99

lexicon 11, 13, 16, 213, 216, 218, 282, 286
– mental 34, 166, 168
Libras 262–3
Liddell, S. K. 110, 253, 255, 262–4
light verbs 150, 158
linear objects 113–14, 117
linguistic categories 12, 17, 129, 191
linguistic categorization see *categorization*
linguistic competence 246, 264
linguistic diversity 1–2, 9, 16
linguistic domains 2, 5
linguistic evidence 28, 69–70, 76
linguistic experience 231, 242–3
linguistic expressions 2, 10, 12–13, 100
linguistic forms 88, 133, 244
linguistic knowledge 134, 222, 231, 235–6, 242, 247
linguistic meanings 10, 133
linguistic relativity 17, 59–60, 119
linguistic structures 87, 96, 247, 253, 284–6
linguistic systems 194, 215, 260–1, 263
linguistic typology 1–2, 11, 101
linking rules 148, 156
links 4, 25–6, 36, 110, 212, 280, 282, 287
– conceptual 114
– metonymic 25, 259
listing 132
literal interpretations 170, 173–4, 177, 180, 186
– salience-based 173, 175, 178, 181, 185
literalness 168
located objects 48, 52
location 48, 58, 70–2, 153–4, 253, 256, 258–9, 261–3
– change of 87
– control 48–50, 60
– object 55, 58, 150
locatives 92, 153–4, 237
Loebell, H. 153–4
Low Academic Attainment (LAA) 235–6, 238
low-salience interpretations 166–7
low-salience markers 166, 176, 179–81, 186
LSC (Catalan Sign Language) 257
LSF (French Sign Language) 257, 263
Lucy, J. 3, 15, 98
Lyashevskaya, O. 204–6, 208

macro-constructions 220, 223
magnitude 73–6, 120–1

Majid, A. 7–8, 10, 12–13, 16, 60
Malt, B. C. 4, 16–17, 98–9
manipulations 55, 256
– of geometry 48–9
– visibility 57
manner 82, 88–90, 92–7, 99–100, 119, 159, 217, 231
– of motion 99, 119
– verbs 91, 94, 99, 119
mappings 45–6, 49, 51, 54–6, 70–2, 149, 155–6, 203
markedness 182–3
– structural 171, 182, 184–5
markers 7, 144, 166, 182, 217–19, 225, 254–5, 263
– low-salience 166, 176, 179–81, 186
– tense-aspect 205
Markman, A. B. 151, 283
masculine 232–3
mass 69–70, 74–5
mass nouns 74, 195
Matrix conception 80
Matsumoto, Y. 90, 94, 110–11
matter 69–70, 74, 101, 131, 136, 139, 226, 265
– constituent structure 75
– substrate 74–5
Matthew effect 243, 245
MCA (multiple correspondence analysis) 31
McNeill, D. 91, 252
meanings
– caused-motion 157–8
– coded 166
– descriptive 10, 13
– grammatical 254, 263
– homonymous 34–5
– lexical 12–13, 24, 148, 263
– linguistic 10, 133
– new 217, 219
– nonsalient 168–9
– prepositional 88
– sentence 148–50, 157, 162
– spatial 27, 219
– subordinate 37
– word 10, 131, 135
Meillet, A. 213–14
Meir, I. 260

membership, category 24, 128–9, 131–3, 135
memory 55, 58, 97–100, 110, 235–6, 243, 280, 286
– capacity 37, 236, 242
– consolidation 280
– middle-term 280
– short-term 279–80
memory game experiments 56, 58
mental achievements 67, 69, 79–80
mental grammars 231, 246
mental lexicon 34, 166, 168
mental representation 28, 31, 82, 130
mental states 6–7, 11
Mental Time Line (MTL) 73
meshing of inputs 280–2, 285, 288
meso-construction 220, 222
metaphorical connections 258–9
metaphorical extensions 4, 218
metaphorical motion 91, 120
metaphorical utterance-interpretation, default 171–3
metaphoricalness 170, 172–3
metaphors 67, 72, 130–1, 191, 193–9, 255, 258–60, 283
– aspect 194–6
– conceptual 15, 67, 70–1, 77, 80, 111, 120
– mood and modality 197–8
– motion-emotion 119
– Moving Observer 71–2
– Moving Time 70–1
– objects 193–4
– and signed languages 255–7
– tense 194
metonymic links 25, 259
metonymical patterns 15
metonymy 15, 25, 131, 191, 199, 219, 257–9, 265
– and metaphor 191, 199, 258–9
– and signed languages 257–9
micro-constructions 220, 222
middle constructions 140–1, 151
middle-term memory (MTM) 280
Miller, G. A. 30, 87, 242
Minkowski space 75
modal expressions 192, 204
modal force 200, 203
modal verbs 192, 197–8, 208, 225

modality 82, 192, 203-4, 207, 252, 255, 267
- epistemic 203
- and mood 197-8
- perceptual 8, 14
- root, epistemic, and speech-act 203-4
modals 192, 197-8, 203, 224
- epistemic 203
models 89, 93, 197-8, 202, 206, 215-16, 218, 279
- competition 282
- criterial 264, 267
- emergentist 275, 285
- Langacker's 197
- prototype 264
- Šatunovskij's 208
- Standard Pragmatic 168-9
- usage-based 134, 231, 241
modularity 287
mood 191-4, 197, 199, 204-5
- and aspect 207-9
- definition 192
- and modality 197-8
- root, epistemic, and speech-act modality 203-4
- and tense 205, 207
Moore, T. 67, 73, 75-6, 80, 114
morphemes 23, 135, 138, 149, 265, 268
- grammatical 254
- lexical 254, 263
morphology
- irregular 232
- regular 233
Mortelmans, T. 197, 203
motion 6, 66-7, 70-2, 77, 80-1, 87-101, 111-12, 117-21
- abstract 111, 116
- in acquisition 95-6
- actual 109, 111-12, 117-18
- applications of typology 89-91
- constraints and variation in lexicalization patterns 93-4
- constructions 6, 118, 158
- events 6, 12, 66-7, 87-92, 94-9
- complex 98-9
- study 88, 97, 101
- expressions, fictive 109-11, 120
- fictive see *fictive motion*
- fleeting sense of 111, 121

- implied 117
- in language and memory 98-100
- lexicalization patterns and semantic typology 88-94
- in linguistics 87-8
- manner of 99, 119
- metaphorical 91, 120
- paths 117, 119
- problems and solutions 91-5
- processing 53, 117, 283
- simulated 111-14, 117-18
- structures 89, 92-3, 96
- subjective 111
- in translation 96-7
motion-emotion metaphors 119
motivation 9, 26, 207, 225, 277, 281
motives 247, 276-7, 280-1
motor control 78
mouth 7, 254, 258-9
move forward time questions 115-16
movement 87, 89, 114, 222-4, 253, 257-8, 261-2, 264
- tough 234, 242
MTL (Mental Time Line) 73
MTM (middle-term memory) 280
multi-dimensional scaling analysis 202, 205
multimedia analysis 285
multiple correspondence analysis (MCA) 31
Murphy, G. L. 33, 35, 129

narrative understanding tasks 112
Narrog, H. 193, 203-4, 214
native speakers 89, 134, 150, 169, 231, 244, 246
- adult 232-4
natural selection 276, 276-8
negated concepts 167, 174
negation 166-8, 171-3, 175-6, 178-82, 184-6, 198, 213
- and structural markedness 182-4
negative constructions 166, 171, 174, 177, 179-80, 182, 185-6
negative items 175, 177, 180, 185
- novel 172, 175, 177, 180
negative polarity items (NPIs) 170
negative utterances 170, 172-5, 177-8, 180-1, 183-4
- novel 172, 174, 177-8, 180

neighbouring categories 128-9, 133, 136
networks 28, 31, 37, 149, 220, 283, 288
– lexical 26, 29, 32
neural network modelling 285
neuroimaging 285, 288
neurolinguistics 37, 118, 161, 279, 282, 285, 288
neuroscience 55, 66, 286
neutral space 253, 258
nominative 195, 232-3
nonce nouns 232-3, 247
non-final positions 173, 175, 178, 181
non-linguistic categories 16, 160-1
non-linguistic tasks 60
nonliteral bias 175, 178, 181
nonliteral interpretations 167, 169-73, 175, 178, 182, 184-6
– conditions for default 169-70, 182, 184
– default see *default nonliteral interpretations*
– generated nonsalient 185
nonliteralness 166, 169-70, 182, 184
non-possessive compounds 141
non-reality 194, 197, 199
nonsalient interpretations 171, 173, 185-6
nonsalient meanings 168-9
nonsalient nonliteral interpretations 166, 185
nonsalient sarcastic interpretations 175, 178, 181
Norvig, P. 25
noun phrase constructions 137, 149
nouns 50, 129-30, 135-7, 142-4, 151, 153, 195-6, 232-4
– deverbal 194-5
– feminine 233
– inanimate 232, 234
– masculine 232
– mass 74, 195
– nonce 232-3, 247
– real 233
novel a-adjectives 159
novel affirmative counterparts 172, 175, 177, 180
novel constructions 159, 186, 222
novel negative items 172, 175, 177, 180
novel negative utterances 172, 174, 177-8, 180

novel nonliteral interpretations 171, 176, 179, 181, 186
novel verbs 151, 156, 160
NPIs (negative polarity items) 170
Núñez, R. 75, 77, 82-3, 114, 116, 120

object properties 58, 70
objective properties 265, 267
objectivity 28, 224
objects 44-58, 69-71, 113-14, 193, 195-6, 232, 255-7, 261
– of conception 224-5
– direct 137, 140, 158, 232
– linear 113-14, 117
– located 48, 52
– location 55, 58, 150
– metaphor 193-4
– physical 24, 70, 114, 225, 256, 261
– reference 49, 51-2
– solid 50, 195
– unfamiliar 58, 232
offline measures, evidence from 172, 174, 177, 180
one-dimensional sorting 150
online measures, evidence from 171, 173, 175, 178, 180
ontological categories 68-9, 77
ontological status 26, 28
open class lexical items 151-2
operators 171-2, 184-5
Optimality Theory 282
organisation, asymmetric 72-3, 75

pairings
– form-meaning 148-9, 220-1, 267
– learned form-function 149
– logical 204
Parallel Distributed Processing 282-3
parasitic gaps 234-5
partitive case 195
parts of speech 31, 135
passive constructions 151, 239-41, 277
passive descriptions 153, 155
passive sentences 153-4, 157, 238, 240
– comprehension 237, 241
passive-attracting verbs 240-1
passives 153-4, 237-42, 245
– implausible 238-9
– unbiased 239

past tense 129, 199–200, 206–7
path prepositions 118
paths 53, 81, 88–91, 93–100, 111–15, 117–18, 219
– sight 116, 118
– traversable 110, 113
– visual 116–17
patterns 1–2, 5, 117–18, 149, 155–6, 159–61, 217–18, 279
– item-based 284
– metonymical 15
– socio-cultural 14–15
perception 4–6, 8–9, 14–15, 17, 81–2, 98, 259, 267
– of duration 67–8
– event 67, 81
– sensory 195, 259
– of space 58
– verbs 5, 11
perceptual modalities 8, 14
perceptual recording 284
perceptual space 55, 57
perfective event-objects 195, 205
perfective interpretations 192, 196
perfectives 74, 110, 192–3, 195–6, 200, 204–8, 254
performance 60, 156, 233, 236–9, 242–5, 252, 264, 266
performatives 205–6
phonological form 32, 220
phonological learning 283
phonology 251, 253, 265, 286
– semantic 261
– and signed languages 253
phrases 139, 144, 149, 169–70, 214–15, 284
physical embodiment 252
physical objects 24, 70, 114, 225, 256, 261
physical space 110–11, 116–17, 254
physical structures 284
Pickering, M. J. 34
pictures 51–4, 59, 113, 115–16, 118, 153–5, 157, 236–7
– selection 236, 239
– target 154–5
– verification 53, 236
Pike, K. L. 12, 251
Pinker, S. 158, 160
plasticity 284, 287

pluralization 135–6
plurals 143, 192, 195, 200
point clouds 36
Polish
– dative 233–4, 245
– genitive singular 232
polysemous adjectives 34–5
polysemous categories 29, 131
polysemous words 34–5, 37, 131–2, 134, 144
polysemy 2, 5, 10, 12–13, 23–37, 46–7, 51, 191
– in cognitive linguistics 23–30
– corpus linguistic approaches 30–2
– desiderata 35–7
– discussion and revision 27–9
– extreme splitting 26–7
– fallacy 28
– in neighboring fields 30–5
– newer developments 29–30
– notion 23
– psycholinguistic approaches 32–5
Poole, K. T. 194, 204–6
Pöppel, E. 78
positions 50, 54–5, 67, 70, 87, 215, 219, 275
– non-final 173, 175, 178, 181
– relative 49, 52–3
– subject 234, 277
possession 11, 141
possessive apostrophe 141
possessive compounds 141–2
possessives, prenominal 141–2
possessors 141–2, 232
poverty of stimulus 287
pragmatic incongruity 170, 185
pragmaticalization 215, 219
predictions 171, 173, 178, 181–2, 197, 206, 266
preemption, statistical 158–9
preferences 51, 100, 171, 173
preferential looking paradigm 156, 159
preferred interpretations 172, 175, 177–8, 180
prenominal possessives 141–2
prepositional dative 153–4
prepositional meanings 88
prepositions 26–7, 29, 46, 48–54, 56, 130–1, 135–7, 232–3
– locative/relational 45

– path 118
– spatial 44–5, 47, 53, 55
– vertical 50–4
priming 35, 133, 152–5, 157
– animacy 153
– constructional 153
– production 154–5
– structural 152–3, 157
processing time 34, 74
production 44, 46–7, 52, 96, 152, 154–6, 162, 252
– language 152–4, 157, 162, 265
– priming 154–5
– sentence 34, 149, 281
productivity 92, 127, 142, 144, 221, 233–4
profiling 199, 201–2, 220
projectionist accounts 148, 155–6
projective terms 45, 51–4
proliferation 275–6, 282
properties 9, 11, 74–5, 132, 136–8, 195, 222, 277
– object 58, 70
– objective 265, 267
– semantic 141–2, 151, 153, 261
– syntactic 148, 155
prosody 2, 17, 263–4, 277, 279
prototype categories 127–31, 138, 265
prototype effects 25, 35, 191
– application to grammar 134–5
– centrality 130–2
– frequency 133–4
– in grammar 127–45
– lexical categories 135–7
– salience 132–3
– syntactic constructions 139–44
– word structure 138–9
prototype models 264
prototypes, category 132, 135, 137
prototypical senses 24, 26–7, 31, 131
prototypical verbs 136–7
prototypicality 134–5, 144, 168, 198
– degrees of 133–4, 168
– semantic 135
protracted duration 68, 76
proximity 36, 45, 71, 172, 174, 177
psycholinguistic experimentation 29–30, 288

psycholinguistics 23, 30, 32–6, 155
psychological reality 26

quantifiers 196, 218, 236–9, 242, 245
questionnaires 11, 237
questions, comprehension 175, 178

radial categories 25–6, 45
Ramscar, M. 72, 114–15, 127, 160
RCC (region connection calculus) 47
reaction times (RTs) 152, 241
reading 76, 112, 140, 167, 170, 207–8, 243, 245
– times 173, 175–6, 178, 181
real experience 67–8, 76
real nouns 233
reality
– immediate 197, 199–200
– psychological 26
reanalysis 212, 214–15, 217
reasoning 72–3, 99, 116, 120, 132, 191–2, 203
– spatial 72–3, 116
– temporal 73, 114–16
recognition 28, 33, 35–6, 99, 140
recursion 275, 286
reference frames 51, 60
reference objects 49, 51–2
referents 99, 129, 140, 232, 260, 276
Regier, T. 51–2, 98
region connection calculus (RCC) 47
regular morphology 233
reification 70, 80, 225
relations 29, 46–7, 59, 66, 141–2, 144, 260, 280
– geometric 47, 54
– spatial 7, 44, 46–7, 50–1, 59, 120
relative clauses 159
relativity, linguistic 17, 59–60, 119
relevance theory 32, 218
repetition 217, 219, 266
representation
– embodied 283
– grounded 51, 78
– mental 28, 31, 82, 130
– spatial 69–70, 72, 82
– temporal 67–9, 72, 75, 77–80, 82
representational systems 8, 82

representativity 128, 130, 136
research, cross-linguistic 6, 8, 10–11, 13–15, 95, 119
resources 17, 80, 88, 90, 97, 135, 240, 276
rhetorical style 90, 96–7
Rice, S. 27, 29, 37, 51, 132
Richards, L. 48–9, 168, 231
Richardson, D. C. 113–14
Roberts, I. 155, 214–15
Rodd, J. M. 35–6
Rosch, E. 24, 45, 127, 129–33, 144
RTs (reaction times) 152, 241
rules 204–5, 232–3, 252, 275, 286
– vs. cues 286
– linking 148, 156
Russian 5, 7, 193, 195–6, 200, 202, 204, 208
– verbs 196, 205, 208
Russo, T. 260

salience 34, 94, 130, 132–3, 166–8, 185, 224
– effects 132–3, 144
salience-based interpretations 166, 168–9, 185–6
salience-based literal interpretations 173, 175, 178, 181, 185
Sandra, D. 27–9, 51, 132
Sanford, A. J. 48–9
sarcasm 170, 175, 177, 179–80, 183–4
– rate degree of 175, 177, 180
– ratings 175, 177, 180, 183–4
sarcasm scale 175, 177, 180, 183
sarcastic interpretations 167, 174–5, 177–8, 180, 186
– nonsalient 175, 178, 181
sarcastic utterance-interpretation, default 174–6, 179, 182
satellite-framed languages 6, 89–92
satellites 88–92, 94, 96
Šatunovskij's model 208
scaling analysis, multi-dimensional 202, 205
schemas
– abstract 156, 239
– low-level 233, 245
– meso-constructional 222
schemata, image 46–7, 51

schematic templates 262
schematicity 221
schematization 28, 37, 221, 224–5, 261
second language learners 237, 244
Sekerina, I. A. 236, 242
selection 33, 275–6, 282
– pictures 236, 239
self-organization 283, 287
Self-Organizing Feature Maps 283
semantic anomaly 170, 172, 174, 177, 180, 184–5
semantic characterization 135, 137
semantic components 88–9, 93–4, 97
semantic differences 17
semantic domains 3, 9, 88
semantic evolution 218–19
semantic extensions 4, 258–9
semantic generality 13, 221
semantic phonology 261
semantic properties 141–2, 151, 153, 261
semantic prototypicality 135
semantic shifts 2
semantic space 35–6
semantic structure 130, 135, 144, 261
semantic typology 1–17, 88
– body from different angles 6–8
– cognition to perception 4–6
– colour 3–4
– further research questions 16–17
– methodological challenges 10–16
– motion events 6
– temperature 8–10, 14–16
semantics 10–11, 27, 30–1, 33, 88, 135, 137, 148–52
– cognitive 2, 10, 23, 32
– conceptual 223–4
– lexical 16, 23, 27, 131
– theoretical 10, 12
senses 4–5, 10, 23–9, 31–7, 45–7, 68–9, 130–1, 140–1
– central 130–2, 134
– dominant 33–4
– multiple 27, 34
– prototypical 24, 26–7, 31, 131
– subordinate 33–4
– word 26, 28, 33
sensory perception 195, 259
sensory-motor experience 67, 80–2

sentence comprehension 149, 152, 237, 241, 245, 281
sentence production 34, 149, 281
sentences 53–4, 113–16, 118, 135, 149–51, 154–5, 157–8, 234–41
– complex 234–6
– control 234–5
– fictive motion 110, 112–14, 116, 118–19
– locative 153–4
– passive 153–4, 157, 238, 240
– structure 150, 154
– target 112, 153
– test 156, 235
– transitive 156, 284
S-handshape 255–6
shifts, semantic 2
short-term memory 279–80
sight paths 116, 118
sign linguists 261, 264, 267
signals 196, 200–202, 206, 252, 281
signed languages 110, 251–68
– and cognitive linguistics 255–61
– and dynamic systems theory 265–7
– and gestures 261–5
– grammars of 253, 260, 265
– and iconicity 259–61
– incorporation of gesture 263
– linguistic systems 261, 263
– and metaphors 255–7
– and metonymy 257–9
– and phonology 253
– structure 253–5
– use of space 253
signers 253–6, 258
– body 253, 255, 260
signs 2, 136, 251, 253–63, 266–7
– ASL 255–6, 259
simulated motion 111–14, 118
Sinha, C. 68, 77, 80, 88
Slobin, D. I. 17, 46, 90–1, 93–5, 97–8, 117
social isolation 287
socio-cultural patterns 14–15
sociolinguistics 246–7, 279, 282
solid objects 50, 195
solutions, embodied 252, 265, 267
sorting 59, 98, 150, 196
– decisions 150
– one-dimensional 150

source domains 71–2, 120, 203, 283
space 14–15, 44–61, 66–7, 69–77, 80–2, 193–4, 253, 255
– conceptual 260–1
– cross-linguistic differences and "linguistic relativity" 59–60
– domain of 69–70, 73–4
– Minkowski 75
– perceptual 55, 57
– physical 110–11, 116–17, 254
– semantic 35–6
– spatial adpositions 44–54
– spatial demonstratives 45, 54–9
– spatial language defined 44–5
– and time 69–75, 81, 114
– distinction 74–6
Spanish 16, 55–6, 59, 92, 94–5, 97, 110, 119
– speakers 55, 98–9, 119
spatial adpositions 44–54
– projective terms 45, 51–4
– topological terms 45–51
spatial concepts 44, 46, 59, 67
spatial constructs 44, 60
spatial demonstratives 45, 54–9
spatial experience 80
spatial expressions 49
spatial language 44–8, 50–1, 54, 58–60, 77, 118, 120
– definition 44–5
spatial meanings 27, 219
spatial prepositions 44–5, 47, 53, 55
spatial reasoning 72–3, 116
spatial relations 7, 44, 46–7, 50–1, 59, 120
spatial representation 69–70, 72, 82
spatial scenes 48, 59
speech 91, 96, 242, 247, 251, 265–6, 275, 287
– adult-directed 234
– child-directed 157, 234
– parts of 31, 135
speech-act modality 203
spillover effects 173, 175, 179, 181
spillover segments 173, 175, 178–9, 181
splitting, extreme 26–7
spoken language 110, 148, 234, 239, 252–3, 262, 264–5, 267–8
Standard Pragmatic Model 168–9
Stanojević, M.-M. 204, 206

statistical preemption 158–9
status 66–7, 128, 136–8, 140, 142, 224–5, 261, 279
– ambiguous 136, 139
– ontological 26, 28
Stefanowitsch, A. 94, 141–2
stems 138, 232–3
stimuli 4, 11, 57, 150, 152, 154, 160, 185
– events 98–9
– poverty 287
– verbal 114–15, 118
– visual 90, 155
Stokoe, W. C. 252–3, 259, 261
structural configurations 139, 153–4
structural markedness 171, 184–5
– and negation 182–4
structural priming 152–3, 157
structures 67–8, 70, 73–4, 81, 235–8, 275–6, 278, 281
– category 25, 35, 129, 131
– complex 94, 266, 287
– events 120, 151
– internal 135, 141, 217
– linguistic 87, 96, 247, 253, 284–6
– mapping 283
– motion 89, 92, 96
– physical 284
– semantic 130, 135, 144, 261
– sentence 150, 154
– signed languages 253–5
– surface 148, 153–4, 217
– syntactic 154
subject position 234, 277
subjectification 203, 212, 215, 223–5
subjective construal 197, 224
subjective experience 67, 143, 207
subjective motion 111
subjectivity 117, 203
subjects 31, 33–4, 132–5, 140–2, 153, 195, 224–5, 277
– of conception 224–5
subordinate clauses 88, 90, 234
subordinate meanings 37
subordinate senses 33–4
subordinating conjunctions 136
subordination 234–6, 242
substrate matter 74–5
succession 75, 77–9, 193, 197

support 28, 30, 44, 46, 48, 59, 117, 286–7
supportive information 170, 185
surface elements 88, 92, 94
surface structure 148, 153–4, 217
syllables 265, 268, 281
synchronicity 79, 266
synonymy 31
syntactic constructions 2, 27, 127, 135
– prototype effects 139–44
syntactic properties 148, 155
syntactic structures 154
syntax 16, 27, 148, 160–1, 198, 234, 236, 238

tactics 179–80
Talmy, L. 6, 69–70, 73–4, 87–9, 91–4, 109–11, 197–8, 201–2
target domain 71–2, 97, 283
target utterances 167, 171–6, 178–9
targets, biased 173, 176, 178–9, 181
task dynamics 265–6
tasks 58, 60, 95, 98–9, 112, 233, 235, 238–9
– narrative understanding 112
– non-linguistic 60
– sentence production 34, 149
– spatial reasoning 72–3
taxonomies 73, 78, 111, 220–1
temperature 8–10, 14–16
– body 68
templates 13, 156, 222, 239, 278
– lexical 241
– schematic 262
temporal boundaries 195
temporal concepts 67, 69, 78, 80–1
temporal experience 68, 73, 76, 78–9, 81–2
temporal processes 81–2
temporal processing 67, 78, 287
temporal reasoning 73, 114–16
temporal representations 67–9, 72, 75, 77–80, 82
tense 2, 191–5, 197, 199, 204–9
– and aspect 204–7
– categories of 191, 204
– definition 191
– metaphors 194
– and mood 205, 207
– past 129, 199–200, 206–7

– present 140, 192, 196, 204, 206–7
– as immediate vs. past as distal 199–200
tense-aspect markers 205
time 35, 66–83, 112–17, 142–3, 158–9, 192–4, 218–19, 235–6
– domain of 66, 69–70, 73–5, 77, 81, 193
– empirical research in cognitive science 82–3
– experience of see *temporal experience*
– homogenous or multifaceted 76–7
– nature and status 66–9
– processing 34, 74
– reading 173, 175–6, 178, 181
– reasons for representation in terms of sensory-motor experience 80–2
– representations universal or not 77–80
– and space 69–75, 81, 114
– distinction 74–6
time-as-such 68, 77, 80
timeframes 275–6, 278–82
timelines 82–3, 156, 191, 193–4, 197, 199
to-infinitive 217–18
tokens 144, 150, 160, 218
Tomasello, M. 155–6, 158, 216, 243, 245, 284
topological terms 45–51
tough movement 234, 242
trained constructions 238–9, 243
training 68, 97, 156, 237–8, 243
– phases 157, 159, 237, 244
– sessions 134, 237, 243–4
transience 73, 76, 78–9
– experience of 78
transitive sentences 156, 284
transitive verbs 140, 195, 277
transitory states 201–2
translation 11, 95–7, 100, 213
Traugott, E. C. 203, 214–15, 217–18, 220–1, 223–4
traversable paths 110, 113
Trousdale, G. 214, 219, 221–4
Tuggy, D. 28
Tyler, A. 27, 29, 47, 49, 132
typological research 1–2, 6, 11
typologists 1, 196
typology 1–2, 55, 89, 94, 288
– grammatical 15
– lexical 2, 13, 15

– linguistic 1–2, 11, 101
– semantic 1–17, 88
– two-way 89, 93
Tyrone, M. E. 266

UG see *Universal Grammar*
unaccusatives 140, 144
unbiased passives 239
undirected activities 201–2
unergatives 140, 144
Universal Grammar (UG) 275, 286–7
usage 4, 29, 142, 144, 156, 195, 279, 286
– events 252, 262
usage-based approach 32, 202, 209, 265, 267, 275, 282, 284–5
usage-based frameworks 89, 218
usage-based models 134, 231, 241
use, language 100, 149, 162, 194, 220, 222, 277, 282
utterances 148, 156–60, 167–9, 173, 178–9, 181–6, 244, 262
– negative see *negative utterances*
– target 167, 171–6, 178–9

Van Gelderen, E. 215
Van Orden, G. C. 33, 35
Vanhove, M. 4–5
variability, cultural 77, 257
variation 88, 92–4, 98, 183, 212, 216, 246–7, 267
– cross-linguistic 10, 13–16, 59
– diatopic 94
– intertypological 93–4
– intratypological 94
verb classes 29
verb classifiers 196
verb roots 88–9, 93
verbal categories 191, 197, 209
verbal stimuli 114–15, 118
verb-independent constructions 152, 157
verbs 88–90, 129, 135–7, 140–1, 148–53, 155–60, 191–3, 195–6
– denominal 151
– imperfective 204–5
– intransitive 27, 195
– lexical 254–5
– light 150, 158
– manner 91, 94, 99, 119

- modal 192, 197–8, 208, 225
- motion 6, 95, 100, 111, 118–19
- novel 151, 156, 160
- passive-attracting 240–1
- perception 5, 11
- prototypical 136–7
- Russian 196, 205, 208
- transitive 140, 195, 277
verification, pictures 53, 236
vertical prepositions 50–4
visibility manipulations 57
visual attention 113–14
visual paths 116–17
visual scenes 47, 53–4, 59
visual stimuli 90, 155
vocabularies 156, 251, 266
von der Gabelentz, G. 213–14, 216
vowel sounds 128

Wallentin, M. 118–19
Walsh, V. 73–4
weighted attributes 129, 131, 133
Whorf, B. L. 251
Wierzbicka, A. 3, 7–8, 12–13
Wilkins, D. P. 4–7, 10–12, 14–16
Williams, J. N. 34–5, 231
word classes 2, 135
word meanings 10, 131, 135
word order 149, 160, 213
word senses 26, 28, 33
word structure 127, 138–9
words
- function 37, 212–13
- -ness 221
- polysemous 34–5, 37, 131–2, 134, 144
- single 76–7

zeugma 24, 34

www.ingramcontent.com/pod-product-compliance
Lightning Source LLC
Chambersburg PA
CBHW021118300426
44113CB00006B/203